Cowley raises ideas by authors ~~...~~ Trotsky, Conrad ~~...~~ Granville Hicks, John Strachey, and H. L. Mencken, illustrate Mr. Cowley's skill in singling out persons of lasting interest. Mr. Piper has included several general essays which discuss the familiar themes of the Thirties—communism in its various forms, the pacifist crusade, the crusade against world fascism, and the collapse of the American economy. Part II, *The Literary Record*, contains articles which deal chiefly with literary values. They are especially important because of the purity and accuracy of Mr. Cowley's artistic judgment. As the editor remarks in his Introduction, "the quality of Mr. Cowley's discernment is seen in the fact that almost no major American or European writer of the Thirties has been overlooked."

Mr. Cowley has written a lively, new, retrospective essay, "Adventures of a Book Reviewer," especially for this volume, describing his experiences as a member of the NEW REPUBLIC staff. This essay not only helps to explain the continuing vitality of these reviews today; it is itself a classic on the art of the book review, and quite apart from its connection with this volume, should be read by every reviewer concerned with his craft.

The collection, in the editor's words, "is a fascinating record of certain issues and problems of a historic epoch as they are reflected in the commentary —week by week—of a gifted observer. They gain by the unity that comes from having been filtered through the intellect and sensibility of one individual. Thus, they have a special value for the student of this era."

THINK BACK ON US . . .

A Contemporary Chronicle

of the 1930's

For the Class of 1967
M. C.
H. D. P.

Think back on us, the martyrs and the cowards,
The traitors even, swept by the same flood
Of passion toward the morning that is yours:
O children born from, nourished with our blood.
From TOMORROW MORNING (M. C. 1938)

THINK BACK
ON US . . .

A Contemporary Chronicle of

the 1930's by Malcolm Cowley

Edited, with an Introduction

by Henry Dan Piper

Southern Illinois University Press

Carbondale and Edwardsville

Feffer & Simons, Inc., *London and Amsterdam*

CONTENTS

2 THE *Literary* RECORD

THOSE OF US who belong to the generation of the 1930's run the risk these days of taking them too much for granted. Have you tried recently to describe to your teen-age son, or to a class of skeptical undergraduates, what it was like to grow up during the Depression? To the average Sophomore born around 1947 the 1930's now seem as remote and old-fashioned as the gas-lit 1900's once did to us.

This volume of uncollected essays and reviews by Malcolm Cowley grew out of my need for a source book of college readings in the intellectual, social, and literary history of the Thirties. I wanted something with more unity—and more continuity—than the usual scissors-and-paste anthology provides. I wanted something that would help the younger generation understand why I and so many of my middle-aged contemporaries think the way we do.

In my search I ransacked the back files of *The New Republic*—the magazine that served more than any other during those years as the intellectual conscience of our generation. I soon realized that the volume I was looking for lay waiting among the literally hundreds of reviews and essays that Malcolm Cowley had written week-in and week-out during the Thirties as literary editor of *The New Republic*. From these *NR* pieces I have chosen those that seemed best suited to my purpose. To them I have added several from the period that Cowley published elsewhere.

The result is a collection of penetrating and extremely readable essays by a gifted commentator that also serves as a kind of topical chronicle of one of the liveliest decades in the history of the American mind. It is also an unintended tribute to the old pre-World War II *New Republic*. For where today is there an American magazine with a roster of editors equalling in eminence the names that adorned the *NR* masthead during those years—John Dewey, Jane Addams, Heywood Broun, Lewis Mumford, Rexford G. Tugwell, H. N. Brailsford, Stark Young, George Soule, Robert Morss Lovett, not to mention its two literary editors, Edmund Wilson and Malcolm Cowley.

Cowley went to work for Wilson in *The New Republic*'s literary department in October 1929, just three weeks before the stock-market crash. Thus, in selecting the essays for this volume I had no choice about the date when they would begin. It was more difficult deciding where to stop. For some people the Thirties ended exactly ten years later in the autumn of 1939 with the outbreak of the European war. But for most Americans the mood of the 1930's persisted until the Pearl Harbor attack two years later plunged us into World War II. By choosing the later date I have been able to include several pieces by Mr. Cowley that belong to the Thirties, even though they were not published until 1940 or 1941.

How important Cowley's literary editorship of *The New Republic* was for the generation that came of age during the Depression has recently been reaffirmed by Alfred Kazin in his memoir, *Starting Out in the Thirties.**

> What young writers of the Thirties wanted was to prove the literary value of our experience, to recognize the possibility of art in our own lives, to feel that we had moved the streets, the stockyards, the hiring halls into literature—to show that our radical strength could carry on the experimental impulse of modern literature. And it was because of this genuine literary ambition that the influence of Malcolm Cowley, then literary editor of the *New Republic,* was so fundamental. For Cowley had lived among the expatriates in Paris, he had just published *Exile's Return* as a chronicle of the lost generation, and each Wednesday afternoon, when I waited with other hopeful reviewers for Cowley to sail in after lunch with a tolerant smile

* Little, Brown and Co., Boston, 1965. pp. 15, 18–19.

on the face which so startlingly duplicated Hemingway's handsomeness, the sight of Cowley in the vivid stripes of his seersucker suit seemed to unite, through his love of good writing and his faith in revolution, the brilliant Twenties and the militant Thirties. . . . The lead review in the *New Republic,* a single page usually written by Cowley himself, brought the week to focus for people to whom this page, breathing intellectual fight in its sharp black title and solid double-columned lines of argument, represented the most dramatically satisfying confrontation of a new book by a gifted, uncompromising critical intelligence. . . . [He] was the last of this era—the last *New Republic* literary editor who dominated "the back of the book," and who week after week gave a continuing authority to his judgments. Cowley made his points with unassailable clarté and concreteness; he *made* an article each week that one had to read and could remember.

Born in 1898 on the family farm in western Pennsylvania, Cowley grew up in Pittsburgh, where his father was an upright but impractical physician. After entering Harvard as a freshman in the fall of 1915, he left in the middle of his sophomore year to enlist as a volunteer ambulance driver. Instead, he ended up driving a truck in the "T.M.U.," the French military transport service. After the war he married and returned to Harvard, graduating in 1920 "as of the class of 1919."

Along with many others, he gravitated to Greenwich Village, where the family set up housekeeping in a cold-water flat costing seventeen dollars a month. While waiting to become a successful free-lance writer, he went to work for *Sweet's Architectural Catalogue.* In 1921 he was awarded a thousand-dollar American Field Service scholarship that—in those days, when it was fantastically cheap to live in France—was enough to take him to the University of Montpellier for a year's study of French literature. Its renewal the following year made it possible for him to move on to Paris, where he met, and was soon writing about, the leaders of the new Dadaist movement —André Breton, Tristan Tzara, Louis Aragon. Later he also translated into English several modern French classics, including Valéry's *Varieté* and Radiguet's *Le bal du comte d'Orgel*. He also helped edit a new little magazine, *Secession*, that had been launched by two other young American expatriates, Matthew Josephson and Gorham Munson.

Returning to New York in 1923, he took up his old job at *Sweet's* and helped Josephson edit another magazine, *Broom*, founded by Harold Loeb in 1921, that soon fell afoul of the U. S. Postmaster General and was suppressed. A $100 prize from *Poetry* served as the down payment on a sixty-acre farm in Connecticut, where the Cowleys' neighbors included Josephson, Allen Tate, Caroline Gordon, Robert M. Coates, Hart Crane, John Brooks Wheelwright, and Peter Blume. Meanwhile, Cowley had quit *Sweet's* a second time in the hope of supporting himself as a freelancer. His first book of poems, *Blue Juniata*, appeared early in 1929. But although it was well received by the critics (and is still remembered), it sold less than a thousand copies. Thus, he was in a receptive mood when Edmund Wilson, literary editor of *The New Republic*, suggested that he join the *NR* staff the following October.

During the months that followed, as the Depression worsened, Wilson began to spend more time writing special articles about the country's economic and social problems, while Cowley gradually took over responsibility for the book department in the magazine's back pages. For this new assignment Cowley proved to be ideally suited. His long apprenticeship in the writing of verse, and his dedicated study of the masters of French literature, had taught him the virtues of economy, simplicity, and clarity. His value as a commentator and critic lay in the close reading he gave a book, in his ability to sum up its main argument fairly and succinctly, and in the intellectual breadth that prompted him to reach out for fruitful, relevant generalizations. To this important task, week after week, he brought a cosmopolitan point of view, a sense of literary style, and an idealistic Swedenborgian conscience. How he went about his job as *The New Republic*'s literary editor and chief book reviewer is the subject of a retrospective essay, "Adventures of a Book Reviewer," written especially for this volume, and included at the end, that is a classic statement about the art of literary journalism.

In justice to Cowley it should be pointed out that the present volume contains only a fraction of his published work during the years 1929–41 and is therefore intended in no way to represent his total literary output. For example, 1934 saw the publication of *Exile's Return*, his memoir of expatriate life during the 1920's. In 1937 he edited and also contributed to a volume of essays by various hands on modern American fiction, *After the Genteel Tradition*. That same year he also joined Bernard Smith, the Marxist critic, in editing a volume of essays called *Books That Changed Our Minds*. In 1941 he published a second volume of poems, *The Dry Season*. Besides these, there are the scores of reviews, essays, and articles published in *The New Republic* and elsewhere, that I have omitted from the present collection.

I have divided this volume into two parts: "The Social Record" and "The Literary Record." In both, the contents are arranged chronologically. Part I is concerned with the issues, problems, and ideas of the period. Some of the books discussed are worth reading about only because of what Cowley has to say about them, and the issues he raises. But the names of the authors of other books—Margaret Mead, Leon Trotsky, Robert and Helen Lynd, Conrad Aiken, Archibald MacLeish, Granville Hicks, John Strachey, H. L. Mencken—remind us how skillful Cowley was in singling out the personalities of most lasting interest.

Besides book reviews, "The Social Record" also includes essays of a more general nature, including his debate with Archibald MacLeish over pacifism and his oft-reprinted account of the flight of the Bonus Army. Again and again certain familiar themes of the era reappear—communism in its various forms (Marxist, Stalinist, Trotskyite); the pacifist crusade and its successor, the crusade against world fascism; the collapse of the traditional American economic system and the quest for alternatives.

The essays to be found in "The Literary Record," although they date from the same period, are remarkable primarily because of the purity and accuracy of Cowley's artistic judgment. Unlike the pieces in "The Social Record," they are concerned almost exclusively with literary values. And yet they are authentic products of their time and place; they could not be written today. They would lack the sense of immediacy, the excitement of discovery. The quality of Cowley's discernment is seen in the fact that almost no major American or European writer of the Thirties has been overlooked: Hemingway, Fitzgerald, Faulkner, Wolfe, Dos Passos, Crane, Farrell, Auden, Spender, Day Lewis, Virginia Woolf, Silone, Malraux, Mann, Winston Churchill the rhetorician—even Mikhail Sholokhov, who would wait thirty years more for the Nobel Prize he already deserved. Whether Cowley is confronting a major work (*Tender Is the Night*, *The Bridge*) or a lesser work by an important writer (Faulkner's *Pylon*, Kenneth Burke's *Towards a Better Life*) his comments have a way of illuminating the author's total achievement.

The choice of the essays included here has been mine. But I have consulted Mr. Cowley extensively and he has patiently taken time from a busy schedule to answer innumerable questions. He also went over the entire text, occasionally altering a word or phrase or inserting a new heading. He suggested the book's title and generously contributed the retrospective essay at the end, now published for the first time.

I am also indebted to three of my students for help in preparing the text, Paul Borgman, Glenn Woods, and Carol Vernetti, as well as to my wife, Roberta, and Vernon Sternberg, Director of the Southern Illinois University Press, for advice and encouragement.

Henry Dan Piper

Carbondale, Illinois
May 9, 1966

THE *Social* RECORD

1

Angry Professors

THE OPPOSITIONS lately encountered by the disciples of More and Babbitt can be explained in part, though only in part, by a confusion in the minds of the American Humanists themselves between humanism with a small "h" and their own sort of capitalized Humanism.

Humanism with a small "h" is a general attitude that is difficult or impossible to define. Partly it is an emphasis on the qualities it considers to be essentially human. Partly it is a defense of human dignity, of human possibilities; partly it is an opposition to all the forces that threaten them, whether these be religious, social, governmental, economic, or those of an anti-human philosophy. This attitude received its name during the Renaissance, when it was revived by the study of Greek and Roman antiquity. The Chinese sages were humanists in their time, and so, it might be added, are vast numbers of thinking men today.

The Humanism we spell with a capital letter is a body of doctrine assembled by Professors Irving Babbitt, of Harvard, and Paul Elmer More, of Princeton. These two men are among the foremost American critics of their generation, and this in itself surrounds their philosophy with a certain prestige. Their system appeals, moreover, to the critics who wish to apply fixed standards to literature; and it is not uncongenial to the somewhat conservative temper of the younger generation. Thus, in the midst of enemies, this doctrinal Humanism has grown in power. Today there are Humanist magazines, Humanist publishers, Humanist professors in all the larger universities; there are Humanist critics, scientists and political thinkers (if not Humanist artists); and the movement has even enlisted the editorial support of *The New York Times*, which doesn't quite know what it is all about, but which feels, somehow, that Humanism is safe. Yet in spite of all these activities, American Humanism is only one school of thought among

An article from *The New Republic* (henceforth abbreviated as *NR*), Apr. 9, 1930. A somewhat longer version of the article was published in *The Critique of Humanism: A Symposium*, edited by C. Hartley Grattan. New York: Brewer and Warren, 1930.

many: it is a movement that may be compared in scope with Ethical Culture, or at the most with Christian Science.

Now, the Humanists themselves have unconsciously confused their specific cult with the general attitude. When Babbitt, for example, speaks of founding a Humanist university or of banding his followers together into a Humanist "communion" from which most of us will be excluded for doctrinal reasons, he is evidently referring to the contemporary cult. When, on the other hand, he speaks of humanism as something comparable in importance with religion in general—when he says that "a more definite feeling of limitation . . . lies at the base of both humanism and religion," or that "the question remains whether the more crying need just now is for positive and critical humanism or for positive and critical religion," or again that "the solution of this problem as to the relation between humanism and religion . . . lies in looking upon them both as only different stages in the same path"—in all these instances he is obviously referring to humanism as a general attitude, and one which is shared not only by Socrates and Confucius but also by many contemporary writers whom Babbitt himself disowns. His followers profit vastly by this confusion. It enables them to claim all the humanist past for their modern doctrine; it enables them to speak of "Homer, Phidias, Plato, Aristotle, Confucius, Buddha, Jesus, Paul, Virgil, Horace, Dante, Shakespeare, Milton, Goethe . . . Matthew Arnold in England and Emerson and Lowell in America" as their own collaborators; and it subjects them to a great deal of justified ridicule which they might have avoided by a little Socratic thinking.

Their philosophy should be considered in itself. And so, in the present essay, I intend to deal chiefly with capitalized Humanism, though I shall sometimes contrast it with other forms of the general attitude which impress me as being more valid.

ii

American Humanism begins with the assumption that life can be divided into three planes: the natural, the human and the religious. It holds that we should cultivate the second of these planes, not in opposition to religion, but rather to the natural plane, which is represented today by the scientific descendants of Francis Bacon and the romantic descendants of Jean-Jacques Rousseau. Thus, says Robert Shafer, writing in *The Book-man:*

> Against romanticism, humanitarian sympathy, mechanistic or vitalistic determinism, the doctrine of progress and the like, has been opposed a skeptical criticism of life and letters which rests ultimately on the proposition that man differs not alone in complexity of organization, but in kind, from the animal, and that his happiness depends upon his recognition and cultivation of that element in his being which is distinctive of him. This is held to be possible; man is held to be, within limits, capable of responsible choice. . . . To choose is to discriminate, and, for this, habituation to self-restraint is essential; it is, indeed, the foundation on which the whole structure of distinctively human life rests.

Everything is reduced, in the end, to the morality of the individual. By practicing self-restraint, by applying the *law of measure*, by the *imitation* of great models chosen from the antiquity of all nations, he can arrive at the Humanistic virtues of *poise, proportionateness, decorum*, and finally attain "the end of ends"—which, Babbitt says, is individual happiness.

These are the general doctrines of Humanism, and it seems to me that they can be accepted, so far as they go, by many opponents of More and Babbitt. They can also be criticized, but chiefly for what they omit. They can be criticized in theory, first, for their incompleteness as a system of ethics, and second, for their total disregard of social and economic realities.

The ethic of Humanism consists of a single precept: namely, that we should exercise self-restraint (or the will to refrain, or the Inner Check, Veto Power, *frein vital, Entsagung* or whatever else it may be called at the moment). We are offered no other guide. But why—we ask like children repeating a Shorter Catechism—why should we exercise self-restraint?

A. In order to achieve decorum.

Q. And why should we achieve decorum?

A. The end of ends is happiness. (Be good and you will be happy. If you can't be good, be careful. With all their paraded learning, all their analysis of texts, all their quotations from the French, German, Latin, Greek, Sanskrit and Chinese, can the Humanists tell us nothing more than this?)

In theory, they can tell us nothing more. In practice, we find them basing their moral judgments on a set of conventions which have nothing to do with their logic. In practice, at this critical point in their philosophy, they renounce a "positive and critical" humanism for tradition and theology. Yet this silent renunciation, which damages their own position without bene-fiting the church, was quite unnecessary. Without ceasing to be strictly humanist, they could have developed a complete sys-tem of ethics, but only by considering man in relation to society. This they have failed to do: in this increasingly corpo-rate world of ours, they have confined their attention to the individual.

Economically, socially, their doctrine is based on nothing and answers no questions. Out of what society does Humanism spring, and toward what society does it lead? Has it any validity for the mill hands of New Bedford and Gastonia, for the beet-toppers of Colorado, for the men who tighten a single screw in the automobiles that march along Mr. Ford's assembly belt? Should it be confined to the families who draw dividends from these cotton mills, beet fields, factories, and to the profes-sors who teach in universities endowed by them? Can one be Humanist between chukkers of a polo match, or can the steel workers be Humanists, too—once every three weeks, on their Sunday off? Has Babbitt any social program?

In his *Democracy and Leadership,* which gingerly touches on some of these problems, he rejects the whole conception of social justice as a dangerous fallacy. He asserts that the eco-nomic problem, including the relations between capital and labor, runs into the political problem, which runs into the philosophical problem, which in turn is almost indissolubly bound up with the religious problem. The root of the whole matter is in the psychology of the individual. For unemploy-ment, low wages, long hours, intolerable working conditions, for all the realities of the present system, he has one solution, perhaps the most unreal that could be offered. "The remedy," he says, "for the evils of competition is found in the modera-tion and magnanimity of the strong and the successful, and not in any sickly sentimentalizing over the lot of the underdog."

Yet it would be incorrect to say that Babbitt offers no social program. For all his hatred of terms like humanitarianism and social justice, he does suggest a mild path toward a Humanist Utopia. "The first stage," he says, "would . . . be that of Socratic definition; the second stage would be the coming together of a group of persons on the basis of this definition . . . the third stage would almost inevitably be the attempt to make this convention effective through education." Babbitt seems to contemplate the salvation of society through a private-school system culminating in a Humanist university. For one of his collaborators, Frank Jewett Mather, Jr., of Princeton, the salvation of the country seems even simpler. He says, in a recent group-statement of the Humanist faith:

> We contributors to this symposium have actually seen a few humanists made, have helped a little to make them perhaps; and we are dealing with spiritual values which transcend ordinary statistics. A few thousand genuine humanists in America would make our society humanistic; a hundred humanist painters, sculptors, architects, musicians and men of letters would make our art solidly humanistic.

A few thousand Humanists in business and the professions, a hundred Humanists in the arts . . . I submit that these rash professors, in their aversion for utopian visions, have produced the lamest utopia ever imagined. The vast economic machine that is America would continue to function aimlessly; great fortunes would continue to grow on the ruins of smaller fortunes; several million factory workers would continue to perform operations so subdivided and standardized as to be purely automatic; two million former workers, the "normal" army of the unemployed, would seek vainly for the privilege of performing the same dehumanizing tasks; the Chicago beer barons would continue to seek their fortunes and slaughter their rivals, revealing once more a deplorable ignorance of the Inner Check; the students in the new Humanist university, after the two-o'clock lecture on Plato, would spend an hour at the talkies with the It Girl—and meanwhile, because of a few thousand Humanists, our society, our government, our arts would be genuinely and ideally Humanistic.

iii

When a philosophy like that of More and Babbitt presents itself as a way of life, it is dangerous for that philosophy to omit important aspects of life. These gaps in thought do not remain empty. They are filled unconsciously, irresistibly, by the conventions that prevail in the world surrounding the philosopher. If these are blind and narrow, the philosophy will be blind and narrow in practice, however enlightened it may seem in theory.

Such has been the misfortune of American Humanism. At birth, the world that surrounded it was the American university of the 1890's, and from this world the Humanists have borrowed their underlying convictions. Economic problems at Harvard or Princeton before 1900 were less urgent than they became after the War: the young instructor was sure of being fed and clothed; he was comfortably lodged; and his salary was fixed by an individual arrangement with the university. The moral problem, however—or at least the problem of self-restraint—was of primary importance. Any sort of enthusiasm was suspicious. Any failure to restrain one's impulses toward frankness of judgment, freedom of thought, sympathy with the dispossessed, and love most of all—love for one's neighbor or his wife—might lead to immediate dismissal. And what was Babbitt's reaction? "The wiser the man," he says, "the less likely he will be to indulge in a violent and theatrical rupture with his age. He will like Socrates remember the counsel of the Delphian oracle to follow 'the usage of the city.' " Even Socrates himself, as Babbitt adds in another passage, "was perhaps needlessly unconventional and also unduly inclined to paradox."

The American Humanists, less paradoxical than Socrates and more faithful to the usage of the city, have adopted the older conventions of the universities where most of them teach. One of these conventions is a snobbery both intellectual and social—a snobbery which does not seem out of place in a professor's drawing-room, but which becomes grotesque when applied to literature and art. Paul Elmer More, for example, damns a whole school of American fiction, partly for literary reasons, but partly because its leading members are men of no social standing, men "almost without exception from small towns sprinkled along the Mid-Western states from Ohio to Kansas . . . self-made men with no inherited background of culture." One of More's disciples, Seward Collins, couples this accusation with another: namely, that some prominent American writers are Jews, "the sons of recent arrivals in this country"! It is as if Parnassus were a faculty club, at the doors of which More and Collins stood armed with blackballs. It is as if the world of letters were a university—one which applied the quota system to Irishmen and Jews and demanded a signed photograph with every request for admission.

Sometimes the snobbery of the Humanists is carried from the sphere of esthetics into that of government, and here it leads them into dangerous alliances. Babbitt, for example, is not unwilling to have his Inner Check on conduct reinforced by the outer check of civil authority: he speaks with approval of the policeman who arrested Raymond Duncan for wearing a Greek costume in the streets. Paul Elmer More, in the same fashion, feels that the cause of Humanism was somehow strengthened by the Princeton officials who "rusticated" a student for his "aspiration towards free morals in literature." Seward Collins vehemently defends the Watch and Ward Society; his only regret is that there are not two such societies in Boston. And this alliance between Humanism and reaction was emphasized some years ago at the Scopes trial, when Bryan took a book on evolution by Louis Trenchard More—who is the brother of Paul Elmer More and who wrote the leading essay in the Humanist symposium—along with him to Dayton, Tennessee, in order to confute the ungodly biologists and support his view that the Bible is the one American textbook of natural science.

So these angry professors, in following the usage of the city, have come to defend the social and intellectual prejudices of the universities where they teach and the churches where some of them worship. To themselves, they seem to play a more distinguished role. Gorham B. Munson claims for his Humanist colleagues the virtue of swimming against the current; but so, apparently, do straws caught in an eddy. Norman Foerster absolves himself and his condisciples from "the pro-

fessorial vices of pedantry, indolence, timidity and . . . sluggish tolerance"; he commends their boldness in attack. Boldness of a sort they have, but it is not the courage of lonely men
treading their own paths: it is the boldness of reactionary
professors in the classroom, lecturing to students most of
whom agree with their ideas and none of whom will rise in
rebuttal.

iv

Partly from the moral atmosphere of our eastern universities
in the 1890's, the Humanists imbibed another quality, one
which their enemies describe as Puritanism. The word is dangerously vague: it connotes or denotes a number of characteristics, good or bad, sentimental or realistic. The single quality to which I refer is clear, definite, unmistakable: it consists in
a profound belief in chastity, a belief which forms no part of
their official theories, which is revealed only in their practice of
criticism, and yet which is so fundamental that it distorts the
moral, the social and especially the literary judgments of the
American Humanists.

Babbitt, for example, in the course of his long attack on
Rousseau, happens to discuss the question of wages. "If a
working girl falls from chastity," he ironically says, "do not
blame her, blame her employer. She would have remained a
model of purity if he had only added a dollar or two to her
wage." I expect this remark to be utilized—perhaps it has
already been utilized—by those of Babbitt's pupils who are
now employing girls in the cotton mills of Fall River and New
Bedford. If chastity is all-important, if chastity is unaffected by
wages, why should they ever raise wages? . . . One might
answer from the standpoint of a humanism just as valid as
Babbitt's, that a working girl may be chaste or unchaste and
still remain human, but that it is almost impossible to be either
human or Humanist on ten or twelve dollars a week.

Elsewhere, in speaking of Goethe, he adopts the same tone
as with the working girl. "Anyone," Babbitt says, "who thinks
of the series of Goethe's love affairs prolonged into the seven-
ties, is scarcely likely to maintain that his *Entsagung* was of a
very austere character even for the man of the world, not to

speak of the saint." By what right does Babbitt summon him to the Dean's office?—a little jestingly, it is true, but still with profound disapproval, as if Goethe were a Harvard or Princeton sophomore with aspirations toward free morals in literature. And by what right does the professor deliver this lecture? Is he speaking in behalf of humanistic standards, to be deduced from the conduct of a hundred generations of sages, including Socrates, Dante and Goethe himself—or is he applying the religious standards of the Reformation? And is he willing to assure us that his opinion of Goethe's books, as books, is not affected by this smoking-room gossip about Goethe's life?

He believes, not without justification, that morality and esthetics cannot be separated, but he destroys the value of his esthetic judgments by confusing morality in general with the one virtue of chastity. "Restoration Comedy," he says with a professorial smile, "is a world not of pure but of impure imagination." "A greater spiritual elevation . . . is found in Wordsworth's communings with nature than in those of Rousseau and Chateaubriand." The reason, he explains, is because in Wordsworth "the erotic element is absent." At other times he delivers lectures on the sex life that could not be surpassed by the professor of Mental Hygiene in a fresh-water college. Yet Babbitt, after all, never quite reaches the heights of chaste absurdity that are attained by Paul Elmer More.

Consider More's "Note on Poe's Method," an essay that mingles some keen literary judgments (and others less keen) with an inexcusable ignorance of the poet's life. At the end, after deciding that "Poe remains chiefly the poet of unripe boys and unsound men," More goes on to say:

> Yet it is to the honor of Poe that in all his works you will come upon no single spot where the abnormal sinks to the unclean, or where there is an effort to intensify the effect of what is morbid emotionally by an appeal to what is morbid morally. The soul of this man was never tainted. [That is, Poe lied, flattered, slandered, drank to excess, took opium; his characters indulged in strange forms of necrophilia; but neither they nor their author committed fornication.] . . . If you wish to understand the perils he escaped, read after "The Sleeper" one of the poems in which Baudelaire, Poe's avowed imitator and sponsor to Europe, gropes with filthy hands among the mysteries of death. [That is, in which he writes of physical unchastity.]

On the next page, after delivering this judgment which reeks of Rufus Wilmot Griswold, S. Parkes Cadman, and all the psychological and literary ingenuousness that could very well be packed into a single paragraph, More turns to a new subject, "My Debt to Trollope." . . . As a "professed Trollopian," he praises the ethical atmosphere of Trollope's novels, regretting only that Trollope the moralist should yield so much to Trollope the entertainer; he exults over the fashion in which the good little Trollopes are rewarded and the bad Trollopes punished by the great Trollope their creator; and meanwhile he pauses to comment on the one class of modern writers who have followed Trollope's example:

> The only form of literature today wherein you may be sure that the author will not play tricks with the Ten Commandments is the detective story; the astonishing growth of which brand of fiction can be traced in no small measure, I suspect, to the fact that there alone murder is still simply murder, adultery simply adultery, theft simply theft, and no more about it.

In other chapters of the same volume, More writes about Joyce, Dos Passos and the Surrealists, but he appears not to have read them carefully. They seem to him unchaste, as do most other contemporary writers. He reads detective stories.

v

Among the Humanists in general, there is a real antipathy toward contemporary literature. They do no "creative" writing themselves, and they hold a grudge toward those who do. Whether it was originally imbibed, like other prejudices, from the atmosphere of the classroom and Faculty Row—where contemporary literature is expounded only by lecturers bent on uplifting professors' wives, and where it is written only by immature students *—would be difficult to decide. We can safely say, however, that a dislike for modern imaginative writing is revealed in the works of almost all the American Humanists. It is shown once more in their recently published symposium, *Humanism and America.*

*   This was hardly an overstatement of the academic attitude toward contemporary writing in 1930, but the attitude was about to change.—M. C.

Out of the fifteen contributors to that volume, there is only one who has written a mature poem; and T. S. Eliot, in point of doctrine, is far from being a strict Humanist. There is not one contributor who has written a serious novel, a drama or even a passable sketch (though I am told that one of them, under an assumed name, turned out a detective story that More probably enjoyed). At the end of the symposium, the editor has collected a sort of White List containing "most of the recent books that are humanistic in a strict sense." The list includes not one novel, one poem or one drama.

Perhaps I am laying too much stress on the importance of "creative" literature. Criticism, too, can express new values in a style that pleases the senses as well as the intellect; it can have form, vision, imaginative power. Perhaps their philosophy has endowed the Humanists with those qualities? —Turning back to the book, we find that with a very few exceptions—notably those of Eliot and of More himself, who is an admirable stylist —the fifteen critical essayists write either colorless prose or prose that is conspicuous for its muddled metaphors, harsh rhythms, awkward vocabulary and lack of original ideas.

Six of them deal directly with modern American literature. Might it not seem that they would find at least one book to praise? They find many; they praise the collected works of More and Babbitt, but they praise not one poem, drama, or novel. No, I am doing them an injustice. I seem to remember that in one essay, "Pandora's Box in American Fiction," Harry Hayden Clark finds a novel to recommend. It is a dull, correct book by a dull, correct and estimable author; it is not the best of her novels, but merely the most didactic; it is *The Brimming Cup*, by Dorothy Canfield Fisher. Read it and see what our arts would become if controlled for their own good by the "hundred humanist painters, sculptors, architects, musicians and men of letters" who are needed to make them "solidly humanistic."

Drought

AS I DROVE WESTWARD through Pennsylvania, by second-
ary roads, the fields were the color of old straw matting. The
weeds in the fencerows, even, had shriveled like rose leaves in
an album. Except in the shaded gullies, there was not a blade
of green grass in all the vast landscape. A fire was burning
somewhere in the second-growth timber, with a haze of blue
smoke over the mountaintop. A little whirlwind of dust, shaped
like a horn of plenty but empty within, moved over the
ground that was being harrowed for winter wheat. The cows
had gathered under the yellow-green maples; some of them
nibbled the grass roots, some lay dispiritedly; their ribs
showed. The streams were pools of stagnant water under the
willows. An empty watering trough still bore a notice explaining that the spring from which it used to be filled had been
inspected by the state department of health and found to be
safe for drinking purposes. "Big Stillwater Creek" was the
name, I think, of a watercourse so dry that even the moss had
turned to powder and blown away.

At the general store where I stopped for a package of
cigarettes, the proprietor could not change a five-dollar bill.
Three farms, with their stock, implements and household fur-
nishings, were advertised for sale at auction in handbills tacked
to the wall. Across the street the ice-cream parlor was closed:
he wouldn't sell city-made cream, the owner explained, and
they wa'n't enough milk in the county to make his own. That
was last October, near Belleville, Pennsylvania, in the center of
a farming district as rich as any in the East.

In southern Ohio, the look of the fields varied from county
to county, depending on whether there had been late summer
showers, but everywhere the streams were lower than they had
been for a lifetime. In Tennessee, the rains had come in time to
save most of the tobacco crop, but the corn was ruined and
there would be no hay to carry the stock through the winter.
In the Shenandoah Valley, through which I passed six weeks
later, the autumn rains had not yet fallen in early November.
The great barns, which carry the look of Pennsylvania far into
that portion of the South, were almost empty of hay. In the

From "Transcontinental Highway." (*NR*, Feb. 25, 1931.)

barnyards, cattle milled about the dwindling strawstacks, which, in a good season, would have been used only for bedding. An old man told me that fodder hadn't been so scarce since Sheridan raided southward from Harper's Ferry and boasted after his passage that a crow crossing the Valley would have to carry his own rations. "The crows ain't none too fat this fall," the old man said.

South-central Pennsylvania, central Tennessee, the Shenandoah Valley: to mention these names is to call up the picture of fat farms and prosperous farmers. These countrysides are among the richest agricultural lands on our continent, and they are also among the districts most impoverished by a drought that has lasted since early spring.

Within these districts, the richest farms are those which have suffered most; their owners are bankrupt, their tenants are starving. The poorer independent farmers, those who till what is known as marginal land, have learned to know hardship as their next-door neighbor; his face no longer frightens them. When the crops fail, they merely run a little farther into debt and patch the old overalls instead of buying a new pair. When there is no grain to give the hogs, they can be turned into the woods to feed on beech mast; the bacon will be leaner this winter, but the flavor better. For a progressive farmer, however—one who tills rich land by modern methods —a crop failure is disastrous. He is a businessman who has borrowed new capital from the bank; he has bought machinery and signed a note, two notes, a dozen; he owns blooded cattle too valuable to butcher, which eat as much in the worst years as in the best. He has listened to the prophets who tell him that the only solution for the farmer in an industrial age is to be an industrialist on the land, to increase his investment, to adhere to the highest standards of living, to follow the latest fashion in money crops. Bad business comes and he is in difficulty; a drought follows and he is ruined. The marginal farm remains a marginal farm; the best land in the East is in many cases the land that is being abandoned by its owners. And—I wondered as I crossed the shrunken Potomac into Maryland—how much more of it will be abandoned next spring, after the milch cows have been sold for beef, the tractors and combine harvesters seized by finance corporations, the notes and mortgages allowed to go unpaid?

"Let's Build a Railroad"

THE FIRST Russian talkie to be shown publicly in this country has none of the technical skill and finish that characterized the silent films of Eisenstein and his associates. *Road to Life* gives the impression of being produced by amateurs, some with a natural gift for acting, others with a mania for preaching, all with a simple and admirable faith in the virtues of the system under which they live. It isn't at all difficult to list the faults of the picture. The story is a mixture of moralizing and melodrama, sweetened with two parts of sentiment. The photography is generally conventional. The titles, which Michael Gold seems to have translated pretty literally from the Russian, are more reminiscent of *Ten Nights in a Barroom* than of *Ten Days That Shook the World*. But in spite of these faults, and half a dozen others, I would rather see this picture than the slickest society drama that ever came out of Hollywood. The Russian films take you somewhere; they rouse your anger or enthusiasm; they get something done.

Road to Life is the story of the wild children, the *besprizorni*, who were such a familiar feature of Russian life in the years just after the War. Homeless and fatherless they ranged the streets, picking pockets, snatching purses, stealing furs, shoes, apples, cigarettes, and sleeping in cellars among heaps of empty bottles. By 1923 they had become such a peril to society that the Soviets determined to "liquidate" them at any cost. Some of the older officials were in favor of jailing the whole lot of them. . . . A younger Communist, a certain Nikolai Sergeyev, puts through a plan of his own. He invites them to join a children's collective, an autonomous workers' republic to be ruled by the *besprizorni* themselves. When they discover that there are to be no guards or prison walls, and that the Soviets will furnish them with tools and raw materials, they set enthusiastically to work as carpenters, joiners, shoemakers —good Soviet citizens. The news of this experiment spreads to the city, and all the other *besprizorni* in their ragged hosts besiege the police station, asking to be accepted as members of the new collective.

Review of the Russian film *Road to Life*. (*NR*, Feb. 10, 1932.)

There are, of course, attacks on the boys' republic by counter-revolutionaries, in this case represented by the fences and Fagins who used to profit from their thefts. These double-dyed, vodka-drinking, guitar-playing villains are the melodramatic element in the picture. But the really tremendous moment, for an American audience, is an episode in the lives of the boys themselves. The ice breaks up in spring; the roads are flooded; no raw materials can reach the collective; all the band saws, lathes and planes are silent; all the young carpenters and shoemakers wander about discontentedly, begging for work. Sergeyev goes to Moscow to see what can be done about it, leaving the boys to their own devices. During his absence they have an orgy, drink themselves into insanity, kill the collective dog, smash the collective windows, break vodka bottles over their own collective heads, and are kept from destroying the valuable machinery only by the efforts of Kolka and Mustapha, formerly known as the two worst boys in the city, but now transformed into collective heroes. At this moment Sergeyev returns. Sitting in the midst of universal disorder surrounded by two hundred half-grown boys with hangovers, he says exactly nothing. Instead he unwraps a parcel containing a toy railroad, which he assembles carefully on the floor. The train runs up and down the track; the boys look on delightedly; at last Sergeyev speaks: "We need a steady supply of raw materials. Boys, let's build a railroad."

There is something overwhelmingly simple in this remark, something close to the heart of everything one admires in the new Russia. "Boys," he says, "let's build a railroad." It is as if he were saying, "Let us plan, undertake, construct; let us reach the most difficult goal that can be attained by all of us working together." Everyone is captured by the boldness of his suggestion; the government furnishes the materials; the boys strip to the waist, take pick and shovel, go digging their way through spruce forests and swamps; finally, in a delirium of emotion, the first locomotive comes chugging into the new collective station. The spectators applaud, then shuffle toward the door, murmuring perhaps, "They do things that way in Russia." It is a long way from the plains of the Volga to those speakeasies near Forty-second Street where the members of this audience will soon be talking about the depression and who's going to be

fired next week, and did you hear what happened to the
girl that Bill met in Paris—and what do you think of Russia
anyway?

Sermon Against War

THIS BOOK is a pictorial sermon against war, suggesting
the illustrated sermons against hell that were often preached
in the Middle Ages. It offers "a silent but heartrending plea,"
says Mrs. Carrie Chapman Catt in her foreword, "that courts,
round tables, conventions and conferences shall speedily become the substitute for battlefields." Specifically it consists of a
hundred-odd war photographs taken from various public and
private collections, which are mentioned by the editor in a brief
introductory note. Conspicuously absent from the list is the
United States Department of War. The use of photographs
from its archives was refused on the ground that they might
cause unnecessary pain to the relatives of fallen heroes, and
might also—though this second thought remained unspoken—
interfere with enlistments during that coming war to which
good army men look forward. The editor's acknowledgment
to the Societäts-Verlag, of Frankfurt, "for permission to include pictures from their publications" seems a very inadequate
way of saying that more than half the material in the book,
including almost all the best of it, is taken directly from two
German works, *Kamerad im Westen* and *Krieg dem Kriege*.
But the pictures, whatever their source, are being presented for
the first time to the American public, and they are shattering
documents.

They were selected, apparently, on the basis of their capacity to arouse horror and moral indignation. Here are photographs of soldiers marching through burning towns, or waiting
with fixed bayonets to go over the top, or burying their fallen

The Horror of It: Camera Records of War's Gruesome Glories,
arranged by Frederick A. Barber. New York: Brewer, Warren and
Putnam. (*NR*, May 4, 1932.)

comrades in mass graves that are immense puddles of water, mud and decomposing flesh; photographs of rebellious civilians hanged from gallows as long as a city block; of famine refugees with distended bellies and fleshless limbs; of mutilated veterans—one of them has his upper jaw and his nose shot away, leaving a great V-notch where his face should be, yet he stares into space with indifferent eyes—and always the photographs of corpses, dog-gnawed, flame-charred, fly-covered, putrefying or headless, as if to enforce the lesson that war is death, always and only death, under every circumstance of violence or degradation. And the same lesson is reëmphasized in the brief snatches of text beneath and beside the pictures.

Precisely because there is so little of it, and because the mind is so well prepared for receiving it by all these mortuary images, the question of text is vastly important in books of this nature. There are several different fashions of titling the photographs. *Kamerad im Westen*, for example, has purely informative titles—subject, place and date, nothing more. One reads, beneath the picture of ten helmeted German soldiers with fixed bayonets, "In a dugout during the barrage—the Vosges, summer of 1918." This is enough to explain the look on the faces of the soldiers, the mixture of dullness and desperation: their still persistent hope of a victorious war and a conquered Paris, even their joy in having their picture taken, are dissolving into the thought of dying in ten minutes, in twenty minutes, as soon as the German drum fire gives way to the tic-tac of Hotchkiss guns. *Krieg dem Kriege* follows another method, that of irony. Thus it reprints the words of a German pastor—"War is absolutely necessary in that it provides us with a means of education by which Youth can be trained up to virtue and national consciousness"—and above them shows the corpse of a youth thus virtuously trained, his arm half torn away, his chest pitted with shrapnel, his face a yellow grin, his bowels escaping from his torn belly.

The present volume follows neither of these methods, the factual nor the ironic. Its fashion of titling pictures is briefly and blindly sentimental. "Bones," "Derelict," "Silent," "Harvest" (of corpses, naturally), "Cannon Fodder," "Watery Grave"—these are fair samples of its signposts to the reader. A photograph of shock troops advancing behind a smoke screen is called, of all things, "Flight." The picture of the ten German soldiers in the dugout is here reproduced under the title of "Cold Steel." The dead boy with his belly torn open is "A Mother's Son"—and why not? Accompanying the pictures are some of the worst war poems ever written, the work of Robert W. Service, Richard Le Gallienne and their lesser imitators— poems which haven't even the strong stench of corpses, but merely smell rancid, like a dead mouse under the floor.

Not only does this sentimental attitude destroy the effect of what would otherwise be terrific documents, by mixing their vitriol with treacle: it also reveals an important weakness of many pacifists, and perhaps of the American pacifist movement in general. One can safely say that the editor of the present volume and most of his like-minded associates don't know what it's all about. They don't know what is the cause of a war, or how it can be prevented, or what is its worst result. Death? We must all die anyway, and there isn't much doubt that cancer and pneumonia, during the twentieth century, have caused more deaths than machine guns or high-explosive shells. War does something else. It destroys not only human lives, but human ideas, emotions, attachments, living standards, means of production, everything that unites individuals into a unity more important than themselves; war is the suicide of a civilization.

And a new world war seems nearer today than at any other moment since 1918. The battle of oil continues in Persia and Venezuela, the battle of rubber in Liberia and Malaysia, the battle of cotton markets in China, of steel and railroads in Manchuria; the battle for mere subsistence continues everywhere among working people who listen to the whisper that the government would feed them all, give them silk shirts and automobiles, if only another war could be declared. Meanwhile the opposition to war, both in this country and in western Europe, is conducted by people who have the best intentions, the noblest indignation, the most Christian sentiments, but don't know what it's all about. Sentiments are easy to deflect into other channels; a noble but uninformed hatred of war is likely to be transformed into a ferocious hatred of the Germans or the Japanese. Many of our most distinguished American pacifists, including the heads of peace societies, were easily convinced that our defense of the Morgan loans and the Dupont munition contracts was a "war to end war." Others have lately been calling for an anti-Japanese embargo which would lead to fighting almost inevitably. If our best minds continue to hold the illusion that war can be prevented by prayers and poultices, by heartrending appeals to "courts, round tables, conventions and conferences," while the struggle for raw materials and export markets continues all over the world, and international debts pile up, and tariffs rise higher week by week—why, then, we might as well resign ourselves to watching the death of our present world society.

The Flight of the Bonus Army

WHEN THE veterans of the Bonus Army first tried to escape, they found that the bridges into Virginia were barred by soldiers and the Maryland roads blocked against them by state troopers. They wandered from street to street or sat in ragged groups, the men exhausted, the women with wet handkerchiefs laid over their smarting eyes, the children waking from sleep to cough and whimper from the tear gas in their lungs. The flames behind them were climbing into the night sky. About four in the morning, as rain began to fall, they were allowed to cross the border into Maryland, on condition that they moved as rapidly as possible into another state.

The veterans were expected to disperse to their homes—but most of them had no homes, and they felt that their only safety lay in sticking together. Somehow the rumor passed from group to group that the mayor of Johnstown had invited them to his city. And they cried, as they rode toward Pennsylvania or marched in the dawn twilight along the highways, "On to Johnstown."

Their shanties and tents had been burned, their personal property destroyed, except for the few belongings they could carry on their backs; many of their families were separated, wives from husbands, children from parents. Knowing all this, they still did not appreciate the extent of their losses. Two days before, they had regarded themselves, and had thought the country regarded them, as heroes trying to collect a debt long overdue. They had boasted about their months or years of service, their medals, their wounds, their patriotism in driving the Reds out of their camp; they had nailed an American flag to every hut. When threatened with forcible eviction, they answered that no American soldier would touch them: hadn't a detachment of Marines (consisting, some said, of twenty-five or thirty men, though others claimed there were two whole companies) thrown down its arms and refused to march against them? But the infantry, last night, had driven them out like so many vermin. Mr. Hoover had announced that "after months of patient indulgence, the government met overt lawlessness as it always must be met if the cherished processes of self-government are to be preserved." Mr. Hoover and his subordinates, in their eagerness to justify his action, were about to claim that the veterans were Red radicals, that they were the dregs of the population, that most of them had criminal records and, as a final insult, that half of them weren't veterans at all.

They would soon discover the effect of these official libels. At Somerset, on the Lincoln Highway, some of them asked for food. "We can't give you any," said a spokesman for the businessmen. "The President says that you're rebels—don't you understand? You're all outlaws now." A veteran's wife and children were refused admission to a hotel, even though they offered to pay for a room in advance. At Johnstown the wealthier citizens were dismayed to hear of their arrival. Possibly half the workmen in the city were unemployed; a fifth or a sixth of the population was in need of charity. Ten thousand hungry people were a threat in themselves, but the editor of *The Johnstown Tribune* was about to conjure up new terrors. He wrote:

> Johnstown faces a crisis. It must prepare to protect itself from the Bonus Army concentrating here at the invitation of Mayor Eddie McCloskey. . . .
> In any group of the size of the Bonus Army, made up of men

gathered from all parts of the country, without discipline, without effective leadership in a crisis, without any attempt on the part of those leaders to check up the previous records of the individuals who compose it, there is certain to be a mixture of undesirables—thieves, plug-uglies, degenerates. . . . The community must protect itself from the criminal fringe of the invaders.

Booster clubs, community organizations of every sort, volunteer organizations if no sectional group is available, should get together in extraordinary sessions and organize to protect property, women and possibly life.

It is no time for halfway measures. . . .

The heroes of 1918, now metamorphosed into "thieves, plug-uglies, degenerates," were preparing to gather in the outskirts of the city, in the camp site offered them at Ideal Park. And the leading citizens, aided by the state police, were planning to use any means short of violence to keep them from reaching it. Mr. Hoover's proclamation had done its work.

At Jennerstown is a barracks of the Pennsylvania State Police, looking for all the world like a fashionable roadhouse. In front of the barracks is a traffic light. The road ahead leads westward over Laurel Hill and Chestnut Ridge; the right-hand road leads nineteen miles northward into Johnstown. It was the task of the state troopers to keep the Bonus Army moving west over the mountains, toward Ligonier and the Ohio border.

In half an hour on Saturday morning, I saw more than a thousand veterans pass through Jennerstown—that is, more than fifty trucks bearing an average of twenty men apiece. Later I was told that the procession continued at irregular intervals until Sunday evening. The troopers would wait at the intersection, twenty men on their motorcycles like a school of swift gray sharks, till they heard that a convoy was approaching; then they would dart off to meet it in a cloud of dust and blue gasoline smoke, with their hats cutting the air like so many fins. One of the troopers stayed behind to manipulate the traffic light. As the trucks came nearer, he would throw a switch that changed it into a mere yellow blinker, so that all of them could shoot past the intersection without slackening speed. They were full of ragged men, kneeling, standing unsteadily, clinging to the sideboards; there was no room to sit down. Behind each truck rode a trooper, and there were half a dozen others mingled with the crowd that watched from in front of a filling station.

The contrast between these homeless veterans, hatless, coatless, unshaven, half-starved—most of them hadn't eaten or slept for thirty-six hours, a few hadn't had so much as a drink of water—and the sleekly uniformed, well-nourished troopers who were herding them past their destination, produced a sharp effect on the crowd of backwoods farmers, who otherwise cared little about the Bonus March.

"Hey, buddies," they shouted, "turn right, turn right. Johnstown"—pointing northward—"Johnstown." The hungry men smiled and waved at them uncomprehendingly.

But a few had seen that something was wrong, that they were being carried beyond their meeting place. They tried to pass the word from truck to truck, above the roar of the motors. As they went bowling through the level village street, there was no way of escape; but just beyond Jennerstown, the road climbs steeply up Laurel Hill; the drivers shifted into second gear—and promptly lost half their passengers. The others, those who received no warning or let themselves be cowed by the troopers, were carried westward. The following week I met a New York veteran who hadn't escaped from the convoy till it passed the Ohio line. A Negro from Washington, a resident of the city for thirty years—he wasn't a bonus marcher at all, but made the mistake of walking through Anacostia in his shirt sleeves—was arrested, piled into a truck, and carried all the way to Indianapolis before he managed to tell his story to a reporter.

As for the veterans who escaped at Jennerstown, they lay by the roadside utterly exhausted. Their leaders had been arrested, dispersed, or else had betrayed them; their strength had been gnawed away by hunger or lack of sleep; they hoped to reunite and recuperate in a new camp, but how to reach it they did not know. For perhaps twenty minutes, they dozed there hopelessly. Then—and I was a witness of this phenomenon—a new leader would stand forth from the ranks. He would stop a motorist, learn the road to Johnstown, call the men together, give them their instructions—and the whole group would suddenly obey a self-imposed discipline. As they turned northward at the Jennerstown traffic light, one of them would shout, "We're going back!" and perhaps half a dozen would mumble in lower voices, "We're gonna get guns and go back to Washington."

Mile after mile we passed the ragged line as we too drove northward to the camp at Ideal Park. We were carrying two of the veterans, chosen from a group of three hundred by a quick informal vote of their comrades. One was a man gassed in the Argonne and tear-gassed at Anacostia; he breathed with an effort, as if each breath would be his last. The other was a man with family troubles; he had lost his wife and six children during the retreat from Camp Marks and hoped to find them in Johnstown. He talked about his service in France, his three medals, which he refused to wear, his wounds, his five years in a government hospital. "If they gave me a job," he said, "I wouldn't care about the bonus."

The sick man, as we passed one group of veterans after another, pointed northward and said in an almost inaudible voice, "This way, comrades, this way. Comrades, this way," till his head fell back and he lapsed into a feverish sleep.

It seemed the ragged line would never end. Here the marchers were stumbling under the weight of their suitcases and blanket rolls, here they were clustered round a farmhouse pump, here a white man was sharing the burden of a crippled Negro, here white and Negro together were snoring in a patch of shade. The road curled downward into the valley where Johnstown swelters between steep hills. On either side of us were fields of golden grain, cut and stacked for the threshers; a moment later we were winding through a forest. It was a landscape not unlike the high hills north of the River Aisne. In that other country, fifteen years before, I had seen gaunt men coming out of the trenches half-dead with fatigue, bending under the weight of their equipment. The men on the Johnstown road that day were older, shabbier, but somehow more impressive: they were volunteers, fighting a war of their own. "And don't forget it, Buddy," one of them shouted as the car slowed down, "we've enlisted for the duration."

At Ideal Park, where the new camp was being pitched, there was the same determination, combined with a hysteria caused by sudden relief from tension. A tall man with a tear-streaked face was marching up and down. "I used to be a hundred-percenter," he said, "but now I'm a Red radical. I had an American flag, but the damned tin soldiers burned it. Now I don't ever want to see a flag again. Give me a gun and I'll go back to Washington."—"That's right, Buddy," said a woman looking up from her two babies, who lay on a dirty quilt in the sun. A cloud of flies hovered above them. Another man was reading the editorial page of a Johnstown paper. He shouted, "Let them come here and mow us down with machine guns. We won't move this time."—"That's right, Buddy," said the woman again. A haggard face—eyes bloodshot, skin pasty white under a three days' beard—suddenly appeared at the window of our car. "Hoover must die," said the face ominously. "You know what this means?" a man shouted from the other side. "This means revolution."—"Yes, you're damned right it means revolution."

But a thousand homeless veterans, or fifty thousand, don't make a revolution. This threat would pass and be forgotten, like the other threat that was only half concealed in the Johnstown editorial. Next day the bonus leaders would come, the slick guys in leather puttees; they would make a few speeches and everything would be smoothed over. They would talk of founding a new fascist order of Khaki Shirts, but this threat, too, can be disregarded: a fascist movement, to succeed in this country, must come from the middle classes and be respectable. No, if any revolution results from the flight of the Bonus Army, it will come from a different source, from the government itself. The army in time of peace, at the national capital, has been used against unarmed citizens—and this, with all it threatens for the future, is a revolution in itself.

Trotsky and the Art of Insurrection

THE FARMER says, "If they don't stop foreclosing our mortgages, there's going to be a revolution." The steel worker says, "They've cut our wages once too often. It's getting to be time for a revolution." The Congressman says, waving a sheaf of letters from his constituents, "Unless the present situation is remedied, we must face the possibility of revolution."—"The situation is improving," the banker says, "but communist propaganda is spreading dangerously."—"We are not reaching the masses," the communist says. "Today the objective conditions are ripe for a revolution, but the subjective conditions are lagging behind. We must demand. . . ." Pouring another drink, the reporter says, "Well, boys, here's to the revolution tomorrow."

With the possible exception of the communist, not one of them has the vaguest idea of what a revolution means. They picture, if they are bankers, a country given over to robbery, murder and the rape of bankers' wives. They picture, if they are farmers or mill workers, a march on Washington, with banners—Congress turned out by military force—a few bankers hanged from the balcony of the Stock Exchange, to encourage the others—then everybody goes back to work at higher pay and wheat sells for $2 a bushel—everything is jake, all the world is hunky-dory.

But a revolution is something definite, tragic, subject to inexorable laws which can be deduced from revolutions of the past and applied to those of the future. "A revolution breaks out when all the antagonisms of society have reached their highest tension." "The fundamental premise of a revolution is that the existing social structure has become incapable of solving the urgent problems of development of a nation." "The most indubitable feature of a revolution is the direct interference of the masses in historic events." "Revolutions take place according to certain laws. This does not mean that the masses in action are aware of the laws of revolution, but it does mean

The History of the Russian Revolution, by Leon Trotsky. Translated by Max Eastman. New York: Simon and Schuster. 3 vols. (*NR*, Apr. 12, 1933.)

that the changes in mass consciousness are not accidental, but are subject to an objective necessity which is capable of theoretic explanation, and thus makes possible both prophecy and leadership." "Insurrection is an art, and like all arts it has its laws."

To all those vaguely anticipating a revolution, or trying to prevent it, or wavering between discontent and fear, I recommend Leon Trotsky's *History of the Russian Revolution*. It is many things in one: a narrative of what happened during eight memorable months in Russia, a natural history of the forces that lay behind the crisis, an incomparable gallery of portraits, a study of mass pressure, a pamphlet against Stalin, the author's *apologia pro vita sua*, an enormous farce with Kerensky as chief buffoon. Not all these elements are of equal value, nor all these people equally well portrayed. The two least successful characters are Trotsky himself and Stalin—the first because he is presented with a modesty too ostentatious, the second because he is pursued with a vindictive hatred that does not carry the reader along with it, but leaves him standing, as it were, outside a window, looking curiously at the gestures of a furious stranger.

Always Trotsky displays that archidiabolical pride which is both his virtue as an individual and his most dangerous quality as a statesman. Lucifer would have written a book like this about the civil war in heaven—but Lucifer, even, would be most compelling when he forgot his self-esteem and his hatred for St. Michael. It is so with *The History of the Russian Revolution*. The book is better when describing events in which neither Stalin nor Trotsky played a part, and is best of all, I think, when the author rises above his immediate subject into the sphere of universal principles—when he sets out to write a hornbook, alphabet and primer of revolutions in general.

Why do revolutions take place? It is not because people are radical or perverse, but for precisely the opposite reason, because human society is obstinately conservative. Institutions cannot be changed "as need arises, the way a mechanic changes his tools." On the contrary, a nation clings to its institutions long after they have become an intolerable hindrance to the productive forces of society. Life changes while governments remain the same. Finally, when all antagonisms have reached their highest tension, there is likely to be a social earthquake. But "the fundamental forces of the historic process are classes"; and a revolution can occur "only in case the society contains a new class capable of taking the lead in solving the problems presented by history." Thus, a revolution might be defined as *a popular uprising which results in the shifting of power from one class to another.*

How does this apply to the so-called revolutions in Latin America? Most of them are simple conspiracies by which power passes from one clique to another within the same ruling class; only the Mexican revolution of 1910–20 really deserves the name which is applied to them all. In England, the Glorious Revolution of 1688 was a compromise which ended a long period of class conflict: the real revolution was fought by Cromwell and is known as the Civil War. Our own Civil War has also been called a revolution, but in this case I think that Trotsky would disagree with Dr. Beard. The effects of it were revolutionary, but it lacked that "most indubitable feature," the direct interference of the masses in historic events.

Modern revolutions have been of three types: colonial (like our own), bourgeois (like the French revolution of 1789 and the February revolution in Russia) and proletarian (like the Paris Commune). Of the many proletarian revolutions, only one has been successful. "Notwithstanding the number of great social and political crises, a coincidence of all the conditions necessary to a victorious and stable proletarian revolution has so far occurred only once in history: in Russia in October, 1917." Just what are these conditions necessary in any country before a proletarian revolution can succeed? Trotsky describes them in a masterly chapter on "The Art of Insurrection":

POLITICAL PREMISES. — Three things take place before an economic crisis transforms itself into a revolutionary situation. First, "the ruling classes, as a result of their practically manifested incapacity to get the country out of its blind alley, lose faith in themselves; the old parties fall to pieces; a bitter struggle of groups and cliques prevails; hopes are placed in miracles or miracle workers." Second, the revolutionary class achieves a new political consciousness, "a bitter hostility to the existing order and a readiness to venture upon the most heroic efforts and sacrifices in order to bring the country out upon an upward road." But between the bankers, industrialists and big landlords on the one side, and the factory hands and tenant farmers on the other, lie broad layers of the population, shopkeepers, sales agents, small manufacturers, teachers, engineers, government employees, the professions in general, all the people whom Marx broadly described as the petty bourgeoisie. "The discontent of these intermediate layers, their disappointment with the policy of the ruling class, their impatience and indignation, their readiness to support a bold revolutionary initiative on the part of the proletariat, constitute the third political premise of a revolution."

THE SOVIETS. — "Just as a blacksmith cannot seize the red-hot iron in his naked hand, so the proletariat cannot directly seize the power; it has to have an organization accommodated to this task." "The organization by means of which the proletariat can both overthrow the old power and replace it, is the soviets . . . or," Trotsky adds elsewhere, "other mass organizations more or less equivalent." "The soviets are organs of preparation of the masses for insurrection, organs of insurrection, and after the victory organs of government."

THE REVOLUTIONARY PARTY. — But the soviets alone cannot solve the problem; they must have leadership. "Whereas the soviets in revolutionary conditions—and apart from revolution they are impossible—comprise the whole working class with the exception of its altogether backward, inert or demoralized strata, the revolutionary party represents the brain of the class. The problem of conquering the power can be solved only by a definite combination of party with soviets."

The role of the party in preparing a revolution—though Trotsky does not discuss this question—is always misrepresented by its enemies. It cannot of itself produce, or even attempt to produce, a revolutionary situation. It cannot incite the masses to rebellion by deliberately worsening the conditions under which they live. Wars are a favorable opportunity for revolution, but the party cannot provoke them. It must, on the contrary, fight to prevent them, since the cost of any war is borne, eventually, by the working class, which the party cannot afford to betray. The task of creating a revolutionary situation can safely be left to the capitalist system and the classes already in power.

To fight for the interests of the workers, to evoke in them a sense of unity and strength, to persuade them to accept its leadership—these alone are the tasks of the revolutionary party during the period of preparation. They are great in themselves, but there are greater tasks ahead. It is after the revolution is under way that the work of the party demands an almost superhuman ability, and during this period, too, that its greatest failures occur. "The general testimony of history—the Paris Commune, the German and Austrian revolutions of 1918, the soviet revolutions in Hungary and Bavaria, the Italian revolution of 1919, the German crisis of 1923, the Chinese revolution of 1925–27, the Spanish revolution of 1931 —is that up to now the weakest link in the chain of necessary conditions has been the party."

INSURRECTION AND CONSPIRACY. — The insurrection is a violent upsurging of the masses and, in a sense, it can no more be evoked at will than a flood or an earthquake. But it can be foreseen and prepared, can be organized in advance. "In this case the conspiracy is subordinated to the insurrection, serves it, makes smooth its path, hastens its victory."

Conspiracy and insurrection are often contrasted, one being defined as the deliberate undertaking of a minority, the other as the spontaneous movement of a majority. It is true that they do not always exist together. There are conspiracies which, without any help from the masses, lead to successful coups d'états—but the defeated rulers are merely replaced by others drawn from the same class. There are insurrections without conspiracies, but they are seldom victorious and never successful—even if the government is overturned, the insurrectionists have prepared nothing to take its place; the power slips from their hands and is usually taken over by intermediate factions.

A genuine revolution, leading to the victory of one social regime over another, must unite insurrection with conspiracy. And, "the higher the political level of a revolutionary movement and the more serious its leadership, the greater will be the place occupied by conspiracy in popular insurrection."

The revolutionary leaders—the party—must foresee the growing insurrection and bring it forth in due season. "The interference of the midwife in labor pains—however this image may have been abused—remains the clearest illustration of this conscious intrusion into an elemental process. . . . Between the moment when an attempt to summon an insurrection must inevitably prove premature and lead to a revolutionary miscarriage, and the moment when a favorable situation has irretrievably passed by, there exists a certain period—measured in weeks, or sometimes in months—when an insurrection may be carried out with more or less chance of success." To recognize this comparatively short period and then choose the definite moment, the very day and hour, for the last blow—"this constitutes the most responsible task of the revolutionary leaders."

THE SEIZURE OF POWER. — The moment chosen must be one when the revolution can rely upon a "genuine majority" of the people. But this majority need not be arithmetical. An insurrection always occurs at a time when it is impossible to hold a referendum. Moreover, people would vote on the same day, whereas, during a revolution, the different layers of the population reach the same conclusion at different moments, perhaps months apart. These discrepancies in time and mood can be resolved only in action—"the majority is not counted up, but won over." (What Trotsky does not add is that a referendum is usually held, after the event, with grenades and rifles. It is called a civil war.)

The theory that a proletarian revolution need not be supported by a majority of the people, that it can be carried through by a few well-trained detachments if they follow correct tactics, is known as Blanquism. It is condemned by Socialists and Communists alike, though for different reasons. A modern form of Blanquism is the "technological coup d'état" described by Guido Malaparte, whose book, so I understand, was read with great interest by the Technocrats. Malaparte asserted that Trotsky himself was the inventor of the method, and that he mastered Petrograd with a handful of men, a thousand at the most, merely by seizing its nerve centers—telegraph and newspaper offices, power stations, the telephone exchange, the State Bank.

Trotsky answers him in a few contemptuous words. It is true, he says, that the capital was seized by a small number of men. "A few thousand Red Guards, two or three thousand sailors, a score of infantry companies . . . there is no action of great masses." But the October revolution was in good truth the most popular mass insurrection in history. The bulk of the population and almost the whole army had already been won over. The revolutionary detachments could go about their work in the confidence of having supporters everywhere. The scattered government patrols were convinced of their own isolation and abandoned the very idea of resistance. There were no barricades, flaming conflagrations, looting, rivers of blood. "In reality a silence reigned more terrible than all the thunders of the world."

THE PERMANENT REVOLUTION. — These ideas briefly summarized from Trotsky's book are not, for the most part, original with him: many of them are the orthodox theories of Marx-Leninism as advanced by the Third International. Trotsky's chief quarrel with the International concerns a later stage in the revolutionary process, the question of what to do when the power has been seized. His answer, stated baldly, is to repeat the process elsewhere. "The Russian revolution," he quotes from Lenin, "is only one link in the chain of international revolution." Socialism cannot be achieved in any one country; it requires a socialist world.

"Trotskyism," as formally condemned by the Third International, consists of three propositions: (1) that the Soviet Union cannot maintain itself indefinitely in a world of capitalist Powers (the problem of military intervention); (2) that it cannot overcome within its own boundaries the disparity between industry and agriculture (the problem of the peasantry); (3) that it cannot create a shut-in-socialist society (the problem of imports and the balance of trade). These are in-

deed the principal difficulties that confront the Soviet Union.
They aggravate every crisis; they help to explain the recent
food shortage, the peasant troubles in the North Caucasus, the
arrest of the British engineers. But it cannot be denied that
astounding progress has been made toward solving these problems. And is there anything else to do but face them coura-
geously with all the resources of Soviet Russia?

Trotsky's alternative policy, with its continual threat of
war, would be justified only in case there was an imminent
chance of proletarian revolution somewhere in the West. Can
it be reasonably expected? What, for example, are the prospects of a successful revolution in the United States, the
greatest of the capitalist nations?

Let us consider one by one, in relation to this country, the
conditions which Trotsky regards as indispensable to a proletarian revolution. The first condition is undoubtedly fulfilled.
"The ruling classes, as a result of their practically manifested
incapacity to get the country out of its blind alley, lose faith in
themselves; the old parties fall to pieces; a bitter struggle of
groups and cliques prevails; hopes are placed in miracles or
miracle workers"—these words of Trotsky's might be written
yesterday or tomorrow by a Washington correspondent. But
the other conditions are far from being realized. A strong
proletariat united in its hostility to the existing order?—Our
proletariat is divided, white against black, native against for-
eign-born, skilled against unskilled, and is disheartened by its
past defeats. An organization by which the proletariat can seize
power?—There is none, and the ruling class, forewarned by its
experience in Russia, will suppress any soviet that springs into
existence. Indeed, the lessons of the Russian revolution have
been conned more carefully by the capitalists than by most of
the workers. A party acting as the brain of the revolutionary
proletariat?—In this country there is only one party, the
Communist, which attempts to be revolutionary or to act solely
for the workers, and the workers have not yet accepted it as
their own. Under these circumstances it is idle to talk about
insurrections, conspiracies or the seizure of power.

But the chief obstacle to a revolution in this country is not
the weakness of the proletariat: it is rather the strength of the
middle classes and their attachment to the old order. In the
United States the petty bourgeoisie is not only numerous but

extremely influential. Its habits of thought extend above it into the owning class, and beneath it into the ranks of what would be proletarians in other countries. Without at least winning the neutrality of professional people and white-collar workers, no proletarian revolution could even be started. It seems unlikely, today, that they will change their allegiance. A war would, of course, produce a new situation, but the nature and results of a war are impossible to predict. A successful revolution in western Europe might also change "the correlation of forces"—but the situation there is not essentially different from our own.

Yet I do not doubt that the United States will have its revolution. Alexander Hamilton saw to that when he contrived to fashion a Constitution difficult to change (except by will of the Supreme Court) and a national legislature slow to reflect the shifts in popular opinion. The Supreme Court prepared us for revolution by its decisions regarding the "due process" clause of the Fourteenth Amendment. But when the revolution comes, in five years or fifty, it is not likely to be a communist revolution. Germany, not Russia, has traced the path which we seem destined to follow if the crisis continues or recurs. Except for a disastrous war, or the happy discovery of new markets, the only thing that can turn us aside from that steep path into the sea is the influence on the middle classes of the Russian experiment, the success of "socialism in one country."

MacLeish *vs.* Cowley:
Lines for an Interment

MR. STALLINGS' title is inaccurate. It is not the First World War he presents, it is the Second. The First World War was the war which the participants thought they saw. It was a war of parades, speeches, brass bands, *bistros,*

The First World War, edited by Laurence Stallings. New York: Simon and Schuster. This review by Archibald MacLeish is reprinted with his permission. Mr. Cowley's contrary view follows. (*NR*, Sept. 20, 1933.)

boredom, terror, anguish, heroism, endurance, humor, death. It matched great cruelty with great courage. It had its fine sights and its unspeakable sights. It was a human war. Its adversaries were men and its stories were stories of men. Mr. Stallings is familiar with that war—more familiar than most Americans. He has saluted it elsewhere.

The Second World War is the First World War as we now reconstruct it. It is the First World War seen through a keyhole, interpreted from a mountaintop, judged in its causes and its effects. It is a very impersonal and terrifying war. It has no heroes. It is not human. Its actors are not men, nor even armies, but nations, continents. Its stories are not stories of men in warfare but of beginnings, devices, forces—the greed of bankers, the treachery of politicians, the rapacity of munitions makers, the starvation of nations, the death of millions, the maiming of millions. Its end is not victory or armistice or acre after acre of graves or village after ruined village, but a spiritual destruction, a world of dictatorships and tyranny, a dislocation of human life, a denouement not yet achieved.

These two wars are very different; so different that they cannot exist at the same time. To have described the Second World War during the progress of the first would not have been permitted. The beliefs of men would not have permitted it. To describe the First World War now that we are committed to the Second is equally not permitted. Beliefs today are as fanatical, as intolerant, as they were in 1918. The vogue among the intellectuals is Marxism in one form or another, with its anti-war convictions. And American intellectual Marxism is as like the Liberty Loan fanaticism of the war years as one opposite can be like another. It is only necessary to notice the hysteria with which the literary Marxist attacks and exterminates (as he believes) his literary enemies to be convinced of the likeness. Nothing which does not conform to the official dogmas will be endured and any man who questions them, and certainly any man who makes fun of them, will be strung up to the nearest lamppost of Marxian invective. The fact that the lampposts are incapable of bearing the weight of a grown man is irrelevant: the will is there, and the spitballs, and the squealing rage.

But that very fact raises a difficult question as regards Mr.

Stallings' book. Mr. Stallings is not a Marxist and neither the smell of their tar nor the sight of their noisy public lynchings can have much terror for him. In his first war play he braved an as yet unregenerate public opinion which was considerably more terrifying than that of the current breed of night riders. It is therefore difficult to understand why he has devoted his present book so religiously to the Second World War. His own feelings in the matter are of course well known. He hates war. He has excellent first-hand reason to hate it. And he has attacked the idea of war with all his very considerable powers over a long period of time, producing in the process one of the most vivid of American plays and one of the few novels of our time which can be said to have a real expectancy of life. But if it was the purpose of the present volume to record the war itself and as a whole, the limitation he has imposed upon himself becomes a defect.

There are two methods of recording the events of human history: the method of the philosopher and the method of the artist. The philosophic method at present in fashion is the method of the economic determinist who bases himself more or less upon those absolute laws of social evolution which Marx, deceived by the absolutism of nineteenth-century science, established in the Darwinian image. The War, to the economic determinist, is the Second World War—the war of economic causes in which human suffering points only an economic moral, in which all events fit into an economic pattern and in which anything irrelevant to such a pattern is dismissed. It is this method which contemporary intellectuals approve and to which they will permit no exception. The method of the artist, on the other hand, is precisely the opposite. It knows no fashions in substance though it knows very well fashions in form. And it knows no preconceived patterns. It has, that is to say, neither morality, nor text nor lesson. It records those things, seen or unseen, which have actually occurred, legibility being its only test of selection. It records them regardless of their effect upon the minds of the young or the minds of the old; regardless of their capacity for arousing anger against the recorder or anti-social enthusiasms directed at others. It records them because they are an expression of the world and because the sole motivation of the artist is an obscure and personal compulsion to arrest, to fix, to make expressive, the flowing away of the world. For the artist is not and never can be an instrument of society. He is on the contrary an enemy of society if by society is meant the particular social and intellectual fashions of his day. It is for that reason that his truth so rarely passes for true in his own generation.

The second method is the method natural to Mr. Stallings. He has used it before. And yet it is the former method he here adopts. From one end to the other his book argues a thesis and argues it ably, eloquently and unanswerably. It is one of the most compelling anti-war tracts ever produced. It avoids with a skill which amounts to genius all those flag-waving, drumbeating suggestions which, in the ordinary anti-war book, arouse, in the young, emotions the precise opposite of those intended. And its thesis is a noble thesis—there could be none nobler. No man in his senses wants another war—not even the civil war between classes which the Marxians except from their condemnations. No man who saw anything of the last war in any of its aspects can help but hate and fear the possibility of a repetition. If propaganda was what Mr. Stallings intended then Mr. Stallings has succeeded as brilliantly as his medium permitted and criticism must turn to the camera itself and to the curious fact that the snapshot which seemed in its early days so much more real, so much more actual, than any work of art is here proved to be much less real. For it is only the literal-minded, those whose senses have been crippled by the cinema, who will react to these pictures as to the written word. It is here possible to say: "That is an actual man. He is actually dead. How horrible!"—and yet feel none of the horror which Mr. Stallings himself has elsewhere put into a phrase no photograph illustrated. It is possible to turn through the whole book and experience all the sensations of loathing and hatred for war which its editor proposes without once recapturing the feel and taste of the time itself, the indelible experience which Mr. Stallings has, in his own office, recalled.

It is difficult, however, to believe that propaganda was in fact all Mr. Stallings intended. It is difficult to believe that with his knowledge and with his great abilities he was not also moved to recall that other, that First World War. I concede that it is today not only immoral but unfashionable as well to doubt that all the dead were victims—to suggest that some few ridiculously believed in the thing for which (or so they thought) they died. But fashions in thinking would not stand in Mr. Stallings' way. And yet these dead are absent.

Archibald MacLeish.

ii

I * agree with Mr. MacLeish to the extent of believing that many poets should not engage in propaganda. Mr. MacLeish himself is an outstanding example. As a poet, he is one of the three or four most distinguished that we now possess, but he is a quite inferior propagandist. Both his verse and his prose comment on *The First World War* exhibit him in this second function. They are bad propaganda, not so much because they lead to false conclusions as because they don't lead to any. One statement cancels off another. "The sole motivation of the artist is an obscure and personal compulsion to arrest, to fix, to make expressive, the flowing away of the world." In simpler words, Mr. MacLeish believes that the artist depicts the world as it is, without criticism. It would follow that the artist is not an enemy but rather a mere recording instrument of existing society. But, "The artist is not and never can be an instrument of society. He is on the contrary an enemy of society, if by society is meant the particular social and intellectual fashions of the day." In other words, the artist is a warrior against the present and a prophet of the future. It doesn't make sense.

But let us summarize his argument as best we can. There were really, he says, two wars, one human, the other inhuman; one partly ugly and yet partly admirable by virtue of the faith that went into it, the other altogether ugly. The first was the war that the soldiers thought they saw; the second was the real war as seen by the Marxists through a keyhole.—It seems impossible today to conduct an argument without mentioning Marx. The more conservative the critic, the more he insists on dragging in Marx by the beard. But the Marx he drags in is a grotesque effigy quite without relation to the author of *The*

* Cowley's reply. (MacLeish's review was accompanied by a poem, "Lines for an Interment," to which Cowley refers in the fourth sentence of this paragraph.)

Communist Manifesto. The real Marx did not believe in economic forces to the exclusion of human emotions. The whole point of Marxism is that it is a doctrine about and for living men. It says, in effect, that under the present system we are ruled by impersonal beginnings, devices, forces—human beings are subjected to things non-human—but that our task is to devise a state of society in which men direct those forces and ride the whirlwind instead of being tossed about by it.

But let us return to Mr. MacLeish's argument. He claims that Mr. Stallings presents the second, the altogether ugly war, and is, for that reason, making propaganda. He should have presented the first war instead: that would have been art. —Sweeping aside all qualifications, are we to understand Mr. MacLeish as saying that it is propaganda to write against war and art to write in favor of it? He would doubtless answer that it is art to tell the truth. But does this consist of parades, speeches, brass bands, heroism and humor?

It happens that Mr. Stallings has previously described the first, the human and partly admirable war. By now we have learned to recognize the political effect of *What Price Glory.* People at first regarded it as pacifist propaganda, but pretty soon the movies got hold of it, and the publicity department of the United States Marine Corps got hold of it, reduced it to its essence, stirred in a few brass bands and *bistros*—and the result was those gay devil-dogs, Captain Flagg and Sergeant Quirt, urging young men by their heroic example to join the Marines and sleep with foreign women. It would seem that Mr. MacLeish is advising Mr. Stallings to produce more Flaggs and Quirts, more Marine Corps recruiting posters. But the lesson of the review isn't quite so simple. Mr. MacLeish is not (communist critics please copy) a Jew-baiter and sword-rattler. He hates war as profoundly as anybody could. What he says in effect is that other artists, out of hatred for propaganda, ought to do their best to bring about that very disaster which they and he most want to prevent. This is either nonsense, or else it is mysticism too deep for most of us to understand.

I suspect that it is nonsense. But I also suspect that the intellectual confusion of this review is to be explained by an emotional conflict lying far beneath it. Mr. MacLeish served through the War as an artillery officer. His dearest friends served in the War and many of them were killed, still believing that they were fighting to defend their own country: now they are rotting in pine coffins, in foreign earth. And echoing through his mind must be those words so often printed on posters stuck up behind the Isonzo or north or south of the Marne, so often shouted by Reichstag members and British M.P.s and American congressmen: *These dead shall not have died in vain.* But fifteen years have passed and these dead are absent.

If they fought purely for adventure, they found it and found that it wasn't as advertised. If they fought, as Americans were urged to do, for Liberty, Democracy and the Fourteen Points, they fought for abstractions now more deeply buried than all the dead of the Argonne. If they fought to save their own country from the invader, to preserve a land of hills and prairies where each man might live securely on his own acres— well, who owns their country now? What if the phantom invader had really come, had crossed the Alleghenies over the trail of Daniel Boone and Meriwether Lewis? Would it matter now if we were paying tribute to the Allgemeine Elektrizitäts Gesellschaft instead of General Electric?—to Fritz Thyssen instead of Mellon and Morgan?—if the farm lands of Iowa were seized by an insurance company in Frankfurt instead of insurance companies in New York and Hartford? The invaders have come and have taken our land in spite of those who died. It is indeed time that we told the whole truth about the War, as Mr. MacLeish demands; my only complaint against Mr. Stallings' book is that he could not tell enough of it. It is time for us to admit that you, MacLeish, and I, Cowley, and Hemingway, Wilson, Dos Passos, Ramon Guthrie, our relatives who crashed in airplanes or died by machine-gun fire, our friends who were crippled—that all of us fought in vain. It is time to inscribe at the entrance to every veterans' graveyard and over the tombs of all the unknown soldiers, *They died bravely, they died in vain.*

Malcolm Cowley.

A Debate Continued:
The Dead of the Next War

My dear Cowley:

(I trust you will permit this more personal address as it is to you as a poet, rather than to you as an editor of *The New Republic* I address myself.)

Your very fair comment upon my review of *The First World War* raises two issues: my personal powers of logic and the attitude to be adopted by our generation—yours and mine—toward those whom the War destroyed.

The first is of minor importance. I will not even debate the epithet of propagandist which you confer upon me. I have been, and shall continue to be, engaged to the extent of my powers in opposing the silly but nevertheless mephitic effort of the Communist intellectuals to reduce all art to propaganda for the Revolution. Propaganda can only be fought with irony and ridicule, and irony and ridicule will appear to be propaganda to the propagandists. From a certain point of view, as you yourself have suggested, anything is propaganda which a man doesn't like.

I may, however, in fairness, suggest that my faults of logic are not perhaps such palpable faults as you make them appear. When I say that "the sole motivation of the artist is an *obscure and personal compulsion*" to depict the world as it is, I do not say, and do not mean to say, that the artist is "a mere recording instrument of existing society." Those words are yours and they are, if you will permit me to say so, quite contrary to the obvious meaning of my sentence. There is therefore no contradiction between my remark and my further remark that the artist is not an instrument of society but is indeed the enemy to so much of society as is expressed by the social and intellectual fashions of the day. Both statements would seem to me to be true and to make up a single truth between them—which is that the compulsion under which the poet writes is an obscure and personal compulsion to arrest, to fix, to make expressive, the flowing away of the world, whether beautiful or ugly,

This letter from MacLeish is reprinted with his permission. A rebuttal from Cowley follows. (*NR*, Oct. 4, 1933.)

whether with praise or with distaste, and that the fashionable intellectual ideas of his time, which forever attempt to distort, to sterilize, that flowing away of the world in their own image, are irrelevant, even hateful, to him. You, as a poet, can testify to this truth. You will declare without hesitation that you have written poetry out of your personal emotion and under a personal compulsion, and never to illustrate, or support, the doctrines which have, from time to time during our forty years of the world, been fashionable.

However, I shall not attempt to defend my logic. If it can't defend itself it should go down. The important issue raised by your rejoinder is the issue touching the War. I am grateful for your assurance to the Communist critics that I am neither a Jew-baiter nor a sword-rattler. I presume you address Mr. Michael Gold, whose attack upon my *Frescoes for Mr. Rockefeller's City* recently appeared in *The New Republic*. Mr. Gold appears to be an intelligent but badly frightened young man whose defensiveness about his politics, his race and his literary career amounts to an obsession. I, for example, am a Jew-baiter to Mr. Gold not because my poem contains a single reference to that race but because Mr. Gold, who suffers from my ridicule of his political ideas, is a Jew. In the same way I am a fascist not because the poem in any way raises the fascist issue but because Mr. Gold, who is hurt by my ridicule of a well-known New York literary type (to which, I may add, he does *not* belong) is himself a Communist. Precisely why a magazine with the liberal traditions of *The New Republic* permitted a reviewer to drag a religious herring across the track I am unable to say.

You have faithfully and justly described my attitude toward war in general and toward The War in particular. My own experience of it was neither heroic nor particularly hard, but it destroyed my brother, many of my friends, two years of my life. My criticism of Mr. Stallings is not that he should have presented the war of Captain Flagg and Sergeant Quirt, but that in presenting a war from which the dead were deleted, save in their corpses, he presented less than the whole truth. I admit that the presentation of the whole truth might be morally dangerous; that the suppression of part of the truth strengthened the force of Mr. Stallings' book as propaganda against war. But as a reviewer of Mr. Stallings' book I could not in honesty ignore the suppression. And I cannot now agree that a distortion of truth, however desirable it may be socially and morally, produces art.

Neither, though I am moved by the sincerity and feeling with which you make your final appeal, can I agree that it is an answer to all this, to the tangled emotions from which we suffer, to the whole spiritual problem of the War, to admit to ourselves now that our friends, those of our generation who died, died in vain. Indeed it was precisely in protest against this point of view that the poem you so harshly criticize was written. Obviously, standing here upon the little heap which time forever pushes up to give a better perspective of the past —obviously you and I, alive in the year 1933 and looking back —obviously we can say in your fine phrase: "they died bravely, they died in vain." The history of the postwar world proves they died in vain. Every economic consideration proves they died in vain. But what, I demand of you as poet, not as editor, what *is* vanity in death? Is it economic frustration? Is it failure to ameliorate the lot of society? Is it historical abortiveness? Or is it perhaps conceivable that death is something between a man and his own soul, a personal and not a social experience? Is it perhaps conceivable that the measure of vanity in a man's death is to be found not afterwards in a history which to him has no existence, but presently in the circumstances in which his death is met? Is it perhaps conceivable that to die generously and in loyalty to a believed-in cause is not, regardless of the success of that cause, regardless even of its validity, to die in vain? I ask you this as a poet.

New York City.   *Archibald MacLeish.*

ii

Dear MacLeish:

—But I haven't the art of being schizophrenic. I am radically unable to divide myself into a series of persons—poet, editor, critic, western Pennsylvanian, survivor of the last war and candidate for the next—each one of them having a different response to life and a different truth. I can give you only one answer.

Speaking in my own person, because I have no other, I can say that the issues between us are not at all as you have stated them. Your personal powers of logic? I would be the first to admit them. I questioned only your exercise of logic in your review of Stallings' book, and I did so only because your apparent confusion there cast light on a deeper confusion. Readers of that review will decide whether there was ground for my questioning.—Art and propaganda? This issue has been debated now for three long years, and there would be some value in the argument if anybody had a clear idea of what propaganda was, or art. Let us leave them both in peace. But I'm surprised to find you still believing, after three years, that irony and ridicule used for political purposes are not propaganda. If the Communists answered your nevertheless mephitic outbursts against them with irony and ridicule, would that be propaganda? Of course it would. Propaganda is what the other fellow writes.—The attitude to be adopted by our generation toward those whom the War destroyed? Here we come closer to the real issue, yet even here there is no argument between us which cannot be resolved by definition. We differ chiefly in emphasis—

And this can be proved by what we remember about any of those young men who died so uncomplainingly in the Argonne or along the wet meadows of the Yser. They were good guys—that's what we said about them in those days—and they entered an officers' training camp partly because it was the right thing to do and partly because they felt a physical need for danger. But danger has a way of justifying the cause for which it is endured. Our friends soon became patriots; they believed in four-minute speeches; they marched to the front convinced that they were fighting for Democracy, that they were risking death to remove the menace of the German Beast, to protect their own land from rape by the invader. You know and I know that they felt pretty good about it.

Theirs, of course, was a special case. Most of the ten millions killed in battle were common soldiers. Most of them served long enough to lose whatever exhilaration they may have felt in the beginning: there remained with them only a dead nausea and the hope that it would soon be ended and that they could get home perhaps with the loss of a foot or a hand.

Some of them mutinied. I happened to be quartered for two weeks with a battalion of Chasseurs that deposed its officers and marched toward Paris. From that one battalion of 1,800 men—subjected as it was to daily casualties, with heavier losses in each attack, but periodically restored to its full complement—the Germans had killed or wounded 15,000 in a little less than three years. The average Chasseur, in other words, could expect three months of active service before he was carried off to a field hospital, if he was lucky, or to a graveyard. After the mutiny the ringleaders were shot by the French. The survivors marched back to the front, where many of them fought with the spirit of steers driven into the abattoir—there might be a chance of life if they went ahead, but it was sure death to run away.

And however they felt about it, they were killed. Patriotism, love of danger, fear, boredom, disgust—all the things that went on inside their heads didn't matter. The shells burst, the machine guns tic-tic-tacked, and presently they became the things that Stallings shows in his photographs—a hand sticking out of the mud, a carcass blown by flies, a unit in a pile of corpses, an entry in a ledger at Headquarters. What shall we say of them now?

We can say, remembering the perished emotions of some of them, that they died generously and in loyalty to a believed-in cause. It is true. Or we can say, measuring their aspirations against the world which their efforts helped to produce, that they died for an illusion, died in vain—and it is terribly true. We can judge their deaths subjectively or objectively. The argument between us, as regards the dead of the last war, is a matter merely of emphasis. But these dead are not the real argument.

The real issue between us is, *How shall we regard the dead of the next war?* In the light of this question, the difference merely of emphasis becomes a gulf of opposed meanings. For, if we emphasize the useless deaths of the last war, we can be certain of our attitude toward the next! But if, on the other hand, we emphasize the happy illusions of these men who died defending their country—from whom? —and saving democracy —for what? —then we can look forward more or less calmly to the battles in which other generous and loyal men, our sons and nephews this time, not our friends and brothers, will die in the same courageous fashion. We may even come to share the illusions of the dead, and we shall in any case defend the system which makes the next war as inevitable as tomorrow.

What are you doing to prevent that war before it is too late? I ask you this as an editor, a man, a poet or anything you please.

Malcolm Cowley.

To a Revolutionary Critic

DEAR GRANVILLE HICKS: I feel too strongly about your book, *The Great Tradition*, to write an impersonal review of it; the author and the critic have too much in common. Both of us believe that the central feature of modern life is a struggle between classes which is also a struggle of the working class against all forms of exploitation. Both of us believe that the battle extends to every front, even the literary front. We don't regard literature as a mere department of politics: that would be silly. But both of us are convinced that literature and politics, art, science and education, all are departments of life, and that no artist or writer can divest himself of his role in life. He takes, or eventually will be forced to take, one side or the other, and both of us have made the same choice.

This doesn't at all mean that we agree on every subject. There is room on our side for many shades of belief, and it seems to me that your own shade is too sanguine. You face the future with entire confidence, saying that "even in the days of stress, revolutionary writers will have a kind of courage that others cannot share. . . . They will know that they are participating in a battle that, in the long run, is for civilization itself, and they will have no doubt of the outcome." A football coach might talk like this at a pep-rally on the evening before a big game—"We can't lose, we simply can't lose." To me it seems

The Great Tradition, by Granville Hicks. New York: The Macmillan Company. (*NR*, Nov. 8, 1933.)

wiser to acknowledge that the other side may win, even though
their triumph would destroy living forces in our present civilization. That civilization itself may disappear in the next great
series of imperialist wars.

It is because the stakes are so high and the outcome is
undecided that I cannot write impersonally about *The Great
Tradition*. Inevitably your book will serve as a weapon in the
struggle. It will perform this service less by direct argument
than by the cogency of its interpretations, less by precept than
by example. If the weapon is bad, it is sure to be used against
us. That is why I demand that it be nothing less than superb. I
am delighted by its virtues, saddened by its faults, and I want
to speak bluntly about one and the other.

The Great Tradition is possibly the first book in which the
history of American literature since the Civil War is arranged
into a simple and intelligible pattern. This in itself is a rare
virtue, and it becomes still rarer when one considers that you
have achieved it without sacrificing your sense of literary values to your political admirations or antagonisms, and without
ever lapsing into that multihorrendous style adopted by most
of those who try to be Marxian critics. The book is full of good
critical writing, sound judgments and illuminating phrases. In
large part, moreover, it fulfills its chief purpose—which was, I
take it, to show that revolutionary writing, instead of being
alien to the American tradition, was always at the heart of it.

These are considerable achievements, and you will forgive
me for treating them more briefly than your faults, which are
harder to define. Chief among them is a certain harshness and
literalness of approach, which becomes most obvious in your
discussion of Henry James. You say of his novels that for the
most part they seem "completely remote from the lives of the
vast majority of men." You say that his characters exist in a
world "of almost complete abstractions," and with such a
world you have no patience whatever. Defending the tradition
of exact, class-conscious realism, you seem to ask that every
novel should present a world as round and unmistakable as the
lid of a garbage can. And you completely disregard the realism
that Henry James achieved by virtue of his very abstractions.

You cannot forgive him for living in exile. As for Robert
Herrick, Upton Sinclair, Frank Norris, the muckraking novel-

ists who stayed at home, you cannot forgive them for remaining middle-class in the midst of their revolt. You judge them, not in relation to the society they tried to express, but rather from the standpoint of a revolutionary critic of the year 1933. With a better sense of historical perspective, your judgments might remain essentially the same, but would lose their dogmatic tone, would become a shade more lenient and persuasive.

In general you ask entirely too much of novelists, and at the same time too little. You ask too much sociological knowledge—as, for example, when you say that "to describe the contemporary scene regional writers would have had to record the breakdown of sectional lines, the growth of extra-regional alliances, the increasing industrialization of agriculture, the steady march of the factory across the continent. They would have had to show how machinery reduced the labor time spent in producing a bushel of wheat from three hours to ten minutes . . . how the shrinkage of the public domain killed the optimism that had thrived while the westward pilgrimage went on." It doesn't seem to occur to you that they might have described and demonstrated all these things, might have thoroughly displayed their sociological insight, and still might have remained inferior novelists for want of other qualities which you do not demand of them—warmth, vigor, imagination, an eye for human oddities, an ear for the good music of words.

Moreover, just as your demands on authors are one-sided, so your explanation of their motives is simplified to the point of distortion. People are poor and do this; people are rich and do that—so runs the easy formula. Thus, speaking of writers in my own college generation, you say that they ignored society and cultivated art in the abstract because, "if a privileged group feels in no danger of losing its privileges, it comes in time to take them for granted." You say that they decided "to make the most of the advantages with which they were blessed. . . . It was the natural response of the members of a privileged group." But later, you continue, after the Wall Street crash, these esthetes in large part become radicals, because, "in the first place, many of these complacent youths were directly affected by the depression, as their incomes or their fathers' incomes declined."

Now I happen to belong, with many of my friends, among these writers whose motives you are trying to set forth, and I can assure you that under Harding and Coolidge they weren't privileged in the least. They were miserably paid white-collar workers who lived in garrets or basements, ate somewhat irregularly and wrote for magazines that were careless about paying for contributions. So far from being an expression of their privileged position in society, their literary opinions were essentially a protest against society—in those days it seemed quite useless to protest by political action. It happens, moreover, that since the depression several writers of this category have lived rather better than they did before, being older and better established in their profession. They had nothing to lose during prosperity; now they have something; yet this has not prevented them from becoming radicalized. Here is a paradox which cannot be explained by the dry formula of economic determinism—which, incidentally, is not the method proper to Marxian critics.

Not at this point, but sometimes at others, you overstep the thin line which separates unfavorable judgment from abuse. Thus, granting the truth of everything you say about James Branch Cabell's books, I can see no justification for your ascribing a "fundamental venality" to their author; phrases like this belong elsewhere than in a history of literature. As for Thornton Wilder, it is simply untrue that "his work merely reflects the cowardice and dishonesty of his spirit." People can disagree with us without being dishonest and fight for the existing order without being cowards.

Faults like harshness, narrowness, dogmatism, are not at all inherent in our position. It is our business, I think, to leave them to our opponents. Let them, lacking sounder arguments, heap abuse on people with whom they disagree. Let *them* be stingy of praise. Let *them* burn books and misrepresent the culture of the past and even, if they choose, set out to destroy it lest it threaten their position; it is our own function to interpret and preserve that culture for a living future. Let *them* be harsh, arid, one-sided and dogmatic. Let them, in a word, write propaganda; they need it in order to justify things as they are and make people accept the bleak world toward which they are leading. Generosity and human warmth are fighting on our side. We need simply discharge our responsibility as critics, we need simply find and set down the truth in its human complexity, being confident that the truth is all the propaganda we need.

Homesteads, Inc.

MR. RALPH BORSODI is at the same time an excellent guide and a dangerous messiah.

There are thousands of middle-class families that want to escape from industrial ugliness and insecurity and build themselves new lives close to nature. For such families, Mr. Borsodi is likely to prove an excellent guide. Provided they have some capital (it needn't be large)—provided the family includes one breadwinner sure of his job (it needn't be a very good one)— provided the wife has a talent for efficient housekeeping (which needn't amount to sheer genius like Mrs. Borsodi's)— provided mother and father and children all have a gift for living next to the soil and are willing to undergo hardships in the early years—then they can safely take Mr. Borsodi's advice.

Others, too, can take his advice if suitable facilities are present. Unemployed and half-employed clerks and mechanics can form themselves into communities, move into the far suburbs and, if anyone advances sufficient capital, can build their own houses and raise most of their own food. Near Dayton, Ohio, Mr. Borsodi has helped to found a Homestead Unit of thirty-five families. If the first unit succeeds—and I think its success depends on whether the thirty-five families can find a small but dependable source of outside income—new units will be established. Their influence may indirectly serve to raise living standards in many other communities.

But Mr. Borsodi isn't satisfied with being a guide to the middle class or an adviser to certain groups of the underpriv-

Flight from the City, by Ralph Borsodi. New York: Harper and Brothers. (*NR,* Nov. 29, 1933.)

ileged. In his new book, *Flight from the City*, he proposes to solve the whole problem of unemployment and insecurity in modern life—and to solve it, moreover, without labor unions, higher wages for the poor and higher taxes for the rich; without the public ownership of a single factory. His proposal will therefore seem especially attractive to those who fear public ownership and higher taxes. The trouble is that instead of solving the problem it might end by making society even more insecure than it is now. That is why Mr. Borsodi is a dangerous messiah.

He belongs to the class of those who might be called push-button prophets. They look at the world and find it full of injustice, and want to remedy the injustice, but without really disturbing anybody. They think that if one switch could be thrown, one button pushed in a row of buttons, one tonic administered from a shelf of tonics, then everything would be vastly improved. For some the proper button is Currency, for others Credit, for others Taxation, for still others Hours of Labor; for Hitler it is the Jews. Each prophet believes in the perfect efficacy of his own button. Thus, Mr. Borsodi broadly condemns "the futile process of trying to produce prosperity by creating new industries, expanding credit, cheapening money, spreading work, shortening hours of labor or establishing unemployment insurance." He attacks social planning and all other means of protecting society from the effects of what he is satisfied to call "that mysterious phenomenon known as the business cycle." He speaks with contempt and hatred of everything done in Russia. Instead he offers his own simple path for reaching Utopia without political action or civil turmoil.

Unemployment, to Mr. Borsodi, is an elementary problem to be solved by elementary means. John Doe and Jane Doe are no longer working. They no longer receive, on Saturdays, a pay envelope containing enough money to provide for their weekly needs. Charity will destroy their self-respect (and Mr. Borsodi regards unemployment insurance as a form of charity). The public control of industry won't give them back their jobs and will, in Mr. Borsodi's opinion, render our economic life even more insecure than private control has rendered it. What then should be done? Why, the answer is simple—let John Doe and his wife produce their own food, clothing and shelter. If they haven't enough capital to build themselves a home in the country, let money be loaned them by the state—they can earn enough in their spare time to repay it, with interest. By this method, "we should not only relieve them temporarily. If we did it on a sufficiently large scale, we should end the problem of unemployment for the whole country and end it permanently."

We should do nothing of the sort. No matter how large the scale on which Mr. Borsodi's proposal was adopted, it could not fulfill his promises to the unemployed. It could not make them self-sustaining or really secure. Even if millions of them raised all their own food, wove all their cloth on hand looms, owned their houses free of mortgage and provided their own amusements—even then, unless they sank to the level of serfs in medieval Europe, they would still be dependent on society, they would still have needs which only the outside world could supply.

First of all, under Mr. Borsodi's scheme, they would need pumps, piping, electric cable, concrete mixers, band saws, pressure kettles, all sorts of mechanical equipment to lighten their domestic burdens. In order to buy this equipment, they would need cheap and abundant credit. In order to operate it, they would need electric power at a reasonable price. They would need medical service and hospitals staffed by trained physicians. They would need education for their children, beyond the rudiments that could be taught at home. They would need good roads maintained by the state. They would need to pay taxes—road taxes, school taxes, miscellaneous taxes to prevent floods and forest fires, drain malarial marshes, maintain hospitals, universities and libraries. Unless they paid them, public revenues would dwindle away and most of these services would have to be abandoned.

In other words, Mr. Borsodi's followers would require money. The less of it they required, the more urgently would they require it. No matter how much they produced for themselves, the subsistence farmers would also need a cash crop—they would have to sell something, whether it was wheat, beef cattle or their own brawn. The price for which the cash crop was sold would depend on the economic condition of the nation as a whole. If that condition became any more unsound than at present, the subsistence farmers would receive so little, they would have to work such long hours producing their cash crop of grain or industrial commodities, that either they would be reduced to serfdom or else their subsistence homesteads would be sold for taxes. In any case, their fate would continue to depend on the "consequences of that mysterious phenomenon known as the business cycle."

This suggests the answer to the correspondent who asked Mr. Borsodi whether his plans could be made continuously operative—"I mean, can a community organized on your principles not only afford a sane, healthful existence to its members, but also, as long as a capitalistic organization of society endures, a modest and constant increment of usable wealth in the form of money, to give access to the world and its goods outside the community, to provide insurance against age and casualty, and to provide some inheritance for the next generation?" It can, but only so long as capitalism endures in a more or less healthy condition.

Mr. Borsodi is betting on capitalism—but at the same time he is trying to sponge his own horse. If I were to write him in turn, I should speak somewhat as follows:

"You are betting on industrial capitalism to provide cheap machinery, abundant credit, low taxes, good markets, jobs at fair wages—everything your followers need to make their homesteads successful. But at the same time, you are urging a course of action which is calculated to cripple industrial capitalism and absolutely prevent it from furnishing those essentials.

"Let us consider the implications of your proposal, as stated by yourself. You say: 'If enough families were to make their homes economically productive, cash-crop farmers specializing in one crop would have to abandon farming as a business and go back to it as a way of life.' That is all very well for the farmers themselves. But this country contains millions of acres—especially in the wheat belt of the Great Plains and in the irrigated regions of the Southwest—that are good for nothing except one-crop farming. Much of this land is mortgaged to banks or insurance companies. If it were all abandoned, the banks would crash, the insurance companies cease payments—then where would be the cheap credit which subsistence homesteads require?

"You say: 'Food is our most important industry. A war of attrition, such as we have been carrying on all alone, if extended on a large enough scale, would put the food industry out of its misery.' And you say: 'The textile and clothing industries, with their low wages, seasonal unemployment, cheap and shoddy products, would shrink to the production of those fabrics and those garments which it is impractical for the average family to produce for itself.' You seem to think that these three great industries—food, textiles, garments—would die cleanly, shrink away to white bones like a thirsty man in the desert. But industries don't die in that fashion. They thresh about, involve thousands in their ruin, infect the whole country with the smell of their corpses. Incidentally, by contracting the market, their death would make it impossible for other industries—'those which would be desirable and essential because they would be making tools and machines, electric-light bulbs, iron and copper pipe, wire of all kinds'—to produce those necessities at the low price which subsistence farmers would be able to pay.

"It is a bleak prospect that you are holding out. Of course it is more than possible that such industrial disasters would goad the workers to the point of taking over all factories and operating them for the common good. In this case alone there would be some hope that, indirectly, your proposal 'would release men and women from their present thralldom to the factory and make them masters of machines instead of servants to them'—that it 'would end the power of exploiting them which ruthless, acquisitive and predatory men now possess' and 'free them for the conquest of comfort, beauty and understanding.' These ends of yours, Mr. Borsodi, are the good ends which all of us desire; the bloodiest revolution of modern times was fought to achieve them. They will never be reached merely by moving to the country and canning spinach."

Art Tomorrow

IN THE course of several articles recently printed in *The New Republic*, I criticized an attitude toward art and life that prevailed in the literary world of the 1920's. This attitude, which I called the religion of art, I tried to describe in terms of the books it produced and the unsatisfactory courses of action to which it led. I said that it now belonged to the past, that it died in theory with the Dada movement and in practice with the world crisis of capitalism, but I gave no more than a hint of the ideas or doctrines that I thought would take its place.

It is part of a critic's job to be honest with his readers, to state his own ideas and not to hide behind a mask of historical infallibility. What were the assumptions from which I wrote?

I might simply present them as the answers to an imaginary questionnaire. Let us suppose that you, the reader, have compiled a list of questions dealing with the problems of artists in the age now beginning. And let us suppose that I, the writer, have undertaken to answer them, not exhaustively, for that would require a book or a library of books, but informally and briefly.

Should artists devote themselves, you ask first of all, to art or propaganda?

In terms of an apparently simple distinction between two familiar words, this question conceals a type of metaphysical thinking that carries us back toward the beginning of German Romantic philosophy. It was Kant, in fact, who advanced the notion that esthetic activity and practical activity (in other words, art and life) are forever separate and that art has no goal outside itself, being "purposiveness without purpose" —*Zweckmässigkeit ohne Zweck*. This notion was elaborated by other German thinkers, and especially by Schopenhauer, who in turn exerted a great influence on the art-for-art's-sake movement in France. Eventually it took the shape of a whole series of things supposed to be in eternal opposition—form against

NR, May 23, 1934. This essay was used as the concluding section of *Exile's Return* in its first edition (New York: W. W. Norton and Company, 1934), but was omitted from later editions.

matter, art against life, artists against philistines, poetry against science, emotion against reason, then vision or imagination against will or purpose, contemplation against action, and finally poetry or art against propaganda. In this last opposition, all the others are secretly contained. "Art" is vision, form, repose, truth and beauty, the eternal, everything that is "good" for the artist. "Propaganda" is effort, change, science, philistinism, falsity and ugliness, everything that is artistically "evil." Once we have accepted these definitions of art and propaganda, the question of choosing between them seems ridiculous.

But the definitions themselves are not to be accepted. They imply a special attitude toward life and, in particular, a metaphysical doctrine that Schopenhauer was the first to put forward. It was his idea that "the world" is evil and changing and animated by universal Will, and that the artist's duty and privilege is to escape from the world into the sphere of "art," of esthetic contemplation, of perfect will-lessness. One cannot say that any metaphysical notion of this sort is now "exploded" in the sense that a scientific theory may be exploded by the accumulated force of observed facts. It is certain, however, that Schopenhauer's metaphysic is sentimental and foreign to the scientific temper.

Today we know as a simple matter of record that the universe is actually changing in all its parts, from star galaxies down to species of microscopic plants, but we cannot say that this process of universal change is either "good" or "evil"; our adjectives aren't big enough to circumscribe the cosmos. Today we know by virtue of our personal experiences, our pains and pleasures, that human society is changing also. We know that men's ideas and ambitions, and the conflicts between them, are part of this changing world, as are also the works of art that men produce. There is no single type of human activity, whether it be painting pictures or smoking pipes or making money, that can be treated as if it existed separately from all the other types of activity. The whole series of oppositions—art against life, poetry against science, contemplation against action—can safely be swept aside. The real answer to the question whether writers and painters should devote themselves to art or propaganda is that the question is irrelevant: writers should devote themselves to writing and painters to painting.

Yet there is a real distinction that partly takes the place of the one supposed to exist between art and propaganda. The real distinction is not metaphysical, but personal and practical, and it depends very simply on the level of mind from which one writes. If one writes only from the top level of consciousness, in the light of beliefs that have been recently acquired and not assimilated, one is almost certain to write badly, to neglect or distort the things that are hidden underneath, to write in a way that is emotionally false and can be dismissed as "propaganda." But if one has fully absorbed the same beliefs, has felt and lived them, one may treat them in a way that is emotionally effective—that is in other words "art."

And now you have another question. *What, you ask, is the function of art? In other words, what will take the place of the religion of art after it disappears?*

I don't know what is the function of art. Is it a "purging," a "refinement of gross experience," a "center of repose"; is it amusement, escape, self-expression, or a useful means of inciting people to good actions? I suspect that on occasion it can be any or all of these. One thing I know for certain. There is no single theory of the function of art that has not finally confined and narrowed and impoverished art, whether the theory be that of Plato, Aristotle, Kant, Schopenhauer, Mallarmé, Plekhanov or the Russian Association of Proletarian Writers. Art is obviously richer, more varied in its purposes and effects, than any of the theories that have tried to reduce it to order and guide it in one direction. When the religion of art disappears, let us hope that no other limiting doctrine will take its place.

And yet—always this qualification creeps in—there is one function of art I should like to see emphasized above the others, and that is its humanizing function. I believe that all good works of literary art have the same fundamental thesis. All of them teach us that life is bigger than life; that life as portrayed by the creative imagination is more intense, more varied, more purposeful (or perhaps more futile), more tragic or comic, more crowded with events and meanings and yet more harmoniously organized than is the life we have been leading day by day. Sometimes we are discouraged by the contrast and try to escape into a dream world that seems to be, but really is not, the world of the artist. Sometimes we merely contemplate the work of art, gratefully and with a feeling of relief from strain. Sometimes, however, we try to reinterpret our daily lives in the light of the artist's vision. The new values we derive from his work, when projected into our own experience, make it seem more poetic, dramatic or novelistic, more sharply distinguished from the world of nature, in a word, more human.

In addition to giving more humanity to our lives, art also has the function of humanizing nature, in the sense of making it more fit for human beings to live in. The prehistoric world must have seemed alien and terrible to the first tribes that wandered over the face of it. Vast portions of the world are alien to their descendants today. Before a man can feel at home in any surroundings, whether those of seaside or forest, metropolis or factory, he must first transform the objects about him by connecting them with human emotions, by finding their purpose and direction, by making them understandable. He repeats the same process in the world at large, by perceiving in it architectural and musical forms, unity and rhythm, by giving it a history, and chiefly by transfusing it with myth. This last phrase is a little pretentious, and yet it describes an essentially simple operation of the mind. It is what a sailor does by calling his vessel "she," and an engineer by giving a name and human attributes to his engine—"Old Ninety-Six is cranky" he says, reaching out to touch the iron side of it affectionately. A poet or a painter does the same thing in a richer and more communicable fashion; he gives things names and values; he makes them touchable.

At any rate this double humanizing function of art, as exercised on the world of nature and the world of society, is a task that is never finished; it has to be repeated with each succeeding age. Continually the natural environment is changing—is being changed by men whose relations with one another are also changing, together with the means by and the ends for which they live. Every age has its own myths to create, but some ages fail to create them. Often it happens that both the human and the natural worlds transform themselves so rapidly that they outrun men's ability to digest them. This undoubtedly is what has taken place since the Great War, with the rapid development of applied science, power machinery and mass production, the splendor and decay of capitalism and the growing self-awareness of the proletariat. What Shelley said of his own age can be applied more truly to ours: "We want the creative faculty to imagine that which we know; we want the generous impulse to act that which we imagine; we want the poetry of life: our calculations have outrun conception; we have eaten more than we can digest." Today we are entering a period when artists of Shelley's stature are more necessary than scientists or engineers.

And now you turn to the political questions that have been playing an always greater part in literary discussions. *Should artists,* you ask, *take part in the class struggle?*

There is no use adjuring them to take part in it or warning them to keep out of it; the adjurations and warnings are so much wasted breath. The artists will and do take part in it, because they are men before they are writers or painters, and because their human interests are involved, and because they can't stay out of the battle without deliberately blinding and benumbing themselves—and even then they are likely to find that they have been led into it without their knowledge and on a side they mightn't consciously have chosen.

And which side do you think the artists will choose?

I hope and trust that a great number of them will take the workers' side, and I think that doing so will make them better artists. On the other hand, I realize that it will be hard for many others not to take the side of the classes now in power. On that side are most of their old friendships and childhood memories. On that side are all the institutions they have been depending on for a livelihood—the press, the stage, the movies, the radio and, in the background, business, the schools and universities, the Army, the Church, the State. On that side, too, there seems to be all the culture inherited from the past, and with it all the mellowness and tolerance of a class grown old in power, the glamor that surrounds men and women in the habit of being served and obeyed. On the other side are ordinary people who never heard of Chaucer, and dress without taste when they don't dress shabbily, and eat their food with smacking noises and pile cups and saucers on top of their plates to show that the meal is over. They are people without manners or distinction, Negroes, hill billies, poor whites, Jews, Wops and Hunkies. If they should win the struggle here as they have in Russia, there are likely to be years of privation and desperate inefficiency, and there are certain to be harshness, narrowness, fanaticism, the eternal vices of a class struggling to power.

Yet the capitalists can in reality promise less than they seem to promise. The audience they offer to works of art is always limited, not only in numbers but also in capacity for appreciation. Under capitalism only a few people can afford to buy books or pictures or attend plays or concerts, and many of them are snobs who don't come to see or hear, but merely to be *seen* in a good theatre, to be *heard* talking about the books they have read. The mellowness and liberalism of the present ruling class are merely the ornaments of its prosperous years; in times of danger they give way to brutality direct and unconcealed. Its cherishing of individual freedom gives way at critical moments to a call for unquestioning blind obedience to the State, and its fostering of science is replaced by dark myths of race and war and destiny. Eventually it threatens the complete destruction of culture, since its inevitable and insoluble self-contradictions are leading it toward wars in which, tomorrow, not only books will be destroyed, but the libraries that contain them, and not only museums, universities, theatres, picture galleries, but also the wealth by which they are supported and the living people for whom they exist.

These are the prospects really held out to the artist by those who rule under the profit system. As for the other side, that of the factory workers and poor farmers and people now looking for jobs, it can actually promise much more than it seems to promise. First of all, it can offer an end to the desperate feeling of solitude and uniqueness that has been oppressing artists for the last two centuries, the feeling that has reduced some of the best of them to silence or futility and the weaker ones to insanity or suicide. It can offer instead a sense of comradeship and participation in a historical process vastly bigger than the individual. It can offer an audience, not trained to appreciate the finer points of style or execution—that will come later—but larger and immeasurably more eager than the capitalist audience and quicker to grasp essentials.

And it can offer something else to the artist. Once he knows and feels the struggles of the oppressed classes all over the world, he has a way to get hold both of distant events and those near at hand, and a solid framework on which to arrange them. Two housewives gossiping on the back porch about their husbands' jobs and the price of groceries, a small merchant bankrupt in the next block, a love affair broken off, a mortgage foreclosed, a manufacturer's rise to power—all these incidents take their place in a historical pattern that is also illuminated by revolts in Spain, a new factory in the Urals, an obscure battle in the interior of China. Values exist again, after an age in which they seemed to be lost; good and evil are embodied in men who struggle. It is no longer possible to write, as did Joseph Wood Krutch only a few years ago, that "we have come, willy-nilly, to see the soul of man as commonplace and its emotions as mean," or to say that the tragic sense of life has been lost forever. Tragedy lives in the stories of the men now dying in Chinese streets or in German prisons for a cause by which their lives are given dignity and meaning. Artists used to think that the world outside had become colorless and dull in comparison with the bright inner world they tenderly nourished; now it is the inner world that has been enfeebled as a result of its isolation; it is the outer world that is strong and colorful and demands to be imaginatively portrayed. The subjects are waiting everywhere. There are great days ahead for artists if they can survive in the struggle and keep their honesty of vision and learn to measure themselves by the stature of their times.

A Russo-Chinese Documentary

A Chinese Testament is the best book I have so far read about China, which in turn is the most interesting country in the world today. Even Russia is less exciting now, because Russia has chosen its direction and gone rushing ahead; for the moment everything is a question of tempo. China is still groping for a path. Feudalism, laissez-faire capitalism, fascism and communism, the old and all the dozen varieties of the new, are engaged in a struggle of which the issue is uncertain. A coolie bending under the weight of a sedan chair looks up and sees an airplane overhead that was manufactured, perhaps, in a Chinese factory with the latest precision instruments. A feudal landlord marches out at the head of his retainers to fight the military commander of a soviet district, educated in Moscow. A thousand years of history may be summarized—in this book they *are* summarized—dramatically in a single life.

But the Chinese are also the hardest people in the world to write about effectively. A double task of translation is involved. Not only must the speech be rendered into a Western language—a difficult task in itself, considering that most Chinese words have an emotional color different from ours, "white," for example, being the color of mourning—but also the very *deeds* must be translated into Western terms, must be explained and motivated so that they retain their human value instead of becoming merely picturesque or quaint. Ideally it takes two people working in collaboration to produce a good book on China. It takes a native to understand the meaning of the life there, and a foreigner to make it intelligible to a Western audience. There are a few exceptions to this rule—as notably in the case of writers like Pearl Buck and Agnes Smedley who had lived in the country and worked on such intimate terms with its people that they have acquired a

A review of *A Chinese Testament: The Autobiography of Tan Shih-hua as told to Sergei Tretiakov.* New York: Simon and Schuster. (*NR*, June 13, 1934.) This review was originally entitled "Holocaust." Here, as in all other instances where the original *NR* title has been changed, the original title is given in quotation marks in the identifying footnote.

double personality, part of it Chinese; the collaboration takes place within their minds. In the present book, however, the collaboration is between two extraordinary men, and the results of it are even more illuminating than a novel like *The Good Earth* or a book of vivid reporting like Agnes Smedley's *Chinese Destinies.*

Sergei Tretiakov, the Russian novelist and playwright, spent a year teaching at Peking University, in the days when the Chinese revolution was at its height. One of his students was a round-faced, solemn-eyed young man with thin, drooping shoulders and a narrow chest racked by coughs—Tan Shih-hua was his name, and he came from a village in Szechuan, far in the southern interior of China. Tan followed his teacher to Moscow, and accepted with enthusiasm Tretiakov's proposal to write an accurate biography of a Chinese student. Every day for six months they held a conference that lasted from four to six hours, while the Russian asked questions and the young Chinese gradually laid bare his heart. This book, Tretiakov explains in his Preface, is really an extended interview; "but since it embraces more than twenty-six years of a man's life, it might be called a 'Bio-Interview.' "

It is characteristic of Tretiakov to undertake a project like this and invent a name for it. He likes to be hard, objective, factual, modern in all things, including dress. More than six feet tall, with his head partly bald and partly shaved, great horn-rimmed spectacles resting on the high bridge of his nose, and specially made clothes with zippers instead of buttons, he looks like the drawings I remember of Mr. Skygack from Mars. He tells visitors that he used to write poems out of his head, but now (tapping his ear) he writes only what he hears and sees. . . . It is likely that Tretiakov foreshadows the sort of extravagances in which many writers will indulge during the years to come. They will be romantically unromantic; they will avoid inspiration as if it were a dangerous drug and will carry objectivity to the same extremes that subjectivity was carried by writers like Yeats and Mallarmé. Of the two forms of excess, Tretiakov's is probably less dangerous, since an objective writer, if he chooses the proper objects, will at least leave valuable documents behind him; whereas a purely subjective writer, unless he has the highest talent, will leave behind him nothing but personal and half-intelligible moans. But objectivity, too, has its dangers: it leads to dryness, hastiness, the mere piling up of facts; and these are faults I understand that Tretiakov has not always avoided. In this book, however, he is saved from them by the object he has chosen—saved, that is, by the intensity and warmth of Tan Shih-hua and by the extraordinary story he has to tell.

In twenty-six years, little Tan saw his world completely transformed, all its old values destroyed and new ones fighting to be established. He was born in a half-feudal household high above the banks of the Yangtze. All the men of his family were scholars; women did the work of the household, hobbling off to market on their little, deformed feet, their "golden lilies." The life they led was peaceful and full of mental and bodily satisfactions, but even a child was conscious of its being menaced by foreigners and by corrupt imperial officials. . . . Twenty years later, when Tan came home for a visit, everything in the village was changed. Szechuan had been ruled by a dozen revolutionary and counter-revolutionary governments, the countryside was overrun with bandits, opium poppies were grown instead of rice, most of the old families had lost their money, and new families had risen. There were no old-fashioned scholars any more. The boys and girls were crowding into modern high schools, learning to talk about nationalism and communism. Even Tan's three-year-old daughter begged him for a foreign dress.

In the course of the book there are several unusually fine passages. There are, for example, the chapters dealing with Tan's early childhood, full of sentiment and unexpected humor. There is the story of how his father came home from Japan to organize the first revolution, and secretly carried on his work while acting as chief of police. Again there is Tan's pathetic romance; his father made him break it off because the girl's family consisted of reactionary officials, and he had to marry an ugly and stupid woman instead. There is the description of life in Peking at the university—the intellectual ferment there, the translations from Tolstoy and Kropotkin, the impression made by John Dewey's lectures, and the part played by the students in the civil war, when, "after a day's work, with our eyes and fingers tired, we would fall into a heavy slumber. We had no time to go to a bath house. We grew filthier and filthier every day." Finally there is the story of how the students lectured on socialism to the coolies, who for the first time received the impression that they were something more than beasts of burden.

And now, with the book ended, Tan Shih-hua has gone back to China and has disappeared. Tretiakov explains that for two years his letters to his student and collaborator have been unanswered. "Perhaps he has become a Communist, and like his father, who once wandered from village to village with his insurgent army, continues to carry on guerilla warfare around the populous villages of Hunan and Kiangsi. Or perhaps he has fallen into the executioner's hands, and his head with its sparse black hair and quiet eyes is peering through the bamboo bars of a basket-cage in some marketplace far in the interior of China." That, we know, has been the fate of hundreds of his contemporaries. Others, including several gifted young poets and novelists, have been kidnaped and tortured, then shot, buried alive or left to die in prison. The bravest spirits of Tan's university generation have died in this fashion and the weaker ones have been terrified into surrendering their aspirations— China during the last ten years has been offering up a vast holocaust of youth. But all these lives haven't been wasted. Younger boys and girls are taking the places of the dead; and meanwhile the great movement that began among the students has been taken over by the coolies, the mill hands and the revolutionary peasants.

Eagle Orator

REGRETFULLY I have to bring in a dissenting opinion. Paul Engle is not, as Stephen Vincent Benét says he is, "a new voice—and the voice of a new generation—in American poetry." He is not any of the fine things that he has been called

American Song: A Book of Poems, by Paul Engle. New York: Doubleday, Doran and Company. (*NR*, Aug. 29, 1934.)

by J. Donald Adams of *The New York Times*. Except in a few passages where he speaks in a sharp homely fashion, he is not a poet at all. He is an eagle orator, a thumping good, tub-thumping Fourth of July congressman. He says all the proper things for a congressman to say when he wants to make his constituents forget about high prices and low wages and remember only that they are free-born Americans. He makes the eagle scream, the bison bellow, the welkin ring and the Pioneer Woman beat out the flames of a burning cabin with her dying husband's bloodstained hunting shirt. He roars out his hatred for skeptics and his contempt for the degenerate nations of Europe that drag their "worn-out bellies on the sun-warmed rock." He feels God stirring within his heart. He assures us that he is young and rich in spirituality and strong with a primitive old strength that "men have called courage and that we call guts." Standing with one hand outstretched toward the sky at sunset and the other thrust deep into the Iowa loam, he wraps himself in the red, white and blue starry folds of the American dream, while his kleagle voice resounds from klavern to klavern throughout the broad American land. Lord, how they love it, those hicks and rubes on the New York newspapers!

Like every true orator, he has a message. It echoes through most of the poems collected in this book, but it becomes clearest and loudest at the very end, in "America Remembers." This long declamation won—and richly deserved to win—the prize awarded by *Poetry* magazine for the best poem about the Century of Progress Exposition at Chicago. Here was a subject that would have embarrassed most poets. To Engle, on the contrary, it was an opportunity for displaying all his forensic gifts and for writing in his most characteristic manner. Let us examine the poem for clues to his popularity.

It begins with America personified vaguely as someone, probably a Greek-robed full-bosomed woman with an olive branch in her hand, who sits on the shore of Lake Michigan among the "buildings shaped with light" of the Chicago Exposition. Here she dreams of her past, remembering "the strange way I have had in this land, the incredible trail I have followed." She remembers the wild continent as it was when the red men called to their gods in the gusty rain (twenty-one lines). She remembers the first Spanish ships landing (five lines), and the English settlers planting their corn with a rotten fish in each hill (nineteen lines). She remembers the Jesuits teaching in the North (eleven lines), and the colonists who rebelled on the seaboard—

> *the English soul*
> *Plunged seven years in flame and steel and become*
> *The American soul—O strange, strong thing! And over*
> *The land ranged the unique American dream*
> *Of the common man and his right before all men*
> *To shape his own peculiar single self*
> *Tempered in the wild flame of beating out*
> *On the huge anvil of the wilderness*
> *A young and iron nation.*

In other words, she proudly remembers Mr. Hoover's wrought-iron individualism. There follow two eloquent pages in which she remembers the myth of the pioneers, the land-hungry men of the Wilderness Road and the gold-hungry men who crossed the Sierras—always westering, always sun-following, till at last they "struck the Pacific and the force of their traveling flung them back over the way they had come." In a dull page, she remembers the Indian dead. In two pages not much brighter, she remembers the Civil War, the rise of industrialism and the years when "the fatal Horsemen rode." She somehow feels that the Great War should have uplifted us —but instead the American

> *Soul, that should have soared, flapped in the driving wind*
> *That blew with the stench of sweat and oil and the fetid*
> *Fat breath that cried for gold.*

She refers scornfully to the materialism of the postwar years, when American ships circled the oceans and American eyes "could not see beyond the diamonds flashing their hands." She says nothing, nothing about these later years when the wind no longer stinks of sweat and oil and the diamonds are pawned. Miss America, grown old and smug, has no eyes or ears or nose for the present. Indeed, she assumes that our material problems have been solved and that all of us now have "shoes for our feet, shirts for our backs" and a fat chicken in the pot. The real problem facing us today is that of finding a spiritual destination. With all the country settled, "Where shall they go now," she asks, "the forever westward-wandering people?"

> *They cannot be quiet, they cannot rest, they would not*
> *Be American if they could do that. I tell them: You*
> *Shall fit again the curved felloe, and with the bucket*
> *Swinging under the wagon, the slouch-gaited hound*
> *Following its restless shade patch, plunge*
> *Into that vaster and more savage West,*
> *The unfamiliar country of your heart.*

Having loaded our possessions into a prairie schooner, and having nowhere else to go, we are asked to drive it into our vast, savage breasts and, I suppose, to build ourselves subsistence homesteads somewhere in the high heart-mountains between the auricle and the ventricle. Seriously, this prospectus for a spiritual dude-ranching trip is Paul Engle's message and his solution for all our troubles. It doesn't offer much hope to those of us who have no wagon to hang a bucket under, nor even a bag of meal with which to make hoe-cakes in the ashes of the campfire.

The spirit of pioneer individualism, the search for gold and land that Paul Engle glorifies as the true American dream, has ended by laying our country waste. It has butchered the timber north and south, it has killed off the game, wasted the coal, crippled the men who mined it, poisoned the streams, exhausted and eroded the rich farmland. After a hundred years it has left us with only the dry crust of the continent that our fathers possessed—and not even that, for other people own it now and continue to gnaw it away. The children of the pioneers, and of the immigrants who followed them, are faced with the task of winning back the land from the people who stole it, and of living in it together, and of helping one another to make it rich again. This is a real adventure and one for which people are being jailed and shot. But Paul Engle wants us, instead, to continue pioneering in the imaginary mountains and prairies of our souls—comfortably, after dinner, thanking God in our hearts that we aren't drab materialists—that we can forge our own "singular vision of eternity" and, with "the American faith" proudly behind us, can discover "the deep spirituality of man." Andrew Carnegie and John D. Rockefeller, Sr., used to talk a great deal about spirituality; it saved them embarrassment when paying low wages. Paul Engle's American muse speaks in the familiar Sunday voice of the robber barons—and perhaps this explains why he is praised by critics who ought to recognize that the voice is harsh and bombastic and full of awkward intonations.

Technically Engle has two accomplishments, both of them rare in young poets: he knows how to build a poem in big square solid chunks and he is able to keep it moving. But his verse is inferior in metrical texture; it alternates between the two extremes of awkwardness and monotony without his ever being able to find a middle passage. His figures of speech are intellectual rather than visual; most of them come out of books. But his real fault as a poet is one of inflation. He started with an honest and admirable emotion, a love for the rich Iowa acres where he was reared, but he has tried to expand the emotion through space and carry it backward through time, until he ends by windily declaiming about things that he has neither felt nor accurately imagined. He has issued too much watered stock on his real assets. Like any overextended businessman, he has been forced to go to the bankers, and he has made considerable loans from Whitman, from Stephen Vincent Benét, from Archibald MacLeish and, I suspect, from McGuffey's Fifth Reader. "Here," says Mr. Benét, "is somebody walking in America in proud shoes." The trouble is that the shoes are borrowed and they don't fit.

Mencken: The Former Fugleman

RECENTLY there appeared two items concerning H. L. Mencken, and I wish that somebody would explain them. Taken together, they don't make sense.

Item 1. The Modern Library has reprinted Scott Fitzgerald's best novel, *The Great Gatsby*. It is a book whose unique value has been overestimated by many people, including T. S.

Eliot, Rebecca West and its own author, but nevertheless it is a fine piece of work, a sentimental poem to the Jazz Age that I was glad to reread in 1934; it hasn't staled or withered. The item about Mencken appears in the preface to the new edition. Here Fitzgerald gives a round scolding to the present race of critics and says that there is no one today who goes to the trouble of discovering and guiding able but unknown novelists, as Mencken used to do in *Smart Set* and in the early days of *The American Mercury*. And it is perfectly true that Mencken not only engineered the success of Dreiser, and helped to put Lewis across, but also had a share in the humbler triumphs of several talented writers who followed them. He wasn't in many cases the real discoverer; somebody else usually performed that function; but Mencken was the only critic out of blinkers who was widely read by people under thirty. He was, to use one of his favorite words, the fugleman of the new fiction.

Item 2. To the October 6 issue of *The Saturday Review*, Mencken himself contributed an article on proletarian writers. A great many of the able young novelists who have appeared during the last three or four years belong to this category. It happens that the literary and human value of their work has been persistently undervalued by critics who don't like their politics. It also happens that the worst attacks against them have appeared in journals which Mencken used to despise for being stodgy. Therefore, on the face of the record, we might expect that he would now come to their defense, would praise them immoderately in order to restore the balance in their favor, would shout and prod and bludgeon a little sense into the heads of the Tory reviewers. This is the sort of thing he used to do often. If he had done it again, the two items would agree, and that would be the end of it.

On the contrary, he takes the side of the stodgier critics. He tries to make us believe that all proletarian novelists are dull beyond description and are writing about factory hands and farmers only because they tried and failed to break into *The Cosmopolitan* with Cinderella stories. He doesn't stop there, unfortunately. He also implies that most proletarian writers are Jews, even though many of them sign their work with "distinguished (albeit largely bogus) Anglo-Saxon names." It is curious how this thread of anti-Semitism runs through his essay. He talks about young men who "took to religion and declared themselves High Church Episcopalians—despite, in many cases, inconvenient surgical evidence to the contrary." Like Reichsbischoff Müller of the German State Church, he evidently believes that nobody is entitled to be a Christian unless he can prove that all four grandparents were Aryans. Mencken speaks of novels "too often done in English that seems to be a bad translation from the Yiddish." In Hitler's Germany there is a movement to prohibit all Jews from writing in any language except Yiddish or Hebrew, on the ground that they have been corrupting German taste and style. This critic who used to think for himself now writes as if he were making a free translation from a pamphlet by Dr. Joseph Goebbels.

And the voice of Goebbels rings even louder at the end of the essay. Mencken suggests that the whole radical movement could be ended suddenly by the declaration of another war—in twenty-four hours all the proletarians would be patriots. Or else, he continues, "on some rather remoter tomorrow, the cops may turn Nazi and get out of hand, and prudence may suddenly consume the passion for Service, as in 1917. There is, indeed, never much heroism in literati." But I don't enjoy this blowing of warlike trumpets by a Baltimore gentleman of sedentary habits who has passed the age for military service. And the physical courage of the literati is not a question of vast importance. I can't remember that Mencken himself has done anything bolder than what H. G. Wells describes Frank Harris as doing—that is, to "sit and talk exuberantly in imminent danger of unanswerable contradiction."

It is true that he avoids some of this danger, in the present essay, by naming no names. He never tells us just which writers he is attacking (nor, for that matter, does he say anything to prove that he knows the work of any proletarian writer whatever). But it would be better to give him the benefit of the doubt. Let us assume that he has actually read some proletarian novelists and that, being fair-minded, he is choosing as target the best or most prominent of those who have appeared during the last two or three years. In that case he is writing about Robert Cantwell (this being the *nom de plume* or pseudonym of a young man from the state of Washington who was christened Robert Cantwell); he is writing about William Rollins (the pseudonym of William Rollins), Grace Lumpkin (the pseudonym of Grace Lumpkin), Albert Halper (the pseudonym of Albert Halper), Jack Conroy (the pseudonym of Jack Conroy) and Fielding Burke (the pseudonym of Olive Tilford Dargan). There is one bogus name in the list of six. There is also one Jew, but the Jew writes under his own name. As a matter of fact, Jewish writers have not particularly distinguished themselves in this particular type of fiction, for reasons that have nothing to do with racial genius or literary talent. Most proletarian novels deal with the struggles of workers in the basic industries. There is not a high proportion of Jews in those industries, and honest writers of any race prefer to deal with subjects they know at first hand.

How much does Mencken know about proletarian novels? He says they are amateurish, preposterous and written in shaky English. Well, in all the books by all the authors I have mentioned, there is not so much downright bad writing, not so much English that sounds like a fancy translation from the Polish, Coptic or Aramean, as there is in any chapter of Joseph Hergesheimer, whom Mencken regards as a fine stylist. He conjectures that the chief charm of proletarian fiction "to those who can endure it at all, is probably the flavor of pornography that is in most of it." Well, there are several proletarian novelists who use coarse language—and rather too much of it for my own studious taste—but in all their books there is not enough real pornography to butter thin a single page of *Jurgen*. If I remember correctly, Mencken was one of those who worked hardest to rescue *Jurgen* from the censor.

No, there is some deep and strange disparity between Item 1 and Item 2, between the atheistic, censor-baiting, freedom-roaring Mencken of 1920 and the pious God-and-Pierpont-Morgan-fearing Mencken of these depression years. Something is gnawing at his vitals, and it would take a surgeon, a psychoanalyst, two Marxian critics and an investment banker sitting in conference to diagnose the disease from which the man now suffers. He has nightmares and delusions. He starts up from an uneasy sleep to cry that the country is going to the dogs and that Stalin himself is in the White House. He

summons the cops and the censors to his bedside to protect him
from pornography. After ten years spent fighting the Ku
Kluxers and making himself feared by kleagles and wizards,
he is ready to swallow the nostrums of Imperial Wizard Hitler and Grand Dragon Goebbels. And he has lost his appetite
for good writing. There was a time when Mencken the critic
used to praise young novelists and Mencken the editor used to
print their work, even though he suspected them of being
Jewish or radical or stony broke. But the critic and the editor
are dead now, and their clothes are too big for Mencken the
politician.

Valuta Girl

SHE WAS a German schoolgirl bored by the War, a flapper thrilled by the revolution in Bavaria, an apprentice banker
in Berlin during the Inflation, a Frenchman's mistress in the
years after Locarno. She was twice married, first to a famous
physician, then to the head of the biggest publishing house in
the Western world. She was the central figure in the worst of
all the scandals before the Reichstag fire. She regards herself
as a free individual, but at all times she has acted as the
creature of her age and status. That is the virtue of R. G.'s
Prelude to the Past. She is so immersed in the time spirit that,
simply by writing the candid story of her life, she has mirrored
the vast decay of the Weimar Republic.

R. G.—Frau Rosie Graefenberg-Ullstein, born Rosa Goldschmidt—was the daughter of the leading Jewish banker in
Mannheim. The Jews in that Rhineland city were "completely
assimilated, and distinguished from their Christian fellow citizens chiefly by their greater interest in things of the mind."
Famous writers and musicians were guests in the Goldschmidt
home. Rosie grew up in "an atmosphere of brilliance, beauty,

Prelude to the Past: The Autobiography of a Woman, by R. G.
New York: William Morrow and Company. (*NR*, Dec. 5, 1934.)

cordiality and stimulation that I have never seen surpassed in any other society in the world."

In the last year of the War, when Rosie was nineteen, she was given her own checkbook and sent to study art in Munich. She was there when the revolution broke out. The revolutionary leaders were professors and poets "with wise gentle faces. . . . They said 'reason' and 'good will' and 'we will have no terror.'" They believed in the brotherhood of man, and for this mistake they were shot promptly when the bourgeoisie got back into power. Meanwhile the students were celebrating the revolution in their own fashion, by drinking and making love. At first Rosie enjoyed this life, then simultaneously she lost her revolutionary enthusiasm and was disgusted with the dancing in half-lit crowded rooms, the lying about on couches and pawing one another. She would never like adultery unless it was wrapped in pink silk sheets.

In 1921, after winning a Heidelberg doctorate *summa cum laude*, Rosie was apprenticed to a banker in Berlin. With the War lost and the revolution suppressed, everyone was bent on making money. The most honorable of the new people she met was Kommerzienrat Guggenheim, of whom her employer said that he "was decent up to 100,000 marks. Nobody is decent beyond that." Soon the inflation would be upon them and nobody would be decent beyond twenty American dollars.

Rosie did not dislike the inflation. "It contained all the elements of the uncertain and of the hectic, which I then felt to be congenial to me." Having finished her banking apprenticeship and having tired of married life with a fashionable physician, she went to work for one of the new kings of industry. He summoned her to his imposing private office:

> It was a few weeks after I had entered the firm. On the blotting pad with its pink sheets lay the drafts which he was going to use to purchase a large stock of goods. They represented several hundred millions. I sat facing him while he signed one after another with his heavy gold fountain pen. The masterful way he pressed down the blotting paper irritated me. He was such a poseur, was Lobkowitz!
>
> "The whole capital of the firm won't be enough to redeem those drafts," I said.
>
> "In three months, when they fall due, they won't be worth a hundredth of their present value," he said triumphantly.

Lobkowitz knew his inflation, and his nerve was magnificent
. . . that afternoon I became his mistress.

After divorcing her husband (who knew nothing about the
affair with Lobkowitz) she went to live in Paris and fell in
love with a French businessman. It was her Franco-German
reconciliation, her own Locarno. From the very beginning, this
affair with René had a political basis. He would often shout,
"*Your* Stresemann is not acting in good faith. *Your* fortifica-
tions on the east! It is clear that *you* are secretly arming."—
After puzzling for a moment over his outbreak she would
understand the cause of it. "Why don't you say at once that I
ought not to flirt with the man at the next table?" René would
laugh shamefacedly, and then a moment later, "*Mon petit
chou*," he would say, "you are adorable. And I own that the
Germans do their level best to pay their reparation debts."
René left her when it became evident that France and Germany were not going to be reconciled.

Back in Berlin her two best friends were a former revolutionist and a Cabinet Minister who had won his office by
betraying the revolution. The first, Paul Levi, was a comrade
of Rosa Luxemburg and had helped her and Karl Liebknecht
to lead the Spartacists when they rose in January, 1919. "I
always had the feeling," Rosie says, "that the murder of Rosa
Luxemburg had broken down his revolutionary energies,
though for a time he remained the leader of the Communist
Party. He did not leave the Party till he had been to Moscow
and discovered that his political aims were incompatible with
those of Lenin. All his German friends—which meant most of
the intellectuals—left the Party when he did." He was now a
lawyer specializing in divorce and treason cases and a collector
of old China, Chinese bronzes and ceramics and Gothic Ma-
donnas. The Cabinet Minister was Robert Weismann, who,
after the first revolution in November, 1918, was head of the
political police "and knew everything about everybody. The
fact that, in spite of this, he took action only against Communists made him acceptable to German Social Democrats and
the German bourgeoisie, and he became Secretary of State for
Prussia." Paul Levi, who fought beside Rosa Luxemburg, and
Robert Weismann, who helped to plan her murder, now
moved in the same circles and Rosie admired them both.

I am not trying to narrate her career; I am merely suggesting a few of the episodes and characters that cast a light on the society in which she lived. It was a society wholly without standards, and by the beginning of the year 1930 she had reached the top of it. She slept between rose-colored silk sheets and went out to dinner wearing more jewels than Al Capone. She was married to one of the richest men in Germany, a publisher twice her age, and was acquiring more and more influence in the great House of Ullstein. But Dr. Franz Ullstein's four brothers, who were also his partners, hated Rosie and were determined to get rid of her at any price. They charged her with being a woman of abandoned morals and a spy for several foreign governments. A scandal burst forth involving so many editors and pimps and statesmen that it hastened the fall of the German Republic.

R. G. doesn't show to much advantage in her own *Prelude to the Past*. She married a rich man in the hope of using his wealth and position to prolong her liaison with a government official who didn't love her. She got all the money she could out of Dr. Franz Ullstein without ever paying him for value received. The best one can say for her is that her morals were those of the crazy world in which she lived. For Rosie and her friends there was nothing to do but plunge forward, backward, up, down, nobody knew where; for it was as if all these ex-Communists, ex-heroes, ex-Jews, ex-Christians, were lacking in those tubes of the inner ear that give a sense of balance; their experiences had made them biologically unfit to survive. After reading this book of hers, you don't like Hitler any better, but you can understand why so many people regarded him as a savior. There are ages so utterly sunk beneath the level of human dignity that they make even a false and vicious messiah seem, for the moment, better than none at all.

Literature and Politics

I AM NOT going to review John Strachey's new essay, except by saying that it is short, clear and has nothing portentous about it except the title. All those who are interested in the hotly argued relationship between literature and politics should read it for themselves; they will find that this booklet of twelve thousand words has more good sense in it than have most critical essays five times its length. But Strachey makes one point about which I am dubious.

The point has to do with the attitude to be adopted by Marxist critics toward writing as a fine art. Here Strachey differs with Granville Hicks. He approaches their difference in the politest manner possible and with the warmest praise for Hicks's critical achievements, yet there is no mistaking the tone of reproof in his voice. "It does seem to me," he says, "that Hicks falls sometimes into an error which, as I was suggesting above, is a tempting one for Marxist critics. He hardly seems to pay enough attention to the merits of writers as writers. . . . It would be a thousand pities if his strong sense of responsibility, as the foremost Marxist literary critic of America, which he certainly is, should force him to stifle his esthetic sensibility."

Strachey himself avoids that error by retaining and exercising a keen sense of esthetic values. Before attacking a writer for political reasons, he almost always stops to explain that he has a high regard for the writer's distinction of style or choice of images. Indeed, he carries his appreciation so far that I wonder whether it doesn't encourage a state of mind and a practice of criticism that are even more dangerous than Hicks's forthright abuse of his political enemies. Take for example the passage that precedes his attack on Archibald MacLeish:

> It would obviously be a sheer waste of time to talk about
> Mr. MacLeish's poem unless its author had the talent to make a
> true poem. . . . It is, as a matter of fact, precisely because Mr.
> MacLeish is a writer of a high order of ability that it is worth
> while to point out what he is writing about. From the very
> outset, our method of criticism must depart from the established

Literature and Dialectical Materialism, by John Strachey. New York: Covici, Friede. (*NR*, Jan. 2, 1935.)

methods of bourgeois criticism. Bourgeois criticism is in the main an attempt to establish a hierarchy of works of art, to say that this poem is better than that, but not so good as a third, etc., etc. We are not primarily concerned with this question. Obviously we shall only discuss works that do succeed in expressing adequately what their authors meant to express. But what we are here and for the moment concerned with is the thing expressed.

In other words, Strachey sets up an arbitrary distinction between "expressing adequately" and "the thing expressed"—that is, between style or form and intellectual content or subject matter. Bourgeois criticism is supposed to evaluate the one; Marxist criticism is here and for the moment strictly confined to the other. Now, it was long ago discovered—and it is rediscovered by each new generation—that nobody can drive a barbed-wire fence through a work of art and divide it like a cattle range. Form and substance are intermingled. A writer's technical equipment almost always helps to determine his choice of subject. Even more fatally, his opinions and ambitions and social allegiances have an effect on his technical equipment; style is the man. If the Marxist critics followed Strachey's suggestion—if they dealt only with works that someone else had declared to be technically competent, and merely discussed their political significance—they would confine themselves to stating partial truths and, eventually, would bore and alienate their readers. The formula of criticizing books solely in the light of the fascist or anti-fascist ideas in them is altogether too easy to follow.

But this method that Strachey seems to recommend—fortunately without himself following it too strictly—has still another danger, in this case arising from a universal human habit of seeing our enemies larger than life. We tend to overestimate both their ability or cunning and their danger to mankind. Strachey, for example, considerably exaggerates the literary value of *Frescoes for Mr. Rockefeller's City*. The poem is not on a level with MacLeish's permanent work: it is a long, vigorous, loose-jointed piece of poetical pamphleteering not likely to outlast the age that called it forth. As for its political significance, Strachey proves beyond a doubt that it contains strong traces of what Michael Gold called "the fascist unconscious," but this fact is losing its importance now that wholly conscious fascism is becoming prevalent among us. In the past, some writers with hidden fascist tendencies have learned to recognize and avoid them. The tactical danger in MacLeish's case is that he will say to himself—and perhaps has already said, who knows?—"These Communist boys are nasty, but maybe they're right after all. They say that I am a very important poet and am getting to be a fascist. Well, the thing to do is to make myself still more of a fascist and thereby become a still more important poet."

Ernest Hemingway, also discussed by Strachey, presents another aspect of what is essentially the same problem. Strachey says that, in his last book, he "has expressed more adequately than ever before his ferocious despair at the condition of the world." After that high praise, Strachey goes on to attack his social philosophy. But the bourgeois critics, who were not interested in attacking his social philosophy, considered that his last book was at best a standing still, and was quite possibly a retreat from his earlier achievements. Not yet having read *Winner Take Nothing*, I am hardly qualified to comment on this difference of opinion. It seems to me, however, that if the Marxist critics want to write about Hemingway they must first judge his last book in relation to the others —give it a place in the hierarchy—and must then decide whether the advance or the retrogression from his earlier work has any relation with the opinions on politics, revolution and the world in general that Hemingway has lately been expressing.

This is the sort of task that Granville Hicks, for example, is always willing to undertake. His judgment of literary values is oversimplified, sometimes distorted, and Strachey's comments on what he says about particular writers are wholly justified. Yet Hicks doesn't make the mistake of limiting himself to one aspect of a writer's work. He does try to bring the whole picture together, style and message and substance, into a coherent whole. In this respect he is on the right track, even though I sometimes feel that he is on the wrong train.

A Note on Marxian Criticism

PLANS are being laid and a call has already been issued for an American Writers' Congress to be held in New York City on May 1. Two or three hundred of the left-wing novelists, playwrights, poets, critics and journalists are expected to attend the sessions, and many of them will talk about their own problems in relation to the revolutionary movement. The discussion will be largely political, dealing with the best means of mobilizing public sentiment against war and fascism, but literary questions will also be argued. I should guess that the Congress will quarrel and grope its way toward some valuable formulations of opinion and also, perhaps, toward practical activities.

Meanwhile there is one literary question that I hope will be considered calmly and at length. It has to do with the nature and scope of what is variously known as revolutionary or Marxian or proletarian criticism. A great many attacks have recently been made against this type of literary analysis and most of them, perhaps, have been based on misunderstandings. But it is unfortunately true that not all the misunderstandings have been on the side of the attackers. The Marxian critics themselves have been too zealous, have used their method too narrowly and in some cases have carried it too far, thus lending color to the charge that they have neglected literary and human values for the sake of political tactics. This is one of the reasons why the limits of revolutionary criticism should be carefully defined, as well as its effectiveness within its proper boundaries.

One of its sharpest limits consists in the fact that it is sociological rather than psychological. It can explain the social effects of a novel or a drama, and can do so, I think, incomparably better than any other critical method, but it cannot always or accurately explain the personal reason for which the novel or drama was written. This distinction between social and personal, between objective and subjective, can be illustrated by an example taken from American history. The *social motive* for the mass migration that settled the prairie states was the existence of cheap, fertile, unoccupied land beyond the Mississippi. But if a sociologist living in those days had stopped a wagon train and asked each member of it why he was moving westward, he would have uncovered a variety of *personal motives*—one man had been disappointed in love, another was looking "for room to stretch my legs in," still another had robbed a henroost and left town three jumps ahead of the constable. The existence of cheap land played a part in all their decisions, but not the most prominent part; its real importance would be revealed only by statistics and averages—in other words, by one of the methods that Marx used throughout his *Capital*. I mention the westward migration because it casts light on a confusion appearing in a good deal of contemporary criticism. One might say, for example, that a certain type of fiction "reveals a petty-bourgeois mentality," and it is possible that the statement would be justified in fact, even though it sounds hackneyed and unconvincing. But if one said that a certain paragraph of a certain novel was written because the novelist had a petty-bourgeois mentality, one would be wrong in three cases out of four. It might have been written because of a death in the family, or a quarrel with his wife, or merely because he remembered something that a man named Jones had told him in a smoking-car outside Chicago. If the social effect of it is to strengthen petty-bourgeois ideals—well, that it a different matter entirely, and one that falls within the scope of the Marxian method.

There is, moreover, a whole group of human emotions that are based on biological sorrows and satisfactions—on birth, adolescence, sexual desire, eating, walking in the country, growing old and dying. In poems and stories that deal with such emotions, there may be no social elements whatever. It is of course true that bourgeois ideas appear in unexpected places. In Marcel Proust, for example, there are perhaps a thousand pages dealing with love, which is supposed to be one of the inalienably personal elements in life. Yet Proust's idea of it is so closely involved with the bourgeois sense of possession—love is so much a matter of owning a woman as one might own a fine racehorse, and jealousy is so much the pain of being robbed, of having thieves break into one's house and carry off a valuable work of art—that I am doubtful whether those long passages will be understood in another age when the sense of private property has grown weaker and less all-embracing. In the same way, our ideas of birth and death embody social judgments and are likely to change in the future as they have changed in the past. The fact remains that there is a vast neutral area of literature, neither social nor anti-social, neither revolutionary nor counter-revolutionary. About the only thing that Marxian critics are justified in saying about it—within the limits of the Marxian method—is that if a writer confines himself permanently to neutral subjects he will narrow his scope, impoverish his sympathies and, in the end, diminish his own literary stature.

There is one other boundary set to Marxian criticism, though in this case it is an advantage rather than a limitation. Marxian criticism is not religious. It does not have its Bible, its theory granted by revelation and fixed for all time. It does not demand the surrender of the intellect to an ancient Authority that cannot be contravened; on the contrary it requires that the mind be constantly alert. It does not demand a mystical immolation of one's personality or a mystical union with some collective entity, with church, nation or class; on the contrary it requires that all personal talents be developed to the highest point they can reach. There are, of course, some opposite tendencies in the revolutionary movement itself, and their presence is only natural considering that, as any movement grows larger, it includes many types of heterogeneous thinking. There are even some communists who talk like characters out of Dostoevsky, transferring his worship of Holy Russia to an equally mystical creation called the Masses. They preach self-abnegation and sometimes, in whispers, they quote the parable of the Grand Inquisitor. It is obvious that their mysticism is absolutely opposed to the Marxian thinking, which emphasizes the value of conscious activity and, in a sense, carries on the spirit of the Renaissance and of the French Enlightenment. There is, however, another theory which holds that individuals should wholly surrender themselves to the Collectivity, should abandon reason for blind obedience to their leaders, should admire books full of self-abnegation, ecstatic darkness and the call of the blood. It is called fascism.

H. G. Wells in the Kremlin

I DOUBT that any other interview of the last ten years was more dramatic, more interesting as a clear statement of two positions or, in a sense, more absurdly grotesque than H. G. Wells's interview with Stalin.

They met in Moscow on July 23 of last year and talked through an interpreter for nearly three hours. Wells gives a one-sided story in the last chapter of his *Experiment in Autobiography*. The official text of the interview can now be had in a pamphlet issued by International Publishers for two cents. A longer pamphlet, costing fifty cents in this country, was published in London by *The New Statesman and Nation*. It contains both the interview and an exchange of letters in which Bernard Shaw is keener and wittier than Wells or J. M. Keynes. There is, unfortunately, no letter from Stalin. We know what Wells thinks about him; it would be instructive to hear what Stalin thinks about Wells.

The drama of their meeting lay in the contrast between two systems of thought. Stalin, with full authority, was speaking for communism, for the living heritage of Marx and Engels and Lenin. Wells is not an official figure and was speaking for himself; but he spoke with the voice of Anglo-American liberalism. Stalin represented the class-conscious proletariat of all countries. Wells claimed to represent the interests of humanity as a whole, but he actually defended the middle-class-conscious technical workers. Stalin advocated revolution and Wells argued against violence. He pictured a new world order achieved painlessly by education and by a sudden miracle of the human spirit. Stalin was too busy creating a new order to disengage its outlines from the excavations of the Moscow subway and the scaffolding that surrounds the House of the Soviets. Furthermore, there was a contrast of age and country between the two men, Stalin representing the iron age in Russia and Wells the hopefulness and trust in the future of England before the First World War.

Marxism vs. Liberalism: An Interview Between Joseph Stalin and H. G. Wells. New York: International Publishers Company. (*NR*, Apr. 24, 1935.)

The burlesque quality of their meeting lay in the purpose that Wells carried to Moscow. During the spring of that year he had visited America and had been enthralled by the New Deal. Brain Trusters familiar with his own books (these, indeed, are among the principal sources of the Brain Trust) had unfolded to him "a view of the world which seemed to contain all I had ever learned and thought." He spent an evening in the White House and decided that Roosevelt was "the most effective transmitting instrument possible for the coming of the new world order." At the same time, he perceived a striking similarity between Washington and Moscow. The two governments differed in method, but the end they sought, "a progressively more organized big-scale production, was precisely the same." Therefore he determined to bring them together. He thought, modestly, "If Stalin is as able as I am beginning to think him, then he must be seeing many things as I am seeing them." He would urge Stalin to forswear Marx, to forsake the proletariat, to forget all his outdated nonsense about class hostility, and immediately to join with Roosevelt in a united front—against what? Against nothing in the world but the "mental tangles, egocentric preoccupations, obsessions, misconceived phrases, bad habits of thought, subconscious fears and dreads and plain dishonesty in people's minds" that are today the sole obstacles standing in the way "to the attainment of universal freedom and abundance." That was his proposal. Imagine a Mohammedan missionary setting out to convince the Pope that he ought to renounce the Bible and make a pilgrimage to Mecca, after being circumcised. Then imagine Wells in the Kremlin, if you can.

Short-legged, long-waisted, smiling, armed with an ingratiatingly candid self-esteem, he makes his proclamations of faith and international good will to the interpreter, who writes them down and repeats them in Russian. Stalin, after politely asking Mr. Wells's permission to smoke, sucks at his big pipe and gives his answers slowly. Wells rushes on to new subjects. The two men are talking in different worlds, Stalin in the iron present, Wells in the golden future; there is no meeting of minds. Yet this failure to communicate is not Stalin's fault. He listens patiently, he considers everything Wells has to say and answers it point by point, without haste or condescension, exactly as if he were trying to explain the aims of the Russian revolution to a slow-witted but influential worker in the Puti-lov factory. Wells listens hardly at all. Wells is the apostle, Wells is bearing a message, Wells is pursuing his own ideas with inexorable deafness. At the end of three hours he goes away, having forgotten nothing and learned nothing, except that Stalin cannot be liberalized.

It is an absurd situation, and it is also mildly tragic. If Wells had asked the right questions and had listened to the answers, he would not have been converted to Stalin's point of view, but at least he would have been able to measure some of his own ideas against reality. Several of the proposals he made in the tracts and novels of his middle period are now being tested in the Soviet Union. Thus, he once suggested that there ought to be a caste of Samurai, men and women who would dedicate themselves wholeheartedly to the task of guiding a new society. Membership in this caste would be voluntary and open to everyone who could meet the qualifications and the severe disciplinary tests. It is obvious that the real organization standing nearest to Wells's Samurai is the Russian Communist Party, and he might have learned how it functioned. Again, Wells has always dreamed of technically trained administra-tors given power to remake the world; they have some of that power under the Soviets. He has always emphasized the ideal of planning, and Stalin could have told him about some of the difficulties that must be overcome when planning is attempted on a continental scale. But Wells in the Kremlin asked no practical questions.

In recent years, such questions have ceased to concern him deeply. He has fixed his mind on the future so obstinately, he has wished and schemed and plotted so long for Utopia, that he is beginning to think it is just around the corner. "The socialist world-state," he says, "has become a tomorrow as real as today." But Wells's world-state of tomorrow will be created suddenly and without shedding blood by an Open Conspiracy of middle-class technicians. It has nothing whatever to do with the socialist state that exists today in a sixth of the world, after being violently created by a proletarian revolution. Stalin can have that real state, with all its problems; Wells would rather clutch his dream.

What the Revolutionary Movement Can Do for a Writer

IT IS IMPORTANT first of all to define what the revolutionary movement cannot do for a writer, so that nobody will hope for miracles that will not be performed. It cannot give him personal salvation. It is not a church that calls upon him to have faith, to surrender his doubts, to lay down his burden of anxieties, and from henceforth to follow a sure path mapped out for him by sanctified leaders. This is an age when messiahs are being invoked not only by unemployed preachers and engineers and by shopkeepers who have lost their shops, but also by bewildered novelists and by poets no longer able to write poetry. Marx and Lenin were not messiahs; they were scientists of action. Their aim was not to convert but to convince.

Again, the revolutionary movement cannot transform writers, men used to walking by themselves and puzzling over personal difficulties, into political leaders of the working class. The working class will furnish its own leaders. And yet again, the revolutionary movement cannot change third-rate bourgeois novelists into great proletarian novelists. It may not be able to transform bourgeois novelists into any sort of proletarian novelists at all.

At this point I am not using the term "proletarian novel" in the very wide sense that Edwin Seaver tried to give it yesterday. I am defining it in a much narrower sense as a novel written from the revolutionary point of view about working-class characters. There is a great need for such novels today, but there is also a considerable doubt as to whether many of them will be written by men who began their career as middle-class novelists. Of course, such men might succeed after a period of years, by living among workers and actively taking part in their struggles and learning to see the world from their point of view. They might also succeed by going around with a notebook, like Emile Zola, and approaching their material from the outside. But Zola's type of objectivity is not wholly

A paper read at the American Writers' Congress. (*New Masses*, May 7, 1935.)

satisfying to most contemporary novelists, who demand more "inwardness," a deeper knowledge of the characters one is describing. That sort of knowledge cannot be acquired in a few months or a few years, since it depends on a long, slow process of acquiring sympathies and associations.

Of course there are examples of great fiction written about the members of one class by a man or woman who belonged to another. Elizabeth Madox Roberts' fine novel *The Time of Man* belongs to this category; it is a book about a tenant farmer's wife written by a woman of the landowning class. Tolstoy, the nobleman, finally succeeded in identifying himself with the Russian peasants. But Joshua Kunitz tells me that Tolstoy once tried to write a novel about a Jew and abandoned the project. His plan was good, his ideas were sympathetic, but he found that he could not feel his way inside the character. It seems to me that some recent books about the proletariat or the lumpenproletariat would never have been written if their authors had been as conscientious as Tolstoy. Two examples are a novel by Catherine Brody, *Nobody Starves*, which had hidden in it a vague sort of condescension and which made the lives of workers seem duller, more hopeless and apathetic, than they are in reality; and Sherwood Anderson's so-called communist novel of three years ago, *Beyond Desire*, which sentimentalized and priapified them.

Good novels about the working class are needed at present more than any other type of literature. But this does not mean that those who can write good middle-class revolutionary novels should feel it a duty to write bad working-class novels. They can serve in other ways.

I have devoted perhaps too much of my brief time to these negative aspects of the revolutionary movement. But it is important to arouse no hopes that cannot be fulfilled. The writers who join the revolutionary movement in the expectation of being saved or being endowed with leadership or being reborn to genius are likely to leave it suddenly—as Sherwood Anderson did after the failure of his novel. Others, who come with more reasonable hopes, are likely to remain. For the fact is that the revolutionary movement can and will do more for writers than writers can do for the movement. It can offer them practical inducements—not financial ones, certainly, for it will never make them rich; but still inducements that are worth more to them than money.

In the first place, it offers them an audience—the most eager and alive and responsive that now exists. We saw part of the audience the other night in Mecca Temple, when for one evening our discussions were carried out of the atmosphere of the study and the back barroom into a bigger world. We heard about the rest of it from the delegates speaking for the Marine Workers and the American League Against War and Fascism. We might hear still more about it from Alexander Trachtenberg, who can tell us how pamphlets issued by International Publishers Company are printed in editions of fifty and a hundred thousand and exhausted almost on the day of publication. But the most impressive testimonial to the quality of the revolutionary audience was given a few weeks ago by Archibald MacLeish.

MacLeish is scarcely a revolutionary writer. Mike Gold once described him as having "the fascist unconscious." I believed at the time that the charge was at least premature, but later it seemed to be justified by other poems and articles that MacLeish was writing. All of us were amazed to hear that he had arranged for a special performance of his play *Panic*, to be given for the benefit of *The New Theatre* and *The New Masses*. After the performance, he partly explained his motives by thanking the audience for its attention, for its applause, for its criticism, for its general lively interest. The whole point was that this poet who had won the Pulitzer Prize, this editor and writer for *Fortune*, had to turn to a revolutionary audience to get the sort of response without which any writer has the feeling of living in a vacuum and writing with invisible ink.

In the second place, the revolutionary movement gives writers a whole new range of subject matter. It seems to me that during the half-century ending in 1930 there was an increasing tendency for serious novelists and dramatists to occupy themselves with a single theme: the conflict between the individual and society, between the Artist and the World. The theme has been treated in hundreds, in thousands of bad novels and in a few good novels that almost all of us have read. James Joyce's *Portrait of the Artist as a Young Man* is perhaps the best of them all—but there are also *The Way of All Flesh, New Grub Street, Of Human Bondage, The Hill of Dreams, Manhattan Transfer, Look Homeward, Angel, Of Time and the River.*

A few characteristics are shared in common by all the novels of this type. One is that the hero usually is presented as a figure typical of all mankind—"a legend of man's hunger in his youth"—whereas in reality he is typical of nothing except the over-educated and under-adjusted young man of the lower middle classes who finds that the dream-world of books is to be preferred to the drab world he actually encounters. Another characteristic is that although these novels portray a conflict between the individual and society, all the emphasis, all the loving sympathy, is placed on the individual. Society, the outer world, becomes progressively dimmer and more puzzling in the artist's eyes. There is an attempt to escape from it into an inner world, into the subconscious, until finally these artist-and-the-world novels are transformed into interior monologues.

Now, the interior monologue was at first saluted and celebrated as a great new device for enriching the texture of fiction. In reality it had the opposite effect. After several years we began to see that the inner world it was supposed to illuminate was really not very interesting, not very fresh. The inner world of one middle-class novelist was very much like the inner world of another middle-class novelist. And the liberating effect of the revolutionary movement has been to carry the interest of novelists outside themselves, into the violent contrasts and struggles of the outer world.

In the third place, the revolutionary movement gives the artist a perspective on himself—an idea that his own experiences are not something accidental and unique, but are part of a vast pattern. The movement teaches him that art is not an individual but a social product—that it arises from experiences in society and that, if these experiences cease and if the artist no longer participates in the life about him, the source of his inspiration evaporates like a shallow pool after the rain.

In the fourth place, the revolutionary movement allies the interests of writers with those of a class that is rising, instead of with the interests of a confused and futile and decaying class. It gives them a new source of strength.

I have said that the revolutionary movement can perform no miracles, and yet with writers, especially with poets, it does sometimes produce effects that appear miraculous. Take Wordsworth, for example. During a few years of his long career he wrote great poems; then at the end of it he settled down to be the most skillful, high-minded and accomplished bore in English literature. Critics and college students have always been puzzled by this phenomenon. It is only during the past few years that some light has been thrown on it—that we have learned how he visited France at the height of the French Revolution, how he was filled with enthusiasm, how he learned to think in universal terms—and then how he became disillusioned, turned his eyes inward, accepted the eternal rightness and triteness of British society, and spent his last years bumbling in a garden.

We might well be skeptical about the source of Wordsworth's strength if it were not that we could find the same pattern in the lives of other poets. William Blake called himself a Jacobin, he paraded the streets of London in a liberty cap, he wrote great poems—then he too became disillusioned, he decided that the first revolution must be "in the soul of man," and he wrote those Prophetic Books that almost nobody reads today. Even Baudelaire had an experience something like this. In 1848, the revolutionary year in France, he fought for the revolutionists. He fought for them both in February, when the middle classes and the working classes rose together, and again in June, when only the workers manned the barricades. He wrote at least one proletarian poem correct enough in its ideology to be printed in *Pravda* or *Humanité* if it had been written in 1935. He wrote many other poems at this period and immediately afterwards; it was the most productive time of his life. But the working class was defeated and Baudelaire lost much of his energy, though not his admirable skill.

Heinrich Heine, Algernon Swinburne—the pattern could be traced through many other lives, and this is a task that I specially recommend to revolutionary critics. But the most striking example of all is Arthur Rimbaud. During four years of his life, from the age of fifteen till the age of nineteen, he wrote poems that are certainly among the masterpieces of French literature; then, for the rest of his life, he wrote nothing whatever. This genuine miracle has always dazzled critics. So far as I know, not one of them has pointed out the obvious connection with the struggles of the French working classes. Rimbaud began to write during the Franco-Prussian War, when Napoleon III was overthrown. At the age of fifteen, he was drawing up the constitution for an ideal communist state. During the Paris Commune, he was in the country, at a distance from the fighting, but he was doing his best to help—he was winning over soldiers in country inns and he was trying to make his way into Paris through the lines of the besiegers. The fierce energy he displayed during the next few years was not his energy alone; it was that of the revolutionary French working classes. But the Commune was overthrown and the reservoir of energy was not refilled. Rimbaud turned away from literature altogether and devoted himself to adventure, exploration, the smuggling of rifles into Abyssinia. His life became a parable of what happens under fascism.

Perhaps I am spending too much time on these examples chosen from the literatures of other countries. But I want to make it clear that our discussions here in this room, tedious as they may sometimes seem, have a direct relation with what has happened or is about to happen in the great world of human affairs. That sense of relationship is, I believe, the final and the principal gift that the revolutionary movement can make to writers. It gives them the sense of human life, not as a medley of accidents, but as a connected and continuing process. It ties things together, allowing novelists to see the connection between things that are happening today in our own neighborhoods, at the gates of factories, in backyards and street corners, with the German counter-revolution, with the fight for collectivization in Russia, with the civil war now being waged in the interior of China; and it connects all these events with the struggles of the past. It gives the values, the unified interpretation, without which one can write neither good history nor good tragedy.

During the past year, as a reader and literary critic, I have had several opportunities to compare books written from a revolutionary point of view with others written from a liberal point of view, when both authors were treating the same subject. In almost every case, the revolutionary books were better, not merely as politics but as literature.

To give one example, both Pearl Buck and André Malraux have written novels about life in Shanghai at the time when the proletarian leaders were being executed. The novels by both writers contain an episode in which the hero is imprisoned and waiting for death. In Pearl Buck's novel, he doesn't really know why he was arrested; the whole thing seems a regrettable and not very exciting accident. In Malraux's novel, the hero knows exactly why he is to be killed; he has deliberately faced death in order to help the revolution. And this keener consciousness, this voluntary purpose, this sense of unity with his comrades, are qualities that transform the story from accident into tragedy.

Again, both Konrad Heiden, a liberal journalist, and Ernst Henri, a Communist journalist, wrote books about the National Socialist Party in Germany. Of the two men, Heiden, the liberal, is better informed and has a better style. Yet the chief impression left by his *History of National Socialism* is one of confusion and bewilderment. Heiden himself, when revising the manuscript for English publication, found that after two years he had to change many of his estimates and prophecies. The curious thing is that his 1934 changes make the first part of his book less interesting and less *permanent* than it was in 1932. As for Ernst Henri, the author of *Hitler Over Europe,* he is only a middling good Marxist—and yet good enough to chart the course of events, good enough to write a book that does not need serious revision even now, since it casts light on the future of National Socialism as well as its past.

Yet again, there are two men who have written factual accounts of the tortures they underwent in Nazi concentration camps. One of them, Dr. Seger, was a middle-class Socialist member of the Reichstag; in this country he would probably be a Roosevelt Democrat. The other, Karl Billinger, was an underground Communist organizer. The impression we gain from Seger's book is that of reading a personal horror story. In Billinger's book there is even more horror, yet the emphasis is elsewhere, being laid on the heroism and solidarity of the

German workers. Seger's book is a document; Billinger's belongs to literature.

I don't mean to suggest that any of us can write a book as good as Billinger's *Fatherland* merely by proclaiming our undying allegiance to the proletariat. There is an ostentatious, just-look-at-me sort of revolutionary spirit that it would be well for us to avoid. For my own part, I am not a proletarian writer and I doubt that I shall ever become a proletarian writer. My background and my family and my education were all strictly middle class. I might be described as a highly class-conscious petty-bourgeois critic. But I believe that the interests of my class lie in a close alliance with the proletariat, and I believe that writers especially can profit by that alliance. Their souls won't be saved and they won't be magically supplied with talent if they have none already. But they will, if they approach the revolutionary movement without pride or illusion or servility, receive certain practical benefits. Literature and revolution are united not only by their common aim of liberating the human spirit, but also by immediate bonds of interest.

News from New Guinea

THE ANTHROPOLOGISTS are coming home. Thirty years ago they began to scatter toward the ends of the earth, in search of tribal cultures still uncorrupted by merchants, missionaries and machine guns. They measured the heads of Papuan head-hunters, they stole the digging tools of Digger Indians, they recorded the sexual rhythm of anybody half-willing to talk about it. Now at last they are applying their desert and jungle lore to the tribal cultures of the German blond Nordics and the white Protestant 100-percent American he-men.

Take Miss Margaret Mead, assistant curator of Ethnology at the American Museum of Natural History. She has been

Sex and Temperament in Three Primitive Societies, by Margaret Mead. New York: William Morrow and Company. (*NR*, June 5, 1935.)

using her anthropological training to study a problem that Stalin and Hitler have studied in terms of politics and Freud in terms of the subconscious. Why do men and women behave differently? Are there certain qualities, such as boldness, aggressiveness and logic, that we can scientifically regard as masculine? Are there other qualities—timidity, submissiveness, intuition—that belong to women by their biological nature? Or, is it possible that both sets of characteristics are socially assigned and imposed, like parts in a community drama? How can we give both men and women freedom to develop their inherent possibilities?

Miss Mead tried to answer these questions by studying three primitive tribes, all living in northwestern New Guinea. Among the Arapesh, a gentle people of the hills, she found that both men and women were trained to be coöperative, unaggressive and trustful. Warfare was practically unknown. Fathers shared the work of child rearing—to such an extent that when Miss Mead referred to a middle-aged man as good-looking the people answered her, "Ye-es? But you should have seen him before he bore all those children." The whole pattern of Arapesh life was soft and maternal. A hundred miles southeast of them lived the Mundugumor, whose pattern was truculent, selfish and male. Miss Mead spent several months among these recently reformed cannibals. She found that both men and women were lecherous, violent, almost completely lacking in tribal or parental feeling. Babies were neglected and often were drowned at birth. The ideal of romantic love among the Mundugumor was for a boy and girl to meet secretly in the jungle and scratch each other till the leaves were covered with blood. Miss Mead observes that neither of the first two tribes she studied showed any contrast between the sexes. "The Arapesh ideal is the mild, responsive man married to the mild, responsive woman; the Mundugumor ideal is the violent, aggressive man married to the violent, aggressive woman."

Traveling a hundred miles farther up the great valley in which the head-hunters ambush their enemies and betray their kinsmen, she studied the Tchambuli tribe of artists and fisher-women. Here there was plenty of sexual contrast. The men were delicate, wheedling, esthetic; they spent their days in gossip or in perfecting ceremonial dances. The women were matter-of-fact and jolly. "Solid, preoccupied, powerful, with

shaven unadorned heads," they sat in groups, laughed together and carried on the work of the tribe. Their attitude
toward the men was "one of kindly tolerance and appreciation." Miss Mead found that what we regard as the normal
roles of the two sexes were reversed among the Tchambuli.

But she also drew a general lesson from her observation of
the three savage tribes. The lesson was that most of the so-
called masculine and feminine traits are social rather than
biological, acquired rather than instinctive. They are no more
closely linked with sex than are women's hats or men's waist-
coats.

> . . . human nature is almost unbelievably malleable, responding
> accurately and contrastingly to contrasting cultural conditions.
> The differences between individuals who are members of differ-
> ent cultures, like the differences between individuals within a
> culture, are almost entirely to be laid to differences in condition-
> ing, especially during early childhood, and the form of this
> conditioning is culturally determined. Standardized personality
> differences between the sexes are of this order, cultural creations
> to which each generation, male and female, is trained to con-
> form.

In the argument leading to this radical conclusion, there
are some links of which the weakness is obvious even to a non-
anthropologist and non-sojourner among the Papuan abori-
gines. Thus, on the basis of Miss Mead's own records, it is not
true that "neither the Arapesh nor the Mundugumor have
made any attitude specific for one sex." The attitude of rest-
lessness, of continually seeking new distractions, is a trait of the
Arapesh men; their wives call them "Walk-Abouts" or
"Never-Sit-Downs." Among the Mundugumor, the attitude of
reckless self-exposure in warfare is specifically male. Among all
three tribes, even the women-ruled Tchambuli, it is taken for
granted that the men will have a monopoly of hunting, trading, fighting, painting and wood-carving, whereas the women
will stay at home and preserve the continuity of tribal life. If
all the researches of all the anthropologists were added together, it might be shown that a few male and female characteristics have prevailed everywhere. After all, the men are
stronger than the women and are unhampered by pregnancy.
The matriarch has to be gentler and more conniving than the
patriarch. Even the Tchambuli women are careful not to rule

their husbands too openly, for, as the men say, "We might become so ashamed that we would beat them."

Yet it seems to me that Miss Mead is essentially right in her principal conclusions about sex and temperament and the lack of a real connection between them. She is right in saying that most of the traits connected with social classes are also non-hereditary, are roles invented as if by a dramatist and imposed as if by a dictator. There is no more biological basis for class distinctions than there is for the belief of the Mundugumor that only a child born with the umbilical cord wrapped round its neck can become an artist. And Miss Mead is justified in her emphasis on the infinite adaptability of human nature. This, indeed, is the lesson pointed by the studies of almost all the modern anthropologists. After scattering over the world for thirty years, they are now carrying home the results of their studies. They have to report that nothing is humanly impossible, that there is certainly no inferno in which man has not managed somehow to live and possibly no Utopia toward which he might not rise.

The Paris Congress of Writers

SIR: The American Organizing Committee of the International Congress of Writers for the Defense of Culture wishes to announce that the Congress, to be held in Paris, has been postponed from June 3 to June 21. The Congress is anti-war and anti-fascist in its ends, and American writers who agree with this general program are urged to attend. If they are going, they should get in touch with the Secretariat of the Congress at 1 Cité Paradis, Paris, France.

Isidor Schneider,   *Malcolm Cowley,*
Van Wyck Brooks,   *Waldo Frank,*
John Chamberlain,   *Lewis Mumford.*
New York City.   AMERICAN ORGANIZING COMMITTEE.

NR, June 19, 1935.

The Writers' International

PAINFULLY, from articles in the French and English press, I have been piecing together a picture of the Writers' International Congress for the Defense of Culture. It met in Paris on June 21 and continued for five days, with public sessions every afternoon and evening. In spite of the sticky, interminable heat, there was an audience of several thousand at all the meetings, a young audience partly composed of students and tourists, but chiefly drawn from the French working class. The delegates sat on a high platform barricaded with microphones. Flashlight bulbs exploded among them, caricaturists made sketches, reporters took notes at long unpainted tables and, hour after hour, the speeches continued, those in German, English or Russian being followed by unusually competent French translations. There were interruptions and disputes, some of them quite interesting, there was the inevitable scandal provoked by the Trotskyites, there was much wandering outside to drink beer or lemonade in the open air. Still, when the Congress ended, a long and carefully studied program had been concluded impressively.

The writers assembled there at the Palais de la Mutualité —about two hundred of them, from thirty-eight countries—included a great many prominent citizens of the world republic of letters. Especially brilliant were the French delegation (Gide, Barbusse, Malraux, Aragon, Bloch, Vildrac and others), the Soviet delegation (with Ehrenbourg, Pasternak, Babel and Alexis Tolstoy) and the German delegation (entirely composed of exiles). Waldo Frank made the principal speech for the Americans; the English were represented by E. M. Forster, Aldous Huxley and John Strachey. The Congress had been organized by a left-wing group composed for the most part of Communist sympathizers, but all sorts of writers had been invited, provided only that they were hostile to fascism. The natural and healthy result was a series of arguments, traditionalists against innovators, liberals against Marxists. And yet, if the speeches are compared, they reveal a curious unanimity in regard to the most important subjects under discussion.

In the first place, nobody spoke in favor of abandoning "bourgeois culture" for the sake of a "proletarian culture" still to be created. All writers of whatever political complexion agreed that the old masterpieces should not only be preserved but should be rendered available to a much wider audience. Most of the argument on this point was provoked by Julien Benda. The occidental tradition, he said, holds that intellectual activity is independent of economic activity; the Communists claim that the two are interlocked; hence, there is a definite break between Communism and the Occident. Several writers answered him by pointing out that Marx and all his ideas belong to the occidental tradition. Paul Nizan, speaking for the Communists, made a more elaborate reply, explaining that the occidental tradition is not a homogeneous mass, but contains all sorts of currents and counter-currents. "Out of the whole cultural heritage to which M. Benda clings, we accept everything that implies a criticism of the existing world; we accept every plea made in favor of individuals who live and think, who hunger and die." On the other hand, "we reject the humanist mythology that asks us to contemplate an abstract human creature, and meanwhile to ignore the real conditions of life." The old culture should be preserved by emphasizing its best elements.

But the old culture—and this was another point made by many speakers—is not a fixed and definite object to be kept like a family heirloom. It is, said Jean Cassou, an *act* that must continually be renewed. Malraux, in the closing speech, went much farther along the same path. "Art, ideas, poems, all the old dreams of man: if we have need of them to live, they have need of us to live again—need of our passion, need of our desires, need of our *will*. . . . Whether or not we wish it, we create them at the same time that we create ourselves. . . . The cultural heritage does not transmit itself, but must be conquered."

Still another point on which there was general agreement was that national peculiarities—what André Gide called "the angles of refraction" proper to each people—are not to be abandoned in favor of a colorless internationalism; they are valuable to the world at large. On the other hand, the types of nationalism current today are hostile to the interests of the nations they claim to preserve, just as individualism is hostile to the freedom of most individuals. They are driving us towards another war which, as Malraux said, "will doubtless mean the end of Europe."

It would be a difficult and not a very useful task to summarize forty or fifty speeches, heterodox and orthodox, witty or windy. I suppose that the word most often repeated was "humanism," which was redefined as a preoccupation with living and suffering men and a hostility towards the abstractions and institutions now weighing them down. For the rest, there was one emotion underlying all the speeches and binding them together more closely than any idea or slogan. It was, briefly stated, a deep sense of *urgency*. No matter how high the speakers might soar into realms of intellectual theory or pure nonsense, they were brought down to earth by the knowledge of what might happen tomorrow, in this city, in this street. Yesterday fascism had triumphed in Germany. There were dozens of exiles in the hall; there were writers still scarred with floggings received in concentration camps. Today France was threatened with the same fate; and if France fell the rest of Europe would tumble after. The writers here would suffer not only in their books but in their persons.

It was a practical danger that brought them together; it was also a practical hope of combating it. In Germany the parties of the Left and the Center had quarreled with one another more bitterly than with Hitler; in France they were trying to unite. The same process was going on in the intellectual world, and this explains why Communists and Catholics and believers in the aristocratic tradition were addressing the same audience of students and workers. The audience was the key—for it was obvious that all these literary men had agreed on still another matter of everyday importance. No matter how united they were among themselves, they would be impotent, easy to gag and stifle, unless they drew nearer to the classes in the population that were actively fighting a big-business dictatorship. It was too late now to scurry back into their ivory towers. Their only salvation was to establish an offensive and defensive alliance with their audience—on the principle that if the working class successfully defended its liberties, the writers could be sure of saving theirs.

The Poet's Privacy

CONRAD AIKEN's "Plea for Anonymity," printed in this week's *New Republic*, is one of those essays that I like tremendously and disagree with violently. I like it because Aiken attacks the whole crazy system of personality puffing and literary ballyhooliganism, and because his own practice agrees with his preaching. He has never let himself be drawn into those nudist camps where authors parade without so much as a last fig leaf of self-respect. But I disagree with Aiken's essay because I think it is based on a questionable theory of art and politics.

Let me choose three quotations for comment and dispute.

First: "What is esthetically 'good' turns out, on examination, to be psychologically useful, and therefore socially useful, and on this basis a hierarchy of values could be worked out which would be both practical and sound."—I wish I could share Aiken's simple faith in the psychological usefulness of the esthetically good. Some of the passages in world literature that are esthetically best—as, for example, the suicide of Kirillov in *The Possessed* and Baudelaire's apostrophe to the two Lesbians: *"Descendez, descendez, lamentables victimes"*— have done a tremendous lot of psychological damage that social historians might trace in diaries and letters and novels. But the point in this sentence with which I really differ is the short phrase, "and *therefore* socially useful." It goes back to the conception of society as an arithmetical sum of individuals, whose psychological patterns add up into the general social pattern. Anthropologists don't hold this conception and even psychologists are ceasing to hold it. They are beginning to say that "the individual," as presented in political speeches and textbooks on moral philosophy—the individual as divorced from the community in which he lives—is a metaphysical abstraction.

But let's pass on to the second quotation, which continues the same argument. "One of the elements in this hierarchy, but by no means the most important, would certainly be the political—the relation of the individual and his class to governmental or social forms at a given time and place. By no means the most important, because its validity is transitory and limited: it is a momentary aspect of a deeper universal, the relationship, simply, of man to man."—I don't know just what Aiken means by the relationship of man to man. But I take it that he means sexual love, parental love, friendship, respect, hatred, etc. The assumption would then be that these relationships were unchanging—in contradistinction to the relationship between social classes, which are transitory. This simply isn't true. A few months ago—to give one item of disproof—I reviewed a book by Margaret Mead, *Sex and Temperament in Three Primitive Societies*. The author was trying to find out whether there were any *constants* in the relationship between men and women in different primitive cultures. She couldn't find any. In one tribe, marriage was a gentle and stable relationship of equals, in another it was an unstable and violent relationship of equals, in still another the women had "male" characteristics and ruled, the men had "female" characteristics and submitted. In one tribe both mothers and fathers loved and cherished their children; in another tribe both mothers and fathers hated and neglected them.

History gives still more striking examples of these changes in personal relationships. There have been patriarchal families, matriarchal families, polygamous and polyandrous families; today there are bourgeois families, experimental families, and each type is distinguished by a different ideal of man's part, of woman's part, of filial obedience. That "deeper universal, the relationship, simply, of man to man," has changed almost as rapidly as the broader social relationships, and is, indeed, almost impossible to understand without them. The simple statements, "He was my father and I killed him," or "She was my sister and I married her," would have an entirely different emotional meaning in different tribes or civilizations. In some, they would be a factual statement of cause and effect. But we are trained to believe that our institutions are eternal and universal, that capitalism is the "normal" economic relationship and the bourgeois family the "normal" relationship of individuals. It is a point of view lacking in perspective and one that prevents us from realizing the changes that are taking place in our own families and professions. A better social theory might also lead to our writing truer fiction.

On account of this intermingling of art and politics, we have to change our arguments against political censorship. What Aiken says on this subject seems wistful and innocent: "Just the same, we must admit that nowadays things are made very difficult for the good artist. In the past few years every sort of attempt, by argument, by intimidation, by exile, by bribery, has been made to coerce him into this or that social or political faction or fashion."—Aiken regards this as being a very bad state of affairs indeed. I should regard it as being a good or at least a promising state of affairs. It shows that political leaders recognize the importance of literature. When they cease to bribe or coerce or intimidate writers, then it is time for the writers to worry. But I also think it is a healthy state of affairs when the writers fight back; when they tenaciously defend their freedom. And they are by no means helpless: they have weapons on their side, if they know how to use them. In the Soviet Union, for example, they have won many intellectual privileges during the last three years and have routed the worst of the censors. The strength of the Soviet writers lies in the fact that the political leaders want and need their support, and are willing to grant a great deal of intellectual liberty as the price of receiving it.* That, too, impresses me as a healthy condition. Freedom is not the result of tolerance, indifference, deadness: it is won and held after a struggle.

* This deluded comment must stand for the record, with others I made about Stalin's Russia. It was written a year before the Great Purge of 1936–38 put an end to literary protests, and to the lives of many protestors. Tretiakov, whose *Chinese Testament* I had warmly praised, would be among the first to vanish. It was not until after Stalin's death that Russian writers would again feel strong enough to do battle with the censors, who might still condemn them to prison, but not to death.—M. C.

And the same is true of an author's privacy. There is one cheap and certain method by which he can preserve it, namely, by never writing anything that bothers people or makes them faintly curious. I doubt that many writers would be satisfied with this state of affairs. They want to be read, they want to achieve success, and any successful writer is, by definition, a public figure. More or less, he has to play the part. He cannot live, as Aiken seems to recommend, in a tower built of glass bricks that are transparent from within but translucent from without, so that he can enjoy the world without being seen. He cannot influence his readers without allowing himself to be influenced in turn. But he can set a limit to their influence on him, and, in particular, he can prevent his personality from being ballyhooed like a new brand of shaving cream. He can keep his integrity by fighting for it; otherwise it wouldn't be worth having.

Footnotes to a Life of Marx

THE MAN OF LETTERS.—In reading Franz Mehring's book—probably the best biography of Marx in any language, and certainly the one good treatment of his character that is available in English—I got the impression that part of his intellectual background has been badly neglected. Marx was of course a philosopher who developed out of Hegel, a political thinker stimulated by the French Utopian Socialists, an economist who adopted and transformed the theories of Adam Smith. "He was above all a revolutionary," as ten thousand people have quoted from Engels' address at his grave. But the same people forget that he was also, by taste and training, a man of letters. During his boisterous youth at the University of Berlin, he wrote three copybooks full of poems to Jenny von

Karl Marx: The Story of His Life, by Franz Mehring. Translated by Edward Fitzgerald. New York: Covici, Friede. (*NR*, Feb. 26, 1936.)

Westphalen. He decided—and rightly, thinks Mehring after seeing these verses—that his talent lay elsewhere; but all his life he continued to read poetry (Æschylus in Greek every year; Shakespeare and Goethe aloud to his children) and to take a poet's pains with the structure and style of his political writings. Indeed, I should guess that their literary form has had a great deal to do with their influence. Each of his books is boldly constructed, most of them are adorned with fine dramatic portraits, and all are rich in figures of speech. For example, *The Communist Manifesto* begins and ends with two subversive metaphors—"A spectre is haunting Europe" and "You have nothing to lose but your chains"—that have been almost as dangerous to the established order as the ideas framed between them.

As a man of letters, Marx was a Romantic of the second generation, the spiritual contemporary of Baudelaire and Flaubert. Like them he toiled at his desk—corrected, recopied, recorrected—and published nothing till he was sure of its absolute rightness. Like them he took pride in his isolation and his neglect by the conventional world; like them he despised the rabble of the half-educated. He reviled the bourgeois in a double sense, both as economic exploiters and as the enemies of honest writing. He suffered both as a rebel among reactionaries and as a genius among the philistines. The revolution he desired was one that would not only free the proletariat from its chains of wage slavery, but also the creative spirit from its chains of convention.

And there is another sense in which he belonged to the Romantic school. It seems to me that he was touched with the spirit of Milton's Satan—a not improbable supposition, considering that the arch-revolutionist of *Paradise Lost* was a popular figure in all the revolutionary literature of the early nineteenth century. There was scarcely a poet who supported the revolutionary cause without invoking Satan: one can trace the line of them from Blake through Byron and Baudelaire down to Rimbaud and to the author of the "Internationale"— of which the second line, translated literally, is "Arise, ye *damned* of earth." The revolt against monarchism and capitalism was quite naturally identified with the revolt of the fallen angels. But in Marx's case, this conception is embodied in his life rather than in his writings; and it becomes especially manifest during the period of his exile and deep poverty in London. Driven headlong from their own country, separated from their families, their means of livelihood, their hopes of the future, the German refugees of 1849 were like Satan's cherubs after their nine days' fall from Heaven, as they "lay rowling in the fiery Gulf." And Marx was like Lucifer proclaiming, "All is not lost; the unconquerable Will"—Lucifer inciting his comrades

> *To wage by force or guile eternal Warr*
> *Irreconcileable, to our grand Foe*

It might have been Lucifer speaking in that last editorial of *Die Neue Rheinische Zeitung*, when Marx addressed the Prussian monarchists who were suppressing his newspaper together with every other democratic activity. "Why bother with your foolish lies and official phrases? We are ruthless ourselves and we ask no consideration from you. When our turn comes, we shall make no apologies for our terrorism. . . ." Again, one hears that Miltonic tone in the answer Marx gave to a deputation which asked by what right he and Engels spoke as the representatives of international labor. Marx told the deputation "that they had received their mandate as representatives of the proletarian party from no one but themselves, and that it had been confirmed by the general and particular hatred manifested toward them by all the parties of the old world."

This Luciferian pride, which Baudelaire and Flaubert would have understood (and which indeed they shared), was a quality that enabled him to survive those terrible years of exile when his friends were emigrating to America, or dying of tuberculosis and starvation, or going down among "the living dead" who had made their peace with the Prussian state. But the pride that sustained him also made his troubles worse by involving him in endless quarrels with those who were less proud and less uncompromising. It caused him to be attacked as "an ice cold demagogue" and "a heartless intriguer." Marx did not answer these personal slanders. Only those nearest to him—Engels, Frau Marx, the children—guessed what he suffered during that period of loneliness and utter destitution.

FRAU MARX. — Of Johanna Bertha Julie Jenny von Westphalen as she was in her youth, nothing survives except a daguerreotype that gives us a cloudy glimpse of white shoulders, a good-humored mouth and sober, big, appealing eyes. She was a baron's daughter, "the prettiest girl in Trier," "the queen of the ball." But she fell in love with a rebellious Jewish student somewhat younger than herself, and married him after an engagement that lasted from 1836 till 1843, seven long years. Then, after a short honeymoon, she followed him into exile, "the home of virtue."

She must have been happy enough in her love for her husband to forget the inconveniences they suffered at first. They had a small income and Karl's family was prosperous enough to help them a little. Besides, there was always a revolution in prospect that would change their world. . . . But the revolution came, and it only meant that Karl squandered everything he had and everything he could borrow to keep his revolutionary newspaper running for a year. When they went back into exile with their three children, they had nothing, not even debts—only a ticket to show that Jenny Marx had pawned the family silver.

During their first years in London, they often went hungry; sometimes they lived for a month on bread and potatoes. Sometimes Karl could not leave the house because he had no shoes and, as she heard him growling to Fred Engels, "no coat to cover my behind." Sometimes the whole family was ill—Jenny and little Jenny and Lenchen their faithful servant; there would be no money to pay a doctor. Frau Marx did not mind for herself—"I am among the lucky ones, am specially favored, seeing that my dear husband is still at my side. But what really crushes me, what makes my heart bleed, is that my husband has to suffer so many paltry annoyances, that so few have come to his help."

Guido, her fourth child, died partly as a result of her tribulations. A few days before his death, she pitied him in a letter to one of their friends who had emigrated to America. "The poor little angel drank in so many cares and worries with his milk that he was always fretting and in violent pain day and night. . . . When thus afflicted, he sucked so vigorously that my nipple became irritated and bled; often the blood streamed into his little mouth." Her fifth child, Francisca, was born in the early spring of 1851 and survived until Easter, 1852. Frau Marx wrote in her diary, "For three days the poor child struggled against death and suffered much. Her small lifeless body rested in our little back room while we all went together into the front room and when night came we made up our beds on the floor. The three surviving children lay with us and we cried for the poor little angel. . . . Her death took place in a period of bitterest poverty. I went to a French refugee who lives near us and who had visited us shortly before. He received me with friendliness and sympathy and gave me two pounds and with that money I paid for the coffin in which my child could rest peacefully. She had no cradle when she was born. . . ." Her sixth child, Eleanor—"Tussy," they called her—was born prematurely; Frau Marx was proud of keeping her alive and thereby spiting all prophecies. But during the same year—1855—she suffered her worst blow with the illness of Edgar, her only son, "the life and soul of the house." He died in his father's arms. On that day and for ten years afterward, Frau Marx kept saying that she wished she were in the grave with her children.

Years later, she wrote a letter of consolation to their friends the Sorges, who had lost two children during adolescence. She said, "I know only too well how terrible it is and how long it lasts before one can recover one's peace of mind after such a loss, but everyday life with its little pleasures and its great troubles, with all its petty worries and its minor torments, comes to our aid and gradually the great suffering is numbed by the troubles and worries of the moment, so that almost unnoticeably the violent anguish diminishes; not that such wounds ever heal completely, and certainly never in a mother's heart, but gradually one recovers one's receptiveness and even one's ability to feel new sufferings and new pleasures, and one lives on and on with a broken but still hopeful heart until finally it is stilled forever and eternal peace is there."

Frau Marx died slowly of cancer, suffering because she could not spend her last days with her husband. "The Moor," as his daughters called him, was dangerously ill with bronchitis and incipient pneumonia; they agonized in separate rooms. Little Tussy wrote, "I shall never forget the morning when he felt himself strong enough to get up and go into Mother's room. It was as though they were young again—she a loving girl and he an ardent youth starting out together through life, and not an old man shattered by ill health and a dying old lady taking leave of each other forever."

Marx survived his wife by fifteen months, but his spirit was broken. Fred Engels had said on the day of her death, "The Moor has also died."

Comrade Trotsky

LAST MONTH, after writing "Footnotes to a Life of Marx," I was reproved by an eloquent and anonymous reader. "Did it ever occur to you," he asked, "that there is a man today in this world who resembles in his destiny 'the Moor' of your admiration? His name, of course, is Leon Trotsky. And what are you doing, Mr. Cowley, to prevent some future poet and critic from bemoaning the lot of a great spirit who died— maligned, hounded, slandered, hated by all the parties of the old world? . . . How could you remain so callous in the presence of the greatest and most sublime single tragedy in our cruel epoch?" I am quoting these few sentences from a perturbed and perturbing letter to explain why, five years after the date of publication, I set myself the task of reading and reporting on Trotsky's *My Life.*

To me it proved a disappointing book, one that partly spoiled a magnificent story. Trotsky has not the gift of writing about himself. That fact was already clear in *The History of the Russian Revolution,* which loses much of its unusual breadth and conviction as soon as the author appears on the scene and begins to argue and expostulate about his own historical role. In *My Life* he is on the scene from the first chapter

My Life, by Leon Trotsky. New York: Charles Scribner's Sons. (*NR,* Apr. 8, 1936.)

to the last, and yet he never makes himself quite clear as a character because (after the chapters dealing with his childhood) he does not look at himself objectively. The other characters in his story are less vivid than those that appear in the *History*. He is able to describe people superbly in their relation to world forces—who could forget his portraits of Kerensky and Tsar Nicholas?—but he cannot describe them in their relation to himself; always in this book he lets us see them vaguely through the colored glass of his own personality.

And that personality seems less sympathetic than the reader had expected. "I am obliged," Trotsky explains with candor, "to speak of myself in a way I should never have done under other conditions"—that is, with more self-praise. "For me it is a question not merely of historical truth but also of a political struggle that is still going on." But even for the purpose of a political struggle, there is too much buttering of his ego, there are too many testimonials quoted not only from his bitter enemies (whose words are most effective here) but also from his allies and camp followers, and principally from N. I. Sedova, who is Mrs. Trotsky. He will not admit that he was ever wrong in any important question. But the least admirable quality he reveals is a vanity that is always striking poses and playing roles—now the role of conspirator, now that of hero quelling a mob, now that of General Phil Sheridan riding twenty miles to Winchester and rallying his defeated soldiers (while his orderly ran at his heels brandishing a revolver and shouting for all he was worth, "Courage, boys, Comrade Trotsky is leading you")—then the role of an invalid helpless while plots were being woven against him (and also woven by him, the narrative makes clear), then the role of Gulliver bound by the Lilliputians (these being the epigones, the followers of Stalin), then finally the role of a martyred leader fighting for his rights—carried down stairs kicking and squirming by a squad of secret agents while his son Lyova rang all the doorbells in the apartment house and shouted to the frightened people who appeared, "They're carrying Comrade Trotsky away!" In all these episodes there is a mixture of profound drama with actor's parade, and sometimes with actor's parade in circumstances that make it seem trivial and unpleasant.

In effect, this book is unjust to Trotsky and makes him

seem smaller than life. In effect, it reduces his tragedy to the
dimensions of a personal quarrel. This is partly the result of a
story that he brings forward to explain his fall from power. It
seems that when he was a second-year student in an Odessa
high school, the boys "gave a concert" to an unpopular teacher.
A dozen of them were caught and punished, but Trotsky, the
bright student, was not suspected. A particularly stupid and
disagreeable boy named Danilov was so jealous of his intellectual prestige and so angry at his going scot-free that he accused
him of being responsible for the whole affair—and the bright
student was expelled, even though several friends came to his
defense. "Such," Trotsky says, "was the first political test I
underwent." He believes that the pattern established in Odessa
was repeated all through his life, and that Stalin, whom he
calls "the outstanding mediocrity in the Party," played the
same ignoble role as Danilov. Other Bolsheviks helped Stalin
because they were becoming self-satisfied philistines and were
made uncomfortable by Trotsky's revolutionary virtue. . . .
But most people accept a different explanation of his fall, and
one that makes him seem more important. Trotsky originated
and refused to abandon the idea of the permanent revolution—
the theory that "a lasting, decisive success is inconceivable for
us without a revolution in Europe" and in fact throughout the
world. The revolution in Western Europe was checked in
1923, with the failure of the last German uprisings. In 1927,
when the Chinese revolution was also suppressed, most Russians decided that their only hope was to develop socialism in
their own country. Trotsky the internationalist was thus defeated by events in Shanghai and Berlin. But he was also
defeated by flaws in his own character—by his vanity, by his
losing touch with popular sentiment and by his persistent failure to recognize Stalin's ability. He was a general who under-
estimated the opposing forces.

Today it seems to me that the nature of his tragedy is
generally misapprehended. To be "maligned, hounded, slandered, hated by all the parties of the old world" is not a fate
that would torture him: he had learned to bear misfortunes
like these in the course of his earlier exiles. To be driven from
power is probably not a lasting sorrow, for he was not deeply
attached to power in the state. It is history that has been his

forum and stage, his purpose in living, one might almost
literally say his God. It is "the judgment of history" that has
been his undeviating standard of right and wrong. On the day
after the October Revolution he thundered to the Mensheviks,
"Go to the place where you belong from now on—the dustbin
of history!" and he was exactly like a pope condemning lost
souls to limbo. Today his tragic burden is that he has been
defeated by historical forces. He has not only been expelled
bodily from the country he helped to win, but also painted out
of its pictures and deleted from its schoolbooks. "The dustbin
of history"—that is the real prison into which he was thrust by
Stalin, to languish until the old animosities have died away.

Hicks's Life of John Reed

I CONFESS to having been mildly perturbed when I
heard two years ago that Granville Hicks was writing a life of
John Reed. The two men had something in common—both of
them went to Harvard and both became Communists—but
apart from these quite obvious resemblances their tempera-
ments seemed to clash beyond any hope of successful collaboration. Reed was a poet and a bohemian by nature; he groped
his way toward instinctive judgments; his picture of the world
was primarily esthetic. Hicks incarnates the spirit of sound and
scholarly prose; his judgments are based on logic and, beyond
that, on the non-conformist New England conscience. It was
hard not to feel that his picture of Reed would be distorted
and made to fit his own pattern.

I now want to apologize to Hicks for these doubts which I
never expressed. His book leaves them with only the faintest
shadow of justification. There are a few moments when the
contrast between the two men seems a little too striking, espe-

"The Making of a Writer." A review of *John Reed: The Making
of a Revolutionary*, by Granville Hicks, with the assistance of John
Stuart. New York: The Macmillan Company. (*NR*, Apr. 22,
1936.)

cially when Hicks is quoting from *Insurgent Mexico*—at such
moments he seems to be slogging along the highway in good
footsoldierly prose, while Reed, mounted on a golden stallion,
is galloping off into the legendary sunset, young, successful,
hated and adored. But this impression fades as the book continues. In the end it becomes clear that Hicks, by patient scholarship, by finding the documents and respecting them, by consult-
ing hundreds of men and women who knew Jack Reed, has
managed to recreate his figure very much as it was in life. In
the process he gives us a new impression of his own talents. His
first book, *The Great Tradition*, was systematic, vigorous, but
at the same time a little cold and unrelenting toward human
weakness. Here there is a surprising warmth, and beyond it a
tolerance achieved without sacrificing the moral feeling that
lends force to Hicks's writing. He shows a forgiving spirit not
only toward John Reed—whose early deviations he might be
expected to condone, in the light of Reed's conduct during the
Russian revolution—but also toward the poet's friends and girl
friends and drinking companions. What emerges is an extraordinarily fine picture of a man's career against the background
of Harvard and Greenwich Village, of war, revolution and the
American radical movement.

As for John Reed himself, the book makes it clear that he
became a revolutionist for reasons that were both profound and
fundamentally literary. He could write supremely well on
only one subject—on men revolting against the institutions that
prevented them from leading human lives. This fact he first
discovered in 1913, when he went to Mexico for *The Metropolitan* and spent three months with Pancho Villa's army. Other
correspondents saw battles, generals on horseback, disgustingly
dirty soldiers; Reed saw beyond all this to the ideal of human
dignity for which the Mexicans were fighting. His imagination
was touched and suddenly, overnight, the romantic poet and
journalist was transformed into a writer who had something
close to genius. The editors of *The Metropolitan* misunderstood the nature of his achievement. They thought of him,
they advertised him widely, as a dashing, white-stocked, cav-
alry-booted war correspondent in the tradition of Richard
Harding Davis. They sent him to the Western front and were
vastly disappointed with the articles he sent home. Reed sim-

ply could not report a mechanized butchery; he was not a
pacifist, but this war in Europe was not his sort of war.

His path in retrospect seems perfectly clear: by his literary
conscience he was continually guided toward the material that
produced his best work. But he had no map, and often he tried
to escape into blind alleys. At Harvard, for example, he narrowly missed being what in Jewish slang is called an "allright-
nik," in this case a conventional member of the Harvard patri-
ciate. In New York after his graduation he was elected to the
Dutch Treat Club and felt almost at home among the high-
priced magazine hacks. In Florence at Mabel Dodge's villa,
and again in Provincetown, he was nearly the perfect bohemian, swimming, loafing, having mad love affairs and writing
paradoxical plays. But all the fruits of these escapades—his
Harvard poems in the Cantabrigio-Victorian tradition, his
monthly-magazine brightness, his Shavian talkodramas—
seemed dry and unappetizing. By his hunger for something to
feed the imagination, he was continually sucked back into the
human struggle where he felt that he belonged.

A favorite theory with regard to John Reed is that he was
a poet lost to the world through his ill advised devotion to the
revolution. Hicks does not argue this point—one of his virtues
as a biographer is that he avoids being controversial—but he
furnishes enough facts for the reader to draw his own conclusions. The truth seems to be that Reed was never much of a
poet—in verse, at any rate. When he ceased to rhyme his
emotions, the world did not lose anything more than another
Carl Hovey or Bliss Carman. On the other hand, his best prose,
which was his revolutionary prose, added a new quality to
American literature. He turned reporting into history, and
history itself into the great poem he had failed to write.

Another theory completely disproved by Hicks is that
Reed as a revolutionist was only a Harvard playboy who never
ceased to be resentful at having to play the new role into which
he had blundered. The fact is that after October, 1917, the
revolution was almost his whole life—he spoke for it, wrote for
it, starved in prison and finally died for it. There was only one
occasion when he seemed to be turning it into a game. After
the second congress of the Communist International (at which
Reed was elected to the Central Executive Committee) he and

two friends walked up to Lenin while the delegates were singing and cheering. The tall Americans hoisted the stocky little man to their shoulders as if he were the captain of a winning football team. Lenin did not understand: at first he protested and then began kicking, leaving a big bump on one American's forehead. Reed went away in high spirits. But it happened that this was his one serious breach of revolutionary decorum: the rest of the time he was working hard for the world revolution that seemed to be as certain as sunrise. On his deathbed, just before sinking into a coma, he was correcting the speech on the Negro Question that he had delivered before the Comintern.

Edmund Wilson in Russia

FOUR YEARS ago Edmund Wilson wrote *The American Jitters,* possibly the most valuable and certainly among the least appreciated of all the books that have dealt with the depression. It contains a series of articles that appeared in *The New Republic,* but the book itself has to be read from beginning to end in order to get the cumulative effect of it. Ostensibly Wilson was reporting the state of the nation in 1931, after one of those transcontinental tours that so many journalists have made since then. But there was another story involved, the story of a traveler in search of a philosophy. At first Wilson was a progressive, mildly hopeful that older progressives like Senators Norris and Cutting would point out a path for him to follow; then step by step he became convinced that Marx was his real guide, that our whole society was bankrupt and would have to be reorganized. The book ends with a succession of powerful chapters, in one of which he expresses at some length his admiration for Soviet Russia.

"Flight from the Masses." A review of *Travels in Two Democracies,* by Edmund Wilson. New York: Harcourt, Brace and Company. (*NR,* June 3, 1936.) The review is continued in the essay that follows.

Wilson has now fulfilled the promise half-made in those chapters: he has gone to Russia and has formed his own judgment of the new civilization there. But *Travels in Two Democracies* also contains some further reports on America, and these I found definitely inferior to *The American Jitters*. The writing is just as good as ever, and there are two passages that are pretty nearly superb—a report on the Oxford Groups called "Saving the Right People and Their Butlers" and a fantasy called "What to Do till the Doctor Comes," full of tepid vice and people too passionless to be damned. But the section as a whole is composed of postscripts and codicils; it lacks the clear direction that Wilson's earlier pieces seem to derive from their sympathy for the working class.

The Russian half of the book, which was printed in part by *The New Republic,* has started an argument that shows no sign of stopping. It seems to me that most of those who have been abusing Wilson, and some of those praising him, have misunderstood what he was trying to do. In the first place, his account of Russia is more favorable to the Soviets than anyone would guess from the separately printed extracts (most of which dealt with Moscow, a city where he felt less at home than in Leningrad or Odessa). In the second place, his habit of relating trivial incidents does not reveal a trivial mind. It is part of a plan which consists in reducing socialism to the scale of daily life, and in writing an account of Russia based on what he saw with his own eyes and heard with his own ears. (The only time his method seems to betray him is in his passages on Stalin, where actually he departs from it to the extent of depending on hearsay.) And, in the third place, Wilson's narrative is valuable not only as a vivid impression of Russian life but also as a mental autobiography written with persistent candor.

In a sense it is a sequel to *The American Jitters,* but this time the stages in his thinking are more difficult to explain. The first stage, I think, was a puzzled disillusionment, never directly expressed but underlying whole chapters. Wilson in his earlier book had spoken of hoping to see "the whole world fairly and sensibly run, as Russia now is run, instead of by shabby politicians in the interests of acquisitive manufacturers, businessmen and bankers." He had condemned his fellow in-

tellectuals for "their extreme skittishness about Russia," and
had said that writers would be better off under socialism. But
he found that Russian writers were either conforming to official standards at some cost to themselves or else were rebelling
at a still heavier cost; and he decided that the intellectual
world had an atmosphere of nervous tension that suggested
New York. The politicians in Moscow were more honest but
hardly more appealing than politicians elsewhere. As for the
Russian masses, he was repelled by their inefficiency and vast
inertia.

Soon his thinking entered a second stage. He became an
American patriot, took pride in American initiative, the American standard of living, and partially forgot the ignorance and
misery that he had chronicled in *The American Jitters*. It was
unfortunate, he thought, that Russia had become the first
socialist country. "The opponents of socialism can always put
down to socialism anything they find objectionable in Russia.
The advocates of socialism are betrayed into defending things
which are really distasteful to them, and which they have no
business defending." With its greater technical knowledge and
its republican institutions, America would have an easier time
developing a collective society.

A third stage in his thinking began on the homeward
journey, even before he crossed the Polish border. He was
suddenly sorry to be leaving Russia and began to think of all
its friendly and human qualities. The sight of fat Polish businessmen, overbearing officers and whining beggars made him
long to be back in a country where nobody seemed rude or
servile or tried to sell you anything whatever. He reflected
that the Soviet Union was "at the moral top of the world,
where the light never really goes out." The Western capitals,
Berlin, Paris, now seemed dead beyond hope of resurrection.

But he had one other reaction to his travels, one that is
important in his mental history, but hard to define because it
was almost purely instinctive. In the old hospital in Odessa,
where he spent six weeks recovering from scarlet fever, he had
his first experience since the War of being with people from
morning till midnight, of living collectively. He liked it in a
curious fashion, yet he violently rebelled against it; and in self-
defense, I should judge, he developed a cult of the genius and

the hero. Lenin in particular became the object of this cult, and Wilson here exalts him at the expense of his countrymen—who are amazed, he says, "with their formless and expressionless faces, when they look down on him and know that he was one of them, and that he invoked from their loose and sluggish plasm all those triumphs to which life must rise and to which he thought himself the casual guidepost." The whole passage is one of the most eloquent that Wilson has written. But in the course of it he seems to forget that Lenin, in addition to creating a new revolutionary Russia, was himself produced by an older revolutionary Russia—that his career was made possible by the sacrifice of other careers, beginning with that of his own brother, who was executed for trying to kill the Tsar; that his mind was sharpened by dispute with minds almost as keen; that his determination was strengthened by his determined comrades; that in short he was the arm and the voice of an idea for which thousands had died obscurely before the first gun was fired in the October revolution. Lenin is the archetype of modern hero, whose individuality grows through his relation to a collective movement. And therefore it seems curious when Wilson exalts him as a genius out of the void, and still more curious when he adjures the rest of us to be like him, in these days "when accuracy of insight, when courage of judgment, are worth all the names in all the books." We have been adjured these two thousand years without being much the better for it. Today the best that can be done is to prepare and organize the events that will give men a chance to reveal whatever insight or courage or judgment they may have within them.

Postscript to a Paragraph

LAST WEEK, after writing about Edmund Wilson's *Travels in Two Democracies*, I felt thoroughly dissatisfied with

Conclusion to the review of Edmund Wilson's *Travels in Two Democracies*. (*NR*, June 10, 1936.)

the final paragraph of my review. It might as well be con-
fessed that this has happened before, and will continue to happen unless I recover with age from the writer's occupational
disease of procrastination. Usually these final paragraphs are
hammered out in the chill dawn of a Monday morning, just an
hour before the irrefrangible and bulletproof deadline. I begin
them with the feeling that, in the review written during the
night, I have expressed not half the ideas that seemed so
important—and I try to crowd the rest of them into a few
blunt assertions; or still worse, I try to suggest ideas which
there is no room for stating directly, as if I were writing a
poem instead of a criticism.

These several faults were more than usually evident in the
final paragraph of the piece on Edmund Wilson. I had been
saying that Wilson's attitude had passed through at least three
stages—at first he was disillusioned with Russia, then he
looked backward and saw new virtues in his own country, then
finally he began to be more sharply impressed by the human
and friendly qualities that had flowered under Soviet communism. All this was clear enough in my review. "But," I added
in the final paragraph that I liked so little:

> But he had one other reaction to his travels, one that is
> important in his mental history, yet hard to define. . . . He had
> his first experience since the War of being with people from
> morning till midnight, of living collectively. He liked it in a
> curious fashion, yet he violently rebelled against it; and in self-
> defense, I should judge, he developed a cult of the genius and
> the hero. . . .

There is no use quoting the whole of the paragraph. Nothing in it is false or exaggerated, and yet on reading it over I
felt that it was so briefly stated, so lacking in supporting
evidence that it raised more questions than it answered. I
decided that it would have to be rewritten. And I am printing
it below as it would have looked in the beginning if it had been
given the time and space that it required:

"But Wilson had one other reaction to the Soviet Union. It
is harder to explain, because partly it was an instinctive response to a new situation—almost a muscular reflex, as if he

had touched a steam pipe and suddenly drawn back his hand.
But the situation was permanent, and the response to it became
fixed in his conscious thinking. . . . In Odessa, Wilson spent
six weeks recovering from an attack of scarlet fever. The
hospital where he was quarantined was not one of the new ones
designed since the revolution: it was the old Odessa pest-
house, built in 1795 and practically never cleaned. It was
understaffed, archaic, crowded with noisily convalescent children; the nurses were most of them incompetent, even though
they were enormously friendly and obliging; only the few
Communists were trying seriously to keep things in order. But
the point of the episode was that Wilson was forced to be
among other people, eat, talk, play, sleep among them day
after day, with scarcely an hour to himself. For the first time
since the War he had the experience of living collectively and,
in a curious fashion, he liked it. He was for a short time very
unhappy when he left the hospital and went to a hotel:

> Alone in the silence of the room, I suddenly dropped into a
> depression of a kind which I had never known all the time that I
> had been in the hospital. It was loneliness: I was missing the
> children and the nurses who had bothered me when I was trying
> to work and from whom I had looked forward to escaping. I
> walked back and forth across the room a few times, then began
> declaiming aloud some old poems of my own composition. I
> found that some need was relieved: my loneliness disappeared. It
> was the assertion of my own personality against those weeks of
> collective living.

"To me this episode seemed to explain a good deal that
had gone before it. More than once Edmund Wilson in the
Soviet Union had been asserting his own personality against
the threat or the temptation of collective life—hence his discomfort in Moscow and his rather hostile attitude toward
Russian writers, especially toward those who lived at peace
with the new society. Back in Washington he had felt and
expressed the same dislike for the New Dealers; his logical
reasons for distrusting them were entirely different, but the
emotional background was the same. He had sheared away
from all sorts of political groups even when their ideas appeared to be similar to his own—first from the Progressives,

then from the Communists, then later, I think, from the American Workers' Party; and I am not aware that he responded to the persistent overtures of the Trotskyites and the Lovestonites. Fundamentally he was an individualist of the old school, without even the need for blind and partial coöperation that is forced on most of us by capitalism. As he explained at the end of *The American Jitters,* his own family of doctors and lawyers and professors had retained the traditions of a precapitalistic era. They were descended from country squires; and Wilson himself, in any large gathering, must have felt very much like a country squire forced to go into town for a lawsuit and rub elbows with greasy politicians.

"Always, retiring into himself, he would declaim 'some old poems of my own composition'—that is, he would remind himself of those defenses built by any sensitive man against the risk of having his personality invaded by the anonymous and colorless throng. But nobody in this age can live alone, can live without help; and Wilson has begun lately to invoke the great men of the age that is passing. He is developing a cult of the genius and the hero that is evident in more than one of his Russian notes—for example, in his tribute to Elinor Wylie and in what he says about Borodin, the man who organized a Chinese army and nearly won the East for Communism. 'I believe,' Wilson wrote after seeing him at a theatre, 'that his moral stature and the attitude that people adopt toward him make him seem bigger and taller than he is. This is what the early race were like.'

"The attitude that Wilson half reveals—the mixture of distrust for the masses and admiration for the 'early race' who tried to redeem them—is even clearer in a final passage, a magnificent tribute to Lenin in his tomb under the Kremlin wall:

> And here we come to gaze down at this shell of flesh, in its last thinness, its delicacy and fragility, before it crumbles and loses the mold—this skin and bone still keeping the stamp of that intellect, that passion, that will, whose emergence has stunned the world almost more with embarrassment at being made to extend its conception of what man, as man alone, can accomplish, than admiration at the achievements of genius. And these countrymen of his are amazed, with their formless and expressionless

faces, when they look down on him and know that he was one of
them, and that he invoked from their loose and sluggish plasm
all those triumphs to which life must rise and to which he
thought himself the casual signpost.

"At first on reading a passage like this one feels an exhilaration compounded of pride and gratitude—pride that one of
our human race could rise so high, and gratitude to the writer
who was moved by Lenin's greatness and expressed it in such
fine prose. But why did Wilson have to emphasize his admiration for Lenin by asserting a contempt for Lenin's countrymen? Is there not a purely subjective emotion mingled with
and falsifying his judgment of history? Why does he forget to
say that Lenin, in addition to creating the new revolutionary
Russia, was himself shaped and forged by an older revolutionary Russia? For it is the simple fact that Lenin's triumphant career was made possible by hundreds of broken careers,
including that of his own brother, who was executed for trying
to kill the Tsar. It is the simple fact that his mind was sharpened by disputes with other minds almost as keen; that his
revolutionary determination was strengthened by his determined comrades; that he could depend on the help of thousands not too humble to die for the cause which he represented; that in short he was the arm and voice of an idea, the
symbol to a nation of that new age in which everything would
be different. Lenin is the archetype of the modern hero, the
man whose individual character is affirmed and enforced by his
very sacrifice of individuality to a common cause. And it seems
now that Wilson has studied his books, has worshiped at his
tomb, has even shared in his heritage, without understanding
the sources of his strength or the dream for which he lived."

Fable for Russian Children

I CAN IMAGINE a group of towheaded Russian children sitting round the fireplace while the night winds howl outside their communal dwelling. "Uncle Karl!" the oldest of them says. "Uncle Karl, tell us a story. Tell us what a patroness of art was like under capitalism."

Uncle Karl, combing his long white beard with his fingers, remembers his youth in the salons of St. Petersburg. He remembers Lenin speaking in the palace of the Tsar's former mistress. He has read all the books in all the languages.

"Let me think, children," he says. "She would be the daughter of a very rich provincial banker and she would be many times unhappily married but always willing to try again. She would have lived in Paris and Florence and learned the gossip of the art world, but she wouldn't care much about pictures or poems, not in her inmost heart. Indeed, her inmost heart would be as dry and cold as a vault in her father's bank. She would try to fill it with color and warmth that she stole from living artists, just as she tried to adorn her body with the brilliance of great paintings. She would have a salon crowded with very famous people, and still her heart and mind would be so empty that she was afraid to be left alone with them, even for a single hour.

"But, children, there is no use trying to invent an imaginary patroness of art. Let me tell you the real story of Mabel Dodge Luhan as I found it written in a book I have just received from New York. Let me tell you how she fell in love with a revolutionary poet and tried to buy him and failed. . . ."

"Tell us, Uncle Karl," the children cried.

"Well, it was two years before the War and Mabel Dodge, as they called her after her second marriage, had just come back from Italy. She hated to live in an uncultured city like New York, but nevertheless she rented a big apartment and

Movers and Shakers, by Mabel Dodge Luhan (*Intimate Memories, Vol. III*). New York: Harcourt, Brace and Company. (*NR*, Nov. 25, 1936.)

furnished it with delicate old gray French chairs and dozens of
white silk embroidered Chinese shawls flung over her big
white bed. That is what she always did when she was lonely or
idle. She rented a new apartment or bought a house—even if
she had many others unoccupied—and she furnished it from
front to back and top to bottom. It was as if she tried to relieve
the emptiness in her heart by filling her rooms with furniture.

"But she still felt lonely and unsatisfied, so she began
collecting people in exactly the same spirit as she collected
china dogs for her mantelpiece. One of them—one of the people, I mean—had a red beard that enhanced her white embroidered shawls. Another was 'a real decoration,' she tells us
in her book, and was 'always charming in his rough, red-brown
clothes, or fuzzy blues, with a late, pinched flower in his
buttonhole.' But she had to have always more people around
her. Soon she was collecting them merely for their air of
eminence, merely because they were the heads of things, the
heads of newspapers, the heads of movements. She was a
species of head-hunter, so she tells us. Even though she had no
convictions in art or politics, her salon became a center of
modern painters and radical labor leaders—and a very interesting center because America was then in the midst of a cultural
awakening like that of our own country in the 1870's.

"But she was still lonely, still unsatisfied. Out of all the
hordes that gathered in her apartment, she chose a young poet,
a friend of the workers. He had poured his great vitality into
the labor movement and had received in exchange for it a new
vitality, which he poured into his poems. Mabel Dodge admired this strength of his and was greedy to possess it. She
carried the poet off to Italy, where for the first and only time
he made her feel like a living woman in a living world.

"And still she was unsatisfied. Now she wanted to separate
her lover from the sources of his strength and reduce him to an
object that was utterly hers, like a delicate old gray French
chair or a china dog. She was jealous of everything that inter-
fered with her unqualified ownership—jealous of stones in
Verona, of the great past in Venice, of newspapers in New
York and of women everywhere. Finally the poet went away
after writing her a letter. 'Goodbye, my darling,' he said. 'I
cannot live with you. You smother me. You crush me. You

want to kill my spirit. I love you better than life but I do not want to die in my spirit.'

"Of course that was not the end. Mabel Dodge threatened to kill herself and the poet came back to her. Then he left her again and came back to her again, because he really loved this woman he had brought to life. She tells us that she herself was responsible for the final separation. At any rate, the poet went away to fight in our revolution and write a great book that many of you children will read, and he is buried near Lenin, beside the wall of the Kremlin. Mabel Dodge rented and furnished a new apartment and three houses in the country.

"She was now lonelier and emptier than ever before and frantic in her search for a new source of vitality. Soon she scented and tracked down and captured a painter of talent. He was as different as possible from the poet she had lost; he claimed to despise politics and what he called 'the mob.' Mabel Dodge overawed him as she had not overawed the poet, and she was cruel to him as a way of revenging her defeat. She was cruel to other people too. She liked to invite penniless artists to stay in her house 'indefinitely,' then wait until they had grown really dependent on her and dismiss them with a curt note. She became really heartless and evil, if we can trust her own story. On one occasion the painter was nearly drowned. She watched the lifeguards trying to revive him and decided that he looked very unesthetic as he lay there limp over a barrel with his arms swinging—so she left without waiting to learn whether he would live or die. On another occasion she burned hundreds and hundreds of letters that the poet had written her from Mexico and Europe, letters that would have made the whole world richer. She had fits of aimless hysteria. She went to psychoanalysts, to faith healers, to fortune tellers, to all sorts of fancy quacks, seeking for anything that would soothe her expensively and without effort on her part. Finally she hurried off with her cook and her chauffeur to find new strength among the Indians of New Mexico."

Uncle Karl paused for a long time, filling the white porcelain pipe which he had carried with him from Vienna and preserved intact through the civil war. At last one of the children asked him, "But didn't the government take her money instead of letting her waste it on quacks and fortune tellers?" Another interrupted, "And didn't anyone punish her for being cruel and destructive?"

Uncle Karl tried to answer the questions in turn. "No, the government didn't take her money, because after all it was her own government, the government of the rich. And nobody punished her except herself, though we might say that she will also be punished by history. For she wrote a book years afterwards, and she tried to make it a great book in which she would appear as a great personality. The book is not great, though parts of it are very interesting to sociologists like myself. But it makes us feel that she had no personality at all, in the strict sense of the word. When she describes herself, it is almost always in electrical or chemical or mechanical terms—she calls herself a live wire, a dynamo, an engine, a vibration, a blue flame, a clockwork in a cage, a magnet, a chemical compound, but never a human being. She had not even the limited freedom that human beings achieve; like any mechanical thing she was utterly at the mercy of her times. And that is why her life is the case history of an art patroness under capitalism—a fable told round the fireside to edify and frighten little Russian children."

On Literature and Revolution

IS A REVOLUTION good or bad for writers? Does it tend to stimulate or retard the production of masterpieces? Such questions have been asked for several years, and have usually been argued with more temper than understanding. Indeed, they are tangled to such a degree in human faith and fears that it is hard even to state them dispassionately, let alone finding answers in anything that approaches the critical spirit. Yet there is no lack of material for research. Beginning with the Dutch war for independence in the sixteenth century, and by no means ending with the battle that continues in the streets of

NR, Dec. 2, 1936.

Madrid, there have been so many revolutions won or lost—so many writers have been caught up in them and have reacted in similar fashions—that it should not be impossible to establish a pattern of response to the different stages of the struggle.

Not the first of these stages, but the first at which connections become easy to trace, is the political crisis that precedes every major revolution. There is plenty of evidence to show that such crises are likely to be periods of literary ferment. This generality is true of many revolutions that failed (1848 in France, 1919–23 in Germany) as well as of almost all the revolutions that succeeded. Russia in 1917 is an exception, but in this case the ferment had preceded the unsuccessful revolution of 1905, which in turn was followed by years of intellectual torpor and a disastrous war. Almost everywhere else the political crisis has been accompanied by a crisis in the arts and by a flowering of all literary forms except perhaps the greatest. There is a feeling of excitement, of urgency, that probably interferes with the writing of epic poems or long, solid novels or dramas of the type that ripen in contemplation. On the other hand, there is a new audience for every sort of writing that bears on immediate problems. A new class is hoping to rule the state and it wants all the privileges of the former ruling class, including the enjoyment of books and pictures. Theatres give experimental plays and are always crowded. Publishers and booksellers have no enemies except the censor. Novels are written as hastily as pamphlets, whereas pamphleteering becomes a fine art (witness Tom Paine and the French Encyclopedists). There is likely to be a new interest in peasant speech (Russia, Ireland) and in folksong (Ireland, Spain). And the growing vitality of literature produces a growing anger against the restrictions laid upon it by the old order. People are saying, "Things can't go on like this."

On the day of a successful revolution, a great and almost involuntary sigh of relief runs through the country. The old institutions, as they hardened with age, had become always more burdensome and confining; now that they are shattered, the revolutionary nation is like a man released from a plaster cast, who takes his first awkward steps and immediately wants to dance for pure delight. He holds the future in his hands: everything seems possible. It was of a time like this that

Trotsky said, "Many could not contain their joy, and wept."
And Marmont, one of Napoleon's marshals, wrote in the
memoirs of his revolutionary youth: "We lived in a radiant
atmosphere; at the age of fifty-five I still feel its power and
warmth as on the first day."

Great poems might well be written during these days of
exaltation (though when I try to think of examples I can
remember only Alexander Blok's "The Twelve"). But usually
the period is too brief to make itself felt except as a glowing
and impossible memory. The next stage comes too soon, with
its factional bickerings, its civil war, its massacre of revolutionists, its terror directed against the rebellious nobles. There
is almost certainly a foreign invasion; there are probably
plagues and famines and general disorganization. Few have
time enough, and almost nobody of talent is sufficiently cold-
blooded, to write polished strophes or cadenced prose in the
midst of the battle against chaos.

Then, if the revolution has been successful, a slow wave of
disillusionment sweeps through the intellectual classes. After
so much heroism and so many wasted lives, there are still
rulers and subjects, there are still bureaucrats and hypocrites: it
seems that nothing has really changed. The writers of the
revolutionary country, now tempted into the chase after money
and honors, look beyond their borders with a patronizing and
reminiscent and painful smile—perhaps at the belated Jacobins
in Naples, or at English intellectuals like William Blake pa-
rading through the streets of King George's London in a
liberty cap. How many years has it been since people wore
liberty caps in Paris? Is it true—the writers ask a short time
later—that Napoleon is planning to suppress all but the official
newspapers? Is it true that literary experiments will soon be
punished as severely as republican deviations?

I am trying to suggest two conclusions about the fate of
writers during a revolutionary struggle. The first is that their
work is likely to suffer—at first from the diversion of energies
into other channels and later, under Cromwell or Napoleon,
from a censorship that writers are too weary or disillusioned to
fight. The second conclusion is that the liberating effects, the
warmth and enthusiasm of the revolution, are likely to be felt
in the literature of other countries before they are felt at home.

This was certainly the case in Germany and England at the end of the eighteenth century. Recent biographies of Blake and Wordsworth seem to show that the whole Romantic movement owes a vast, unrecognized debt to the French rebels. Moreover, the debt continued to grow. During Napoleon's last years as emperor, the English could read the early poems of Byron and Shelley, glowing with republican ideals, while the French were being afflicted with copybook odes and pseudo-classic tragedies. It was not until 1830 that French literature began to express the new forces and classes liberated by the men of 1789. In this sense, Balzac and Stendhal were the novelists of the revolution, and Victor Hugo was its greatest poet, the first to celebrate those beardless soldiers of the year II before whom the thrones of Europe, "rolling like dead leaves, were scattered to the wind." With Hugo, the revolution returned to its fatherland.

Such, in its simplest and baldest outline, is the pattern that revolutions have left in the literature of several European countries. Certainly it does not justify those sentimental radicals who call for a revolution at any price and trust that their literary problems will be washed away in other people's blood. But neither does it justify those timid critics who, in their fears of a future castastrophe, are moved to attack the revolutions of the present and the past—not only the Spanish and Russian revolutions, but also those in France and America (and if they say nothing about Cromwell's revolution in England, it is only because they are so ignorant of history that they think the English solved everything by compromise and never cut off King Charles's head). Men of middle-class families, these critics are in debt to revolutionists for almost all the advantages they enjoy. If the American revolution had not opened a continent to settlement, if the French revolution had not sent feudal institutions scuttering like dead leaves, they doubtless would have been tied to their fathers' trades—they would have been selling goods over the counter to the landed gentry or, with ancestors like my own, would have been hoeing a hillside potato patch in Ulster. Yet they continue to proclaim the utter wickedness and futility of all revolutions with a fear that is hard to distinguish from the fear of life itself.

Marx and Plekhanov

AFTER several years of incessant fighting over Marxian criticism, two of the essential texts have at last been published. One of them is Jean Fréville's collection and translation into French of Marx's and Engels' opinions on the art of writing. The other is an English version of two essays by George V. Plekhanov, by far the most important of the Marxist critics in Russia before the revolution.

The first thing that strikes you about Fréville's collection is its briefness. Almost everything that Marx or Engels said about literature and literary theory is contained in a book of two hundred pages, with nearly half of it devoted to comments by the editor. Moreover, the texts are fragmentary, often consisting of a sentence or a paragraph and rarely extending to more than a thousand words. It is evident that Marx never developed a general system of esthetics. He had planned such a work when he was young, but he got no further than taking notes, and the notes have disappeared. His books and his correspondence with Engels are full of salty and sometimes peppery remarks on literary subjects. Nothing that the two friends wrote in this connection was meant to be taken as holy writ. On the other hand, they stated and restated certain principles that are extremely useful as a guide to critics.

Art and literature, they said, do not exist by themselves; human life must always be considered in the richness of its interrelations. Economics is ultimately the determining factor in art as in other forms of human activity, but it is by no means the only factor, and its effect is exerted in complicated and devious fashions. Thus, it is only when the history of art is studied over long periods and wide territories that its curve begins to parallel the curve of economic development. Eras of transition are generally favorable to the flowering of great talents—and the great talents are men like Dante, Cervantes,

Sur la Littérature et l'Art: Karl Marx, Friedrich Engels, edited by Jean Fréville. Paris: Editions Sociales Internationales. *Art and Society*, by George V. Plekhanov. Translated by Paul S. Leitner, Alfred Goldstein and C. H. Crout. New York: Critics' Group. (*NR*, Dec. 30, 1936.)

Shakespeare, Goethe (but not Schiller) and Balzac (but not Hugo) who mirror the complex life of their times. For Marx, vigor, richness and truth are the ultimate standards of literary judgment.

Toward propaganda or *Tendenz* literature, Engels stated their attitude in a letter to Minna Kautsky. He was commenting rather harshly on a book of hers that would now be called a proletarian novel. "Probably," he said, "you feel the need of publicly taking sides in this book, of proclaiming your opinions to the whole world. But that has been done; it belongs to the past, and you needn't repeat it in this form. I am not at all opposed to propaganda poetry as such. The father of tragedy, Æschylus, and the father of comedy, Aristophanes, were both very clearly poets with a thesis, as were Dante and Cervantes. . . . But I believe that the thesis must inhere in the situation and the action, without being explicitly formulated; and it is not the poet's duty to supply the reader in advance with the future historical solution of the conflicts he describes."

That is about as far as Marx or Engels went in propounding the general principles of art. But their comments on individual novelists and poets are always illuminating; and what they say about Eugène Sue and Balzac is likely to discourage any of the left-wing critics who may have been judging books in a spirit of partisan politics.

Eugène Sue was "on our side"; he had to go into exile for his political opinions. He was also the most prominent of the many French proletarian or pseudo-proletarian writers who flourished before the revolution of 1848. He claimed that in his novels he plunged into the shadowy depths of society, there to uncover its secret crimes and reveal the causes of the ills from which it suffered. His longest book, *The Mysteries of Paris*, was praised by many devout communists, but Marx loathed and despised it. Analyzing the story at great length, he found that it was inspired by a windy middle-class idealism, and that it assumed a pitying and patronizing air, thereby insulting the proletarian characters whom Sue was pretending to cherish.

Balzac was "on the other side"; he claimed that his novels were composed "in the light of two eternal truths: Religion and Monarchy." Yet Marx admired his work and planned to

write an extended study of it just as soon as he had finished
Capital—which was always to be "next year." Engels said, in a
letter to a young English left-wing novelist, that Balzac was "a
far greater master of realism than all the Zolas, past, present
or future." The letter also explained the basis for his judgment, saying that Balzac describes, "in chronicle fashion, almost year by year from 1816 to 1848, the ever increasing
pressure of the rising bourgeoisie upon the society of nobles
that established itself after 1815. . . . Around this central
picture he groups a complete history of French society from
which, even in economic details (for instance, the rearrange-
ment of real and private property after the French Revolution), I have learned more than from all the professional
historians, economists and statisticians of the period together.
Well, Balzac was politically a legitimist; his great work is a
constant elegy on the irreparable decay of good society; his
sympathies are with the class that is doomed to extinction. But
for all that his satire is never keener, his irony never bitterer,
than when he sets in motion the very men and women with
whom he sympathizes most deeply—the nobles. And the only
men of whom he speaks with undisguised admiration are his
bitterest political opponents, the republican heroes of the
Cloître-Saint-Merri, the men who at that time (1830–36)
were indeed the representatives of the popular masses." It was
in this same letter to Margaret Harkness, only a first draft of
which survives, that Engels scribbled on the margin: "The
more the opinions of the author remain hidden, the better for
the work of art."

The final impression left by Fréville's collection is that
Marx and Engels were men of exceptionally sound taste who
read for recreation and solace and enjoyed literature for its
own sake. Sometimes they pointed out the deep underlying
connection between art and politics. Thus, in long letters to
Ferdinand Lassalle, both of them criticized the plot of his
sixteenth-century historical tragedy, *Franz von Sickingen*.
They explained convincingly that his misjudgment of the role
played in Germany by the knights and the rebellious peasants
had weakened the dramatic conflict—both the matter and the
form of Lassalle's play had suffered from a political error. On
the other hand, the two friends did not censor the political

conduct of writers they admired. Marx felt—so Mehring his biographer tells us—"that poets were peculiar people who should be permitted to go their own way and must not be measured with the standards of ordinary or even extraordinary mortals. If they were to sing they must be flattered; it was no use belaboring them with severe criticism." The severe criticism was likely to be reserved for stupid people who attacked literature from the standpoint of the higher ethics. "I have tried as long as I could to preserve my respect for the fellow," Engels wrote about an eager Russian socialist, "but it is no longer possible. What can one say of a little gentleman who, after reading his first novels by Balzac (and to make it worse the novels were *Le Cabinet des Antiques* and *Père Goriot*), speaks of them in a toplofty fashion, with utter disdain?"

Sometimes Engels seems to be addressing the Marxian pedants of today, in deep-voiced imprecations rumbling from the grave. "It happens all too often that people think they perfectly understand a new theory and can apply it without effort after merely grasping its essential principles. That isn't always true in practice. More than one of our recent 'Marxists' cannot be absolved from this fault—and they have done some really curious things."

ii

The first of two essays in the booklet issued here by the Critics' Group is shorter and less ambitious than the second; but it is a beautiful example of Plekhanov's method. Its subject is the class struggles of eighteenth-century France as revealed in the French theatre. At first, Plekhanov explains, the rule of the aristocracy was unquestioned, both on the stage and in the street. Classical French tragedy, with its stateliness and decorum and strict adherence to artificial rules, was an expression of the aristocratic standards. As the middle classes gained new power, after 1750, tragedies became less popular than middle-class sentimental comedies. This phenomenon has been ob-

Art and Society, by George V. Plekhanov. Translated by Paul S. Leitner, Alfred Goldstein and C. H. Crout. New York: Critics' Group. (*NR*, Jan. 6, 1937.)

served by many French critics whose point of view was not Marxist in the least. But why was it, Plekhanov asks, that sentimental comedies lost favor and artificial tragedies regained it—and this at the very moment when the revolution was ready to explode? He answers that sentimental comedies were unable to express the heroic mood of the times. The new tragedies that took their place were classical in form, but they dealt with leaders like Spartacus and William Tell; they were revolutionary in subject matter. And—Plekhanov adds to clinch his point—French painting passed through almost exactly the same process: it was courtly with Le Brun, domestic with Greuze and heroic with David. The whole eighteenth century is an excellent illustration of Marx's theory that the history of art, when considered over long periods and wide areas, tends to parallel the curve of economic development.

The second essay is a long and generally impressive historical criticism of the doctrine of art for art's sake. That doctrine is likely to be advanced, Plekhanov says, at any time when a hopeless contradiction exists between the aspirations of artists and their social environment. Often during the nineteenth century—for example in Russia after the Decembrist revolt of 1825, and in France after the unsuccessful revolution of 1848 —artists hated the ruling class but saw no hope of its being overturned; so they defended themselves from official standards by claiming that whatever they wrote or painted had absolutely no social meaning. In this way, Plekhanov tells us, they managed to achieve a limited freedom; their doctrine was successful in practice. But it ceased to be successful at a later stage in their careers, because it cut them off from human sympathies and caused them to take refuge in various illogical notions that damaged their work esthetically as well as intellectually.

Up to this point, Plekhanov's argument seems to me pretty nearly incontrovertible. If his essay had been translated five or six years ago, the American left-wing critics might have been saved an endless lot of arguments, the principal result of which has been to lead them to substantially the same position that Plekhanov had reached in 1905. Moreover, this Russian revolutionary critic has certain clear advantages over his younger colleagues in this country. His knowledge of European literature is prodigious; so too is his knowledge of general history. He has a keen time-sense that keeps him from judging the writers of 1830 by the political standards of 1905 or 1918. But still he is interested primarily in politics rather than literature; and this becomes an element of weakness when he deals with his own contemporaries.

It is in the latter part of the essay on "Art and Society" that his faults are most apparent. There he lumps together a number of French or Russian artists—cubists, mystics, futurists—and condemns them indiscriminately on the ground that they represent a decaying society. His judgment of them seems colored partly by moral preconceptions, and partly by the plain philistinism that has afflicted the socialist movement—not in the persons of the socialist leaders or the plain workers, but frequently in the party functionaries. A worse fault is that he tries to deduce an entirely too immediate connection between art and economics. And when he tells us that "the art of a decadent epoch *must* be decadent," I can imagine Marx calling him back to order and explaining to him that modern society is too complicated for such easy generalities—that one class might be rising while another decayed, and that both classes might have their representative artists.

As for the American left-wing critics, it seems to me that they have followed Plekhanov rather than Marx.

André Gide's Retreat from Moscow

LAST SUMMER André Gide went to Russia for the first time. He found much to admire and even love, he saw whole countrysides that already have "the laughing look of happiness," but in general he was disillusioned. And because he had felt such exalted hopes for Russia—because he is more respected, in a half-reluctant fashion, than any other living

Retour de l'U.R.S.S., by André Gide. Paris: Gallimard. (*NR*, Mar. 17, 1937.)

French writer, and because the French conservatives have been talking and fearing revolution—the little book he wrote about his travels has been read and quoted and lovingly misinterpreted by the very people who neglected his earlier works. It is announced for American publication late in the spring, and extracts from it may appear in *The New Republic*. Meanwhile, from the French text, let us see what the book contains.

Roughly the first third of it is filled with praise for the Soviet Union. Most of the French critics have slighted this section in their eagerness to discuss the more sensational chapters that follow, but it is essential to Gide's plan. He is trying to give an accurate picture of his impressions, and part of that picture is the enthusiasm he felt for Russian factories and coöperative farms, for the vigorous life of Russian cities, for the beaches of the Crimea, the forests of the Caucasus, but most of all—since he loves people more than landscapes—for the warmth and human friendliness of Russians everywhere. He did not feel that anything was being concealed from him. "Several times," he says, "it was our luck to blunder unexpectedly into village schools, nurseries or clubs that nobody expected us to see and that were doubtless in no way distinguished from many others. And these are the ones that I most admired, precisely because nothing there had been made ready for display."

Nevertheless he was continually tormented by the comparison between Soviet life as it was actually lived and that ideal culture for which he had been scanning the future. More and more doubts piled up in his mind. First of all he was worried by the terrible mediocrity of the merchandise displayed in the Moscow stores. Were these ugly cottons and these tasteless melons the best that an enlightened government controlling all industry and agriculture could offer its citizens? Then he was depressed by the uniformity of the crowds in Moscow, all dressed in summer white, and by the cottages on the collective farms, identical buildings each with the same factory-built furniture, the same picture of Stalin, and absolutely nothing else. The uniformity of minds was even worse: everybody seemed to take his opinions from the latest edition of Pravda, and this without the least sign of intellectual rebellion. Gide was full of love for the Russian youth: some of his happiest days were spent with Komsomols or in the summer camps of the Young Pioneers. But he was disquieted by the growth among them of a "superiority complex," of a national pride so intense that they were willing to remain in ignorance of other nations. Some of the Pioneers—and some of their elders too—refused to believe that there were subways in Paris or that the French workers were not completely and uniformly miserable. And the same children and elders showed unmistakable signs of class feeling—they were intellectually gifted and therefore privileged; they expected other Russians to be content with lower living standards. This growth of bourgeois pride and inequality was what disturbed Gide most of all. "The Soviets have shown us," he says, "that they are capable of making sudden changes of direction. But I greatly fear that in order to put an end to this 'bourgeoisification,' which is now approved and encouraged by the rulers, there will soon have to be a sharp about-face that runs the risk of being as brutal as the one that ended the New Economic Policy."

Another of Gide's complaints is summed up in a story that has already become famous. Driving from Tiflis to Batum, his party passed through Gori, the little town where Stalin was born. Gide thought that it would be only simple politeness to send a telegram thanking Stalin for the splendid welcome he had received everywhere in the Soviet Union. He stopped at the post office to dictate a message: "Passing through Gori in the course of our marvelous journey, I feel the cordial impulse to address you. . . ." But here the translator halted to explain that Gide could not speak in this fashion: the simple "you" was not enough when that "you" was Stalin; the proper form was "you, chief of the workers," or "you, master of the peoples." Gide protested that Stalin was above these mean flatteries, but there was nothing he could do; his message could not be, and was not, accepted for transmission until he had agreed to observe the proper forms of Soviet courtesy.

In many ways his *Retour de l'U.R.S.S.* bears a curious resemblance to Edmund Wilson's *Travels in Two Democracies*. Both books are written in a simple style, colloquial and negligent by careful design. Both give an impression of complete candor. Both are based, not on general statistics, but rather on personal experience and the daily incidents of travel. Both authors reach almost the same conclusions, but these are based on subjective reactions so different in the two cases that sometimes they cancel each other off. Thus, Gide loved to wander through the Park of Culture and Rest in Moscow; he had never seen a place of public amusement that seemed so full of friendliness and essential goodness. Wilson found the park depressing and tried to keep away from it. Gide thought that all Russians were cast in one identical mold. Wilson, during his six weeks at the contagious hospital in Odessa, collected an album of striking and eccentric characters that would not be easy to match in any city west of the Russian border. In his direct comments on Russian society, Wilson seems less naïve than Gide, who was always looking for Utopia and being desolated when he failed to find it. But Gide has a somewhat better grasp of international politics: he realizes that the compromises he dislikes are not the work of a personal devil named Stalin, but rather the effects of a policy forced on the country by the hourly danger of war. This danger, so he tells us, helps to explain the progressive restoration of the family, of private property, of the right of inheritance: Soviet citizens now have personal possessions to defend against an invader, as well as their abstract pride in revolution. And yet, Gide adds, "It is thus that the original impulse is progressively weakened and lost, and eyes cease to be fixed on the future. . . . One is forced to admit in so many words: that is not what we wanted. One step more and we should even say: it is exactly what we did not want."

Yet even though Gide reaches this harsh conclusion (and others still harsher), his book is more confused and contradictory than anyone would imagine from this brief summary. Out of it one could extract an essay filled solely with praise for the Soviet Union. Out of it one could extract a slightly longer essay filled solely with condemnation—and this is exactly what the conservative French newspapers have been doing. I hear that Gide himself is deeply disturbed by the fashion in which his book has been used by the enemies of everything he loves. He is still a revolutionary, though a Utopian revolutionary, and his book remains somewhere within the extreme limits of revolutionary self-criticism. One might say that the real tone of it is set by the last few lines: "The aid just furnished to Spain by the USSR shows us the happy revivals of which it remains capable. The USSR has not done with teaching us and surprising us."

Still Middletown?

IN JUNE, 1935, just ten years after the end of the Lynds' first "venture in contemporary anthropology," Robert Lynd returned to Muncie, Indiana, with a staff of five assistants. He wanted to learn the sequel to the earlier story. How much had Middletown-Muncie actually changed as a result of the boom and the depression? Had the basic texture of its culture been tough enough to remain intact? Were people returning sharply to the old faiths, or were they moving out to embrace new ways of thought?

Middletown in Transition, written in collaboration with Mrs. Lynd, tells what the investigators found on their second visit. Muncie had become much more attractive. Many public improvements had been carried out with government relief money. A new interest in flower gardening had been encouraged by the leisure time that was so abundant during the depression years. The wealthier business folk had moved westward into new suburbs that reproduced Westchester. Good times were coming back and the streets were crowded with smiling people.

There were other changes of a more fundamental nature. Back in the 1890's Muncie had been a community of glass workers and mechanics, highly skilled, strong in their unions— "one of the best organized cities in the United States." When Samuel Gompers came to town, in 1897, he was dined by the mayor before addressing a great crowd in the Opera House. But slowly the skilled mechanics were displaced by machines,

Middletown in Transition: A Study in Cultural Conflicts, by Robert S. Lynd and Helen Merrell Lynd. New York: Harcourt, Brace and Company. (*NR,* May 12, 1937.)

and the labor unions were too snobbish or too short-sighted to organize the machine-tenders in the new mass industries. In 1924, when the Lynds began their first survey, there were only 800 organized workers left in Muncie. The unions had lost whatever influence they once possessed. The businessmen had seized power and were determined to share it with nobody. They had a little trouble during the first year of the NRA. There was a vigorous organizing campaign that brought in two thousand new union members; but the campaign was obstructed and, so it would seem, deliberately betrayed by old-line labor officials. "The agitators were making real headway," said *Business Week* in its own survey of Muncie. "You've got to give the A.F. of L. credit for turning that trend. It's an unwritten chapter of history."

"Middletown businessmen," say the Lynds, "are coming out of the depression with their asset of being an 'open-shop town' nailed to the city's masthead—and they mean to keep it there." They are not at all discouraged by the fact that Detroit and Toledo and South Bend have been organized under the CIO. This means, so they say, in private, that more and more factories will move to Muncie—like the big new General Motors plant—in order to get away from labor difficulties. But it also means that Muncie since 1924 has ceased to be a typical American city and has become a specialized city instead. Lacking other advantages, it now intends to prosper by virtue of its cheap labor.

During the depression, the very rich got richer, the middling businessmen got poorer, and the unemployed workers got relief, but not too much of it. "The impression was clear in the investigator's mind at the end of the field work in 1935 that the line between working class and business class, though vague and blurred still, is more apparent than it was ten years before."

In Muncie the working class includes about 65 percent of the population. It lives in the South Side, "on the other side of the tracks," and it has much less social life than the business class. The workers rise before six in the morning and spend their days in tasks involving chiefly the manipulation of *things*. They live in fear of being laid off or permanently discharged and, in addition, they run the risk of industrial accidents that may kill or cripple them. But perhaps their chief handicap is that, in a culture which places all its emphasis on "going up in the world," they have little chance of climbing even to a foremanship. Few of them can reach the first rung of "the ladder to success."

The business people of Muncie compose about 35 percent of the population; they live "north of the tracks." They rise after seven in the morning and spend their days in tasks that involve chiefly the manipulation of *people*. Their hourly earnings may be less than those of the employed factory hands, but they are much surer of their jobs and they run little risk of industrial accidents. Perhaps their chief advantage is the chance of "getting ahead." The ladder to success is harder to climb than it used to be, but at least the first rungs of it are still within their grasp.

The investigators found signs of a growing class-consciousness, especially among women and children on the two sides. They also found that the two big social strata are being split again into thinner slices. The working class now includes a top layer of foremen and skilled mechanics, a middle layer of semi-skilled factory workers, and a bottom layer of untrained laborers—"hill-billies" or "green peas" without regular jobs. But the new divisions in the business class are much more significant. Part of that class has remained largely as it was in 1924. A less privileged group, composed of clerical workers, salespeople and small retailers, is being set aside as a new middle class. Finally, at the top of the scale, there is a "business control group" that is emerging as a local aristocracy. And this group, in turn, is dominated by a single family, which the Lynds have chosen to call the "X family" (it is of course the Balls, the biggest local industrialists, who got their money by making mason jars). A Muncie man told the investigators:

> If I'm out of work I go to the X plant; if I need money I go to the X bank, and if they don't like me I don't get it; my children go to the X College; when I'm sick I go to the X hospital; I buy a building lot or house in an X subdivision; my wife goes downtown to buy clothes at the X department store; if my dog stays away he is put in the X pound; I buy X milk; I drink X beer, vote for X political parties and get help from X charities; my boy goes to the X Y.M.C.A. and my girl to their

Y.W.C.A.; I listen to the word of God in X-subsidized churches; if I'm a Mason I go to the X Masonic Temple; I read the news from the X morning newspaper; and, if I am rich enough, I travel via the X airport.

The "X family" has vastly extended its wealth and power during the last ten years. Under its well-intentioned but strict control, Middletown seems to be developing into an industrial feudalism tempered by philanthropy.

Yet in spite of these shifts in economic power and class alignments, the Lynds conclude that the institutions of the city and its pervasive "Middletown spirit" are the same as they were before. A broad answer to the questions asked in their first chapter "is that basically the texture of Middletown's culture has not changed. . . . Middletown is overwhelmingly living by the values by which it lived in 1925." The only real difference is that these individualistic, get-ahead, Rotarian values have less and less to do with life as is actually lived. And now the Lynds wonder "how obvious the disparity needs be between symbols and reality before Middletown may cease to believe in inevitable progress—and what may happen then within the lives of these busy, hopeful people?"

I found their new book of absorbing interest. It is warmer and more human than the original *Middletown;* it corrects some of the mistakes that were inevitable in a first survey. Yet somehow the general effect is less impressive. The Lynds explain that their second investigation was conducted on a less ambitious scale and involved only a tenth as many man-days of research time. Of course each of these man-days counted for more because the basis for work had already been established. On the other hand, the whole nature of the research was changed by the fact that it had to be done quickly. There was less time for the staff to wander through North Side and South Side collecting the remarks of ordinary housewives. They had to get their information where it was most available—from census reports, from newspaper files and from interviews with "key people." In other words, they had to depend chiefly on the articulate part of the population. Since the working class is less articulate than the business class, it receives much less attention in the present volume. Between the second *Middle-*

town and the first, there is almost the same difference as between the *Literary Digest* poll, mailed to a selected list, and the Institute of Public Opinion poll, obtained chiefly by interviews. The Lynds went wrong at exactly the same point as *The Literary Digest*. They failed to predict an earthquake.

Muncie in national politics had always been a standpat Republican city. In 1924 La Follette got only three percent of the votes in the county. In 1932 this same county was the only one out of ninety-two in the state of Indiana that "went down the line" for the Republican ticket. In 1936 everybody, including the Lynds, thought that the old pattern would be repeated. All of Roosevelt's favorite policies were contrary to "the Middletown spirit" of business enterprise. Landon, "the careful Kansan," was exactly the sort of man the city admired—and "the weight of frightened hope with which the city's leading businessmen backed Landon to defeat Roosevelt was almost literally beyond exaggeration." Yet Roosevelt got 59 percent of the city's votes—a majority of six to four against "the Middletown spirit." It seems to me that if the investigators had spent more time with the working class, they would have been less surprised and puzzled by the election returns.

It seems to me too that this one mistake in emphasis suggests the possibility of others. Perhaps the social values of Middletown aren't so unalterable—or so unaltered—as the Lynds assert in their final chapter. Perhaps they haven't talked enough about the new "intelligentsia" that has developed in Muncie since 1925. Rebellious college graduates can no longer solve their problems by moving to Chicago or New York, and they now form an opposition group at home. Still more important is the fact that "the Middletown spirit" is no longer being accepted at its face value by the younger generation, even among the businessmen. They have developed a "wary cynicism"; they sing the Rotary songs with their fingers crossed. Usually this attitude of cynicism is a prophecy of social changes.

What direction will the changes take when they come? —In their answer to this question the Lynds seem on surer ground. Underlying all their conclusions is the fear that cultural conflicts in a town like Muncie may be solved violently and may lead to "an eventual coercive control which in Europe today

goes under the name of fascism."–"If President Roosevelt
moves to the right . . . Middletown business leaders will 'go
along.' Should the present tension continue unabated, the
mood of men of power and ability such as these may conceivably lead to explosive action." The danger is there; I hardly
think that the Lynds exaggerate. But it is quite possible that
they fail to realize the strength of the liberal opposition,
especially in the working class. We may get fascism in this
country after all, but we won't get it without a fight.

Three Spanish Kids

THIS IS mostly a story about three Spanish children, war
orphans, two little girls and a boy. I never saw them and don't
even know their names. Last summer I came close to becoming
their legal father.

At dinner in Valencia on July 3, I met an old acquaintance
from New York, a Spanish writer who used to teach at New
York University and sometimes wrote articles for *The New
Republic*. For the last year he had been the editor of an
important Madrid daily. He told me that he had been married
just a few months before the war began–"to a very nice girl,"
he said, smiling in desperate embarrassment. Last April his
wife had a baby. It was thin and sickly and all the doctors told
him the same story: the mother herself was undernourished
and couldn't give it enough to eat; it would have to have
supplementary feedings, a pint of milk a day. He found that
there wasn't a pint of fresh milk or a tin of condensed milk to
be had in the whole city, even on a doctor's prescription. Yes,
the baby was still alive, but that was only by a stroke of luck: at
the last moment he had met somebody who knew somebody
else who had a whole case of condensed milk that he would
sell for a consideration. There must be thousands of parents in
Madrid who had been less fortunate.

NR, Sept. 22, 1937.

The conversation changed to other subjects. What about some old friends of his on University Heights, and why wasn't Roosevelt doing something for Spain? He was hungry for news of the States. He had been working very hard and needed a rest; maybe after the war the government would send him to New York on a mission. . . . I listened to him a little distractedly, for he had set me to thinking about the Spanish children.

On the road to Madrid, the writers' congress stopped for lunch at Minglanilla, a little town just off the highway. A hundred unexpected guests must have taxed the resources of the councilmen, who entertained us in the second story of the town hall. There was plenty of food, as in almost all the towns and villages behind the lines—the harvest this year has been excellent—but there were hardly any knives or forks or glasses; we ate the potato omelets with our fingers and sopped up the salad dressing with crusts of bread. Under the window we could hear the voices of many children singing the "International." Half a dozen of us stepped out through the French window, crowding the little balcony. All the children of Minglanilla, perhaps two hundred boys and girls, had gathered in the little square. Their mothers stood in the background, dressed in black. There were no men at all, except two or three very old ones leaning on their long canes. The children gave us the clenched-fist salute and we returned it. Then we went back to our potato omelets, while the singing continued. The next time I looked down from the balcony, a Dutch Catholic professor named Brouwer was leading the children in the new Spanish republican anthem (which, to my taste, seems too much like a music-hall song). They sang the "International" once more, and once more; they raised their clenched fists and shouted "Salud!"

When we went down into the square, we were surrounded by girls and boys, by mothers and grandmothers. The women were saying something very earnestly: all I could catch were the words "friends" and "help us, help us." Towering above the crowd was Stavsky, the Russian writer with a shaven head who looked like a Mack Sennett comedy convict. He made a gesture that nobody would have expected of him: he took the hand of an old woman, bent very low from the waist and kissed it. I saw with amazement that there were tears in his eyes, and in the old woman's too, and in my own—except for the children, everybody there was furtively weeping.

It was one of those moments of direct feeling, transmitted almost without speech, that you find in Spain and nowhere else in the civilized world. Only afterwards did I learn what the women had been saying. They were asking us to go home and tell our own countries that the Spanish people needed guns and airplanes. One of the old men explained that Minglanilla had suffered heavily in the war. Most of the younger men were in the army, but many of them had been massacred in far-off Badajoz, where they had gone to look for work. Some of the children who sang for us were refugees from Madrid. Nicolas Guillén, the Cuban Negro poet, talked to a boy of ten who had lost his father at the front during the first weeks of fighting. His two little brothers had been killed by an airplane bomb while playing in the streets. On each of his skinny brown arms he had an inscription pricked out in ink: "Death to the Fascists" and "They shall not pass."

As our motor caravan drove out of town, a woman in rags begged for money. Stephen Spender gave her a *peseta,* but the chauffeur knocked it out of her hand. "Spaniards don't beg," he said, and then in a lower, apologetic voice, "She is a Gypsy." An old man hobbled up to show us a very dirty newspaper clipping about the massacre in Badajoz. His daughter and his son-in-law had been killed there, he said. They had left three little girls.

Madrid was full of children, in spite of the scores of thousands who had been evacuated. They were everywhere in the streets, selling papers, watching the soldiers drill, stealing rides on the backs of trolley cars. Even at the west of the city, in streets that were barred to traffic because they were visible from the Fascist lines, there were children playing war games in the ruins of houses knocked to pieces by artillery fire. They were nice kids, too—barefooted, bareheaded, burned dark brown by the sun, with wiry hair, clear gray or chestnut-colored eyes and engaging grins that kept you grinning back at them. After eight months of living under siege, they seemed to be absolutely without fear. When the fascist planes came over, their mothers called them into the houses, but they didn't always obey; it was much more exciting to watch an air battle from the streets.

Louis Fischer came to the hotel late one afternoon, just after an attempted air raid. He had watched it from the Plaza Mayor. Three big Fiats came over, looking for a convenient place to drop their bombs. Suddenly half a dozen *chatos,* the little snub-nosed Russian pursuit planes, appeared from nowhere. The Fiats zoomed away at top speed, with the *chatos* maneuvering to bring them down. And the people watching them, the soldiers, the mothers, but especially the children, began dancing in the square and singing new words to the tune of "La Cucaracha":

> *Los chatos, los chatos,*
> *Ya se quieren caminar.*

I repeated the story to Dick Mowrer, who had just arrived from Valencia. He told me that last winter Madrid was almost completely without firewood, or fuel of any sort. Nobody touched the shade trees that stand in double rows along the principal streets. Nobody touched them, that is, so long as they were living and whole. But if a tree was hit by a bomb or a shell, all the kids of the neighborhood swarmed out with hatchets and set to work on it. Within a few hours it had disappeared, even the stump and the roots. Other kids chopped planks and beams out of the ruined houses. But it was dangerous work, because sometimes another shell hit the same spot.

Switchmen, firemen, policemen, women standing in line for food and children playing in the streets: these were the usual victims of a bombing or a shelling. Perhaps the children had suffered most of all.

On the morning after the bombardment of downtown Madrid, about twenty writers drove out for a visit to the lines northeast of Guadalajara. It was an uneventful journey. Every village through which we passed had suffered from air raids; every wall, so it seemed, was peppered with bomb fragments and every fourth or fifth house was totally demolished. But most of the raids had occurred last spring, when the fascists were trying to avenge their defeat. Since then the Guadalajara sector had relapsed into a calm that was almost somnolence. We parked our cars within a short stone's throw of the front-line trenches. These ran along the northern rim of a plateau and looked out across a pleasant valley where the wheat was ripening: that was no man's land. About 2,000 yards away was the enemy's country: another plateau exactly as high as the one on which we were standing and guarded by an exactly similar line of trenches. Neither side had rifles or machine guns that were accurate beyond 500 yards and neither side had much artillery, so that life on this front was quieter and substantially safer than life in Madrid.

The commanding officer was General Hans, a big, amiable, efficient German exile whose real name is a state secret. He speaks at least five languages and needs them all to communicate with the men on his staff. One of his chief assistants is a Frenchman who fought against him at Verdun. Hans told us that the Loyalist front lines and those of the fascists were equally impregnable. He had tried a frontal attack after the battle of Guadalajara, but his tanks got stuck half way up the steep slope and a lot of his men were killed. His shock troops were fighting now in the offensive west of Madrid. He kept the others in training by making occasional raids under cover of darkness and by sending them down each night to occupy the village in the valley. The peasants had been moved out of it only a month before. Until that time, both sides used to go there at night to buy eggs and to trade the unsmokable Loyalist cigarettes for the almost equally unsmokable fascist cigarettes.

One of the writers claimed that he saw a fascist across the valley. Hans looked through his field glasses and found that it was only a tree. But he thought—although he couldn't be quite certain—that he saw two fascists off to the right of the tree. As we stood there on the trench parapet talking idly, they might as well have been in China or the moon.

We went on to Brihuega, a town that for two weeks had been the headquarters of an Italian division. The road ran eastward straight across the battlefield. When Hemingway drove along it four months earlier, he had seen hundreds of Italian corpses dotting the sparse live-oak woods and lying in gray clusters around the tumbled heaps of stones that they had used for machine-gun nests and that proved to be worse than no protection against the Loyalist tanks. The corpses were buried now; the tanks were fighting west of Madrid; there were no relics of the battle except little clean shell holes the size of preserving kettles. Brihuega itself had been more than half destroyed by an air raid just after the Loyalists recaptured it. We stopped at a fountain and Anna Louise Strong took pictures of a little Spanish boy against a background of utter ruin and desolation. Looking at his thin face, I thought of the children in my own Connecticut village.

"Listen, Anna Louise," I said very quickly. "Why couldn't I adopt some Spanish children and take them back to the States—four of them, perhaps, or three? I think they're the finest kids in the world."

"Yes," she said, "there's no reason why it couldn't be arranged. If you are really serious about it, I can take you around to the children's bureau in Madrid."

The kindly woman in charge of the war orphans put me through a long series of questions. What was my profession? Was I married and had I children of my own? Could I support three others? Would they have a good school in Connecticut? Did I intend to bring them up as American citizens? That, she explained, was contrary to the usual custom. The government hoped that all children sent to foreign countries would come back after the war. But in this case she was sure that an exception could be made—there were so many orphans in Madrid and so few good homes to put them in; the chance of sending three of them to America simply couldn't be overlooked. "Of course," she said, "they will be the children of workers, not of rich people or intellectuals. You understand that." I answered that I wasn't expecting to adopt the Spanish Infanta.

In less than an hour all the arrangements had been completed. I would go to Valencia and reserve passage for the

children on the big air liner that flies into France. I would talk
to the American consul and make sure that there would be no
difficulty over their passports. Back in Madrid, the authorities
would go over their records and pick out two little girls and a
boy between the ages of three and five—indeed, they would
pick out several children so that I might have a choice among
them. The adoption papers could be signed on my return and
the children could be made ready for their long journey.

In Valencia two days later I found that there would be no
serious difficulty about passage on the air liner. Then I went to
the American consulate, which occupies an upper floor of the
Hotel Venecia, overlooking the central plaza. Getting into the
consulate was like getting into a speakeasy: you rang the bell,
waited, rang again; a tiny barred slit opened in the door; an
eye goggled at you suspiciously and a voice demanded who you
were and why you were here anyway. It turned out that the
vice-consul in charge of the office was home with a touch of
grippe. But the embassy was here too, behind the same barred
door. If I so insisted, I might talk to the chargé d'affaires, Mr.
Walter C. Thurston.

Mr. Thurston was quite amiable. He didn't know about
getting passports for the children, as that sort of business
wasn't in his line, but he had no doubt that the matter could be
arranged with the vice-consul when he returned next morning. Meanwhile he had read in the newspapers that I had been
attending a writers' congress in Valencia and Madrid. That
was very interesting indeed. Would I mind telling him
whether I had a visa for Spain and just how I had managed to
obtain it?

I explained that I was here primarily as a correspondent
for *The New Republic* and therefore was entitled to a passport
without the usual restrictions on travel in the war zone. Would
I care to show him the passport? Ah, yes, he was pleased to see
that everything was in order. But would I mind writing him a
brief biography of myself, with some account of my activities,
so that he could send it back to Washington? Mr. Thurston
was polite and even friendly in making this request. Still, it
seemed strange to me that an American diplomatic agent,
supposedly in Spain to protect the interests of his fellow countrymen, should begin by putting them through a cross-exami-
nation.

And the examination was only beginning. Mr. Thurston had heard that there was some difficulty about the passports of the English delegates to the congress. Did I happen to know whether they were in Spain legally? I answered that I hadn't asked them, that it was certainly none of my business. Well then, what about the Lincoln Battalion? How many Americans had joined it? How had they sneaked across the border? How many of them had been killed? Had the government forces really taken Brunete? Mr. Thurston had been listening to reports from the Seville radio station and didn't believe that they had. He wanted to know about losses in the big offensive: was it true that the International Brigades had been cut to pieces? His questions went on, a trifle insistently. At first I answered them to the best of my knowledge. Then I began to feel like a prisoner being examined, with a show of politeness, by the enemy's general staff. Some of the questions were designed to call forth answers that would scarcely interest Washington but would certainly interest General Franco's agents in Valencia. I blamed myself for carrying my suspicions too far—but still I reflected that Mr. Thurston had no business arousing them.

A little awkwardly I changed the subject and began talking about other countries. It turned out that Mr. Thurston had been stationed in Mexico City during the revolution there and had developed a deep contempt for natives and revolutionists. Here in Valencia he seemed to be completely cut off from the world. I pictured him sitting alone in an empty office, disliking the Spanish government, distrusting the Americans in Spain for fear that they had become infected with popular enthusiasm, and in general knowing and learning less about the Spanish war than if he had stayed at a desk in Washington and read the daily papers.

Next morning I saw the vice-consul, Mr. Milton Wells, who inspired more confidence, being less discreet. Quite frankly he despised both sides in the civil war, though he seemed to despise the government more than the rebels. He warned me against letting my feelings be touched—war, he said, was always like that; it was a very unpleasant business. As for the children, he was very much afraid that he couldn't help me. Under the American immigration law, merely adopting a child had no effect on its prior nationality—did not make it an

American citizen or entitle it to a non-quota visa or even give it preference under the quota. The child was treated like any other immigrant. For all of Spain, both loyal and rebel, the quota for immigrants was only 252 per year. There might possibly be some quota numbers remaining—one or two per month—after the preference visas had been allotted, but Mr. Wells wouldn't know about that for several weeks, and in any case he didn't propose to encourage me in what he regarded as a sentimental gesture. "If the children stay in Madrid," he said, with an obvious effort to be just and reassuring, "I'm sure they'll be taken care of."

I remembered the ambulances clanging through the empty streets at night. "Yes," I said, "Franco's bombers will take care of them." But there was no use losing my temper.

That is the end of the long story. When I got back to Madrid, I asked Anna Louise Strong to go to the children's bureau and explain how matters stood; I simply couldn't face them. For once I felt ashamed of being an American citizen. If I had been French or English or Siamese I might have helped, but the American Congress had passed a law against kindness to Spanish children. Just a short time ago the State Department was trying to prevent us even from sending them milk or money, but that little, thank God, can still be done.

There Have To Be Censors

THE ARGUMENTS FOR and the arguments against the political censorship of works of art both seem to me substantially unassailable.

On the affirmative side there is one argument that is a basis for all the others and even makes them superfluous. Art does affect society. That is, it affects people by changing their stand-

NR, Apr. 27, 1938.

ards of value or heightening their emotions, and thus helps to determine their future actions. It used to be argued that art existed in its own world and had no practical results of any sort; but that was in the days before the movies were really popular and before the law-enforcement agencies had a chance to observe that certain types of pictures—desperado, gangster, racketeer and "snatch"—had an almost statistical effect on the prevailing types of crime.

After such evidence began to accumulate, the art-for-art-sakers shifted their arguments. Some of them tried to make a distinction between the "lower" arts and the "higher" arts, placing the movies, popular songs, illustrations and cartoons on the one side, and novels, plays, poems, symphonic music and painting on the other. The "lower" arts were the only ones that affected practical life and hence the only ones rightly subject to censorship. But this is a distinction that, in practice, is very hard to enforce—especially since a movie may be higher art than the play or novel from which it was made. Political cartoons and murals may be done by the same man, and it has often happened that the cartoons were better esthetically than the murals. And why should we choose to believe that great novels—to mention only one of the "higher" arts—have no effect in action? That such effects may be subtle and long delayed and even quite opposite to those intended by the author—as in the case of Dostoevsky, whose anti-revolutionary novels helped to inspire the Russian revolutionists—is no excuse for denying their existence. Artists in general should object to being told that their patient efforts to formulate ideas and transmit emotions are absolutely fruitless, by definition. They have nothing to gain by a theory that offers them a degree of irresponsible freedom at the price of their being regarded as harmless people, quite beneath the notice of the state.

But if artists are not harmless or helpless, then society has the right to judge their work by its effects, to encourage it, guide it into new channels and even suppress it if its effects are evil. Indeed, that right has always been exercised, and I should guess that it will be more widely exercised in the future. Planned social controls are becoming always more elaborate and are being extended into fields that used to be ruled by custom or chance or whim. Censorship is one control among many, and it is likely to grow like traffic regulations.

Not without well grounded opposition. . . . Although justified in theory, censorship has in practice been harmful not only to the arts but often to the general social structure as well. I don't want to repeat the familiar arguments against it, some of which should be questioned. It is said, for example, that censorship defeats itself by calling attention to the books it wants to suppress. That statement may apply to partial or ineffective censorships, but not to those enforced by the new fascist states. Nor is it true that censorship is always stupid. In Soviet Russia it has been both popular and intelligent in its aims, but that has not made it ideal for the artists who work under its direction. Dr. Kurt London's book on *The Seven Soviet Arts*, reviewed here two weeks ago, suggested without directly stating a new line of attack.

Briefly, censors and artists can never understand each other because they speak different languages. The censors may be conservative or radical, ignorant or learned, but in any case their language is that of political logic, which is based on what used to be called "the intellect" and is now described as the conscious mind. The arts are based on it too, in large part, but they also depend on something that used to be called "the instincts" or "the passions"; it is now described as the unconscious. There is no way of forcing the two into agreement at any given time. The result, under an effective censorship, is a whole series of difficulties and real disasters.

Both the censors and the political critics make demands that many artists cannot honestly fulfill. Often their arguments are so persuasive that the artists assent with their intellects; but unless they assent with their instincts as well, their work will be either shallow and mediocre, written off the top of their minds, or else it will have what the Soviet critic Yuri Yuzovsky calls a "subtext" conveying a meaning opposite to that which was consciously intended. The censors think politically, in terms of the present situation, whereas the artists have to feel chiefly in terms of the past. This means that in Russia the party press now calls for books dealing with Stakhanovism or counter-espionage or the Second Five Year Plan, whereas the artists, moving more slowly, have not yet digested the First

Five Year Plan, not to speak of the revolution itself. The censors want effects that are measurable and immediate; they tend to disparage the books whose influence is exerted over long periods, deeply rather than broadly. They reward those works of art that comply with their instructions; in other words, they often reward mediocrity and favor the careerists and politicians of art at the expense of the honest artists. As for the people at large, they will get the books and pictures that the censorship thinks is good for them. But the censorship may be quite as mistaken about the psychology of the audience as about the psychology of the artist—with the result that the art it recommends for making people happy may simply bore them or rouse them to revolt.

The arguments for and against censorship are convincing on both sides, and I can see no logical solution to the dilemma that they pose. Should we simply abolish censors? That experiment was tried in Germany just after the War, but it was not successful. Outside of its practical effects on the public order it would have a theoretical weakness, in that artists would be the only members of society permitted to influence others without being controlled or influenced in their turn. Should we say that only moral as opposed to political censorship can be justified? It would be hard to distinguish between them in a world where every department of life is becoming part of politics. Ireland has a censorship that is supposed to be purely moral, but besides being stupid and oppressive it is rapidly assuming a political nature. Should we then insist on having intelligent censors? They might be worse for artists than the stupid ones, who in practice have a lot to recommend them. Intelligent censors in Tsarist Russia would have suppressed Dostoevsky's novels instead of allowing them to affect the ideals of a whole generation. What then? Should we say that a censorship is justified so long as it is imposed by our own party and agrees with our own ideals? That might be satisfactory for the present, and necessary too, in revolutionary conditions. But it is certain to weaken the artists of the future by suppressing that conflict among theories and methods and purposes of art out of which the future is born.

My own humble suggestion is that although the dilemma cannot be solved in theory, it might conceivably be solved in practice. Instead of trying to end the conflict between artists and censors, let us regard it as normal and even desirable. Let us say that both sides are right, not in any particular skirmish but in the battle as a whole. The censors are right in attacking books and pictures which they regard as immoral or subversive. The artists are right in counter-attacking the censors and in fighting not only to save but to widen their own freedom of expression. There is no final decision to be reached, but there is a temporary stability to be achieved as the result of struggle. . . . This, I might add, is not a Utopian proposal. It is a fairly accurate description of what has happened in several democratic countries, including our own, when the artists were strong enough to fight for their privileges.

American and English Journals of Opinion

THE WINTER ISSUE of *Scrutiny,* an English quarterly review published at Cambridge by a group of the younger instructors, carries a leading article on "The New Republic and the Ideal Weekly." The article was written by H. A. Mason, but there are grounds for believing that it also represents the opinion of his colleagues, including the redoubtable Mr. Leavis. Although flattering on the whole—much too flattering, I think—it shows a real insight into our problems and contains some pretty sharp criticisms. I should like to summarize it at length before making a few comments of my own.

Mr. Mason's purpose is "to suggest an approach toward the formulation of a standard for a weekly journal of opinion." The approach he suggests is to examine the files of *The New Republic* for one complete year. He has chosen 1931 "as being sufficiently recent and at the same time far enough removed to insure a proper critical balance"; but his judgments are checked and verified by reference to more recent years. "I propose," he says, "to review the contents of the copies I have

NR, Jan. 18, 1939, where it was titled "Transatlantic View."

selected . . . and in suggesting where *The New Republic* attains or falls short of its standard, to come near to an ideal that . . . will serve as a criterion by which our English weeklies can be measured."

He believes that the signed articles in *The New Republic*, by way of contrast with the English periodicals, are its most praiseworthy feature. He divides them into five general categories. First come those dealing with "matters which are engaging or should engage the immediate attention of the government. As far as I can judge they are extremely competent and present a wealth of technical detail and such acquaintance with the problems of government as comes rightly from experts who expect to be read by an intelligent public and by fellow experts. . . . I risk the observation that they are more impressive on questions of internal administration than on long-term policy. The occasional supplements that I remember struck me as models."

The second category consists of articles on general economic questions. These, Mr. Mason says, "maintain an equally high standard. When descending to the details of business, *The New Republic* shows a particularity that I suppose our libel laws would prevent." He supposes rightly. An English editor told me that to print a page like John T. Flynn's in his own paper would cost a minimum of twenty thousand pounds a year in libel suits, the truth being no defense in England. The third category consists of articles on general social questions. "The selected year is rich in examples. . . . In this field *The New Republic* appears more lively than any English journal and manages to throw light on so many aspects of American life which do not come up for comment in England." On the other hand, Mr. Mason believes that the articles on foreign politics "are often more naïve and presuppose a public less well informed than ours." The fifth and last category consists of articles on the sciences, arts and philosophy, which "do not call for separate consideration under this head. They are in fact merely an opportunity to treat at greater length topics which arise from the general reviewing."

This leads Mr. Mason to the section of the paper that most closely concerns me. "In many respects," he says, "though with reservations, as will appear, the reviewing pages are a model of what weekly criticism should be. At any rate a strict comparison of a review of the same book from *The New Republic* and *The New Statesman* provides an exercise in comparative criticism which supplies its own comment. Quite an anthology of opinions that would hold today could be taken from this one year. . . . *The New Republic* reviewers are not handicapped by the belief general in England that no useful service can be served by trying to assess the importance of contemporary literary figures. They are constantly engaged in sorting out of their recent history those writers who have something important to say."

Mr. Mason concludes his preliminary investigation by saying: "A reader who is chiefly interested in the criticism of American writers is presented over a period of years with a gradual crystallization of opinion about the important contemporary writers. . . . *The New Republic* enables its readers to participate in the best opinion of the day and not to be twenty or fifty years behind the times as in England."

In the second part of his article, where he tries to assess the general virtues and failings of this magazine, Mr. Mason is less definite and harder to summarize. Perhaps the picture of the ideal weekly is still too vague in his mind to serve as a standard for judging the imperfect weeklies that exist. In any case, he knows what he likes and doesn't like. He quotes with admiration the editorial note that preceded a series of articles: "They are the outcome of conversations among the editors of *The New Republic* that have been occurring for several months and the gist of which may be of interest to our readers as raw material for thought and discussion." The note reminds him once more "that there is a continuous interchange of criticism among those responsible for *The New Republic*. . . . Such criticism, apart from its value in securing unity, has the equally useful result of clarifying differences. A sickly feature of English periodicals—the overindulgent treatment by fellow reviewers of any book written by the fraternity—is almost wholly absent." He likes our "healthy bias towards referring all questions to present needs," an attitude that he contrasts with the "quaint and delicate dilettante antiquarianism" of many English reviewers. He also likes what he calls "the Middletown approach to society," which enables the New Republicans, so he says, "to blend skillfully the economic, social and cultural in their presentation of America." This approach, "with all its limitations, makes possible a kind of synthesis mutually illuminating and transforming all its elements." He compares it with the divided purpose of the English weeklies, where the editorials seem to be marching firmly in one direction and the book reviews in another.

But this is precisely the point at which his criticisms begin. *The New Republic* synthesis is not the one that he would adopt for his ideal weekly. He thinks that political opinions—and especially Marxist opinions—play too great a part in it. He would prefer a unity based on values derived from literature instead of politics, and one, I gather, in which the politics was much more conservative than our own. He thinks that our literary criticism is terribly uneven. "Poetry in particular comes in for the most uncertain treatment. . . . A *New Republic* reviewer is capable of swerving from good sense to elementary fallacy in the course of a single article. One may of course retort that good criticism of poetry is rare enough anywhere. Yet it remains true that the central theme which should give sharpness and delicacy to the whole body of criticism functions fitfully and as it were coarsely." A graver charge, however, is that some of us are getting tired. "A review must finally be judged by the quality of its chief writers. Often they are too few and (as happened with that excellent organ *The New Frontier*) they write themselves out." *The New Republic* has escaped this fate, but some of its best contributors are now writing beneath the level of their best work. "One may tentatively suggest (with a due and sufficiently grim awareness of the situation in England) as a possible reason for this decline the poverty of the critical milieu. No weekly journalist can hope to produce good work regularly without the support of more leisured writers."

Mr. Mason's final judgment should be quoted at length:

> *The New Republic* with all its faults does at least succeed in providing a certain standard firmly enough maintained for deviations from it to be easily detected. Moreover it does supply with all its deficiencies the essential material for the irrigation of

public opinion. The best available thought is sooner or later
reflected in its pages. And—a note which has not been sufficiently
heard in this survey—it presents its material in a lively, flexible
way. It has carried on for twenty-four years in an environment
bleaker than ours, with a circulation smaller in proportion to the
size of the reading public than that, say, of *The Spectator*. And
it has carried on with such relative success in spite of having at
times to do the work of a quarterly as well as that of a
weekly. . . . The existence of *The New Republic* is a standing
challenge to the intelligent public of this country. Why have we
no such paper here?

I suspect that this judgment is somewhat affected by the
pathos of distance. Our achievements loom up to Mr. Mason
like clouds on the western horizon; our faults are partly veiled
in the sea mist. Seen from this side of the water, *The New
Statesman and Nation*, which is closest to us of our English
contemporaries, is also an approach to the ideal weekly. The
difference between us is not primarily the work of the editors,
English or American (although no survey of this paper would
be complete unless it mentioned the lasting influence of Her-
bert Croly). It is not the result of a model displayed before us,
like an ideal bag of oats. Chiefly it depends on the different
publics for which the two weeklies are written.

The public of *The New Statesman* seems to me amazingly
definite and homogeneous. I picture it as composed of teachers,
civil servants, journalists and perhaps lawyers spending their
days in London and their evenings in a Sussex cottage where
they smoke well-seasoned briars and potter about in the pot-
ting shed. They are not a numerous class—the circulation of
The New Statesman is the same as ours or a shade smaller—
but England is a smaller country and they play a fairly important role. Advertisers recognize their need not only for books
but for stout walking shoes, safe investments, small cars, progressive schools and Virginia cigarettes. Their intellectual center is Bloomsbury, and I have heard it said in England that
The New Statesman reflects the tone and opinions of a good
Bloomsbury dinner. The remark was offered a little conde-
scendingly, but it made me feel envious rather than superior.
A good English weekly is a hydrometer that records a whole
streamflow of opinion. An editorial paragraph in *The New
Statesman* may summarize an evening of argument, with half

a dozen people contributing to the final judgment. And that judgment gains in persuasiveness by being expressed in the tone of good conversation.

The level of literary competence—I did not say of literary talent—is higher in England. The average page of *The New Statesman* is written with more ease, with shorter words and looser sentences, than the average page of *The New Republic*. The task of assigning a book for review is easier for the English editor, since any one of a hundred writers might pass a sound judgment on it, in a printable style, whereas the American editor must choose from no more than a dozen. On the other hand, too many of the English critics write in a tone of supercilious indifference, as if they were afraid to speak out on any subject that matters. Perhaps that fear is not unconnected with the general fear of change and the future that is spreading through English society. And always there is the English law of libel, as omnipresent and conducive to timidity as was the Tsar's official censorship.

In this country the chief difficulty for a weekly journal of opinion is the lack of a unified audience. Our readers are scattered over the country from Maine to the Mexican border, with more of them in New York than in any other city, but not more proportionately than in Los Angeles or Washington. They are of different groups and professions, young and old, rich and poor, to judge from their letters, but most of them belong to the intelligent left wing of the middle class. The trouble is that the members of this intelligent left wing do not form a class by themselves, to be identified and numbered. The qualities that distinguish them are real but difficult to measure. Many of them live in comparative isolation, and there is no one locality where their opinions are orthodox, as those of *The New Statesman* are in Bloomsbury.

It would be impossible for *The New Republic* to reflect the tone of their dinner-table conversation. There are few dinners here, in the English sense, and there is comparatively little intelligent conversation. Americans talk to exchange information, but seldom to amuse themselves; instead they drink or play games. Anyone here who writes about ideas tends to write like a prophet in the wilderness. And he also tends to write badly, in the sense that the language he uses is not that of his

everyday speech; the words he uses come out of books and go
back into books, like documents returned to a filing cabinet.
Perhaps this situation also explains Mr. Mason's remark that
"a *New Republic* reviewer is capable of swerving from good
sense to elemental fallacy in the course of a single article."
Some of the fallacies are simply points where we disagree with
Mr. Mason. The others might have been recognized in advance if the reviewer had been able to test his opinions conver-
sationally.

I don't want to paint too bleak a picture. The American
audience, as contrasted with the English, is serious, patient,
full of curiosity. It listens to shop talk, which in England is
bad form, and it even listens to economists and philosophers.
The American writer is not afraid to get mad or enthusiastic,
or to risk his reputation for his opinions. There is no skeleton
in his closet—nothing, I mean, to compare with the English
feeling that their society mustn't be handled too roughly for
fear of its falling apart. The American hasn't lost his eagerness
to experiment or his sense of working toward ends that can be
reached in the future.

Indeed, most of the virtues that Mr. Mason ascribes to
The New Republic are those of its writers and readers. The
other virtues are partly caused by the shortcomings of our
audience—in the sense that we are trying to compensate for its
geographical dispersion and its difficulties of communication.
We hope that our readers will never agree with one another,
will never be intellectually *gleichgeschaltet*. But it is one of
our ambitions to maintain among them a general level of taste
and information, a *consensus* to which a magazine can fruit-
fully appeal. We feel that such a consensus is necessary not
only in the arts but also in politics and economics. And this aim
of ours, much more than "the Middletown approach," explains the unified impression that Mr. Mason admires.

Of course there can be no "ideal weekly," any more than
there can be an ideal house. The weekly exists in relation to its
public, just as the house exists in relation to its site and its
tenants. When Mr. Mason gives praise to *The New Republic*,
together with some blame, we deduct only our proper share
of both, our commission as agents. The rest we pass on to our
contributors and our sometimes overburdened readers.

Exiles of the Arts

FIRST CAME THE YEARS when American writers and painters went to Europe, hoping to find a climate where works of art could ripen. That happened just after the War, in the midst of a political and intellectual reaction here that was a mild foretaste of fascism. The Americans in Paris were called expatriates, but they regarded themselves almost as refugees. The movement toward Europe continued for a decade, then suddenly reversed itself. After 1930 the expatriates came drifting home again, chiefly because they no longer had money enough to live in France. But that wasn't the end of the story. The same ships that carried the Americans homeward also carried the first European writers into exile. They too hoped to find a climate congenial to works of art, but first of all they were coming to New York to escape from the shadow of the concentration camps.

The Germans, of course, have been the central current of the new migration. They have reached this country in successive waves—first the political refugees, in 1933, then the racial and religious refugees (who have never stopped coming), then the liberals who had hoped to find an audience in Vienna, then the more uncompromising anti-fascists driven out of Prague, then a whole assortment of people who had grown discouraged in Paris or London—with the result that New York today is full of German intellectuals; there are said to be more German writers of distinction here than have stayed in Berlin. But the Germans have been accompanied or followed by the intellectuals of other nations under fascist rule—by the Italians, Hungarians, Czechs, Spaniards, whoever was lucky enough to find a loophole in our immigration laws. And the movement has by no means been confined to political refugees. There are, for example, more than a few French painters working in New York. There are Germans who have remained on good terms with their own government. There are English artists and stage people who are glad to escape from the wartime psychology that is interfering with any sustained efforts. As for English writers, who used to come here only to lecture and hurry home, they now insist on making a grand tour of the States—much in the spirit, I suspect, of Rimbaud exploring Abyssinia.

I am discussing only the cultural side of this new immigration, but even so I should be wrong to confine myself to literature and the fine arts. The learned professions are represented too, along with the practical arts, the folk arts and the world of sports. There are physicists, philologists, concert singers, night-club singers, animal trainers, blue-ribbon chefs, industrial designers and dress designers; there are even *skimeisters* like Hannes Schneider and Benno Rybizka, who are trying to create another Tyrol on the slopes of the White Mountains. These people have brought with them not only their skills but as many of their material possessions as they could smuggle past the border guards. Stroll up Madison Avenue, look into the windows of the little shops or the picture galleries, and you will see Tyrolean costumes, old family silver from Cologne and Frankfurt, fine cameras, first editions, Goethe manuscripts, paintings by the German masters, the spoils of Central Europe.

People still not middle-aged have seen it all happen in their lifetime. First New York was a sort of provincial capital, bigger and richer than Manchester or Marseilles, but not much different in its essential spirit. Then, after the War, it became one among half a dozen world cities. Today it has the appearance of standing alone, as the center of culture in the part of the world that still tries to be civilized. And even though the reality is more modest than the appearance, it is still sufficiently impressive. During the last ten years New York has become the central marketplace for most forms of artistic production and at least the temporary home of the international style in art and life.

Yet when I meet some of the new exiles and catch hints of their illusions about New York, I feel a little abashed—like a host who hears visitors praising his house when he knows that the roof leaks and the bathroom is out of order. I want to greet the exiles warmly, as if they were my own guests. I want to console them for what they have suffered and thank them in advance for all the contributions they can make to the art and business of living in America. At the same time I want to give them a warning that is difficult to put into words.

It isn't a warning about the money troubles in front of them; on that score they have been warned already. They know that there are no restrictions on their finding work, such as exist in almost all the European countries, but they also know that work is hard to find. Hundreds of exiles would have starved during their first months in America if they had not been kept alive by various private charities (the Jews have been particularly active in helping both Jews and gentiles). Hundreds of others, trained in the professions, have taken whatever jobs they could get—often as gardeners, cooks (after a degree in dietetics), handy men or maids of all work. On the other hand, there are hundreds who manage to live much as they did in Europe and even, in some cases, to better their positions.

Apart from the personal element, their success in New York depends largely on the market that exists for their particular skill. Magazine photographers are a case in point. Their profession was highly regarded in Germany, which during the 1920's had the best illustrated magazines in the world, and which still has the best cameras. In the days of the Weimar Republic they would have found no market in this country. But shortly after Hitler, five or six American picture magazines were founded almost simultaneously, so that there was a sudden demand here for skilled photographers. Many Germans and Hungarians—both exiles and simple immigrants —have been hired at good salaries; and they have helped to transform American pictorial journalism. The German industrial designers have also been fortunate, since many of them reached this country at the beginning of the vogue for streamlining, when all sorts of products and packages were being remodeled and new designs were salable.

The scientists belong to a special category, since they speak a universal language and are at home wherever there are facilities for research. The best of them quickly found places in American university or industrial laboratories. The professors of history, economics and political science have not been too unlucky, provided they were able to lecture in English that students could understand: they are teaching now in at least fifty American colleges. At the New School for Social Research, the graduate faculty is a "university in exile," entirely composed of anti-fascist Germans, Italians and Spaniards. The former Spanish ambassador will teach there next year.

The members of other professions allied with literature and the arts have been less fortunate. The musicians, for example, have come to a country whose own musicians are unemployed; only the more famous of the exiles have been able to find regular engagements. The actors, after learning a new language, have to face a new audience whose reactions are unfamiliar; they don't know when to expect applause or laughter. The writers are probably the most unhappy of all. Besides suffering the same losses as the others—their homes, their livelihood, their audience and their means of reaching it —they have lost some of the essentials of their art. If they are accustomed to dealing with contemporary life in the homeland, they can no longer broaden their experience or refresh their memories. In any case they have few opportunities to hear or speak their own language, the instrument which they have spent their lives perfecting. Some of the older writers, it is true, have found a new audience in translation. But many of the younger ones have grown discouraged: they say it is no use for them to go on writing when there is hardly anyone to read their work even if they succeed in getting it printed. A few are learning to write in English. Most of these are political and economic writers, who deal in ideas that are comparatively easy to render in another language. At any rate they write effective English; and I think they are partly responsible for the increasing sophistication of American political journalism.

In general one might say that the financial prospects of the exiles are black with streaks of sunlight. Their moral prospects are actually more threatening.

A great defeat—like that suffered by humanism in Germany and Spain—does not bring people together. It does not unite the factions that used to struggle for power. In exile, each faction tends to justify itself and blame all the others, thinking that if only the Communists or the Socialists or the Democrats had acted more wisely, the tragedy might have been averted. Quarrels that began on the floor of the Reichstag or the Cortes are continued in West Side rooming houses, in an atmosphere of stale cigarette smoke and delicatessen sandwiches. Even the strongest of the exiles become embittered; the weakest lose their sense of reality and sometimes their honor as well. But this is another subject on which it is useless to give a warning. What the exiles don't know from experience, they can easily learn by reading the story of Karl Marx and his friends in London or Bakunin in Switzerland.

No, my warning is addressed to those among the exiles who come here with illusions, who believe that this is really a new world, and in any case too robust a world for the diseases of old age that are attacking Europe. I want to make them understand that New York is merely another great European city. It is younger than Paris or London; much too young to have developed the traditions of intellectual hospitality that have flourished in London since the eighteenth century and in Paris since the Middle Ages. On the other hand, it has been a great city longer than Berlin, and it seems tired and almost senile as compared with Moscow. It is a colony of European capitalism, a very old colony that has become a richer metropolis than any in the homeland, but without curing itself of the ills that capitalism suffers everywhere. The exiles ought to be warned that by coming here they will escape none of the problems that defeated them in Europe. On an unfamiliar battleground they will have to fight the same enemies.

Notes on a Writers' Congress

I WAS FAGGED OUT on the last day of the American Writers' Congress. Having attended seven meetings, not to speak of parties, business luncheons and a reception; having joined in some lively discussions and listened to more papers than could be remembered, I felt justified in going back to my unweeded garden without waiting for the final session at which

NR, June 21, 1939.

resolutions were to be adopted and officers elected. Still it was a good congress, by far the best of the three that have been held by the League of American Writers.

This time there were more writers present, including more from foreign cities like Dublin and Copenhagen and Hollywood. There was more attention paid to strictly literary matters. Except for the public meeting at Carnegie Hall, where ex-President Benes told what had happened to Czecho-Slovakia since the Germans marched in, there was not much talk of the political situation; it was an ominous background that was taken for granted. The problem around which most of the discussion centered was that of finding a wider audience for good books and plays and poems.

The closed sessions, held at the New School for Social Research, were chiefly devoted to the different literary crafts—fiction, poetry, criticism, stage, screen, radio—although there was also a session organized for and by the exiled writers. Some of these meetings were planned with real ingenuity. The fiction session was one of them; it consisted of five-minute papers by novelists and short-story writers, each of whom discussed his own type of narrative. Thus, Sylvia Townsend Warner talked on historical fiction, Dashiell Hammett on tempo in fiction and Christina Stead on the many-charactered novel, to choose three examples from more than a dozen. With the story-tellers speaking for themselves, the usually voluble critics were invited to listen and be silent. But the critics had a chance to talk at their own session, where they were properly segregated. There were no prepared papers. Instead a single novel, *The Grapes of Wrath*, was taken as a subject for almost clinical dissection, with each critic approaching it from his special point of view and judging it as symbolism, American folktale, heroic legend, social drama or political pamphlet. I was glad that John Steinbeck wasn't there to listen, not because the general verdict was unfavorable—far from it—but simply because he would have been so confused by conflicting ideas and subtle distinctions that it might have become impossible for him to write another novel.

The poetry session, which I didn't get a chance to attend, was concerned with the new and old mediums through which poets might reach more than their present quite specialized audience. The screen session listened to some rather jubilant reports from Hollywood, besides watching rushes of the new Paul Strand film on civil liberties. The most carefully prepared of all the craft sessions was the one on writing for radio, with complete sound equipment furnished by CBS and editors present from all the broadcasting systems to explain and demonstrate just what could be done over the air. But the fact is that the whole congress had the air of being planned with foresight and judgment. Considering that it had been organized as a collective undertaking by writers, who are individualists by definition and quite unused to organizing their own lives or anything else more complicated than a chapter in a novel, it was something to feel proud about.

Afterwards, hoeing between the bean rows in my garden, I reflected that this congress, in addition to the high aims that were set for it and partially achieved, might serve an humble and unexpected purpose. It might help to establish human relations among writers.

If someone asked what I meant by that, I might answer him by referring to the way writers lived during the 1920's. In those days they met one another chiefly at publishers' cocktail parties (always described in the invitations as teas). Judging from what could be heard and seen at those functions, I should say that most writers attended them to boast about the sales of their latest books, to complain about reviews and royalties, to exchange compliments or veiled insults, to flirt and to get free drinks. All these acts could of course be called human relations, but they might be described more accurately as feline relations —considering that cats also come together to boast, quarrel, make love and sniff catnip. Writers, like cats, regarded every colleague as a rival.

From those days I don't recall hearing much literary conversation, either at publishers' teas or anywhere else (except among the Dadaists in Paris). It wasn't that writers weren't seriously interested in their own profession; quite on the contrary they burned with an almost religious enthusiasm. But they hesitated to talk about anything so close to their hearts as literature. Like cats they regarded themselves as solitary animals and kept their thoughts to themselves.

Of course the Writers' Congress didn't change all that in

three days; it was merely the sign of a change that had already taken place. It was, however, the first occasion on which I heard a great many writers talking about their own problems without being boastful or snickering or self-conscious—simply talking because they had something to say. Such an interchange of ideas will certainly transform none of them into geniuses, but it will keep some of them from making mistakes that others have made already, and learned to avoid. It will help to create a general pattern of ideas and thus make it easier to produce good books in certain fields—for example, novels and dramas dealing with contemporary problems. And it will certainly encourage writers to think of one another not as rivals, but as partners in the same undertaking and as human beings to be treated with consideration.

There is a story that might explain just what I don't mean. It happened at a writers' meeting in 1932 or 1933, during those comic-opera days when everybody in New York seemed to be talking about the revolution that would come tomorrow. The meeting broke up late. One writer, since distinguished as an ultra-radical politician, stepped into the street and slammed the door in the face of a pregnant woman. I don't think he saw that she was pregnant; he was absorbed in his revolutionary dream and may not even have noticed that she existed. But from that moment I began to find something false in his literary pleas for the working class. You can't lead them toward a better society by slamming the door in their faces.

Sixteen Propositions

ALL DURING THE 1930's, many Americans kept their eyes fixed obstinately on Moscow. Some followed Stalin, some favored Trotsky or Bukharin, some liked to think of themselves as impartial friends of the Soviets. All factions quar-

An unsigned editorial by Cowley. (*NR*, Feb. 26, 1940.) Reprinted by permission of *The New Republic*, © 1940 Harrison-Blaine of New Jersey, Inc.

reled bitterly, and all were united in believing that Russia was the center of the world struggle; that what happened there would decide the future of other countries, including our own. From the beginning, this paper has tried to point out that they were mistaken. Yet even today, in the midst of a Red scare that recalls the days of A. Mitchell Palmer, we cannot believe that they were bad Americans.

In most cases, it was their Americanism that urged them eastwards. When Lincoln Steffens wrote from Moscow, early in the decade, "I have seen the future and it works," he showed by his choice of words that his enthusiasm was based on two solidly American traits: his optimism ("the future") and his pragmatism ("it works"). The Russia of the Five Year Plan had replaced the United States as the country of industrial progress and large-scale pioneering. And although the famine and the purges soon proved that the future in Russia was not working to the pattern of their dreams, many Americans kept looking stubbornly beyond the Baltic. This time it was because they believed that Russia was the only great power whose foreign policy conformed to the best American ideals.

Such an obsession with one country had its obvious dangers. Those who kept straining into the distance began to suffer from presbyopia; they could no longer see clearly what was close at hand. At first they disparaged the New Deal and the American labor movement, and later they judged them in terms of Russian history or Russian foreign policy—Roosevelt, for example, began by being "a Kerensky," but later was praised as a bulwark of collective security. Russian factionalism played an entirely disproportionate part in American labor politics and American literature, with those who declaimed against it often being the worst offenders. All through this period there was a tendency to neglect Western scientific and social ideas in favor of those imported from Moscow. Western scholarship seemed timid and inconclusive, whereas Russo-Marxism was a dogma that admitted no doubts and answered all questions.

The worst danger, however, was that a blind enthusiasm might lead to an equally blind revulsion. Since the Stalin-Hitler pact and the Finnish war, that is exactly what has happened to many of the Americans obsessed with Russia. Some of them have been reduced to a condition bordering on shell-shock. Some, in agreement now with their former enemies, are calling for a holy war on all the dictatorships. Some are repeating the old radical slogans, but without conviction. Some are reverting to the sort of cynicism and indifference popular during the 1920's, while forgetting the catastrophe with which the 1920's ended. Some have turned their values upside down, believing that they will thereby rid themselves of all their illusions; in reality they are merely trading one set of illusions for another. It is as if they were watching a play in which the actors have changed their roles, with Stalin playing the villain instead of Chamberlain or Trotsky, while the essential plot remains the same.

A much more fundamental change is needed. In view of what has happened in the world, neither the liberalism of Woodrow Wilson's day nor the optimistic radicalism of the 1930's seems any longer a valid position. Russia has still to be studied; perhaps it has to be studied more carefully than ever before. This time, however, it is not as a portent and working model of the future, but rather for the lessons to be drawn from Russian mistakes and Russian achievements. With the help of these lessons, and others drawn from our own experience, there are new foundations to be laid for the American progressive movement. And we offer the following propositions—sixteen of them—as a step in the process and a basis for discussion:

1. That during the last twenty years, faith in socialism has for many people become identified with faith in Russia.

2. That such faith has been justified, in so far as the Russians have proved that socialism can produce vast improvements, even when working under handicaps and in a backward country.

3. That it has not been justified by Russian socialism as an economic system, in so far as Russian industry has been overorganized, overcentralized and has so far yielded insufficient returns to the workers.

4. That it has not been justified by Russian socialism as a

political system, in so far as that system has failed to make a place for opposition groups, for the conflict and compromise of opinions, and hence for individual freedom.

5. That many developments in Russia—notably the famine of 1932–33, the purges of 1937–38 and the dictatorship of Stalin and his Politburo—suggest a complete reexamination not only of Russian practice but of Marxian theory from the beginning.

6. That orthodox Marxism, as preached today by the Comintern, has lost the experimental spirit and the hospitality to new ideas that were shown by Marx and Engels.

7. That it excludes the discoveries in the social sciences made since 1890, particularly in psychology, sociology and comparative religion.

8. That it is psychologically weak in its fashion of providing for many human needs—notably those for loyalties, rituals and symbols—and in its attempt to impose a unified pattern of conduct on people with different backgrounds.

9. That it is sociologically weak in failing to provide many of the customs and institutions necessary to a smoothly functioning society.

10. That in spite of its opposition to religion, it has become an established church—with a pope, a priesthood, a theology, a code of ethics and a heaven placed in the future.

11. That it has inspired countless acts of self-sacrificing devotion, but nevertheless has proved to be a religion less satisfactory in many respects than Christianity.

12. That it has failed in practice to provide even a partial check on pride, jealousy, heartlessness and the lust for power.

13. That it has encouraged certain vices, among them fanaticism and hypocrisy, with one set of principles for the ruling caste, another for the Russian masses and still another for sympathetic foreigners.

14. That the published text of the evidence at the Moscow trials, no matter how one interprets it, reveals a widespread moral breakdown.

15. That these faults of the Russian system—emphasized here at the expense of its many virtues—are no justification for advocating social systems based on inherited privilege and revealed religion; a democratic socialism is still our goal.

16. That although the Russian experience casts light on our own problems, these must be solved at home.

These sixteen propositions are not intended as religious dogmas; they are not, like Luther's ninety-seven theses, to be nailed on the doors of a church. Each of them needs to be tested by all the available evidence. They are offered here as the groundwork of a discussion which we plan to continue, and in which we hope that many of our readers will join. In European countries already fighting or threatened by invasion, there is no time to argue about ideas that might serve as a basis for future action; there is only time for action here and now. In this country, however, we still have leisure to make up our minds.

Mr. Eliot's Tract for the Times

T. S. ELIOT also has written a tract for the times, and one intended to have a permanent value. Like Waldo Frank, whose *Chart for Rough Water* I reviewed last week, he believes that the world can be saved only by religion. At this point the resemblance between them begins and ends. The religion proclaimed by Waldo Frank is deeply felt but intellectually vague and never completely defined; it is apparently to be achieved by individual acts of conversion. T. S. Eliot's religion, though also deeply felt, is primarily intellectual and institutional; it is orthodox Anglicanism as set forth in the Thirty-nine Articles.

His book begins by saying that our present society—in the democratic countries—is neither Christian nor pagan; it is negative and therefore essentially unstable. Mr. Eliot believes that it must follow one of two courses. It must either proceed,

"Tract for the Times." A review of *The Idea of a Christian Society*, by T. S. Eliot. New York: Harcourt, Brace and Company. (*NR* June 17, 1940.) Reprinted by permission of *The New Republic*, © 1940, Harrison-Blaine of New Jersey, Inc.

he says, "into a gradual decline of which we can see no end, or (whether as a result of catastrophe or not) reform itself into a positive shape." If that positive shape turns out to be pagan, we shall have inflicted on us "the puritanism of a hygienic morality in the interest of efficiency; uniformity of opinion through propaganda, and art encouraged only when it flatters the official doctrines of the time." The one way of avoiding totalitarianism—the one hope for control, balance and creative activity—is to build for the first time a positive Christian society.

Such a society, Mr. Eliot says, would be completely different from present-day capitalism, under which people have been finding it harder and harder to lead Christian lives. Yet the change would not necessarily be one of government; a Christian society might be a democracy, a monarchy or even a corporative state of the type recommended by the late Pius XI. The rulers of a Christian society might be infidels in their private lives—that would be their own concern—but they would have to accept Christianity as the system under which they governed. The ordinary citizens would accept it as a matter of behavior and habit. But there would have to be a third group, to compensate for the inertia and self-seeking of the others. That group, which Mr. Eliot calls the Community of Christians, would be composed of people distinguished by their intelligence and spiritual devotion. The church itself would include all three groups. It would be established by law, but would remain independent of secular politics and would be united to the Christian churches in other countries. Thus, every citizen would have a double allegiance, "to the State and to the Church, to one's countrymen and to one's fellow Christians everywhere. . . . There would always be a tension, and this tension . . . is a distinguishing mark between a Christian and a pagan society." As the alternative to totalitarianism, Mr. Eliot offers us the dualism of church and state. He insists that his readers should make their choice: "If you will not have God (and He is a jealous God) you should pay your respects to Hitler or Stalin."

To a reader trained in the liberal tradition, the weakness of Mr. Eliot's argument seems to be that he is confusing religion in general with Christianity (and sometimes with the Church of England). The advantages he claims for a Christian state might also be claimed for a Buddhist or Brahman or Mohammedan state; indeed, I suspect that there is a good deal of Buddhist resignation mixed in with Mr. Eliot's orthodoxy. Even liberalism, the frame of mind that he says is leading us to chaos, has of late years developed its own faith, the religion of humanity, which is not a wholly ineffective shield against fascist doctrines. Among Christian sects—with due apologies to Mr. Eliot and the devout Anglicans I knew at college—the Church of England seems one of the most perfunctory and almost the least qualified to create a new world order.

All these are reasons why I did not expect to like *The Idea of a Christian Society,* and yet in the end I was greatly impressed by it. Once you have granted Mr. Eliot his doubtful premises, the rest of his argument moves toward logical conclusions. And you find, even when you are hostile to the main trend of it, that it is full of moderation and worldly wisdom. He does not make Waldo Frank's mistake of expecting too much faith from too many people; nor does he believe that society as a whole can be saved by the conversion of individuals. Although he makes no effort to be original, his statements of more or less familiar ideas often have the force of axioms, like Poor Richard's. "Behavior," he says, "is as potent to affect belief as belief to affect behavior."—"Out of liberalism itself come the philosophies which deny it."—"Good prose cannot be written by a people without convictions."—"If anybody ever attacked democracy, I might discover what the word meant." Sometimes, by approaching a problem from the standpoint of Christian doctrine, he casts an unexpected light on it. "I have never seen any evidence," he says, "that to be a Buchmanite it was necessary to hold the Christian faith according to the Creeds, and until I have seen a statement to that effect I shall continue to doubt whether there is any reason to call Buchmanism a Christian movement."

Mr. Eliot uses the first-person singular pronoun almost as frequently as Waldo Frank, but with a curiously different effect. His is not the prophetic pronoun of "I say unto you," but rather the self-defining and self-deprecating pronoun of expressions like "I am not here concerned," and "I am not qualified to," and "I do not mean primarily." Mr. Eliot's "I" is the least personal pronoun in English literature; it tells us almost nothing about the author except his limitations. Yet one feels from page to page that he would like to express not only his public ideas but also his heart; one feels that strong emotions are being held in check by equally strong convictions. It is this tension between the personal and the impersonal that gives a special quality to all his work, including his poems. Often it lends emotional force to simple statements of fact; and when Mr. Eliot drops his reserve, even for a moment, he impresses us more than another writer might do by screaming and beating his breast. Such a moment of personal confession occurs at the very end of *The Idea of a Christian Society*. There, speaking in his own voice, the author speaks for a whole generation that was betrayed by its statesmen—and by itself—before it heard the German bombers in the skies:

> I believe that there must be many persons who, like myself, were deeply shaken by the events of September, 1938, in a way from which one does not recover; persons to whom that month brought a profounder realization of a general plight. . . . The feeling which was new and unexpected was a feeling of humiliation, which seemed to demand an act of personal contrition, of humility, repentance and amendment; what had happened was something in which one was deeply implicated and responsible. It was not, I repeat, a criticism of the government, but a doubt of the validity of a civilization. We could not match conviction with conviction, we had no ideas with which we could either meet or oppose the ideas opposed to us. . . . Such thoughts as these formed the starting point, and must remain the excuse, for saying what I have to say.

From the Finland Station

TO THE FINLAND STATION took at least six years in the writing and is based on a plan that may have been conceived as early as 1932. That was the year when Edmund Wilson published *The American Jitters*, an account of what he had seen during the second year of the depression. In the course of his travels he had been impressed by the way in which American business was confirming the predictions made by Karl Marx. He was hoping to see this country and the whole world "fairly and sensibly run as Russia is now run, instead of by shabby politicians in the interests of acquisitive manufacturers, business men and bankers." The Russian revolution seemed to him the climax of modern times; and he determined then or shortly afterwards to study the historical theory on which it had been planned and executed.

As he continued working with the idea, it assumed a more definite form. His new book would study the development of historical thinking as a guide to political action. It would begin in 1824, at the moment when Michelet, the great historian of the French revolution, discovered the neglected writings of Vico, who had been the first to say that "the social world is certainly the work of men." From this marriage of revolution and sociology, there was born a new tradition in historical writing, and Wilson planned to follow it through its period of greatness to its decay in the writings of Anatole France. Next he would study a second tradition, that of the Utopian socialists, from Babeuf and Saint-Simon to the Oneida Community. Getting to the heart of his subject, he would tell the story and expound the ideas of Marx and Engels; and finally he would explain how Lenin prepared himself intellectually and morally for the Marxist revolution. The moment of Lenin's arrival at the Finland Station, in Petrograd, would be the moment when the writing of history passed over into the acting of history.

To the Finland Station: A Study in the Writing and Acting of History, by Edmund Wilson. New York: Harcourt, Brace and Company. (*NR*, Oct. 7, 1940.) Reprinted by permission of *The New Republic*, © 1940, Harrison-Blaine of New Jersey, Inc.

The plan was harder to execute and required more extensive reading than Wilson had anticipated. Michelet's *Histoire de France* was only one of a thousand books he had to digest, yet it consists of twenty-seven volumes. The collected works of Marx and Engels are even bulkier, besides requiring closer attention; and the general literature of Marxism, including the quarrels among disciples, is as endless and complicated as the Peloponnesian War. Moreover, Wilson did not confine himself to studying French and English texts. He spent six months in Russia, nearly dying there of scarlet fever; he studied Russian and German in order to read the great Marxists in the original. Always he was finding new sources or revising chapters already written; it seemed that the book would never be completed. Had it been published in 1936 as originally planned, it would have been not only a scholarly study but also a call to action. In 1940 it appears in a different context as a purely historical work, solidly planned, solidly documented, solidly and often brilliantly written.

Perhaps its principal weakness is a defect in structure that goes back to a defect in theory. Michelet plays much too large a part in this book whose destination is the Finland Station. From reading the table of contents, one would assume that it deals with three authors who are in a direct line of succession, and that Marx is based on Michelet in the same fashion that Lenin is based on Marx. No such claim is made in the text; and the truth seems to be that Marx and Lenin would have written the same books and performed the same deeds if Michelet had never lived. The real line of succession runs back from Marx to Hegel, who was most certainly the man responsible for the conception of history as an organic development. That was the conception at the heart of Marx's thinking, as it was later at the heart of Lenin's; yet Hegel receives only passing mention in a book that devotes five chapters to Michelet, a chapter each to Renan, Taine, France, Lassalle, Bakunin, and two chapters to Trotsky.

But the neglect of Hegel does not end with the failure to discuss his ideas at any length or to acknowledge that they helped to shape the historical movement that is the subject of Wilson's book. When Hegel does appear he is presented as a stuffy wizard living in a cloudland far from reality, yet exercis-

ing a baleful influence on Marx. It was from Hegel that Marx
borrowed the idea of thesis, antithesis and synthesis; and this,
Wilson says, was "simply the old Trinity, taken over from the
Christian theology, as the Christians had taken it over from
Plato." In other words, Hegel diverted Marx from science into
supernaturalism; and the result of his influence was that the
whole Marxian theory of historical or dialectical materialism
became "a religious myth, disencumbered of divine personality
and tied up with the history of mankind"—a myth that
differed from Christianity only by lacking the sense of sin and
by situating heaven in the future.

This version of the dialectic, apparently derived from a
book by Max Eastman, is one that Marx and Engels would
have violently rejected. When Engels in his old age was asked
for an explanation of historical materialism, he advised people
"to study the theory from its original sources and not at second
hand. It is really much easier. Marx hardly wrote a thing in
which this theory does not play a part. *The Eighteenth Brumaire of Louis Napoleon* is an especially remarkable example
of its application." Curiously enough, Wilson shares this admiration for *The Eighteenth Brumaire* and indeed for Marx's
historical writing in general, saying that it is "a product of his
mature genius at its most brilliant" and "in fact one of the
great cardinal productions of the modern art-science of history." We are left to assume either that Marx, usually so
perspicacious, deceived himself about his use of the dialectic in
The Eighteenth Brumaire or else that the modern art-science
of history is based on a theological myth.

But the real answer is of course more complicated. The
Marxian dialectic does indeed have the mythical side that
Wilson presents as its only side; its promise of a future heaven
is deceptive. As applied to the natural sciences, it is only a
metaphor. But for statesmen and journalists dealing with contemporary problems, it offers a rough working diagram of the
fashion in which political situations actually develop—that is,
by the growth of contradictions and by "jumps" into new
situations that are qualitatively different. The rise of German
fascism is an excellent example, though it is one that contemporary Marxists are glad to avoid. Moreover, on the theoretical
level, the dialectic is a means of viewing history in motion

instead of at rest; as a process instead of a structure; and as a totality composed of interrelated parts no one of which can be understood without reference to the others. In this broader sense, which Wilson fails to consider, it is at the basis of modern historical thinking, even among the anti-Marxists.

His book has other weaknesses that might be mentioned. For example, it neglects the English economists who preceded Marx, just as it neglects the German metaphysicians. Considering that it is a book dealing with revolutionary leaders, it pays too little attention to the revolutionary masses, by whom the leaders were sometimes led. But these faults are relatively unimportant because they do not interfere with Wilson's real achievement, which lies in a different field from that of economic theory or revolutionary practice.

Essentially it consists in approaching the communist leaders from a new point of view. In one place he observes that "Marx and Engels have been inadequately appreciated as writers" and that there has been a boycott against them "on the part of literary historians as well as on the part of economists." He might have added that Marx and Engels have rarely been written about in good prose; almost always they have been approached in terms of adulation or abuse and—by their followers at least—in a language so purely abstract that it transforms the people with whom it deals into pure theories (Trotskyism, Kautskyism, Machism) and so dogmatic that the unbaptized reader feels as if he had wandered into a secret meeting of the Early Christian Brothers. Wilson is neither abstract nor dogmatic and he does not belong to any sect. He is, I believe, the first to write about Marx and the Marxists in an extraordinary clear and easy-running style, English rather than Latin and distinguished by its use of the sharp detail and the absolutely right quotation. The result is that he has removed the communist fathers from the realm of dogma and carried them into his own world of letters; he has stripped them of the pedantries that covered them as thickly as Marx's whiskers and has revealed them as remarkable men who never ceased to be human beings.

Part of his originality consists in approaching their **work** with the same critical equipment that he formerly applied to Proust and Eliot. The longest and to me the most successful chapter in the book is the one in which he considers *Das Kapital* as a work of art and Marx himself as a "poet of commodities," driven like other poets by selfless aspirations and obscure grudges. Another fine passage deals with Marx's early poems and still another with Lenin as a prose writer. But besides being a critic, Wilson is also a novelist, a dramatist and a poet. He has the novelist's gift for revealing personality in action, the dramatist's gift for bringing characters into conflict, the poet's gift for finding concrete symbols to express abstract ideas and complicated psychological states; and yet he does not give the impression of being specialized in any of these fields. In reality he is something one rarely finds in this country, a generalized man of letters.

Like André Gide, who is also a man of letters and whose later style often makes me think of Wilson, he has a profound respect for moral values that goes back to Protestant ancestors. The quality in Marx that affects him most deeply is "the serenity of moral ascendancy" that appears in his later photographs—"with the deep eyes and the broad brow, the handsome beard and mane, now whitening, that bend from the defiance of the rebel into the authority of the Biblical patriarch." In Lenin he admires "the sure dignity of the respected headmaster who deals directly and frankly with his charges, yet who stands on a higher ground and always preserves a certain distance between him and them." But Lenin himself, Wilson says, was only the greatest of the great Russian revolutionaries, all of whom were trained in a school of repression that developed both intellect and character.

> Forced to pledge for their convictions their careers and their lives, brought by the movement into contact with all classes of people, driven to settle in foreign countries whose languages they readily mastered and whose customs they curiously studied with a quick and realistic observation, compelled by long sojourns in prison to accommodate themselves to the criminal outlaw and therefore to understand him, while the months or the years of confinement in the solitude of the Peter-Paul Fortress or the gloom of the Arctic Circle have imposed upon them the leisure to read and to write—these men and women combine an unusual range of culture with an unusual range of social experience and,

stripped of so many of the trimmings with which human beings have swathed themselves, have, in surviving, kept the sense of those things that are vital to human life.

One could quote page after page from the book without exhausting the good things in it. Yet one feels in reading even the best passages that they would not only have produced a stronger effect but would in themselves have been stronger and sharper if they had been written at some other time. *To the Finland Station* has suffered from the misfortune that threatens any detailed and scholarly treatment of a world issue: the world changed while the scholar was busy among his books. In 1940 Lenin's arrival at the Finland Station has no longer quite the same meaning; part of the drama has gone out of it, and the name of Finland suggests not so much a glorious revolution as a war for railheads and naval bases in which Lenin's heirs tried to copy the heirs of Bismarck.

Wilson himself, changing with the world, has partly lost faith in his own theme. Eight years ago he had written that "Karl Marx's predictions are in process of coming true," but now he is not so certain, and his statement of 1940 is curiously involved and restricted. "What Marx and Engels were getting at, however, was something which, though it may sometimes be played off the stage by the myth of the Dialectic and though an insistence on the problems it raises may seem to reduce it to disintegration, came nevertheless in its day as a point of revolutionary importance and which may still be accepted as partly valid in our own."—"However . . . though . . . and though . . . nevertheless . . . may still be accepted as partly valid"—this is an affirmation so feeble, so undecided in style and content, that it carries the force of a negation. And the same doubts are present throughout the book, so that many of the solidly written pages give the impression of dealing with something in which the author has ceased to be interested.

To the Finland Station is not a book that Wilson would undertake to write in 1940. The question that probably concerns him today, and certainly concerns the rest of us, is not the evolution of communism up to Lenin, but its devolution in the writings and acts of his successors. How was it that the almost selfless revolutionaries of Lenin's day were transformed into (or executed and replaced by) the present Soviet and Comintern officials, the timid and inefficient bureaucrats, the ferocious pedants, the finaglers, the fanatics and the party hacks? They all started out bravely, full of the highest intentions, warned by the mistakes of the past; yet they have made errors far worse than those they condemned in Kautsky or Plekhanov, and the result of their unremitting efforts has been to create a world very different from the one they planned. Where did the original weakness lie—in Lenin, in Marx himself, or in the application of Marx's and Lenin's theories by people who lacked their singleness of purpose and their genius? The book we should like to read today is one that would try to answer these questions. It might be called "From the Finland Station."

The People's Theatre

THESE LAST TWO YEARS have been a period of confessions and self-justifications. By now the publishers' lists are full of books by ex-officers of beaten armies and ex-statesmen of conquered nations; by ex-Nazis who have quarreled with Hitler, ex-Communists who have escaped from the Russian secret police and ex-New Dealers who have decided that Roosevelt wasn't really being fair to businessmen. *Arena* doesn't at all belong in that category, in spite of the fact that Hallie Flanagan is ex-director of the Federal Theatre Project and hence is describing a venture that ended in defeat. Unlike some of the others I have mentioned, she has no apologies to make and no uneasy sense of guilt to conceal. Instead she feels what I think is a wholly justified pride in the work she helped to accomplish, besides gratitude toward most of her collaborators and an immense liking for the actors who worked under her direction—"the best actors in the world," she says, quoting Polo-

Arena, by Hallie Flanagan. New York: Duell, Sloan and Pearce. (*NR*, Jan. 13, 1941.) Reprinted by permission of *The New Republic*, © 1941, Harrison-Blaine of New Jersey, Inc.

nius, "either for tragedy, comedy, history, pastoral, pastoral-comical, historical-pastoral, tragical-historical, tragical-comical-historical-pastoral, scene individable, or poem unlimited." By talking little about herself and a great deal about the Federal Theatre, she gives us an extremely favorable impression of both. And she can write, too, another circumstance that sets her apart from most of the people now publishing their disgruntled memoirs.

Her story reminds us that the Federal Theatre under her direction had three great achievements to its credit. In the first place, it provided steady work for eight thousand penniless theatrical people. That was its primary purpose, under the law setting up the WPA, and was quite enough to justify the money spent on the project. But in the second place, it also brought stage shows, at a low price or none at all, to people who were starved for entertainment and in many cases had never seen a living actor. It gave regional pageants, comedies specially written to be played in the barracks of CCC camps, tent shows, marionette plays for children and Living Newspapers for the broad public; and much of what it did was tied up with the daily lives of people watching the performance. The Federal Theatre was creating an entirely new audience, just as free libraries had created a new audience for books; that explains why the commercial theatre tried hard to defend it later, when it was being attacked in Congress. And in the third place, it produced an astonishing number of good plays, old and new, highbrow and popular, everything from Marlowe and Shakespeare to surrealism and *The Swing Mikado*. It was for a time the center of almost everything that was fresh and experimental on the American stage. More than that, it came closer than anything else we have had—perhaps closer than anything we shall get in the future—to being an American national theatre.

If this is so, how did it happen that the Federal Theatre was stopped after four years, and stopped completely?

To judge by Hallie Flanagan's story, which is charitably written but often quite revealing in its incidental remarks about human motives, the theatre project had the misfortune to focus on itself much of the antagonism aroused by the work-relief program as a whole. And this program, in turn, conflicted with prejudices that lie so deep in American society that they are almost part of a national religion. Americans tend to think that wealth is a divine reward for thrift and self-denial. In the same way, they tended for a long time to regard poverty and unemployment as God's inexorable punishment meted out to the lazy and shiftless. This feeling had changed by the end of Mr. Roosevelt's second term, to the extent that even conservative congressmen were willing to admit, in principle, that the destitute should be fed; perhaps they should even be clothed. But to give them work relief was flying in the face of Providence. And to give them play relief was worse than that, in the eyes of those congressmen: it was an obscene violation of every principle expounded by the Founding Fathers and Horatio G. Alger.

Besides conflicting with ancient doctrines, the Federal Theatre revealed the strength of class hatreds that are usually half-concealed. Since it charged low admissions, it attracted workers and the unemployed—a class of people who, by the standards of prosperous Americans, deserve no entertainment at all, and certainly none provided at public expense. One excuse given for the suppression of *The Federal Theatre Magazine*, in 1937, was that "there was too much emphasis on poor audiences, too many pictures of squatters in Oklahoma and shirt-sleeved crowds in the city parks." The state director for Washington said, "I don't think we should try to get any other class of people except the usual type of theatre-goers, because an audience that looks poor is apt to give the impression of being radical." The adjective most frequently applied to the project was "communistic." The only justification for it was that there were actually a few Communists among the actors employed. Some of them made the position of the project even less secure by working harder for the revolution than for the theatre; that was their duty as they conceived it, but it was shortsighted as a political policy.

A further handicap to the Federal Theatre was the fact of its being involved in the long standing distrust of the lower middle classes for the theatre as a whole. This is a sentiment that survives from the seventeenth century, when the stage, to good Puritans, was not only the devil's workshop but also the chief amusement of their enemies the aristocrats. Thus, the theatre project was damned for its royalist antecedents as well as for its working-class sympathies. And the speeches against it made by some congressmen were also inspired by a violent philistinism, a hatred not only for actors and playwrights but for every human activity faintly tinged with intelligence.

Even this combination of antagonisms might have been evaded if the Federal Theatre had been less successful. The trouble was that some of its plays attracted huge crowds and were widely discussed in the newspapers, so that the resentment against it grew with the publicity. In Washington the bureaucrats began to get frightened; they thought that the quarrel over the theatre project might end by destroying the whole WPA, and with it their own jobs. Miss Flanagan was indirectly warned a hundred times. Several of the state administrators told her that the ideal plays for their jurisdictions would be the sort that didn't get talked about in the papers. After Harry Hopkins left the WPA, more and more trouble descended on her; there was endless obstruction and, though she doesn't use the word, outright sabotage. The wise people among her assistants resigned one after the other, but Miss Flanagan was not wise in that political fashion, and she stayed on in Washington to fight for her beliefs. Until almost the end, she was not even permitted to defend herself and her actors from the irresponsible charges of the Dies and Woodrum Committees. It seems that officials had decided that the theatre project was to be made a scapegoat, in the exact sense of the word—all the sins of the WPA were to be loaded on its back and it was to be publicly stoned to death, in order that other relief projects might live on in happy obscurity.

Looking back over this story she tells so well, with affection and wry humor and a surprising absence of ill feeling for those who made her life miserable, I get a curious impression. I cannot feel that the principal blame for the death of the Federal Theatre rests with the newspapers and magazines that attacked it as a means of "soaking the raw deal." Nor does it rest with the congressmen who hated it so much that they refused to be told the truth about it—not even with Joe Starnes of Alabama, who thought that Christopher Marlowe was a

Communist; maybe he wasn't so far wrong after all, considering that Marlowe belonged to the secret police of Queen Elizabeth's revolutionary government, which Catholic historians tell us was almost as ruthless as Stalin's. Nor does it rest with the bureaucrats in Washington who were quite willing to sacrifice the project so long as their own jobs were saved. The curious impression I get is that the principal blame rests with ourselves—with you the reader, and me the writer, in so far as we represent progressive opinion in the United States.

We liked the idea of the Federal Theatre; we went to some of the plays when they were sufficiently recommended by Brooks Atkinson of *The New York Times* (whose record was much better than our own), and at the very end, when it was too late, we perhaps signed protests against its suppression. That has been the career of too many progressive people, signing indignant protests when it was too late. Afterwards we were properly regretful and perhaps wrote editorials ridiculing Mr. Starnes of Alabama. But during the four preceding years, when we might have helped to build up a sentiment for the Federal Theatre so strong that Congress would not have dared to abolish it; when we might have proved to Mr. Roosevelt that his always good intentions were receiving wide popular approval, we had done, well, not exactly nothing, but not really enough to matter.

And, in a sense, this failure is typical of the whole decade that has just ended. In 1933 progressive opinion in America received a chance that it had never been given before—a President in sympathy with its aims and a business community so frightened that for once it was willing to accept liberal measures. Brave things were done in the following years, but not enough of them; and some of the bravest attempts were permitted to fail through lack of intelligent support. The progressives had their chance and most of them lost it—sometimes because they failed to see it, sometimes because they saw but failed to grasp it, and sometimes because they were so busy quarreling among themselves that after grasping it they let it slip from their hands. The story would have been different if more of us had been as imaginative and hard-working and self-forgetful as Hallie Flanagan.

The Michael Golden Legend

THERE WAS SOMETHING to be explained, an apparent defeat for the Communist movement, and a myth about it had to be created. During the 1930's, first scores and then hundreds of American writers had accepted Communist doctrines and, what is more, had written and acted on their new beliefs. Although few of them had joined the Communist Party, many had acknowledged its leadership, and the Party liked to put them on display. Then, in the early 1940's, most of these semiconverts had turned against Party policies; they had continued to attack Hitler and even to call for war against him at a time when good Communists were silent about Hitler and were saying that Churchill and Roosevelt were the great enemies of the revolution. How could this process of partial conversion and total alienation be presented for the benefit of the still faithful? There had to be a story that would fit into the general body of Communist legends, a mock-heroic myth that would absolve the Party of its errors while covering the renegades with shame and ridicule.

It was Michael Gold who furnished the necessary myth. His series of articles in the *Daily Worker* was expanded into a short book, *The Hollow Men,* which has been enthusiastically reviewed in the Party press. Last month at the American Writers' Congress, his story was further embroidered by Samuel Sillen of the *New Masses,* and Sillen's speech in its turn was warmly applauded by the delegates. I have not heard that anyone cast doubt on a word of it.

Here is the myth, as Mr. Gold presents it. The 1920's had been a vulgar and futile period dominated by the prose of H. L. Mencken and the poetry of T. S. Eliot, both parvenus. Then came the crash of 1929, and the followers of Eliot found themselves intellectually as well as financially bankrupt, while the Menckenites were jumping out of penthouse windows. Having gambled and lost their money, writers at last discovered their ties with the working class. It was, however, the Communist Party which provided a pattern and philosophy

First published in Klaus Mann's monthly magazine, *Decision,* July 1941.

for their otherwise formless disillusionment. Thousands of
intellectuals found themselves attracted to Marxism as the
answer to their own problems; and when a congress of American writers was called in 1935, under Communist leadership, it
proved to be the nucleus of a great cultural movement. The
government was forced to create the Federal Arts Projects.
What followed was a period of fruitful activity in all fields, of
high achievements in fiction, of brilliant criticism, of a new
audience for poetry and plays—in brief, an American renaissance. It lasted, says Mr. Gold, "until Roosevelt came to his last
gasp as a liberal in 1940, and the Franks and Mumfords joined
him in scuttling the bread and culture of the American people,
in favor of an imperialist war."

But why did the Franks and Mumfords and hundreds of
other writers turn against Communism? Mr. Gold sweeps
aside the many good reasons they have offered, claiming that
these are hypocritical excuses. His own explanation, given at
great length, is that the middle-class intellectuals really hate
and fear the people. They have a deep strain of lackeyism that
makes them always subservient to the great. This is, he says,
"the heart of all petty-bourgeois renegadism, from the Granville Hickses and Edmund Wilsons down to the mangiest
yellow dog who ever peddled his honor and his *Confessions of
an Ex-Communist* to Hearst and the Dies Committee for
thirty silver dollars." And the results of their treachery are
now, he believes, apparent in our cultural life. The renaissance
of the 1930's is coming to a tragic end; most books and plays
are thoroughly trivial; the pro-British intellectuals are preparing the way for an American fascism. "We seem to be entering
a twilight zone, obscure and sinister as that which was lit only
by the Nazi bonfires that burned the books." But Mr. Gold
ends his story on a note of rather forced optimism, assuring us
that the renegades are only a small minority, "the darkness
against which the heroic profile of the People is more strongly
limned." The People will rise again

> . . . *like Lions after slumber*
> *In unvanquishable number—*

while the petty-bourgeois renegades go scuttling off to their
holes.

This story has the advantage of strong and simple outlines, of bright colors and deep shadows, like a Currier and Ives print. It has the advantage of Mr. Gold's slapdash energy and his gift for withering phrases—for example, the editors of *The New Republic* are "men with perpetual slight colds" and Lewis Mumford is "a pure spirit . . . who lives in a cave on coarse goat cheese and an occasional nut." Most of all, it has the advantage of his deep religious feeling, his abiding faith in Communism as the militant and soon to be triumphant Church. Indeed, for all his insistence that Communism is not a religion, his whole argument can be reduced to terms of Christian theology. Thus, during the 1930's, great progress was made by the Church on Earth, which was ushering in a golden age. But a period of hardship was sent by Providence (that is, by history) in order to test men's souls. The Elect (that is, the workers) stood firm as always. But the Laodiceans (that is, the intellectuals) were weighted down by their burden of Original Sin, which to Mr. Gold is the surviving taint in them of bourgeois standards. They had, moreover, lost Divine Grace (that is, the discipline of the Communist Party), and hence they fell into temptation, with the result that their last state is worse than their first. Yea, verily, "the venom of the apostate is an old horror in the soul of man. . . . There is a disintegration of personality and the renegade loses much of his humanity, and can no longer distinguish good from evil." Let others be warned, lest by chance they follow the same steep path into the abyss.

Quite apart from the theological nature of this legend—which provides no test of its truth or falsehood—there are several points at which it departs from the real events that many of us remember.

In the first place, Mr. Gold starts out by putting entirely too much emphasis on the private financial affairs of writers. It is a grotesque mistake to imply that they were attracted to Communism in the beginning because "nearly everyone" in the literary world had been gambling and had lost his money in the Wall Street crash. Most writers had no money to lose, and among those who had it and lost it I personally knew of

only one who became a Communist, although there may well
have been half a dozen others. Nor is it true that writers
changed their political beliefs because "publishers failed, taking the royalties of authors down with them"; only one failure, that of Horace Liveright, caused any serious hardship.
Nor is it true that they became radical because "magazines
retrenched or were wiped out," or for any other reason solely
dependent on their personal incomes. Mr. Gold is trying to
draw the customary parallel between poverty and radicalism.
In the American literary world of the 1930's such a relationship simply did not exist.

What do we learn from the actual record? In the early
years of the depression, there was much talk about revolution
in the literary slums east and west of Greenwich Village, but
there was even more talk about it in Park Avenue drawing-
rooms. The first large group of writers to "go left" was composed of boys and girls in their twenties who had joined the
John Reed Clubs; at that time they had scarcely seen their
names in print. The second group was composed of men whose
position was fairly secure—editors, professors, novelists, sala-
ried critics—in other words, people who could afford the risk of
joining committees organized under Party sponsorship. The
third group—but there is no use continuing the catalogue. At
all times during the decade, the membership of literary organizations close to the Party was changing; at no time after the
death of the John Reed Clubs was it composed chiefly of the
impoverished or unsuccessful. Quite on the contrary, the authors most friendly to Moscow were likely to be the authors of
best-selling novels and autobiographies, of plays that were
smash hits on Broadway; or again they were Hollywood script
men struggling along on a thousand dollars a week while
contributing a tithe of their earnings to Spain or China or
Harry Bridges in order to maintain their self-respect at the
risk of their jobs. Communism in the American literary world
has usually involved financial sacrifices for individuals. It has
been a luxury that could most easily be afforded by the well-to-
do or by those so poor that they had nothing to lose, and both
these classes were represented in the movement. During the
People's Front period, however, the more impoverished writers were beginning to desert it in order to join what Mr. Gold

likes to call "the Zinoviev-Bukharin-Trotskyite gang of wreckers, assassins, saboteurs and Fifth Columnists."

In the beginning it was the economic situation of the country as a whole, and not of writers as individuals, that led them to adopt radical ideas. As individuals they were puzzled, yet they were eager to perform their duty if only they could be sure what it was. They were asking themselves questions of a fundamentally religious nature—what is the purpose of all this suffering? or, how can we help to create a more sensible society? or again, how can the world be saved from war and fascism? One reason why the Communist Party became influential was that it seemed to provide all the answers. And its influence began to wane among writers with the coming of new events to which its answers had ceased to apply.

A second point at which Mr. Gold departs from reality is in his entirely too glowing picture of the cultural renaissance and of the Communist share in producing it. A sort of renaissance there was, and it is now being unjustly disparaged by critics eager to celebrate a new period at the expense of the immediate past. Most branches of American literature were flourishing; almost the only exceptions were poetry and strictly imaginative writing. The 1930's were a vigorous age for criticism, an experimental age for the drama, a really brilliant age for the realistic novel. And the Communists played a great part in this activity, especially at first; their doctrines helped to deepen the sympathies of novelists and broaden their intellectual horizons.

But in the last years of the decade, those doctrines began to seem confining. The change came about for several reasons, some of them connected with the new political atmosphere in Moscow. For the first time, the Russian government had adopted an official theory of esthetics which all the artists in sympathy with Communism were expected to follow. Socialist realism was not in itself a bad theory as applied to the novel, though in painting and music it produced some lamentable effects. The real trouble was that it demanded the suppression of all other theories as anti-democratic and even counter-revolutionary; in practice it was hostile to any sort of writing that could not be understood by the broad masses. All these remarks apply to socialist realism in Russia. When imported to the United States, it proved especially embarrassing to poets, whose literary training demanded that they write in one tradition whereas their political training demanded that they write in another; the result was that they wrote nothing very well. But even the novelists connected with the Communist movement were made to feel that there were certain ideas they shouldn't express. A doctrine that began by liberating writers had ended by making them even more academic and inhibited than before.

Mr. Gold also departs from the simple facts in his attempt to explain why so many intellectuals became renegades to Communism. Searching for ultimate answers, he goes far back into history, while neglecting the events of the last five years. He has nothing to say about the Russo-German pact or the invasion of Finland. When he mentions the fall of France, it is only to condemn "the Lavals, Daladiers, Blums and Reynauds"—what a curious combination!—for having oppressed the French workers. He believes that these events and the Moscow trials had no real effect on writers' minds; they are being used merely as "political alibis"; they are "theatrical masks concealing a deep and more prominent truth; a class truth." He therefore embarks on an extended search for this truth, quoting at length from Dostoevsky's notebooks, and from the official *History of the Communist Party* (for the reaction in Russia that followed the revolution of 1905), and from the wartime writings of Randolph Bourne. He gives the impression that Dostoevsky's world and the revolution of 1905 and the First World War are much more real to him than the events that are now taking place. He cannot admit to his readers or himself that we are facing a new situation. Everything can still be explained for him by an official and time-hallowed text—as if, in a time of troubles, he turned back to his well-thumbed Bible.

And this mental inertia, so typical of the Communist movement today, is what distresses me in his story. His silly and complacent attitude toward the war—an attitude he continued to hold until the moment when Hitler crossed the Russian border—is only the symptom of a weakness that lies deeper in his mind. Mr. Gold and others like him seem to have lost the capacity for fresh observation or independent thinking; they wait for directives from Moscow, and if new directives fail to come, they simply follow the old ones. Fascism, he tells us in two places, is "a tightening of the rule of monopoly capitalism, by any and all means, including the destruction of democratic forms. That is what the Communists said ten years ago, and what they said today." It is a sublime faith speaking here, without recourse to worldly evidence, and it is a faith that Hitler shattered in one day. As another example of inertia, consider Mr. Gold's remarks on America's part in the struggle. Lenin had said that the war of 1914 was a war of empire, conducted by the monopolists of all the countries concerned. Therefore, "if the social characteristics of that war now repeat themselves in America, it must be because the same monopolists are again in control." It *must* be, in spite of the demonstrable fact that many monopolists have been trying to appease Hitler; it *must* be, for otherwise Lenin's writings would have to be revised. Rather than finding new theories to meet a new situation, the Communists have preferred to believe that the situation merely repeats the past; then the old theories can still be used. And, until Russia was invaded, they displayed a curious affection for the word "merely." A world that is our own world is dying before our eyes, and they have insisted on telling us that it is *merely* something that has always happened, *merely* a reason for standing aloof, *merely* an event to be tagged and dismissed with a phrase from Lenin's *Imperialism*.

A few nights ago, I began thinking of a book that I had read twice in my boyhood: *The Lost World*, by Sir Arthur Conan Doyle. As I remember it now, it was a story about a group of scientists who discovered a line of almost unscalable cliffs in the Amazonian jungle. Reaching the top by what means I forget, they found a humid region in which the great saurians had survived from the Mesozoic era. And it occurred to me on reading *The Hollow Men* that the United States today was a lost world, like the one imagined by Conan Doyle. Here, in an especially favored location, protected by two oceans that take the place of the Amazonian jungle, an older civilization has survived that almost everywhere else is in full collapse. Here very ancient animals continue to flourish—not the brontosaurs or stegosaurs or *tyrannosaurus rex,* but rather Henry Ford and Norman Thomas, Oswald Garrison Villard, Senator Taft, General Wood and Comrade Michael Gold. These prehistoric monsters are not friendly to one another; they meet and growl and fight and sometimes are killed, while their enemies feast on their bodies; but all of them were produced by the same conditions and depend for their survival on the same biological environment—yes, all of them, flesh-eating capitalists and liberals like peaceful herbivores and Communists sailing through the air on leathery wings like pterodactyls; all of them resemble the saurians at the beginning of a colder and dryer age in having lost their power of adaptation. Yet all of them, however much they differ on other subjects, are determined to believe that their lost world will continue to exist. That is the basis, that is the meaning of the Michael Golden legend.

THE *Literary* RECORD

2

A Preface to Hart Crane

"THE POETRY of Hart Crane is ambitious," said Allen Tate at the beginning of his valuable introduction to *White Buildings*. Four years later, in reviewing Crane's second book of poems, I can only make the statement again, but this time for a different reason. The ambitiousness of his earlier work was shown partly in tone, in its assumption of the grand manner, and partly in its attempt to crowd more images into each poem—more symbols, perceptions and implications—than any few stanzas could hold or convey. The result in some cases was a sort of poetic shorthand which even the most attentive readers could understand with difficulty. In this second volume, merely by making the poems longer, he has made them vastly more intelligible. His ambition, which has grown with his achievement, is now shown in his choice of subject.

The Bridge is a unified group of fifteen poems dealing primarily with Brooklyn Bridge. But the bridge itself is treated as a symbol: it is the bridge between past and future, between Europe and the Indies; it is the visible token of the American continent. And, although this book of poems—this one massive poem divided into eight sections and fifteen chants —begins with a modest apostrophe to a bridge over the East River, it ends bravely as an attempt to create the myth of America.

We might well conclude that such an attempt was foredoomed to failure. An ambitious subject is by definition a subject rich in platitudes; nor is this its only danger. A poet who chooses such a theme and who, by power of imagination or intensity of feeling, escapes the platitudinous, is tempted to assume the role of a messiah. Many ambitious poems are both messianic and commonplace, but *The Bridge*, I think, is neither. In its presumptuous effort the poem has succeeded— not wholly, of course, for its faults are obvious; but still it has succeeded to an impressive degree.

The faults of *The Bridge* I shall leave to other reviewers.

The Bridge, a Poem, by Hart Crane. Limited edition. Paris: The Black Sun Press. Trade edition. New York: Horace Liveright. (*NR*, Apr. 23, 1930.)

As for the causes of its artistic success, they are not mysterious; they are complicated. They depend on the structure of the volume as a whole, which in turn is too elaborate, too much a fabric of interwoven strands, to be explained in the present review. Instead of advancing a few vague statements, I prefer to suggest Crane's general method by describing in detail one of the fifteen poems. But which? . . . The poem that suggests itself is possibly his best; probably it is one of the important poems of our age, but it is not immeasurably better than others in the book—"Cutty Sark," for example, or "The Dance," or "Ave Maria"—and its method is neither too simple nor too complex to be typical of his work. Let us confine ourselves, then, to "The River."

It occurs in the second section of the book, a section bearing the name of Pocahontas, whom the poet has chosen as an earth-symbol to represent the body of the American continent. She also represents its Indian past. The section dedicated to her consists of five poems, each of which progresses farther into the continent and into the past, till the Indian tradition fuses, in the fifth poem, with that of the settlers. It should be noted, however, that the progression is not geographical or historical: it is a progressive exploration of the poet's mind. Thus, in the first poem of the series, he awakens to the dim sounds of the harbor at dawn; in the second he walks to the subway attended by the imaginary figure of Rip Van Winkle. In the fourth poem, he will picture a corn-dance held by the Indians before the first settlers landed on the marshy banks of the James. The third poem, with which we are dealing to the exclusion of the others, must serve as a link between the second and the fourth —between present and past, between New York City and the Appalachian tribes. Thus, it must have a movement both temporal and spatial, a movement like that of a river; and the subject Crane has chosen to perform this double function is the Mississippi.

His treatment of the subject is oblique; he does not proceed logically, but rather by associations of thought, by successive emotions. Since the preceding poem has ended in a subway, it seems emotionally fitting to begin the present one, not on the Mississippi itself, but on a train westbound from Manhattan into the heart of the continent. From the windows of the Twentieth Century Limited, the poet watches the billboards drifting past. And the first eighteen lines of this long poem are a phantasmagoria of pictures and slogans, an insane commentary on modern life, an unstable world as seen in glimpses by a moving observer.

Suddenly the angle of vision changes. The poet is no longer on the train; he is standing beside three ragged men "still hungry on the tracks . . . watching the taillights wizen." The rhythm of the poem changes at the same moment: it is no longer nervous and disconnected; it settles down to the steady pedestrian gait of hoboes plodding along a railroad. The next ninety-three lines, by far the longest section of the poem, will deal with the Odyssey of these unshaven men, "wifeless or runaway," of whom Crane once said in explaining his methods: "They are the leftovers of the pioneers. . . . Abstractly, their wanderings carry the reader through certain experiences roughly parallel to those of the traders and adventurers, Boone and others."

From the long passage that deals with these wanderings, I remember many lines, some for their vividness or wit, some for their music, and some for the imaginative quality that is poetry in the strictest sense:

> "*There's no place like Booneville though, Buddy,*"
> *One said, excising a last burr from his vest,*
> "*For early trouting. . . .*"

> *John, Jake or Charley, hopping the slow freight*
> *—Memphis to Tallahassee—riding the rods,*
> *Blind fists of nothing, humpty-dumpty clods.*

> *—They know a body under the wide rain;*
> *Youngsters with eyes like fjords, old reprobates*
> *With racetrack jargon—dotting immensity,*
> *They lurk across her, knowing her yonder breast*
> *Snow-silvered, sumac-stained or smoky blue—*

Lurking across immensity, they wander wherever the Mississippi "drinks the farthest dale." In Ohio, "behind my father's cannery works," they squat in a circle beside the tracks. They remember "the last bear, shot drinking in the Dakotas." Drifting through the Missouri highlands, they linger where—

Under the Ozarks, domed by Iron Mountain,
The old gods of the rain lie wrapped in pools—

and inevitably they gather at Cairo, where the waters gather. "For," says the poet addressing these belated pioneers—"For you, too, feed the River timelessly." The poem, after wandering over half the country, has found its proper subject. And at this point the rhythm changes once more; it becomes slower, more liquid; and finally, in a series of eight majestic quatrains, the river and the poem flow southward together, passing De Soto's burying place, passing "the City storied of three thrones," and mingling with the Gulf.

Even from this bare outline of one poem, one can glimpse the qualities by which the ambition of the volume is transformed into realization. Here is the conceptual imagination that resolves a general subject into an individual experience— one which it again dissolves into something universal and timeless. Here is the concrete imagination that reveals itself in terms of sound, color and movement. Here, lastly, is the constructive imagination that makes each separate poem play its part in a larger plan. As for the place of "The River" in this plan, I think I have shown that it succeeds in the two functions it was called upon to perform. At the same time, considered apart from the volume as a whole, it has a life of its own; and it has a separate structure also, one which might be compared to that of an ideal Chrysler Building. Just as the building stands broadly in a rubble of houses, narrows to a tower, rises implacably story after story, and finally soars upward in one clean shaft; so the poem, which began as a crazy jumble of prose and progressed by narrowing circles into the Great Valley, develops finally into a slow hymn to the river, a celebration of the Mississippi as it pours "down two more turns—"

And flows within itself, heaps itself free.
All fades but one thin skyline round. . . . Ahead
No embrace opens but the stinging sea.
The River lifts itself from its long bed,

Poised wholly on its dream, a mustard glow
Tortured with history, its one will—flow!
—The Passion spreads in wide tongues, choked and slow,
Meeting the Gulf, hosannas silently below.

Cummings: The Last of Lyric Poets

E. E. CUMMINGS, the son of a Cambridge minister, attended Harvard University during a period which has never been properly described, that of the Harvard esthetes. It followed the period of Jack Reed and Walter Lippmann, when socialism had a brief vogue at Harvard and H. G. Wells was perhaps the most popular author. The esthetes, for their part, had no interest whatever in social problems. They read Casanova's memoirs and *Les Liaisons Dangereuses,* both in the original French, and Petronius in Latin; they gathered at teatime in one another's rooms, or at punches in the offices of *The Harvard Monthly;* they drank seidels of dry gin topped with a maraschino cherry; they discussed the music of Pater, the rhythms of Aubrey Beardsley and, growing louder, the voluptuousness of the Church, the essential virtue of prostitution. They had crucifixes in their bedrooms, and ticket-stubs from last Saturday's burlesque at the Old Howard. They were trying to create in Cambridge, Mass., an after-image of Oxford in the eighteen-nineties. They wrote, too; dozens of them were promising poets, each with his invocation to Antinous, his mournful descriptions of Venetian lagoons, his sonnets to a chorus girl in which he addressed her as "little painted poem of God." Most of this bustle would soon be overwhelmed in the vaster bustle of the War; but Cummings, like his friend Dos Passos, would have a different fortune. It was precisely the emotions evoked by the War that stimulated him into a period of enormous productivity.

The War, of course, was only a partial explanation; there were also technical reasons for his sudden flowering. The technical problem obsessing all the esthetes, in the midst of their simultaneous gestures toward sin and salvation, was that of originality—how, after three thousand years of written literature, to say anything new, or anything old in a new way. Many of them were inclined to deal with experiences so marginal as to have been neglected by writers of the past; others tried to achieve originality through scholarship, a department in which

VV (Viva), by E. E. Cummings. New York: Horace Liveright. (*NR*, Jan. 27, 1932.)

the modern writer can obtain an easy advantage over his predecessors. Neither of these solutions appealed to Cummings.
Fundamentally he is a lyric poet, in the tradition, let us say, of
Catullus and François Villon and Robert Burns. His message
is their message: that life is vastly enjoyable, and the world
beautiful in spring; that he loves Lady X or Madam Y as
nobody has loved anybody; that "a pretty girl who naked is, is
worth a million statues"; that death comes strolling through
the April fields, "also picking flowers." About the time he
sailed for France, early in 1917, he had discovered that these
old truths could be expressed in other terms—those of "roses
and locomotives (not to mention acrobats Spring electricity
Coney Island the 4th of July the eyes of mice and Niagara
Falls)." He was inventing a new language, an E. E. Cum-
mingsese, in which he would soon be able to personalize the
most familiar emotions. And War conspired with technique by
conferring a new value on the commonplace.

Having sailed for France in April of the same year, I can
remember moments when the senses were immeasurably
sharpened by the thought of dying next day, or possibly next
week. The trees about me were green, not like ordinary trees,
but like trees in the still instant before a hurricane; the sky was
a special and ineffable blue: the grass smelled of life itself; the
image of death at twenty, the image of love, mingled together
into a keen, precarious delight. It is the virtue of Cummings'
poems to capture and accurately preserve the color of moments
like this, to guard them from mutilation by the blunt hands of
time, to save them from the cloudburst of shrapnel which, in
another instant, will obliterate love and sky.

The five years after 1918 were a period of fertility which
seems all the more remarkable when we reflect that Cummings
devoted probably half of his working hours to painting or
drawing, and that, during the remaining time, he completed
The Enormous Room, besides writing an uncomputable number of poems—more than enough, in any case, to fill the four
books of verse he published between 1923 and 1926. Let us
admit that the mere standard of quantity is meaningless: we
have all known poets who could turn out four passable sonnets
of an afternoon and fall asleep in the evening over the twenty-
seventh line of a ballade. The impressive thing about Cum-

mings during those postwar years is not so much the number of poems he wrote as the number of his experiments, inventions, real discoveries. But periods like this, which occur in the lives only of fortunate poets, are likely to be of short duration. When verses no longer rouse the poet from sleep and write themselves before coffee in the morning, demanding only to be corrected; when fresh images no longer confront him like landscapes from a pullman window; when he has ceased to be the mere stenographer of the muses, he may possibly turn from poetry, as poetry has turned from him; or he may, on the other hand, go struggling consciously, by an effort of will, toward the greater achievements that lie in front of him. In the second case, what methods will he adopt, what direction will he follow?

To this question, *Viva* provides a sort of answer—neither heartening nor at all discouraging, not very definite, in fact, but still an answer.

The book contains seventy poems, some consisting of four lines, others of forty, but each of them printed on a separate page so as to present a separate picture. Thanks to the author's arrangement of lines and to S. A. Jacobs' typography, these pictures are generally pleasing. Every seventh page-picture, including the sixty-third, is a sonnet; the last seven form a group of sonnets. The poems were written in different years; many are obviously recent; more, perhaps, are older poems recently revised. Technically, they show a development toward a more arbitrary and geometrical use of language, toward greater ingenuity and complexity—in other words, toward the calligram and the cryptogram.

The word "calligram" has come to have a meaning hardly justified by its two Greek roots: it is applied to an arrangement of words that pictures the thing described, like the mouse's tale in *Alice*. Poem XLV in the present volume deals, for example, with a man looking in winter through a dirty windowpane. The poem is printed in the shape of a diamond, like an old pane of glass. Poem XXXVIII describes a thunder shower, and its typography is lightning-jagged as it tells how the world "iS Slapped: with; liGhtninG." There have been critics who defended this aberrant typography on the ground of its being an aid to the reader—giving, as they say it gives, the exact timing and pronunciation of each word. But how, precisely, is one to pronounce "liGhtninG"? Or the word "n, o; w:" occurring in the same poem—how can it be read aloud as written? The conclusion is that the typography of these words has no relation to the sound of them; the effect intended is purely pictorial. They are more or less successful calligrams.

As for the cryptogrammatic tendency in Cummings' poems, it can generally be identified with his effort to be "simultaneous." Thus, instead of writing his sentences or phrases in their logical order, he is likely to divide two or three of them into fragments, which are then shuffled together and repeated in a single breath. Sometimes the device is wholly effective, as in the poem describing how he stood outside his door at twilight, with his lady, and watched a flying bat. The last lines read, when printed as prose, "i say 'won't you' (remembering) knowing that you are afraid 'go first' of dreams and little bats & mice (and you, you say 'let's' going in 'take hands' smiling 'coming up these dark stairs')." It requires no serious adjustment on the part of the reader to understand that the lady is not afraid of "go first," but merely of dreams and little animals. Sometimes, however, the poet offers a more difficult problem by dividing words instead of phrases, and by jumbling their parts like syllables drawn from a hat. The reader's perplexities are further increased by Cummings' trick of making some words serve two simultaneous purposes, of omitting other words entirely, and of writing whole phrases in a medium which Kenneth Burke described as "fonetty kinglish"—though here it is likely to be a more or less phonetic transcription of French words as currently pronounced in New York. It takes a deal of puzzling to decide that "Lays aytash unee" is simply "les Etats-Unis"; it takes more puzzling to discover that "the hoe tell days are teased" means something after all, being the name of the studio building on Sixty-seventh Street where Harry Crosby committed suicide. When these various forms of cryptography are combined with Cummings' tendency toward making calligrams, it is sometimes impossible to decipher the result.

But the general obscurity of Cummings' work is easy to exaggerate. In *Viva* there are only three poems—including the first—which baffled me completely. There are about a dozen others which had to be untangled like a fishing line. The remaining poems—fifty or more—should present no difficulty to the careful reader. It is quite possible, in fact, to write a criticism of Cummings without any reference to his famous unintelligibility.

He is a wit: this much is apparent in all his work, and one finishes *Viva* with the conviction that he is one of the wittiest poets in the English language. He is a satirist, too, as bitter and biting as anyone since Pope: witness his lines on the death of President Harding and his apostrophe to blond Olaf, the conscientious objector. He is depending more on anger— against politicians, officials, soldiers, against literary fakirs, against humanity in general—as a source of poetry. He is paying more attention to public matters like Einstein's theory and the Russian revolution, but his reaction to them remains private and unsocial. When (in "is 5") he describes a riot between Communists and policemen, his sympathy is with the first, but for reasons inacceptable to the Communists—because they "have very fine eyes. Some are young, some old, none look alike"; whereas the policemen, "tidiyum, are very tidiyum reassuringly similar." In general he remains the poet of love and death, of flowers under the April rain, of moments whose freshness can never be duplicated. More than ever, he is able to record these momentary emotions in memorable lines—iambic-pentameter lines, the most familiar and difficult medium in English. I doubt that any of his contemporaries could have written verses like these:

> *put off your faces, Death: for day is over*
>
> .   .   .   .
>
> *day being come, Love, put on your faces.*
>
> *prouder than all mountains, more than all*
> *oceans various*
>
> *the voice of your eyes is deeper than all roses*
> *nobody, not even the rain, has such small hands.*

This rebel, this innovator—and here is the paradox—is distinguished by his fidelity to the subject matter of lyric poetry through the ages, and by his ability to write in that heroic meter which has been the basis of English poetry since Chaucer. His experiments and inventions are in most cases too personal to be of service to other poets, except as a general example of courage. What chiefly impresses the reader of his best poems is the thought that he is perhaps the end of a great tradition.

There is at present no real doubt that lyric poetry is losing the vitality it once possessed. One would hesitate to say that it faces unfriendly criticism; hardly anybody bothers to attack it; the malady from which it suffers is lack of conviction on the part of its friends. Somehow the focus of interest has shifted. The question whether Miss Y and Mr. X will end by sleeping together still agitates the minds of individual poets, but they are coming to regard it as a private matter, not to be dignified with a memorable sonnet; either they translate their concerns into regions of high philosophy, like Mr. Eliot, or else they write about more public issues. I have known a poet somewhat younger than Cummings who discovered that he had irrevocably lost the woman in whom his life was centered; he stumbled home and wrote, with tears gumming the keys of his typewriter, an elegy on the death of Rosa Luxemburg. Once I asked him what he thought of Cummings. He said, "A fine poet, a very fine poet, but, I mean—there's nothing more up that street."

Kenneth Burke: Unwilling Novelist

THE AUTHOR began this book with the intention of writing a novel; he ended by writing a novel in spite of his most diligent efforts. Between this beginning and this ending there intervened a long process of thought which is partially described in the preface. Three times, Burke says, he sat down to write the opening scene, a conversation in a Greenwich Village speakeasy. Two men conversed "for a fitting period, telling each other a few things which it was very necessary for the reader to know; a bell rang, the waiter's steps could be heard

Towards a Better Life, by Kenneth Burke. New York: Harcourt, Brace and Company. (*NR*, Feb. 17, 1932.)

going down the hall, a peephole was opened; next the slinging of a bolt, then the unlatching of an iron grate; the newcomer, after low-voiced words at the door, could be heard striding along the hall; he entered the room where the two men were talking; 'Hello,' he said—and for the third time your author tossed Chapter One into the discard."

For the qualities that distinguish the ordinary novel—for suspense, verisimilitude, headlong action, the feeling of immediate participation in events of an exciting nature—Burke felt himself to be unfitted by temperament. He had no interest whatever in the problem of getting people in and out of situations, in and out of doors. The problem on which he was working was that of rendering emotion. "Lamentation, rejoicing, beseechment, admonition, sayings and invective—these seemed to me central matters, while a plot in which they might occur seemed peripheral, little more than a pretext, justified not as 'a good story,' but only in so far as it could bring these six characteristics to the fore." In order to focus attention on them, "I reversed the process, emphasizing the essayistic rather than the narrative, the emotional predicaments of my hero rather than the details by which he arrived at them. . . . In form the resultant chapters are somewhat like a sonnet sequence, a progression by stages, by a series of halts." And yet these chapters, these eighteen "epistles or declamations," together make a true novel—with plot, movement, suspense, verisimilitude and, at the end, a feeling of participation in a terrifying tragedy.

This novel, however, is of a sort that is almost unknown in English letters and rarely encountered even in France. Its great prototype, the one book to which, in spite of all differences, it bears a striking spiritual resemblance, is *A Rebours*. Huysmans, in his most famous novel, was concerned with the search for refuge of a man incapable of living in society. Despising the people of his time, both the bourgeois and the aristocrats, the skeptical and the devout, this hero devoted the remnants of his ducal fortune to the task of creating an individual paradise, a paradise of the senses. It took the shape of a house on the outskirts of Paris. Here, in the midst of erudite pictures, flesh-eating plants and fantastic Latin authors, the owner lived in the company of his dreams, trying feverishly to enjoy himself in spite of the real and imaginary diseases that made him a slave to the doctors, and hence to society as a whole.

The story of *Towards a Better Life* is essentially the same. John Neal, like Jean des Esseintes, despises the people about him, the successful ones blind to their own abjectness, the tame radicals who can safely be admitted to bankers' houses "like castrated lion whelps." Incapable of living in society, he determines to create an individual refuge, and goes about this task by methods proper to himself. He is too intelligent to believe that he can build a physical paradise by decorating any house whatever with books, paintings and hallucinations; he is in fact wholly indifferent to his physical surroundings. His refuge will be mentally constructed and will be defended by two categories of thinking. First, he will transvaluate all values, so that the busy, complacent people about him are shown to be mentally sluggish, morally evasive, while he himself, the ingrate and smell-feast, assumes his true role as an active and courageous prophet. Second, he will protect himself from misfortune by running forward to meet it, or else by imagining worse catastrophes than could ever occur, so that real blows will fall upon him harmlessly.

He is in love with Florence and yet, when a happier man pays court to her, he contrives that his rival shall triumph. Since this rival is rich, Neal squanders his little fortune to give the impression of having a great one. Then, taking flight to an unknown village, he marries and becomes a local dignitary. Florence reënters his life; she is traveling from county seat to county seat with a company of penniless actors and is ready, now, to accept John Neal's advances; but he, on discovering that she has been deserted by his rival, dismisses her also—and thereupon feels that a chapter in his life is definitely ended. He wanders back to New York with a girl named Genevieve, always lamenting, rejoicing, beseeching, admonishing and inveighing, always rich in aphorisms. He says: "God pity the man or the nation wise in proverbs . . . for there is much misery and much error gone into the collecting of such a store."

The end of the story and that of *A Rebours* are similar in implication. Des Esseintes, like most self-centered people, became a hypochondriac; his imaginary disorders were aggravated by real ones. The doctors ordered him back to the world of ordinary people; the waves of human mediocrity were about to engulf his refuge. "O Lord," he prayed, "pity the Christian who doubts, the skeptic who would believe." The choice before him was either the arms of the Church, as a French critic said, or the muzzle of a pistol. John Neal is also defeated by himself. He now loves Genevieve all-absorbingly; his passion is returned; but he has ceased to be capable of normal happiness. "Through living under difficulty," he says in explaining why he drove her away, "one learns the mode of thinking, feeling and acting best suited to cope with difficulty. No wonder he prizes a discovery which he has made at so great inconvenience to himself, and will not relinquish it but calls upon it to maintain precisely those adversities which it was at first designed to remedy." Thus, inevitably, he cuts the last tie that binds him to the world. His character begins to disintegrate; he has delusions of persecution and grandeur; he has entered a vicious circle from which he cannot escape. He fancies that there are several choices before him, "madness, travel, drugs, the Faith, death by one's own hand," but in reality there is no choice whatever; John Neal is hopelessly insane.

The book is disturbing, sometimes perplexing, always stimulating. Whatever the author's intentions, his story has a moral, and one that is identical, moreover, with that implied in *A Rebours*. There is no salvation apart from society. The individual paradise—whether we seek to create it on the outskirts of Paris, in Abyssinia or Tahiti, in a mythical Axel's castle, or simply behind the parapets of the mind—proves in the final test to be a fool's paradise. The end of the attempt is written in the beginning. The end, for the creator of Des Esseintes, was to surrender himself to society as represented by the Church. The end for John Neal is to sink through squalor and delusions into a final speechless separation from mankind—"not only not responding, but even refraining from soliloquy—for if we tell no one, the grave burden accumulates within us. Henceforth silence, that the torrent may be heard descending in all its fullness."

Dos Passos: The Poet and the World

JOHN DOS PASSOS is in reality two novelists. One of them is a late-Romantic, an individualist, an esthete moving about the world in a portable ivory tower; the other is a collectivist, a radical historian of the class struggle. These two authors have collaborated in all his books, but the first had the larger share in *Three Soldiers* and *Manhattan Transfer*. The second, in his more convincing fashion, has written most of *The 42nd Parallel* and almost all of *1919*. The difference between the late-Romantic and the radical Dos Passos is important not only in his own career: it also helps to explain the recent course of American fiction.

The late-Romantic tendency in his novels goes back to his years in college. After graduating from a good preparatory school, Dos Passos entered Harvard in 1912, at the beginning of a period which was later known as that of the Harvard esthetes. I have described this period elsewhere, in reviewing the poems of E. E. Cummings, but I did not discuss the ideas which underlay its picturesque manifestations, its mixture of incense, patchouli and gin, its erudition displayed before bar-room mirrors, its dreams in the Cambridge subway of laurel-crowned Thessalian dancers. The esthetes themselves were not philosophers; they did not seek to define their attitude; but most of them would have subscribed to the following propositions:

That the cultivation and expression of his own sensibility are the only justifiable ends for a poet.

That originality is his principal virtue.

That society is hostile, stupid and unmanageable: it is the world of the philistines, from which it is the poet's duty and privilege to remain aloof.

That the poet is always misunderstood by the world. He should, in fact, deliberately make himself misunderstandable, for the greater glory of art.

That he triumphs over the world, at moments, by mystically including it within himself: these are his moments of

1919, John Dos Passos. New York: Harcourt, Brace and Company. (*NR*, Apr. 27, 1932.)

ecstasy, to be provoked by any means in his power—alcohol, drugs, madness or saintliness, venery, suicide.

That art, the undying expression of such moments, exists apart from the world; it is the poet's revenge on society.

That the past has more dignity than the present.

There are a dozen other propositions which might be added to this unwritten manifesto, but the ideas I have listed were those most generally held, and they are sufficient to explain the intellectual atmosphere of the young men who read Arthur Machen's *The Hill of Dreams*, and argued about St. Thomas in Boston bars, and contributed to *The Harvard Monthly*. The attitude was not confined to one college and one magazine. It was often embodied in *The Dial*, which for some years was almost a postgraduate edition of *The Monthly*; it existed in earlier publications like *The Yellow Book* and *La Revue Blanche*; it has a history, in fact, almost as long as that of the upper middle class under capitalism. For the last half-century it has furnished the intellectual background of poems and essays without number. It would seem to preclude, in its adherents, the objectivity that is generally associated with good fiction; yet the esthetes themselves sometimes wrote novels, as did their predecessors all over the world. Such novels, in fact, are still being published, and favorably reviewed: "Mr. Zed has written the absorbing story of a talented musician tortured by the petty atmosphere of the society in which he is forced to live. His wife, whom the author portrays with witty malice, prevents him from breaking away. After an unhappy love affair and the failure of his artistic hopes, he commits suicide. . . ."

Such is the plot forever embroidered in the type of fiction that ought to be known as the Art Novel. There are two essential characters, two antagonists, the Poet and the World. The Poet—who may also be a painter, a violinist, an inventor, an architect or a Centaur—is generally to be identified with the author of the novel, or at least with the novelist's ideal picture of himself. He tries to assert his individuality in despite of the World, which is stupid, unmanageable and usually victorious. Sometimes the Poet triumphs, but the art novelists seem to realize, as a type, that the sort of hero they describe is likely to be defeated in the sort of society he must face. That society is rarely presented in accurate terms. So little is it endowed with reality, so great is the author's solicitude for the Poet, that we are surprised to see him vanquished by such a shadowy opponent. It is as if we were watching motion pictures in the dark house of his mind. There are dream pictures, nightmare pictures; at last the walls crash in and the Poet disappears without ever knowing what had led to his failure; he dies by his own hand, leaving behind him the memory of his ecstatic moments and the bitter story of his failure, now published as a revenge on the world of the philistines.

The art novel has many variations. Often the World is embodied in the Poet's wife, whose social ambitions are the ostensible cause of his defeat. Or the wife may be painted in attractive colors: she is married to a mediocre Poet who finally and reluctantly accepts her guidance, abandons his vain struggle for self-expression, and finds that mediocrity has its own consolations, its country clubs and business triumphs—this is the form in which the art novel is offered to readers of *The Saturday Evening Post*. Or again the Poet may be a woman who fights for the same ambitions, under the same difficulties, as her male prototypes. The scene of the struggle may be a town on the Minnesota prairies, an English rectory, an apartment on Washington Square or Beacon Hill; but always the characters are the same; the Poet and the World continue their fatal conflict; the Poet has all our sympathies. And the novelists who use this plot for the thousandth time are precisely those who believe that originality is a writer's chief virtue.

Many are unconscious of this dilemma. The story rises so immediately out of their lives, bursts upon them with such freshness, that they never recognize it as a familiar tale. Others deliberately face the problem and try to compensate for the staleness of the plot by the originality of their treatment. They experiment with new methods of story-telling—one of which, the stream of consciousness, seems peculiarly fitted to novels of this type. Perhaps they invest their characters with new significance, and rob them of any real significance, by making them symbolic. They adopt new manners, poetic, mystical, learned, witty, allusive or obfuscatory; and often, in token of their original talent, they invent new words and new ways of punctuating simple declarative sentences. Not all their ingenuity is wasted. Sometimes they make valuable discoveries; a few of the art novels, like *The Hill of Dreams,* are among the minor masterpieces of late-Romantic literature; and a very few, like *A Portrait of the Artist as a Young Man,* are masterpieces pure and simple.

Dos Passos' early books are neither masterpieces nor are they pure examples of the art novel. The world was always real to him, painfully real; it was never veiled with mysticism and his characters were rarely symbolic. Yet consider the plot of a novel like *Three Soldiers.* A talented young musician, during the War, finds that his sensibilities are being outraged, his aspirations crushed, by society as embodied in the American army. He deserts after the Armistice and begins to write a great orchestral poem. When the military police come to arrest him, the sheets of music flutter one by one into the spring breeze; and we are made to feel that the destruction of this symphony, this ecstatic song choked off and dispersed on the wind, is the real tragedy of the War.

Some years later, in writing *Manhattan Transfer,* Dos Passos seemed to be undertaking a novel of a different type, one which tried to render the color and movement of a whole city; but the book, as it proceeds, becomes the story of Jimmy Herts (the Poet) and Ellen Thatcher (the Poet's wife), and the Poet is once again frustrated by the World: he leaves a Greenwich Village party after a last drink of gin and walks out alone, bareheaded, into the dawn. It is obvious, however, that a new conflict has been superimposed on the old one: the social ideas of the novelist are now at war with his personal emotions, which remain those of *The Dial* and *The Harvard Monthly.* Even in *1919,* this second conflict persists, but less acutely; the emotional values themselves are changing, to accord with the ideas; and the book as a whole belongs to a new category.

1919 is distinguished, first of all, by the very size of the project its author has undertaken. A long book in itself, containing 473 pages, it is merely the second chapter, as it were, of a novel which will compare in length with *Ulysses,* perhaps even with *Remembrance of Things Past.* Like the latter, it is a

historical novel dealing with the yesterday that still exists in
the author's memory. It might almost be called a news novel,
since it uses newspaper headlines to suggest the flow of events,
and tells the story of its characters in reportorial fashion. But
its chief distinction lies in the author's emphasis. He is not
recounting the tragedy of bewildered John Smith, the rise of
ambitious Mary Jones, the efforts of sensitive Richard Robinson to maintain his ideals against the blundering malice of
society. Such episodes recur in this novel, but they are seen in
perspective. The real hero of *The 42nd Parallel* and *1919* is
society itself, American society as embodied in forty or fifty
representative characters who drift along with it, struggle to
change its course, or merely to find a secure footing—perhaps
they build a raft of wreckage, grow fat on the refuse floating
about them; perhaps they go under in some obscure eddy—
while the current sweeps them onward toward new social horizons. In this sense, Dos Passos has written the first American
collective novel.

The principal characters are brought forward one at a
time; the story of each is told in bare, straightforward prose.
Thus, J. Ward Moorehouse, born in Wilmington, Delaware,
begins his business career in a real-estate office. He writes
songs, marries and divorces a rich woman, works for a newspaper in Pittsburgh—at the end of fifty-seven pages he is a
successful public-relations counselor embarked on a campaign
to reconcile labor and capital at the expense of labor. Joe and
Janey Williams are the children of a tugboat captain from
Washington, D. C.; Janey studies shorthand; Joe plays baseball, enlists in the Navy, deserts after a brawl and becomes a
merchant seaman. Eleanor Stoddard is a poor Chicago girl who
works at Marshall Field's; she learns how to speak French to
her customers and order waiters about "with a crisp little refined
moneyed voice." All these characters, first introduced in *The
42nd Parallel*, reappear in *1919*, where they are joined by
others: Richard Ellsworth Savage, a Kent School boy who
goes to Harvard and writes poetry; Daughter, a warm-hearted
flapper from Dallas, Texas; Ben Compton, a spectacled Jew
from Brooklyn who becomes a Wobbly. Gradually their careers draw closer together, till finally all of them are caught
up in the War.

"This whole goddam war's a gold brick," says Joe Williams. "It ain't on the level, it's crooked from A to Z. No matter how it comes out, fellows like us get the shitty end of the stick, see? Well, what I say is all bets is off . . . every man go to hell in his own way . . . and three strikes is out, see?" Three strikes is out for Joe, when his skull is cracked in a saloon brawl at Saint-Nazaire on Armistice night. Daughter is killed in an airplane accident; she provoked it herself in a fit of hysteria after being jilted by Dick Savage—who for his part survives as the shell of a man, all the best of him having died when he decided to join the Army and make a career for himself and let his pacifist sentiments go hang. Benny Compton gets ten years in Atlanta prison as a conscientious objector. Everybody in the novel suffers from the War and finds his own way of going to hell—everybody except the people without bowels, the empty people like Eleanor Stoddard and J. Ward Moorehouse, who stuff themselves with the proper sentiments and make the right contacts.

The great events that preceded and followed the Armistice are reflected in the lives of all these people; but Dos Passos has other methods, too, for rendering the sweep of history. In particular he has three technical devices which he uses both to broaden the scope of the novel and to give it a formal unity. The first of these consists of what he calls "Newsreels," a combination of newspaper headlines, stock-market reports, official communiqués and words from popular songs. The Newsreels effectively perform their function in the book, that of giving dates and atmospheres, but in themselves, judged as writing, they are not successful. The second device is a series of nine biographies interspersed through the text. Here are the lives, briefly told, of three middle-class rebels, Jack Reed, Randolph Bourne and Paxton Hibben; of three men of power, Roosevelt, Wilson and J. P. Morgan; and of three proletarian heroes. All the biographies are successful both in themselves and in relation to the novel as a whole; and the passage dealing with the Wobbly martyr, Wesley Everest, is as powerful as anything Dos Passos has written.

The Camera Eye, which is the third device, introduces more complicated standards of judgment. It consists in the memories of another character, presumably the author, who

has adventures similar to those of his characters, but describes
them in a different style, one that suggests Dos Passos' earlier
books. The Camera Eye gives us photographs rich in emotional detail:

> Ponte Decimo   in Ponte Decimo ambulances were parked
> in a moonlit square of bleak stone workingpeople's houses
> hoarfrost covered everything   in the little bar the Successful
> Story Writer taught us to drink cognac and maraschino half
> and half
>   havanuzzerone
>   it turned out he was not writing what he felt he wanted to
> be writing   What can you tell them at home about the
> war?   it turned out he was not wanting what he wrote he
> wanted to be feeling   cognac and maraschino   was no
> longer young   (It made us damn sore we greedy for what
> we felt we wanted tell 'em all they lied see new towns go to
> Genoa)   havanuzzerone?   it turned out that he wished
> he was a naked brown shepherd boy sitting on a hillside playing
> a flute in the sunlight

Exactly the same episode, so it happens, is described in Dos
Passos' other manner, his prose manner, during the course of a
chapter dealing with Dick Savage:

> That night they parked the convoy in the main square of a
> godforsaken little burg on the outskirts of Genoa. They went
> with Sheldrake to have a drink in a bar and found themselves
> drinking with the Saturday Evening Post correspondent, who
> soon began to get tight and to say how he envied them their
> good looks and their sanguine youth and idealism. Steve picked
> him up about everything and argued bitterly that youth was the
> lousiest time in your life, and that he ought to be goddam glad he
> was forty years old and able to write about the war instead of
> fighting in it.

The relative merit of these two passages, as writing, is not
an important question. The first is a good enough piece of
impressionism, with undertones of E. E. Cummings and Ger-
trude Stein. The style of the second passage, except for a
certain conversational quality, is almost colorless; it happens to
be the most effective way of recording a particular series of
words and actions; it aspires to no other virtue. The first
passage might add something to a book in which, the plot

being hackneyed or inconsequential, the emphasis had to be placed on the writing, but *1919* is not a novel of that sort. Again, the Camera Eye may justify itself in the next volume of this trilogy—or tetralogy—by assuming a closer relation to the story and binding together the different groups of characters; but in that case, I hope the style of it will change. So far it has been an element of disunity, a survival of the art novel in the midst of a different type of writing, and one in which Dos Passos excels.

He is, indeed, one of the few writers in whose case an equation can accurately and easily be drawn between social beliefs and artistic accomplishments. When he writes individualistically, with backward glances toward Imagism, Vorticism and the Insurrection of the Word, his prose is sentimental and without real distinction. When he writes as a social rebel, he writes not flawlessly by any means, but with conviction, power and a sense of depth, of striking through surfaces to the real forces beneath them. This last book, in which his political ideas have given shape to his emotions, and only the Camera Eye remains as a vestige of his earlier attitude, is not only the best of all his novels; it is, I believe, a landmark in American fiction.

Hemingway: A Farewell to Spain

JUST WHY did Ernest Hemingway write a book on bull-fighting? It is, make no mistake, a good book on bull-fighting, full of technical writing as accurate as anything printed in Spanish newspapers like *El Sol* or *A. B. C.* and general information presented more vividly and completely than ever before in Spanish or English. Hemingway writes for those who have seen their first bull-fight, or shortly intend to see it, or are wondering whether to do so if they ever visit Spain. He tells them what, where, when, how—the seats to buy, the buses or

Death in the Afternoon, by Ernest Hemingway. New York: Charles Scribner's Sons. (*NR*, Nov. 30, 1932.)

trains to take, the things to watch for and which of them to applaud, which to salute with a volley of oranges, empty bottles and dead fish. He tells how the bulls are bred and tested, how the matadors are trained, glorified and, in the end, killed off like bulls. He illustrates the text with dozens of good photographs. In appendices, he gives further information, the dates of the principal *corridas* in Spain, Mexico and Peru, the reactions of typical Anglo-Saxons and the achievements of Sidney Franklin, the one American matador. Everything is there, even a store of pathetic or hilarious stories to read during dull moments of the fight, if there be any. In a word, he has written a Baedeker of bulls, an admirable volume, but—

Being a good artist, he does a good job, never faking, skimping or pretending. He often talks about himself, but meanwhile keeps his eye on the thing outside, the object to be portrayed; by force of prolonged attention, he makes the object larger than life, fills it with all his knowledge and feeling, with himself. His book about bull-fighting thus becomes something more, a book about sport in general and, since this particular sport is really an art, a book about artistic appreciation and literary criticism, yes, and the art of living, of drinking, of dying, of loving the Spanish land. But all this being said—

Like every good artist, Hemingway employs a double process of selection and diversification, of contraction and expansion. He says: "Let those who want to save the world if you can get to see it clear and as a whole." Writing in Anglo-Saxon words of one syllable he is sometimes more difficult than Whitehead or Paul Valéry, but what he means in this case is made clear enough by the addition of two more monosyllables and a comma. Let those who want to do so save the world, if *you* can get to see it clear and as a whole. Then, he continues, "any part you make will represent the whole if it's made truly." This book, being truly made, represents in its own fashion the whole of life. But all this being said, one must add that the whole it represents is discolored and distorted by the point of view; that the book is full of self-conscious cruelty, bravado, pity and, especially when dying horses are concerned, a sort of uneasiness that ends by communicating itself to the reader.

Death in the Afternoon is a less important book than *A Farewell to Arms;* its style is often labored and sometimes flowery (and isn't rendered any less so by Hemingway's apologies for fine writing; apologies never help); its best descriptions of bull-fights are less moving than the briefer description in *The Sun Also Rises.* For three years, in the midst of a world more tumultuous and exciting than any bull-fight, Hemingway has been writing and repolishing this book. Why did he choose this particular subject, this part to represent the whole?

The answer carries us back fifteen years. During the War, Hemingway served on the Italian front as an ambulance driver; he was seriously wounded and received two medals. The War, to judge from his books, has been the central experience in his career; he shows the effects of it more completely than any other American novelist. In an article recently printed in *The New Republic,* I tried to describe these effects in their relation to the writers of Hemingway's generation, which is also mine, reader, and possibly your own. I said that the War uprooted us, cut us off from our own class and country; that it taught us to assume what I called a spectatorial attitude toward life in general; that it encouraged us to write once more about old themes, simple themes like love and death; and, though I did not emphasize the point, that it gave us a sense of self-pity and self-esteem, a bitter aloofness in the midst of armies. The War, I said, "infected us with the slow poison of irresponsibility and unconcern for the future—the poison of travel, too . . . and the poison of danger, excitement, that made our old life intolerable. Then, as suddenly as it began for us, the War ended"—leaving behind it desires and habits which were difficult to satisfy in a world at peace.

Bull-fighting perhaps could serve as an emotional substitute for war. It provided everything, travel, excitement, crowds like armies watching the spectacle of danger. Hemingway says on the second page of his new book, "The only place where you could see life and death, *i.e.,* violent death now that the wars were over, was in the bull ring and I wanted very much to go to Spain where I could study it." His motives were not merely emotional; he was "trying to learn to write, commencing with the simplest things," and bull-fighting was an ideal subject; it dealt with fundamentals; apparently it was independent of morality, of social implications, of any connection with politics. "So I went to Spain to see bull-fights and try to write about them for myself. . . . It might be good to have a book about bull-fighting in English and a serious book on such an unmoral subject may have some value."

But the book when he came to write it ten years later disproved a good many of the ideas that he carried with him into Spain. There are contradictions between Hemingway's ideas and the ideas suggested to readers by his narrative. To give an obvious example, *Death in the Afternoon* is not at all an unmoral book, nor does it treat bull-fighting as an unmoral subject. If Hemingways praises the performance of a great matador, almost all his adjectives are rich in moral connotations: they are words like true, emotional, not tricked, pure, brave, honest, noble, candid, honorable, sincere. Other matadors are not merely inartistic; they are low, false, vulgar, cowardly; they are even "cynical."

A second contradiction is more important. "All art," he says, "is only done by the individual. The individual is all you ever have." But almost from beginning to end, *Death in the Afternoon* is a refutation of that idea. It is true that the art of the matador, the great individual, provides the "moment of truth" which is the climax of a good bull-fight, but Hemingway makes it clear that the matador's performance would be impossible without the collaboration of nameless people, dozens of them, hundreds, thousands, in circles gradually widening till they include almost a whole nation and a culture extending for centuries into the past. The matador, to begin with, must depend on the work of his own team, his *cuadrilla*, which is charged with the function of conducting the bull through the first two stages of the fight, of regulating his speed and carriage, of preparing him for the "moment of truth" when the sword goes in between the shoulder blades and bull and matador are for the moment one. But the bull, too, must play his part; he must be a brave, "candid" bull of a type that can be raised only by breeders of knowledge and integrity, encouraged by audiences that howl at the sight of inferior animals. The audience, moreover, must appreciate the finer points of the art, must know when to throw small dead animals of all sorts, including fish; it must hold a certain attitude toward bravery and death; it must, in short, be the sort of audience that exists only in Castille, Navarre, Andalusia and perhaps in Mexico City. The government, finally, must grant at the very least an intelligent toleration if the art of bull-fighting is to survive. The government might easily abolish it, not by jailing the matadors, but simply by seizing the ranches where bulls are raised and sending the animals to the slaughterhouse. As for the bull-fighters themselves, they grow up unencouraged, "having a natural talent as acrobats or jockeys or even writers have, and none of them are irreplaceable. . . ." And so the author has described a complete circle. He began by saying that the individual, in art, is all you ever have; he ends by deciding that the individual, even the greatest matador, is replaceable and nonessential.

Hemingway is a master at not drawing implications. In this respect as in others, it is interesting to compare *Death in the Afternoon* with *Les Bestiaires,* a novel about bull-fighting written by a Frenchman of the same age. Henry de Montherlant sees implications everywhere. The modern *corrida de toros* implies the ancient sacrifice of a white bull to Mithra, which in turn leads him to consider the beauties of ritual, the mysteries of sacrifice, the glories of tradition, Royalism, Catholicism, patriotic ecstasy, till shortly the bulls, the author and his readers together are lost in a haze of emotion. Montherlant is inferior to Hemingway in hardness, honesty, freshness, keen perception, and yet in a sense I think he is justified. Bull-fighting really does imply a certain attitude toward life, a willingness to accept things as they are, bad as they are, and to recompense oneself by regarding them as a picturesque tragedy. Bull-fighting does, I think, imply an aristocracy, an established Church, a proletariat resigned to suffering pain in return for the privilege of seeing pain inflicted on others, and a rabble of gladiators, bootlickers and whores; but I am just as glad that Hemingway does not consciously draw these implications.

I don't mean to say that the book is without political meanings or contradictions. Hemingway detested the dictator Primo de Rivera—for many reasons, probably, but he mentions only one: Primo insisted on protecting the horses with belly-pads and thereby spoiled one part of the *corrida.* Hemingway hates policemen. Hemingway had many friends among the republican politicians when they were being hunted through the Pyrenees, but now they have come into power he is beginning to detest them also: he suspects them of wishing to abolish bull-fights "so that they will have no intellectual embarrassments at being different from their European colleagues when they meet at the League of Nations." Hemingway is disturbed by the peasant jacquerie in Andalusia, which is threatening the bull-breeding ranches, but at the same time he feels an instinctive friendship toward the peasants. I think he realizes the possibility that the Spanish people themselves, and not their government, might put an end to the bull-fight, replacing it by sports and arts more appropriate to a revolutionary society. On this matter, however, he takes no stand. To do so would force him to think about the present and the future, and he has fallen into the habit of writing with his eyes turned backwards.

This habit, revealed engagingly in all his books, is now becoming a vice. During the War, he dreamed about his boyhood in Michigan, where trout lay thickly in the cool streams in July. "One year they had cut the hemlock woods . . . You could not go back"—but you could write about it nostalgically; and later, in Paris and Spain, you could write about the brave days of the War; and still later, in Key West, you could write about Madrid and Pamplona and the bull-fights, always with an elegiac note, a tenderness for things past and never to be recaptured. All through the present book, but especially in the last chapter, one finds this note repeated, this regret for "the one year everyone drank so much and no one was nasty. There really was such a year." "Make all that come true again," he cries. But, "Pamplona is changed . . . Rafael says things are very changed and he won't go to Pamplona any more . . . Pamplona is changed, of course, but not so much as we are older." Always there is this grief for something that has died within us, for a state of security or felicity existing in youth or in the mind. "We will never ride back from Toledo in the dark, washing the dust out with Fundador, nor will there be that week of what happened in the night of that July in Madrid." It is all very brave, hard-boiled and wistful, but there are other chords for Hemingway to strike.

In a sense, every book he has written has been an elegy. He

has given us his farewell to Michigan, to Montparnasse, his *Farewell to Arms;* his new book is a sort of elegy to Spain and vanished youth and the brave days of Belmonte and Maera. Hemingway's talent is great enough to justify us in making demands on it. Will he ever give us, I wonder, his farewell to farewells?

Fitzgerald's Goodbye to His Generation

Tender Is the Night is a good novel that puzzles you and ends by making you a little angry because it isn't a great novel also. It doesn't give the feeling of being complete in itself.

The theme of it is stated in a conversation among the three principal characters. "What did this to him?" Rosemary asks. They are talking about Abe North, an American composer who became prominent shortly after the War. He was shy and very talented; often he came to stay with Dick and Nicole Diver in their villa near the Cap d'Antibes and they scarcely knew he was there—"sometimes he'd be in the library with a muted piano, making love to it by the hour." But for years now he hasn't been working; his eyes have a hurt look; he gets drunk every day as if trying to escape from nobody knew what. And Rosemary wonders, "Why does he have to drink?"

> Nicole shook her head right and left, disclaiming responsibility for the matter: "So many smart men go to pieces nowadays."
> "And when haven't they?" Dick asked. "Smart men play close to the line because they have to—some of them can't stand it, so they quit."
> "It must lie deeper than that. . . . Artists like—well, like Fernand don't seem to have to wallow in alcohol. Why is it just Americans who dissipate?"

"Breakdown." A review of *Tender Is the Night,* by F. Scott Fitzgerald. New York: Charles Scribner's Sons. (*NR,* June 6, 1934.)

There were so many answers to this question that Dick decided to leave it in the air, to buzz victoriously in Nicole's ears.

The question remains victoriously buzzing in the reader's ears long after the story has ended. Fitzgerald tries to answer it, but obliquely. He tells us why Dr. Richard Diver went to pieces—because he married a rich woman and became so dependent on her money that his own work seemed unimportant and he no longer had a purpose in living; that is the principal reason, although he is also shaken by his love for Rosemary and by Nicole's recurrent fits of insanity, during one of which she came near killing not only her husband and herself but also their two children. Dick's case seems clear enough—but what about Abe North, whose wife was poor and sane and devoted? What about the other nice people who ended as lunatics or drunkards? Fitzgerald is continually suggesting and reiterating these questions that he leaves in the air.

The Divers and their friends are, in reality, the characters he has always written about, and written well. They are the richer members of his own generation, the young women who learned to smoke and pet in 1917 and the Yale and Princeton men who attended their coming-out parties in new uniforms. In his early books, especially in *This Side of Paradise*, he celebrated the youth of these people in a tone of unmixed pride —"Here we are," he seemed to be saying, "the children of the conquerors, the free and beautiful and very wicked youngsters who are setting the standards for a nation." Later, when he described their business careers and their life in great country houses on the north shore of Long Island, his admiration began to be mixed with irony and disillusionment. In the present novel, which chronicles their years of exile, the admiration has almost completely vanished; the prevailing tone is one of disillusionment mixed with nostalgia. "We had good times together," Fitzgerald seems to say, "but that was a long time ago." Dick Diver is now an unsuccessful drunken country doctor, divorced and living somewhere in central New York State. Rosemary is an empty and selfish movie star; Abe North is dead, killed brawling in a speakeasy—all the kind and sensitive people of their circle have gone to pieces, and there remain only the "wooden and onanistic" women like Nicole's

sister, only the *arrivistes* like Albert McKisco and the cultivated savages likes Tommy Barban. A whole class has flourished and decayed and suddenly broken into fragments.

Here is a magnificent subject for a novel. The trouble is
that Fitzgerald has never completely decided what kind of
novel he wanted to write—whether it should center round a
single hero or deal with a whole group. Both types of approach
are present, the individual and the collective, and they interfere with each other. We are conscious of a divided purpose
that perhaps goes back to a division in the author himself.

Fitzgerald has always been the poet of the American upper
bourgeoisie; he has been the only writer able to invest their
lives with glamor. Yet he has never been sure that he owed his
loyalty to the class about which he was writing. It is as if he
had a double personality. Part of him is a guest at the ball
given by the people in the big house; part of him has been a
little boy peeping in through the window and being thrilled by
the music and the beautifully dressed women—a romantic but
hard-headed little boy who stops every once in a while to
wonder how much it all cost and where the money came from.
(Fitzgerald says, "There is a streak of vulgarity in me that I
try to cultivate.") In his early books, this divided personality
was wholly an advantage; it enabled him to portray American
society from the inside, and yet at the same time to surround it
with an atmosphere of magic and romance that exists only in
the eyes of people watching at the carriage entrance as the
guests arrive in limousines. Since those days, however, the
division has been emphasized and has become a liability. The
little boy outside the window has grown mature and cold-eyed:
from an enraptured spectator he has developed into a social
historian. At the same time, part of Fitzgerald remains inside,
among the dancers. And now that the ball is ending in tragedy,
he doesn't know how to describe it—whether as a guest, a
participant, in which case he will be writing a purely psychological novel; or whether from the detached point of view of a
social historian.

There is another reason, too, for the technical faults of
Tender Is the Night. Fitzgerald has been working on it at
intervals for the last nine years, ever since he published *The
Great Gatsby* in 1925. During those years his attitude has

inevitably changed, as has that of every other sensitive writer. Yet no matter how much he revised his early chapters, he could not make them wholly agree with those written later— for once a chapter has assumed what seems to be a final shape, it undergoes a process of crystallization; it can no longer be remolded. The result is that several of his characters are self-contradictory: they don't merely change as living creatures change; they transform themselves into different people.

If I didn't like the book so much, I shouldn't have spoken at such length about its shortcomings. It has virtues that deserve more space than I can give them here. Especially it has a richness of meaning and emotion—one feels that every scene is selected among many possible scenes and that every event has pressure behind it. There is nothing false or borrowed in the book: everything is observed at first hand. Some of the minor figures—especially Gausse, the hotel keeper who was once a bus boy in London, and Lady Caroline Sibley-Biers, who carries her English bad manners to the point of viciousness— are more vivid than Rosemary or Dick; and the encounter between Gausse and Lady Caroline is one of those enormous episodes in which two social castes are depicted melodramatically, farcically and yet convincingly in a brief conversation and one gesture.

Fitzgerald says that this book is his farewell to the members of his own generation; I hope he changes his mind. He has in him at least one great novel about them, and it is a novel that I want to read.

Malraux on Man's Solitude

MAN'S FATE is a novel about the Chinese revolution written by a soldier of fortune who risked his life in the revolutionary cause, and yet it is not in essence a revolutionary or even a political novel. Brutal, tender, illuminating, it ends

"Man's Solitude." A review of *Man's Fate*, by André Malraux. Translated by Haakon M. Chevalier. New York: Harrison Smith and Robert Haas. (*NR*, July 4, 1934.)

by casting more light on our own bourgeois society than on the Chinese Communists who died to change it.

This doesn't mean that it shows political events in false perspective. Malraux is writing about two days that helped to decide the history of China. On March 21, 1927, the Communists of Shanghai declared a general strike and, acting in alliance with Chiang Kai-shek, seized control of the largest city on the Asiatic mainland. Many people then believed that all China would go Communist quickly and without much bloodshed. Chiang Kai-shek had Russian officers training his troops and Russian political advisers; the great formless mass of peasants and coolies was leavened with Communist ideas. But three weeks later, on April 11, Chiang betrayed his Communist allies, dissolved their labor unions, captured their local posts and executed all his prisoners after torturing most of them; the Communist leaders were boiled in vats of oil or thrust living into the fireboxes of locomotives. The streets of the big cities ran with blood, but the revolution continued to live in the countryside, where the peasants were beginning to organize their own soviets. Malraux not only participated in these events: he has since reflected on their political meaning and has learned to estimate the part that was played in them by personal ambitions, by foreign money, by class antagonisms. Everything he says about the Chinese revolution seems keen and convincing.

But the revolution, instead of being his principal theme, is the setting and the pretext for a novel that is, in reality, a drama of individual lives. It is true that these lives are bound together by a single emotion, but it is not the desire to revolt or to achieve justice. Malraux's real theme is a feeling that most men nurse, secretly, their sense of absolute loneliness and uniqueness, their acknowledgment to themselves of inadequacy in the face of life and helplessness against death—that is what he means by *la condition humaine*; it is man's lot, his destiny, his servitude. And he has chosen to depict this emotion during a revolutionary period because it is then carried, like everything else that is human, to its pitch of highest intensity.

All of his characters, though drawn from different nations and ranks of society, are obsessed by this feeling of personal solitude. All of them try to escape from it, either through dissipation or else through establishing a bond with others at the cost of no matter what sacrifice. Thus, little Ch'en, the former student in a missionary college, escapes from his loneliness by adopting terrorism as a career; he wants to found a religion of political murder and self-immolation—finally, clutching a bomb in his hand, he hurls himself under the automobile in which he thinks Chiang Kai-shek is riding. Ferral, the banker and exploiter, tries to escape from his own sterility by dominating others, and ends by despising them only a little more than he despises himself. Clappique tries to evade his personality by playing imaginary roles; he keeps repeating that "the Baron de Clappique does not exist." May finds her escape in love, and Katov finds his in an absolute devotion to the revolutionary cause. Old Gisors, the French philosopher who used to teach at the University of Peking, has two means of avoiding himself: opium and his love for Kyo, his son by a Japanese wife; after Kyo's death, he has only opium.

As for Kyo Gisors, the hero of the novel, "his life had a meaning, and he knew what it was: to give to each of these men whom famine, at this very moment, was killing like a slow plague, the sense of his own dignity." It was through his love for human dignity that Kyo became a Communist, and through dignity, too, that he met his death. On April 11, the one man who might have saved his life was König, the German commander of Chiang Kai-shek's secret police—and König, have forfeited all respect for himself during the civil war in Russia, had learned to hate every man who was not self-seeking and a coward. When Kyo refused to betray his comrades, König ordered him to be taken to Section A, the part of the prison reserved for those who were to be burned to death.

Man's Fate is a novel packed tight with contradictions: one feels in it the dilemma of people ill prepared by a peaceful childhood to face one of the brutal and cataclysmic periods in human history. It is a philosophical novel in which the philosophy is expressed in terms of violent actions. It is a novel about the East that expresses the soul rather of the West. It is a novel written sympathetically about Communists by a man whose own mentality has strong traces of fascism (perhaps this explains why it has been so popular in Italy) and a novel about proletarian heroes in which the technique is that developed by the Symbolists of the Ivory Tower. It is a good novel too, extraordinarily rich in characters and perceptions, and yet it becomes difficult to read—the emotions are so taut that one feels the need of laying down the book, lighting a cigarette, turning on the radio, doing anything to break the intolerable tension.

But if one persists, one comes at last to a scene as tragically stirring as anything in modern literature. It might be compared with the terrible chapter in *The Possessed* in which Kirillov is ordered to commit suicide and finally obeys, except that Malraux is describing several suicides and around them two hundred prisoners waiting for the firing squad—the whole thing is magnified to the point of intolerable melodrama, and yet is rendered true and humanly bearable by the feeling of brotherhood existing among the prisoners. . . . Katov, the old revolutionist, is lying wounded in the famous Section A, which is nothing but a half-empty space along the wall of a crowded prison yard. Beside him in the darkness lies the dead body of Kyo, who has taken the cyanide that all members of the Communist Central Committee kept hidden in their square belt buckles as a final means of escaping their tortures. Katov, too, has his cyanide and is waiting to use it. Two new prisoners, young Chinese, are brought into Section A; they have no poison and know that for them there is no possible escape from being thrown into the firebox of the locomotive whistling outside the prison (all this, I might add, is a faithful picture of what happened that night in Shanghai; Malraux doesn't exaggerate). The two young men are weeping and Katov gives them his cyanide to divide between them; it is his supreme sacrifice.

But the scene doesn't end there; if it did, one might conceivably forget it instead of lying awake to brood over it. One of the young men has been wounded in the hand; he drops both the little packages of poison; and the three of them grope in the darkness among the pebbles and bits of broken plaster that litter the prison yard, looking for death as if they were looking for diamonds. This is the picture that sticks in one's mind—this and the sense of pitiful fraternity among the three searchers, expressed in a few words whispered by one of the young Chinese when he suddenly took Katov's hand, pressed it and held it. "Even if we don't find it. . . ." he said. A moment later the two boys clutched the poison and gulped it down.

Malraux is saying that here in the prison yard, the effort to escape from man's solitude and the search for a purpose by which life is dignified both found their goal. The individual dramas and the great revolutionary drama merged into each other. Here in the darkness, Katov poured himself out in "that absolute friendship, without reticence, which death alone gives"; and here among his comrades condemned to be burned alive, Kyo felt that "he was dying, like each of these men, because he had given a meaning to his life. What would have been the value of a life for which he would not have been willing to die? It is easy to die when one does not die alone."

Spender and Auden

THERE HAS BEEN a great beating of drums and clashing of cymbals to announce these two poets; perhaps there has been more noise than is justified by their work so far. Neither Stephen Spender nor W. H. Auden has yet written a long poem that belongs with the English classics, even with those of the second rank. But they have done something else, something that seemed next door to the impossible: they have brought life and vigor into contemporary English poetry.

They appeared in a dead season when all the serious young men were trying to imitate T. S. Eliot and weren't quite bringing it off. Eliot himself, after writing *The Waste Land*, had entered a territory that was supposed to be watered with springs of spiritual grace, but most travelers there found that the waters were subterranean and the soil brittle with drought. Reading his new poems was like excavating buried cities at the

Poems, by Stephen Spender. New York: Random House. *Poems*, by W. H. Auden. New York: Random House. (*NR*, Sept. 26, 1934.)

edge of the Syrian desert; they were full of imposing temples and perfectly proportioned statues of the gods, but there was nothing in the streets that breathed. Say this for Spender and Auden: they are living in an actual London; they walk over Scotch moors that are covered with genuine snow; they are not in the British Museum pressed and dried between the pages of a seventeenth-century book of sermons.

Still more important, they do not stand alone. They are merely the vanguard of a group that includes Charles Madge, John Lehmann, Cecil Day Lewis (in some ways the most promising of all), Richard Goodman, Julian Bell and others. All these poets are young, gifted in their various fashions, and seem to know what they are doing. All of them are able to write about political issues, not dryly or abstractly, but in terms of human beings. Most of them are radical without being proletarian. It is a matter of simple good sense that a proletarian poet ought to begin by being proletarian, just as a Catholic poet ought to be Catholic; otherwise he runs the risk of becoming as empty and affected as the hangers-on of the Oxford Movement. These young men, graduates of the English universities, don't pose for the newsreel men in the role of mechanics, dressed in greasy overalls; but nevertheless their sympathies are with the workers, and their sympathies have sharpened their perception of what is going on in the world around them. They are able to convey the sense of violence and uncertainty that we gulp down with the headlines of our morning papers, and of disaster waiting, perhaps, outside our doors.

So far Auden and Spender are the only members of the group whose work has appeared in this country (and incidentally their publisher deserves credit for giving them two handsome volumes). In a curious way they remind me of two recent American poets. Auden suggests E. E. Cummings: he has the same crazy wit, the same delight in playing with words and the same indifference to whether he is being understood. Spender suggests Hart Crane, more by a quality of outpouring emotion than by any specific mannerism. Auden, with his sharper tongue and quicker eyes, has more to teach his fellow poets, but Spender, on second reading, is the one I prefer.

Let us call him a humanist. That is the best word I have found to describe the atmosphere of his poems, but it is a word so much abused that it has to be redefined. Spender's human-

ism has nothing to do with the bookish doctrine that was
cricket-chirped by the followers of the late Irving Babbitt. It
does not consist in advocating golden mediocrity or the Inner
Check or the emendation of Greek manuscripts. It is a humanism not of the letter but of the spirit, and that spirit is simply,
in Spender's words, "The palpable and obvious love of man
for man." He isn't one of those poets who can write about
people only after they are dead, only after our memories of
them have been properly mellowed by time and forgetfulness,
like port wine sent on a voyage round Cape Horn. Spender
writes about living men, their laughter, their voices singing,
the cities where they crowd and the great machines made by
their hands. He writes too, but this time with loathing, about
the institutions and abstractions that are turned against men:
the Church, the press, the bankers' state, the columns of figures
in ledgers and the people who profit by them, the ghosts
prisoned in big houses:

> those ladies like flies perfect in amber
> those financiers like fossils of bones in coal.

In our generation we have seen human things increasingly
subordinated to inhuman things, men to systems, writing and
painting to principles of scholarship, tragedy to statistics, and
even revolution to the quoting of texts about revolution.
Spender calls back a note of human warmth into all this
aridity. He is interested in politics, as nobody but an intellectual eunuch could fail to be in this age of ours, and there is no
doubt which side he has chosen. When he speaks of Germany,
for example, he is sure to mention

> the parliament their own side set afire
> and then our party forbidden.

He is explicit; he will fight with "our party," with the unemployed and the communists, against "their side," the Fascists
and the money barons. But his reasons for choosing communism are human, not statistical. "Oh young men, oh comrades,"
he says—

> Oh comrades, step beautifully from the solid wall
> advance to rebuild and sleep with friend on hill
> advance to rebel and remember what you have
> no ghost ever had, immured in his hall.

Spender is serious, straightforward; he can use words like "love," "bravery," "honor," without having them turn mealy in his mouth. The serious defect to be found in his poems is a sort of fogginess that sometimes makes his meaning doubtful. I think it comes from two principal sources. For one thing, his vision of the physical world is not clear enough and his images are not sufficiently precise. Too often he writes like a short-sighted man looking at distant mountains. But he is sometimes ambiguous for another reason—because he is honestly uncertain of his direction, and gropes. It is significant that his more recent work has been sharper and clearer. Spender is one of those poets who improve technically, in sonority and precision, as they become more radical.

W. H. Auden is a battle poet. His boyhood was spent among rumors of war, troop movements, lists of officers dead on the field of honor; his career as a poet belongs to the gray depression years. In his poems he has made a synthesis of these two adventures. The results of unemployment are projected forward into another war, this time a war between social classes fought against a background of decaying industrialism. He gives us a sense of skirmishes in the yards of abandoned factories, of railroads dynamited, ports silted up, high-tension wires fallen to the ground, of spies creeping out at night or stumbling back to drop dead of their wounds (it is curious how often he mentions spies) and always a sense of mystery, of danger waiting at the corner of two streets:

> *But careful; back to our lines; it is unsafe there,*
> *Passports are issued no longer; that area is closed.*

Along with this goes a sanguinary sort of wartime humor that is best illustrated in his burlesque account of a revolution in England. On the second day of fighting, "A white-faced survivor informs the prison governor that the convicts, loosed, storming the execution shed, are calculating the drop formula by practical experiment, employing warders of various weights." On the third day, famine attacks the upper classes— "For those who desire an honorable release, typhoid lice, three in a box, price twopence, are peddled in the streets by starving corner boys." There are pages of Auden that have the irresponsible savagery of the Dada Manifesto.

His principal fault, I think, is his damnable and perverse obscurity. Partly this is the result of his verse technique, of his habit of overusing alliteration and thus emphasizing the sound of words at the expense of what they signify. Partly it is the result of literary tradition—the famous tradition of "opacity" that Eliot and Pound did so much to spread, and the plain-reader-be-damned tradition that was part of Dadaism and Surrealism. There are times when Auden deliberately befogs his meaning, and other times when he obviously doesn't mean anything at all; he is setting down his perceptions for their value in themselves and if they don't fit together into a unified picture, well, so much the worse for the reader. But there is another reason for his obscurity, a psychological reason having to do with his own position in that class war about which he is always writing. By birth and training Auden belongs with the exploiters. When he says "we," the people to whom he refers are the golf-playing, every-morning-bathing, tea-at-the-rector's-taking type of Britons. When he says "they," he is thinking of the workers; but he admires "them" and despises "us." He believes that his own class is decaying from within, is destined to be overthrown, and he looks forward to this event with happy anticipation:

If we really want to live, we'd better start at once to try;
If we don't, it doesn't matter, but we'd better start to die.

And that, I think, is the principal source of his ambiguity: he regards himself as a class traitor, a spy, a Copperhead. For this reason he is forced to speak in parables, to use code words like a conspirator in a Vienna cafe who wants to deliver a message but knows that the bulls are listening. He is on his guard, wary—till suddenly he gets tired of being cautious and blurts out a condemnation of everything he hates. I like him best when he is least self-protective.

What shall we say of both these poets? They have a good many obvious faults, their appeal is partly a snob appeal (and this is true of Auden in particular), but there is life in them always, and reading them is a stimulating experience. They are opening up a new territory. The best of them is the feeling that they will call forth other poets, not merely to follow in their footsteps, but perhaps to go beyond.

Silone's Villagers

Fontamara is a novel that takes its name from a village. The village stands on a dry hilltop in the barren country east of Rome; it consists of a church with broken windows and about a hundred one-story houses. Most of these have only a single opening, which has to serve as doorway, window, chimney and vent for smells. Inside, on the dirt floor, are men, women, children, donkeys, pigs, goats and chickens, all eating, sleeping, procreating and complaining together within four walls. Fontamara is known as the poorest and most backward of the Marsican villages, but a few years ago it had its revolution, it fought against Rome. How the revolution came about is the subject of the novel.

It all began on the day the lights were turned off. For nearly a year, nobody in Fontamara had paid for electric lights; nobody had money to pay for them. Lately the agent hadn't even come round to present his bills; on his last trip somebody had shot from ambush and barely missed him. The Fontamarans had begun to think that electric lights were a gift of nature; then suddenly, on the evening of June 1, the lights went out and didn't come on again.

While the peasants were standing in the square before the church and discussing this extraordinary event, a soft-faced stranger appeared on a bicycle and ordered them to sign a petition to the government. He wouldn't tell them what the petition was, but he assured them that it had nothing to do with taxes and wouldn't cost them any money and so, after an argument, the Fontamarans obeyed. A few days later they learned just what the favor was that the government had granted at their humble request. There was a stream that for centuries had irrigated their fields and made it possible to grow corn and beans enough to keep them alive through the winter. The petition was supposed to be presented "in the superior interests of high production." It asked that the water be turned away from their own fields and used to irrigate a vineyard

"Donkey Town." A review of *Fontamara*, by Ignazio Silone. Translated by Michael Wharf. New York: Harrison Smith and Robert Haas. (*NR*, Oct. 10, 1934.)

whose new owner, the Promoter, was "in a position to bring greater resources of capital to bear upon its development." Already workmen were busy diverting the stream.

The Fontamarans were fools; they were renowned as the greatest fools in Marsica and perhaps in all Italy. On one occasion when they petitioned to have a priest of their own, the townspeople sent them a donkey decked out in holy vestments. Another time—but there is no use repeating all the funny stories that were told about the Fontamarans. The point is that they were foolish enough to be gulled, but not foolish enough to starve to death willingly. All the women of the village went to the Promoter's house and began breaking his windows when he wouldn't listen to them, and might have burned the house down, too, if they hadn't been stopped by Don Circonstanza, the lawyer. He had a compromise to offer. "These women claim," he said, "that half the stream is not enough to irrigate their fields. Right they are, ten times over. So there is just one single solitary solution. Our alderman"—this was the Promoter himself, who had just been named to administer the township— "our alderman must have his three-fourths of the stream water, and the three-fourths of the water that remains will go to the Fontamarans. Thus the one party as well as the other will have a three-fourths share, that is, a trifle more than half."

The Fontamarans were fools, donkeys who deserved a donkey for their priest. They went away believing that they would actually receive three-fourths of their own stream, and not three-sixteenths of it. But when the division of water was made and their fields began to dry up and their corn turned yellow, the Fontamarans knew soon enough what had happened; this time they were even ready to attack the town hall and fight the Fascist militia. Don Circonstanza, the lawyer, stopped them by offering another compromise: after a reasonable period, the water should be given back to them. How long was a reasonable period? The Promoter said fifty years, the priest forty, the notary public twenty-five, but Don Circonstanza argued for a shorter period and insisted that the water should be turned back to Fontamara after "ten quinquenniads." So the agreement was written, and the Fontamarans went home half-satisfied. They couldn't bring themselves to believe that ten quinquenniads would be longer than ten months.

The Fontamarans were fools and their foolishness had a legendary quality; they resembled the youngest brother in the fairy tales. Like him they could see at least as far as the ends of their noses. They could see that times were getting harder for them every year, and taxes higher, and wages lower. They could see that none of them had a chance any longer to rise in the world and buy a piece of land. In the old days the Fontamarans used to emigrate to Brazil or the Argentine and come back with money enough to set themselves up as farmers, but now emigration was forbidden and there was even a law against going to look for work in another Italian province without special permission from the alderman. The Fontamarans had nothing left to depend on but their fields, and their fields henceforth were barren.

Fools as they were, they had learned two lessons. The first was that the farmers of Marsica had to forget their ancient feuds, house against house, village against village, and unite against their common enemies: the promoters, the Fascist militia and the government of the rich. The second was that the question they had to ask in each new situation was not "To whom shall we turn?" or "Who ever heard the like of it?" but "What must we do?" This was what Lenin used to ask, and people said his mind was like that of a peasant; the bright men like Kerensky despised him for being slow-witted. The Fontamarans, though they had never heard of him, were beginning to follow Lenin's path; they were laying plans, choosing leaders, writing a farmers' newspaper and making alliances with the neighboring villages. But before the first issue of their newspaper was distributed, the fascist cavalrymen came galloping up the road that led from the valley and—

The story goes no further. Some of the Fontamarans were killed, some were imprisoned, but nobody knows their names or what happened afterwards. At least three of the peasants escaped in the darkness. Helped by the Unknown Hand, they made their way northward for hundreds of miles and crossed the border into Switzerland. One night Ignazio Silone found the three of them—father, mother and grown son—sitting on his doorstep in Zurich. Silone is an Italian writer who used to live near Fontamara, until he defended the peasants too warmly and had to go into exile. He took the refugees into his house and listened all night while they told him what had happened in the countryside where he had spent his boyhood. Now the father talked, now the mother or the son, but there was no break in the narrative; always the whole village was speaking through their lips.

That, he tells us, is how *Fontamara* came to be written. It is a political novel that deals, apparently, with life in a single village, and yet this village is a concave mirror in which the whole of Fascist Italy is reflected in miniature. The book is so simple and quickly moving and full of hill-country humor that it seems shorter than it really is; you read to the end without laying it down and are surprised to find that it is long past midnight. Afterwards you reflect that although the story begins as broad farce and ends as tragedy, the underlying tone of it is neither one nor the other. Beneath the events of the story is a lyrical sadness, the longing for home of a man who loves his own country and can't go back to it until the present government is overthrown. Perhaps Silone won't have to wait until his hair turns white.

Jesse Stuart: Man with a Hoe

HERE IS a new sort of book about the Kentucky hills. The others were written from the outside, by townspeople who had spent a few months or years among the hillsmen and had learned something about their customs, their ballads, their dialect. Usually these "furriners" were kind and sympathetic, but there was showmanship in their gestures, and in their voices a creeping hint of condescension. They seemed to be asking, "Aren't these people lovably quaint? Aren't they pitiable in their ignorance and rags? Can't we *do* something for them?" Charity visitors, they reined their horses outside a mountain cabin and benevolently watched the barefoot chil-

Man with a Bull Tongue Plow, by Jesse Stuart. New York: E. P. Dutton and Company. (*NR*, Oct. 31, 1934.)

dren scampering in the dust, without ever getting down from their own high saddles. Jesse Stuart is a poet who lives inside the cabin and writes about the life he knows best. He writes about side-hill farmers, moonshiners and loggers, not because they are picturesque but because they are his own people. More often he writes about the land itself—

> *The land of oak trees and the scrubby pine*
> *And sawbriars under the persimmon tree*

—because it is his own land, because he knows the smell of it when his plow turns it over and the feel of it between his bare toes.

Jesse Stuart was born in 1907; he comes from W-Hollow, in Greenup County, in the far northeastern corner of Kentucky. He says that "my father's people, the Stuarts and Stewarts, are, and have been, feudists, killers, boozers, country preachers, Republicans and fine soldiers. My mother's people, the Hiltons, are, and have been, country school teachers, moonshiners, rebels and Democrats. They have all been pioneers in the Big Sandy Valley and the mountains of Kentucky." There is an easy American myth which holds that the pioneers, after crossing Cumberland Gap with Daniel Boone, pushed westward—or rather their grandsons pushed westward—to dig for gold in California and later to become the ancestors of the great American industrialists. Justice is mystically done—men died to open the Middle West, to conquer a continent, and lo! their descendants are rewarded with a controlling interest in Midwest Utilities and Continental Can. But the truth is that the great Western fortunes were made by men who crossed the mountains after the country was safely settled and the Indians herded away. The pioneers themselves were mostly poor men, driven onward by their poverty and never able to rise out of it. Today their children's great-grandchildren are digging coal in southern Indiana or sharecropping in the Arkansas river bottoms, or perhaps plowing a hill farm in eastern Kentucky. They have never seen anything but the underside of American business enterprise. Jesse Stuart himself, who paid for his education by digging ditches and mowing hay, says that he is "the first of my people to finish college." More important, he is the first spokesman that the pioneers of the Kentucky hills have found among themselves.

His book contains 703 poems, all of about the same length, that is, from fourteen to sixteen lines. Jesse Stuart calls them sonnets, but they are not sonnets by any rules that Petrarch or Shakespeare would recognize: rather, they are short lyrics, sometimes with refrains, often with repetitions that take the place of rhymes. *Man with a Bull Tongue Plow* is approximately seven times as long as an ordinary collection of verse, yet I should judge that it contains no more than half the poems written by this young man of twenty-seven; I have seen many others in manuscript, and some of them are better than any of those included here. He writes entirely too much for his own good or the reader's. At least half the time he is careless, trite or perfunctory; but always he is speaking in his own words about his own people, and he doesn't know how to lie.

He shows us the mountaineers, huge families of them, living in one-room pine-pole shacks on the hillside, with gourd vines growing over the porch and two or three hound dogs sleeping under it in the warm dust. He gives us the feel of the dooryard, with its "paths worn bare enough for feet to tell," and the look of the picket fence outside, where glass fruit jars are upturned on the palings. With the "country ikes" we ride into town on muleback; we learn to share their hatred for the merchants, the Pin Hooks, who rob them of their profits from a crop of Burley tobacco. We hear stories about feuds and lynchings and shotgun marriages. We visit country dances where Blind Frailey the fiddler plays "Girl with the Blue Dress On" and "Waltz the Hall"; we are there when the boys drink white corn liquor and begin fighting in the moonlight. Best of all, we take part in the work that keeps these people alive. We help to burn sprouts from the new-ground fields before the spring planting, and in summer we march out with the whole family, from the grandmother down to the boys of six or seven, "to peck our hoes deep in the golden clay." Anybody who has driven through the Kentucky mountains has seen these families working together on the steep hillside, all of them ragged as beggars and lean as foxes, the men in overalls and worn brogans, the women and children barefoot. Anybody could describe them vividly or write eloquent addresses to the Men with Hoes, but Jesse Stuart gives us the accurate notation of how it feels to be working among them:

The loam is hot to filter between toes,
It's smothersome in tall corn to use hoes
And cut pusley and careless from the rows.

At their best, his poems have the springtime freshness of medieval ballads. Their worst fault is that they are written without effort or economy. Jesse Stuart says everything at least twice. The lines come to him quickly and he sets them down as they come, without seeming to know the difference between the good and the bad ones, between the thoughts that are his own and those that have been expressed, not once before but ten thousand times, by every poetaster since the first bastard children of Homer. It is true that by using new images he can sometimes lend new color to a very old conceit. Thus, when he describes the beauty of his lady (whom the medieval poets endowed with skin white as snow, lips red as blood, hair black as the raven's wing), he invents a whole set of fresh comparisons:

Her teeth were bloodroot white—her hair was black
As thick rain clouds—her lips were soft as new
Bark peeled from a slippery elm and her back
Was straight as a horseweed upon the shore.
Her legs were brown as the buff-colored corn.

He can even dress the moon in a new epithet—"the sliced muskmelon moon"—but there are times when he simply parrots what other poets have said. There are times, too, when he is not only conventional but colt-awkward, tangled in his feet; at his worst this Kentucky poet is scarcely better than the Sweet Singer of Michigan. He shows little power of organization, even in the separate poems. The book as a whole would be vastly improved if it were arranged on some coherent and simple theme—the life of a hillsman, for example, or the cycle of the Kentucky seasons. As it is, the poems are tossed at us helter-skelter until they end by beating down our enthusiasm. Half of the book, yes, three-fourths of it, could be destroyed without loss to its author or to the world; but even if we saved only twenty of the best poems out of seven hundred we should still be left with a considerable body of fresh and honest writing. The Kentucky hillsmen have offered their first contribution to American literature, and I hope they profit from this gift they have made.

Outline of Wells's History

H. G. WELLS is one of the very few British writers who belonged to the lower middle class and yet managed early in their careers to reach a place of acknowledged eminence. Dickens, I think, was his only great predecessor, and the two men have several qualities in common, notably a certain copiousness and raw vigor of invention. Yet even Dickens had a little higher social rank than Wells: his father was at least a clerk in the Navy pay office. Wells's father was a gardener who lost his job and scraped together money enough to run a china shop, unprofitably. His mother had been a lady's maid before declining into an unpaid household drudge; she wanted her children to lead a better life, but her highest ambition for them was to make them drapers' apprentices. The family lived over and behind their shop, in an old brick house that smelled of squashed bedbugs, with an outside toilet twenty feet from the pump that gave them drinking water. Not many people have stayed long in a background like this without being forever scarred, or have risen from it without sacrificing their integrity.

But Wells was lucky, even in the calamities that rained down on him. He says, "Probably I am alive today and writing this autobiography instead of being a worn-out, dismissed and already dead shop assistant, because my leg was broken." It was a broken leg, at the age of seven, that first gave him the habit of reading. Later a whole series of accidents and blunders rescued him from the half-dozen false starts he made before launching out as a writer. But perhaps the luckiest event of his whole career was his choice of a year to be born in. After 1866 England was developing its first jumbled system of universal free education, with new schools being started everywhere. By the time Wells was sixteen, there were teaching positions open even to conceited boys who couldn't get along as drapers' apprentices; and by the time he was twenty-one, there was a vast new public, lately disfranchised and illiterate, that was learning simultaneously to vote, read and do a little thinking. The market for ideas was a sellers' market. Wells could earn a

Experiment in Autobiography, by H. G. Wells. New York: The Macmillan Company. (*NR*, Nov. 14, 1934.)

living as a writer because new magazines were being founded
and had empty columns to fill; he could rise quickly because
whole sections of his own class were rising along with him. He
doesn't claim to be the sort of genius who would have made his
own opportunities. He had, so he often tells us, "a rather
ordinary mind"; he was the representative man of his time,
and the time was well chosen.

With all his luck, he came near going under. He haunted
employment agencies and lost one job after another; he was
undernourished and tubercular, to say nothing of being di-
vinely ignorant of the world in which he was trying to get
ahead; probably it was his toughness and self-conceit that
saved him. But his struggles seem brief in retrospect and, by
his twenty-sixth year, the worst of them were over. This again
was vastly fortunate. He had risen so fast that instead of being
exhausted by his ascent he had gathered impetus; instead of
feeling bitter toward mankind he was happy and grateful; he
wanted the whole world to rise along with him, from mean
streets into seaside villas with concealed plumbing, from ignorance and disorganization into an international planned society.
At the turn of the century, the middle classes were enjoying a
great burst of optimism. All good things had been spreading—
knowledge, wealth, comfort, tolerance—and there seemed to
be no reason why they could not continue to spread indefinitely. The coming revolution would be peaceful and would be
directed by middle-class scientists and engineers, who would
reconcile the poor with the rich by helping both of them.
Wells gave definite shape to ideas like these; he painted the
bright picture of things to come. By the time he was forty, his
influence was wider than that of any other living English
writer, and he was fortunate in his audience: it was the generous young people who read and followed him.

Wells's luck has persisted even to the present. Just at the
moment when it seemed that he was going to fade out a little
less spectacularly than Bennett, Galsworthy and Shaw, publishing a long series of volumes each one of which was reviewed a little more briefly and read a little less carefully than
its predecessor—now, in his sixty-eighth year, he has come close
to performing a miracle. He has written a book that stands
with the best of his earlier work. For my own part, I vastly

prefer this outline of Wells by Wells to his three ponderous outlines of human knowledge. *Experiment in Autobiography* is to be valued chiefly as a work of art; it is, I think, the best of his novels.

It is even a whole collection of novels, bigger and more satisfying than most of the current trilogies and tetralogies. It begins as a sort of David Copperfield story about a Cockney boy who lived among all sorts of bad smells and quaint characters and managed somehow to get an education. Then there is a second novel, the love story of a young science instructor who married his cousin and deserted her for one of his pupils, thereby putting an end to his teaching career. These early adventures are told without shame or reticence, but also without any attempt to dramatize the hero. A third section, "Fairly Launched at Last," is good in a quite different way. Wells was now (1895–1900) a rising young novelist, and the drama of his story was centered in his meetings with other writers and his interchange of ideas with them. He reminds us here of something we had almost forgotten: the vigor and ferment of intellectual life at the turn of the century, the passion with which ideas were put forward and debated, the feeling that all these projects would be realized in the better society of the future. Those were the great days of liberalism, and Wells makes them live again.

But his autobiography has also a final section, a chapter of fifty thousand words that deals with his career since 1900 and his picture of the world in which we live. It is obviously and immensely inferior to everything that has gone before. Partly, I suppose, the sudden loss of richness and sympathy is explained by causes personal to the author. He has lived so much in public that he has almost ceased to have any private life (or at least any private life that he can now write about candidly, without hurting the reputations of people still alive). He is dealing, moreover, with recent events that he hasn't had time to digest. Even so, I think that he could and would have done a better job if he had not been held back by the fear of saying the last word about himself and his world, and so being left at sixty-eight with no more books to write. The beginning of his autobiography is too good; it must have frightened him into making a weak conclusion.

There is, however, another and less personal reason for the positive dullness of the last chapter. Wells regards this book as being essentially a story about "the awakening of world citizenship in a fairly normal intelligence." From this point of view, the chapter in which his "citizenship" takes its final form ought to be the climax of an intellectual drama. But the climax is botched and unconvincing. His dream of an Open Conspiracy of millionaires and technicians that would take over the world and run it intelligently is a dream that has nothing to do with the shape of things as they are. Instead of serving as a reasoned guide to conduct, it ends by being a religion, one that consoles him for his personal inadequacies and one whose "releasing and enveloping relation to the individual *persona* is . . . almost precisely the same" as that of other religions. It is a faith that blinds him to everything real and threatening in the present situation—to the lassitude and fear of the future that are spreading through the Western world, to the bitterness of the ambitious young students who would like to rise like H. G. Wells but find that their path has been blocked, to the desperation of the working classes, the uneasy fear that attacks the rulers, the almost universal violence that is the most evident feature of life in these middle decades of the twentieth century. Wells is happy in his faith. He believes that civilization still is marching upwards and onwards, that the goal is now in sight, and that merely by education, without blood or class conflicts, we can attain the Great Good Place of which he dreams, where men like himself will "supply teaching, coercive and directive public services to the whole world."

Wells's Utopia belongs to the happy days before the War. Today it is less alive, and less skillfully embalmed, than Lenin's corpse in his tomb outside the Kremlin. Still, Wells himself lives on and ends by impressing us with his own sort of greatness. He is like the survivor of a prehistoric time, a warm, ponderous, innocent creature ill adapted to the Ice Age in which we live, and yet overshadowing the smaller animals that shiver behind rocks without ever venturing into the open.

The *Smart Set* Legend

THE REAL *Smart Set* was a much less inspiriting and imposing magazine than Burton Rascoe implies in his lively introduction to *The Smart Set Anthology*. He pictures it as bursting like a bombshell in a Methodist graveyard, as frightening and coaxing American literature out of the tomb where the Comstocks had buried it, as continually discovering new talents and as printing nearly everybody worth printing in the ten years before 1923. That is the *Smart Set* legend and there is a kernel of truth in it, but the truth is surrounded with a shell of sentiment and a thick husk of exaggeration. Indeed, my chief surprise on reading the present collection, with its 850 pages of stories, poems, plays and horseplays, was at finding how many good American writers had never appeared in *The Smart Set* or mailed even an angry letter to the editors.

Anderson, Dos Passos, Brooks, Hemingway, Sandburg— there is no use mentioning names when figures are available. Last summer Carl Van Doren published his anthology of *Modern American Prose*, which included extracts from the work of what he regarded as the sixty best prose writers since 1915. Van Doren has always praised the former editors of *The Smart Set* and has concurred in most of their judgments. Yet of the sixty writers he selected—of fifty-eight, to be utterly fair, since two of them began publishing after 1923—only twenty-one ever appeared in *The Smart Set*, and most of these were represented by neither their earliest nor their mature work. The situation among the poets is even more striking. Mark Van Doren edited an anthology that contains, in its final pages, the work of thirty poets born since 1875. Only four of these ever had poems printed in *The Smart Set*. There is no confirmation here for the legend that Mencken and Nathan were foster parents to the younger American literature.

Yet the *Smart Set* legend has a basis in fact and in time. There happens to have been a brief period when no other American magazine was so interesting or influential, and Rascoe tells the whole story in his introduction. Early in 1913 the

The Smart Set Anthology, edited by Burton Rascoe and Groff Conklin. New York: Reynal and Hitchcock. (*NR*, Jan. 16, 1935.)

owner of the magazine was buffaloed into signing a year's contract with a young editor named Willard Huntington Wright. The contract specified that Wright was to have an absolutely free hand in selecting manuscripts and a generous budget with which to pay for them. He had the intoxicating sense of being able to do just what he pleased, and what he pleased was to print the recent European writers—Schnitzler, Joyce, Lawrence, Max Beerbohm, Wedekind, Artzibashev, d'Annunzio. Not one of these men had ever before been published in an American magazine; the public scarcely knew that they existed. When they were gathered together and printed in twelve successive issues, each more brilliant than the last, their impact on younger readers was tremendous; I can offer this testimony out of my own experience. It seemed that a new world was being revealed to us, that it was time to smash the Victorian gods, open all the windows, go floating off on a cloud of dream toward golden Vienna and Paris the City of Light.

Rascoe is possibly right in saying that *The Smart Set* for 1913 was "the most audacious, the best edited and the best remembered of any magazine ever published on this continent." Unfortunately it was not the most profitable. The publisher was disturbed by the attacks of ministers and editorial writers; he was not reassured by looking at his ledgers. He waited for the contract to expire, showed Wright the door, and then, in the issue of March, 1914, he announced a change of policy in a document that is worth quoting at length. After explaining that "to gather laurels is one thing; to publish a successful magazine is another," he described some of the laurels gathered during Wright's editorship. "But," he continued,

> . . . together with this academic approval we have received stout protests. Many of our most valued readers have written us that they did not like the innovation; some of the stories, though written by distinguished English, Continental and American authors, have struck them as too somber; the frankness of certain others has displeased them. In short, we have been too serious as regards the relation of literature to life.
>
> We admit a certain force in the criticism, and so, while modestly wearing the bays we have gathered during the past year, we announce, not a less discriminating realism in such realistic stories as we may publish, but a good round measure of

romantic and humorous relief, to the end that our friends, old
and new, may find in us that variety they ask of a magazine
which, above all, seeks to entertain. We shall continue to make
our appeal especially to the well educated, thinking, appreciative
alert-minded class of Americans who like fiction with a little
tang to it; who relish a bit of subtlety now and then; who like to
be surprised; who enjoy stories of ideas; stories with a strong
dramatic flavor; stories containing an occasional thrill; in a
nutshell, stories different from those found in the usual magazine.

There are thousands upon thousands of such readers in this
country—readers to whom the word "smart" in its best sense of
acuteness, nimble-mindedness, up-to-dateness, makes a strong appeal—yet who are not ultra in any respect. These are the readers
we want, even though they may not be ahead of modern literary
currents. We shall be satisfied if they are merely abreast—with
us.

I think this document should be studied in every school of
journalism: it offers the best possible program for painlessly
suffocating a magazine. When editors begin to talk about being
romantic without ceasing to be realistic—about being subtle and
a little sexy while remaining innately wholesome—about pleasing the radicals and the conservatives simultaneously—then it
is time to call for oxygen tanks and blood transfusions; the
patient is about to expire. The only marvel is that *The Smart
Set* lived on for ten years.

Partly it lived because the legend refused to die; but
chiefly it lived because of Mencken and Nathan, who became
joint editors a few months after Wright's contract expired.
They were not much interested, I suspect, in his program of
publishing the most brilliant work of the best European writers. Nathan wanted to say what he thought about the new
plays; Mencken wanted to write literary criticisms and pursue
his long crusade against rural Baptists. As long as they were
given their own pages to fill as they pleased, as long as they
could print a few stories they really admired, they were willing to edit the rest of the magazine for people who like fiction
with a little tang to it and relish a bit of subtlety now and then
—in other words, for drugstore cowboys.

The Good Earthling

MRS. BUCK's new novel, *A House Divided*, is honest, rich, full-bodied and in general good enough to justify the adjectives that reviewers will lavish on it. Nevertheless it would have seemed a great deal better if it had appeared twelve months ago, before the publication of *Man's Fate* and *A Chinese Testament*.* This doesn't mean that she has been even slightly influenced by Malraux or Tretiakov. On the contrary, she has completed her trilogy of Chinese life exactly as she must have planned it from the first, taking what she regards as the three most vigorous Chinese types—the farmer, the war lord, the student—and treating them in three long novels that together summarize fifty years in the life of a family and a nation. It happens, however, that the student-hero of her new novel strongly resembles the student-hero of *A Chinese Testament*—not for any reason of literary derivation, but simply because the type is widely prevalent in China and because both Tretiakov and Mrs. Buck have portrayed it honestly. It also happens that the first section of *A House Divided* deals with the same period of the Chinese revolution that was more fully treated in *Man's Fate*. The two comparisons force themselves on the reader. Mrs. Buck suffers in both cases, for the other books, in their different ways, are better as literature, more vivid, more compelling.

I would not say that they are truer to Chinese life. Mrs. Buck has spent so many years in the country, has studied the language so well, has lived on such terms of friendship with the people, that she makes Tretiakov and Malraux seem like tourists dropping ashore from a round-the-world cruise. She has a truly extraordinary gift for presenting the Chinese, not as quaint and illogical, yellow-skinned, exotic devil-dolls, but as human beings merely, animated by motives we can always understand even when the background is strange and topsy-turvy. The Chinese themselves are in general eager to praise

A House Divided, by Pearl S. Buck. New York: Reynal and Hitchcock (a John Day book). (*NR*, Jan. 23, 1935.)

* Cowley reviews *Man's Fate* on page 228 and *A Chinese Testament* on page 63.

her work; many of them say that no native writer has painted
a more accurate picture of their country. A few Chinese critics
have attacked her, but usually because they stood to the left or
right of her politically—either they were communist sympathizers or else they were the violent sort of patriots who hate
all foreigners and want to go back to the good old Confucian
customs. Mrs. Buck instinctively takes a middle course. She
seems to know China so well that she no longer judges it even
from the standpoint of "the native Chinese"—whoever he may
be—but rather from the standpoint of a particular class, the
one that includes the liberal, three-quarters Westernized scholars who deplore the graft and cruelty of the present government but nevertheless keep their heads on their shoulders and
hold their noses, and support General Chiang Kai-shek because
they are afraid of what would happen if he were overthrown.

The hero of *A House Divided* belongs to this class. Mrs.
Buck presents him with deep sympathy, but she does not
succeed in making his character seem admirable or even lika-
ble. Wang the Student is the grandson of Wang the Farmer,
described in *The Good Earth;* he is the son of Wang the
Tiger, described in *Sons;* but he has lost the simple sense of
direction that held his ancestors to their path. He is a neither-
nor sort of person. Thus, he can neither take the side of the
new ruling classes, whose cruelty offends his heart, nor work
beside the proletarians and peasants, whose smell offends his
nostrils; he can neither wholly adopt Western customs nor
revert to the ways of his fathers. Unable to fight toward any
fixed goal, he must always hesitate, see the good mingled with
the evil without being able to weigh them in the balance. He
could never be the hero of a great drama, for, being blind to
his own destiny, he can neither accept it nor rebel against it.

In the classical age of Corneille and Racine there was a
rule that only kings or queens could be the subject of tragedies.
The rule, I think, was not entirely nonsense, for it meant that
tragedies enacted themselves on a high stage built, as it were,
of human conflicts and aspirations. Translated into modern
terms, it would mean that novels and dramas should deal
preferably with men and women who are in a high degree
conscious of themselves, of the parts they play in the world, of
the social conditions by which they are molded (and which in

turn they help to mold). They should deal, in other words, not with the typical or average but with the *representative*. Particularly in a novel that describes a revolutionary crisis, it is a mistake, I think, to present a hero who sees only the blank underside of events and cannot even choose the side he wants to fight for. The real dramas take place among the planners, the agitators, the new leaders thrown up violently by the masses like rocks from a volcano—and, on the other hand, among the capitalists and generals who are organizing their counterplots and trying to buy or bully a mass support for themselves. This is the sound principle that André Malraux followed in writing *Man's Fate*, and it is one of the reasons why the climax of the novel has the power of a great tragedy. His revolutionists are in a prison yard waiting to be burned alive—but they have all known the cause they were fighting for, they have calculated the risks they were running, and now, at the moment of death, they find a bitter and exalted reward in their feeling of nearness to one another. . . . It happens that Mrs. Buck describes a similar scene in *A House Divided*. Scores of Chinese students are arrested for having revolutionary literature; they are kept moaning in a cell overnight and then, in the morning, they are driven out to be killed. It is pathetic and strong enough, but it is also rather futile, for the victims have no very clear idea of the cause for which they are dying. The cutting short of all their lives seems less a tragedy than a regrettable and essentially meaningless accident.

As for the other book I mentioned, *A Chinese Testament*, it suggests a different lesson. It is not a novel at all; the author calls it a "bio-interview," and explains that he gathered his material by talking every day for six months to a typical Chinese student. Artistically his experiment was altogether successful. The lesson his book suggests is that, if a writer wishes to describe a typical rather than a representative figure, he might do so in the form of a life-document based accurately on real events. A life-document has several advantages over a novel. It does not require a formal plot ending, for example, with Wang the Student embracing his beloved Mei-ling outside the hut where Wang the Farmer began his life and Wang the Tiger now lies dying. It can begin anywhere and end anywhere; it can introduce all sorts of relevant material; and it permits any type of interpretative treatment—provided only that the writer remains faithful always to the truth that is not necessarily stranger than fiction, but is likely to be richer in color, contrast and meaning.

Letter to England

I SAID that most of the stories and poems and knowing epigrams reprinted in *The Smart Set Anthology* are beginning to smell of mold and lavender. I said that reading them today is like pawing through a trunk in the lumber-room of a rented house and wondering who could have been thrilled by these preposterous gowns and artificial flowers—and who in the world ever thought that these white nainsook drawers with imitation-lace frills at the bottom were unmentionable! But *The Smart Set*, I said, made a great noise in its time and did a lot of good along with incalculable damage. . . .

I was writing an article on contemporary American literature for one of the London weeklies. Quite naturally, in addressing readers on the other side of the Atlantic, one adopts a different point of view. The writer takes three steps backwards in order to gain a longer perspective; he tries to emphasize the outlines of the picture at the expense of the details; he generalizes and pontificates. Sometimes the simple and definite pattern that results is of interest to readers in his own country. I hope it is, at any rate, for I intend without more apologies to copy most of the American letter that I wrote for a recent issue of *Time and Tide*.

Better than any other magazine [I said], better than any book whatever, *The Smart Set* typifies the second of three distinct stages through which American literature has passed since 1900.

NR, Feb. 13, 1935. See page 248 for review of *The Smart Set Anthology*.

During the first of those stages, which lasted till 1918 or thereabouts, the atmosphere was predominantly British and provincial. New York and Boston were like Liverpool and Edinburgh. Writers here chose British models to imitate, mostly those of the Victorian era. But because there are some types of cultural influence that grow stronger as they travel outward from the center—and also because disciples are more dogmatic than their masters—the reign of belated Victorianism in New York was even stiffer and stuffier than Victoria's English reign. In Burton Rascoe's introduction to *The Smart Set Anthology*, there is a story that symbolizes the whole period. It seems that Robert Louis Stevenson, passing through New York, paid a visit to *The Century Magazine*. The editor would not admit Mr. Stevenson to his office on the ground that Mr. Stevenson was not respectable. Everyday life in general—anything that felt or smelled or tasted of reality—was barred out of American magazine offices on the same principle.

The book publishers, then as now, could afford to be more lenient. A few good novels and scores of promising novels were printed in the years before the War. But there was one generality that applied to most of the talented writers as well as to the bad ones, namely, that they expressed and represented only one stratum of American society. Their morals and manners, their virtues and limitations, were those of prosperous people living near the Atlantic seaboard. Literature was regarded as an effeminate upper-class affair open chiefly to men with a Harvard education. There were a few mavericks like Dreiser and Jack London, there was a vast literary underworld of poor devils freezing in garrets, but most of the successful and widely copied writers were well-to-do men used to sitting at the tables of millionaires. They imposed a general level of respectable dullness.

The Smart Set helped to introduce a second stage in American literary taste. It aimed to be a little disreputable (though without ever going far enough to run the risk of suppression by the incredibly strict post-office censorship). It was "A Magazine of Cleverness" whose prime purpose was "To Provide Lively Entertainment for Minds That Are Not Primitive," and its editorial policy was un-British, even anti-British. Especially after 1912, the stories it imported and the great models it held up for imitation were likely to be German, Austrian or French. *The Smart Set* began to have a vast prestige among the younger writers; it set them to making 2.75-percent Nietzschean epigrams and to dreaming of beery-romantic picnics in the Vienna woods.

But it also had a social side and one that presented a rather significant paradox. Originally it was intended as an upper-class literary magazine. Its founder was an—except to his victims— entertaining rogue who got most of his income from a society blackmailing sheet. Long after *The Smart Set* had passed into other hands, it continued to talk a great deal about aristocracy and to ridicule the respectable middle classes. The paradox lay in the fact that, after 1914, its editors, its contributors in great majority and at least nine-tenths of its readers were obviously and unalterably middle-class. They were young for the most part, the sons and daughters of small lawyers, ministers, physicians or businessmen. They wanted to escape from their class limitations, they wanted to be cosmopolitan and sophisticated, but they didn't quite know how to go about it. For that reason the stories they read and wrote and edited had a quality of strain and falseness sometimes rising to high burlesque. Of a typical *Smart Set* heroine it would be said that "None of her attributes could be designated the Menteith's most living charm, neither the timbre of her caroling laugh, the poise of her carriage, nor her green eyes' *chatoyant* allure." The heroes would be "long, lean men, decadent aristocrats, high-bred indolents, subtle, bored, indifferent, dispassionate souls." They were all ghosts dressed in clothes from Bond Street or the Rue de la Paix. But I am rather tempted to believe it was the clothes that were insubstantial and ghostly; inside them could be recognized the bodies of nice corn-fed boys and girls from Ohio or Alabama, strutting the boulevards, bursting with eagerness to prove that they were subtle, bored and indifferent.

All this happened toward the beginning of the second literary period. Before the end of it—that is, by 1929—*The Smart Set* had disappeared along with most of the affectations it helped to inspire. The corn-fed boys and girls had either grown into their imported clothes or else had learned the wisdom of dressing to resemble themselves. Aristocracy wasn't so much talked about. It was evident that American literature had become chiefly a middle-class product, without the manners, the reticences, the it-can't be-saids that ruling classes generally cultivate.

Then, beginning in 1930, there was another swift and striking change. It was as if literary values had been listed on the stock exchange, as if they had been offered and bid for like shares in the automotive industries or in public utilities, and as if, on Black Thursday, they had all come tumbling down. Several of the writers who had distinguished themselves during the preceding decade suddenly fell silent; they had the air of being dazed. All the ideals they had fought for were being called into question; nobody any longer showed an interest in cosmopolitan sophistication or significant form or probing the unconscious or building a castle of beauty remote from the world. New questions were being argued—more bitterly than the old ones, since the quarrels rising ordinarily from vanity and temperament were now mingled with class hatreds. At the same time, a whole new generation of novelists was appearing.

Many of these were distinguished in point of social origin from the writers who preceded them. During the prosperous years there had been a wider diffusion of education: not only small businessmen but also farmers, railway workers and skilled mechanics had been sending their sons and daughters to the state universities. Some of the students from poorer families had literary talent and new things to write about. At other times they might have been absorbed into the great middle classes, but after the depression there seemed to be no more chance for rising in the world, and accordingly they retained their working-class loyalties. . . . This may or may not be a sufficient explanation for what has been happening in the literary world. There is the fact, in any case, that many of the talented writers who have appeared since 1930—Erskine Caldwell, Jack Conroy, Robert Cantwell, William Saroyan, James Farrell, Grace Lumpkin, Albert Halper and others—either come from what we have learned to call the proletariat or else have allied themselves with it by writing about strikes from the standpoint of the strikers.

And so the last thirty years of American literature make such a neat pattern that I hesitate to define it, out of an habitual distrust for neat patterns and a consciousness of the thousand and one exceptions that distort them. First there were the upper-class writers, then the middle-class writers, and now, since the depression, there are the proletarian writers, though they cannot claim to dominate even the field of fiction, let alone those of poetry and criticism. First there was the English influence, then the Continental influence, mostly French, with a touch of German through *The Smart Set,* and now. . . . It can scarcely be said that the new foreign influence is Russian so far as technique is concerned. There is no doubt, however, that many of the younger novelists and poets are being inspired by the world revolutionary movement, that political ideas play a large part in their writing, and that their politics are those of Lenin rather than T. S. Eliot, let us say, or Ramsay MacDonald.

A Hope for Poetry

HERE ARE two more books to show that the hope for poetry in England is not a mirage. The palms on the horizon are only half-grown, but they are real. Their roots are watered by a genuine spring.

Stephen Spender, whose shorter poems were published here last September, has been living in Vienna while writing a longer and more ambitious work. In his boarding house he was surrounded with old maids and retired actors dead in the midst of life, people "printed in papers and cut out with scissors." In the streets he talked to the unemployed, whose eyes never met his, being "fixed upon an economic margin"; or else he listened to speeches by the official leaders, with smiles on their thin ministerial lips as transparent as thin glass—"the glass is dashed down suddenly and murder glares." He walked through the working-class quarters, where the great municipal apartment houses were pitted with machine-gun fire and cracked open by heavy artillery; he talked with survivors of

Vienna, by Stephen Spender. New York: Random House. *Poems,* by C. Day Lewis. New York: Random House. (*NR,* Feb. 27, 1935.)

the street fighting. And he incorporated all these encounters into a single poem, an elegy of eight hundred lines to the men who died in last year's revolution and a tribute to those who, burrowing like moles among the ruins, are carrying on the work of the dead.

Vienna is not technically faultless. The verse is obscure at moments when it ought to be straightforward, involved when it should be simple; it contains several chunks of nearly undigested prose. Yet it shows that Spender has a talent for symphonic structure and for sustained movement that he had not revealed in his earlier work; it adds to his stature as a poet.

Cecil Day Lewis is the writer most commonly linked with Spender and Auden. He has much in common with both of them, but he resembles Auden more closely—to such an extent, in fact, that many of his poems could be printed over Auden's signature, and vice versa, without changing the reputation of either. The whole group of younger English poets—not only the three who have been published here, but also others like Julian Bell, Louis MacNeice, R. E. Warner—are connected by common literary sources and political enthusiasms, by a tangle of personal friendships, and also by the use of what is almost a private language, with special values placed on words that are used repeatedly: "ancestors," "kestrels" as a symbol of free delight, "pylons" that stand for electrification, "the railhead" as a place from which paths diverge into unknown country. But each of these poets makes his own contribution to the common store; and that of Day Lewis is in certain ways greater than the others.

His *Poems* in the volume issued by Random House include three short books of verse and a long prose essay, all of which were published separately in England. "Transitional Poem"—really a sequence of thirty-four lyrics representing "phases of personal experience in the pursuit of single-mindedness"—is the first and least satisfying of these books. It proves that Day Lewis can be as metaphysical and pedantic as T. S. Eliot, and to my mind it does not prove much else. "From Feathers to Iron," dedicated to his wife, is simpler and better poetry. It is another sequence, this time consisting of thirty lyrics that deal with his thoughts and feelings during the nine months before the birth of his first child. Rarely in contemporary literature does one find love poems like these, at once passionate and intelligent and, in the best sense, manly. His third book, "The Magnetic Mountain," shows how his interests have broadened from the self to the family and at last to society in general. It consists of poems that are definitely political—"communist," they were called, although they are no more communist in the strict meaning of the word than any other honest appeals to build a new social order among the ruins. The book is well planned, splendidly put together, and it contains the best of his verse—as, for example, his description of the vessel that will carry us toward the future:

> *Peerless on water, Oh proud our palace,*
> *A home for heroes, the latest of her line;*
> *A beater to windward, obedient to rudder,*
> *A steamer into storm, a hurricane-rider,*
> *Foam-stepper, star-steerer, freighter and fighter—*
> *Name her, release her, anoint her with wine!*

In his prose essay, "A Hope for Poetry," he explains the social and literary background, the aims and poetical technique, of the group to which he belongs. He is a sharp critic, a clear, reasonable, undogmatic expounder, and his essay is almost indispensable to anyone who wants to know what Auden, for example, is trying to say in his more obscure poems. One of the ideas explained at length is that of "ancestor worship." It consists, Day Lewis says, in the feeling "that each of us has some personal link with the past, some natural or quasi-supernatural being from whom we draw power and refreshment, someone with whom a sudden recognition takes place." He adds that it is "of first importance" to all the poets of his circle. The trouble is that their favorite "ancestor," Gerard Manley Hopkins, has bequeathed them too rich a legacy of poetic mannerisms. It is only with the greatest difficulty that they are assimilating Hopkins' double epithets and cross rhymes and "sprung rhythm" into a personal style that is calculated to convey their own picture of the world.

Meanwhile the various roles of these young English poets are becoming more definite. Spender is above all the Man of Feeling, the poet who writes best when expressing his "palpable and obvious love" for his fellow creatures. Of the three, he comes nearest to having a universal appeal. Auden is the Man of Sensation, and he suffers, as Day Lewis points out in the midst of sincere praises, "from an extreme sensitiveness to the impact of ideas combined with an incapacity to relate them with any scheme of values." As for Day Lewis himself, he is the Man of Intelligence and the Man of Character. He is older than the others, more mature and level-headed; he has more critical sense and is able to develop a theme with surer logic. Politically, philosophically, every way but poetically, he is the best of his group, but he rarely touches Spender's warmth of human emotion or Auden's sharpness of perception. Still, he adds solidity and reasonableness and good humor to the unfinished structure on which they are jointly engaged.

The Forty Days of Thomas Wolfe

I HAVE just read Thomas Wolfe's new novel, all of the 912 big, solidly printed pages, almost every one of the 450,000 words, and, like a traveler returning safely from Outer Mongolia, I am eager to record what I heard and saw during forty days in the wilderness. It isn't so much a book review I should like to write as a topographical description of the regions newly explored, with a list of deserts and oases.

I have to report that the good passages in the novel are, first of all, the picture of Uncle Bascom Pentland, originally published by itself and now partly deprived of its effectiveness through being sawed and mortised into another framework, but still grotesque and vastly appealing; then the description of the little people in Professor Hatcher's course in dramatic writing; then the burlesque adventures of Oswald Ten Eyck in search of food and fame; then the death of old Oliver Gant, a tremendous Dostoevskian scene; then the comedy of Abe Jones, the melodrama of the consumptive cuckold, the tragedy of the Coulson family at Oxford; then the disintegration of

Of Time and the River, by Thomas Wolfe. New York: Charles Scribner's Sons. (*NR*, Mar. 20, 1935.)

Francis Starwick, whom I knew at college under his own name, and whose story is long enough to form a good novel in itself; then finally the train ride to Orléans and the episode of the old humbug countess. Together these scenes compose at least a third of the book, and they are extraordinarily strong and living. Thomas Wolfe at his best is the only contemporary American writer who can be mentioned in the same breath with Dickens and Dostoevsky. But the trouble is that the best passages are scattered, that they occur without logic or pattern, except the biographical pattern of the hero's life, and that they lack the cumulative effect, the slow tightening of emotions to an intolerable pitch, that one finds in great novels like *The Possessed*.

I have to report that the bad passages are about as numerous and extensive in area as the good ones. There is the description of Eugene Gant's vast aloneness at Harvard, there are Eugene's reveries about time and death and the ever-flowing mysterious river of life, there is his drunken police-station brawl in South Carolina, there are his anxieties as a teacher and his European musings on the lonely American soul. In particular there are the beginning of the book, in which he flees like Orestes into the North, and the end, in which he returns to set his Antæus feet on native soil. And, just as the good parts of the novel are massively and overwhelmingly good, so too the bad parts are Brobdingnagianly bad, are possibly worse than anything that any other reputable American novelist has permitted himself to publish.

The good and the bad can both be expressed in a general statement. When Wolfe is writing about people that his hero loved or hated or merely observed with delighted curiosity, then he writes with real vigor and with an astonishing sense of character; he writes clear, swinging prose. But when he is dealing with the hero, Eugene Gant, he almost always overwrites; he repeats himself, grows dithyrambic, shouts and sings in blank verse, scatters his adjectives like a charge of rock-salt from a ten-gauge shotgun. He is prayerful and solemn; all his grand wild humor is hidden away. One could scarcely say that *Of Time and the River* becomes a bad novel whenever the hero appears on the scene, for he is always there; but the author's style goes flabby as soon as attention is taken away from the outside world and concentrated on the hero's yearning and hungering soul.

The truth is that although Eugene Gant has many individual and warmly human traits, they scarcely add up into a character. He is not anyone that we should immediately recognize in the street, like his father or his Uncle Bascom Pentland. Rather than being a person, he is a proud abstraction, "a legend of man's hunger in his youth," and his actions are magnified to such an extent that they cease to resemble those of ordinary young men. Never, in the course of this novel, does Eugene go for a walk: no, "like an insatiate and maddened animal he roamed the streets, trying to draw up mercy from the cobblestones." Never does he study a textbook: no, "he would prowl the stacks of the library at night, pulling books from a thousand shelves and reading them like a madman." If he receives a polite letter of rejection, he is not merely downhearted: no, "he stood there in the hallway . . . his face convulsed and livid, his limbs trembling with rage, his bowels and his heart sick and trembling with a hideous gray nausea of hopelessness and despair, his throat choking with an intolerable anguish of resentment and wrong." Then, when he begins to write once more, "the words were wrung out of him in a kind of bloody sweat, they poured out of his fingertips, spat out of his snarling throat like writhing snakes: he wrote them with his heart, his brain, his sweat, his guts." He is Goethe giving birth to Werther, he is Orestes in flight before the Furies, he is Young Faustus, Telemachus, Jason, he is Antæus seeking his own life-restoring soil—and at the same time he is a tall young man from Asheville who studied at the University of North Carolina and at Harvard, taught at Washington Square College, spent two years abroad, came back to Brooklyn—he is unmistakably Thomas Wolfe himself, and there are at least two occasions, on pages 186 and 466, where the author refers to Eugene in the first person singular.

Of Time and the River might have been a better book if the author had spoken in the first person from beginning to end. It seems to me that frank autobiography is a safer form than the disguised autobiographical novel. When the writer says "I felt this" and "I did that," he is forced, paradoxically, to look at himself from the outside. There are common rules of courtesy that compel him to moderate his boasts, to speak as one person among others, even to invent a character for himself. On the other hand, if he speaks of "me" under the guise of "him," all his acts are made conveniently impersonal. He is encouraged to regard himself, not as a character among others, but rather as a unique and all-embracing principle—in youth as the universal Boy, in manhood as the universal Poet. He is tempted to exhibit and magnify and admire his own adventures, till perhaps he reaches the point of wondering how he could ever "find a word to speak the joy, the pain, the grandeur bursting in the great vine of his heart, swelling like a huge grape in his throat—mad, sweet, wild, intolerable with all the mystery, loneliness, wild secret joy, and death, the ever returning and renewing fruitfulness of earth." In other words, he reaches the point of writing like a God-intoxicated ninny.

Such are the reports and ideas that I carried back from my forty days in the wilderness. This book of Thomas Wolfe's is better and worse than I have dared to say—richer, shriller, more exasperating. Cut down by half, it would be twice as good. Strangely, in the midst of its gigantic faults, it gives you the idea that Wolfe might and could write a novel that was great beyond question. But he will not write it until he chooses some other theme and some other hero than a young Faustus and Orestes squeezing out his blood, his sweat, his guts and not enough of his brains to produce the fabulous great American novel.

MacLeish's Poetic Drama

LAST WEEK a drama in verse by Archibald MacLeish was published in Boston and performed three times in a New York theatre. I read the book, I saw the play on its last evening, and I came away with mixed but chiefly favorable impressions. Say this for *Panic*, that it brings a new intelligence

"Men and Ghosts." A review of *Panic: A Play in Verse*, by Archibald MacLeish. Boston: Houghton Mifflin Company. (*NR*, Mar. 27, 1935.)

to the theatre and embodies the results of the experiments made by modern poets. Say this for the author, that he has achieved a style, has written verse that is quick, flashing with images and fit to be spoken on the stage. Say this, too, that he has chosen a major subject and has written about his own time instead of describing court life in Provence or the tribulations of George Washington or any other of the subjects that have been romanticized, glamorized and thoroughly predigested for the audience. There is nothing easy or cheap about his work; even its faults are painstakingly honest.

Panic is a play about the banking crisis of February, 1933. Its protagonist is McGafferty, described as "a sort of composite, non-historical, Ford-Morgan-Carnegie industrialist and banker, the most powerful figure of his time." He is trying to form a money pool in order to prevent the ruin of the banking system. A little mob of radicals bursts into the board room and confronts the little mob of bankers. Among the intruders is a blind man, who puts his hand on McGafferty's face and tells him that the old order is ended, that "The will is made in your own mind to die." McGafferty from that moment feels subconsciously that the blind man is right. Though he struggles at first honestly and later by fraud to save his great bank, everything fails him, everyone betrays him—and most of all he fails and betrays himself. Meanwhile another drama is being enacted by the shapeless and nameless crowd that follows the news on the electric bulletin outside McGafferty's office. The crowd begins by putting its faith in the great banker, then hopes for an unknown savior, and then, after it learns that McGafferty is dead by his own hand, suddenly feels a sense of release and abandons itself joyfully to the deep tidal flood of events. The play ends with many voices crying:

> *March!*
> > *Shout!*
> > > *Run with the*
> > *Marching men: with the thunder of*
> > *Thousand heels on the earth . . .*
>
> *Man's fate is a drum!*

I was surprised to find that, in spite of its mysticism and abstraction and unrelieved tensity of emotion, *Panic* was effective on the stage. "Effective for whom?" you might ask after reading the generally hostile reports of the dramatic critics. Well, it was certainly effective for those who saw the play on its last evening—that is, for a strange audience composed partly of society people, partly of second-string critics, but chiefly of radicals, readers of *The New Theatre* and *The New Masses*, the two magazines for whose benefit the performance was given. I have to report that even this audience found some passages tedious or unmotivated; one could hear coughs and rustling papers. In his last scene, however, McGafferty was as wintry and tragic as King Lear; and a moment later the triumphant mood of the chorus swept over us, even though we could not always understand what was being said. There was a long ovation after the curtain fell, interspersed with half a dozen boos and fifty shouts of "Author!"—agreement, sharp dissent, enthusiasm; in short, the definite reaction for which any writer hopes.

Yet everybody who read or attended the play—the book reviewers, the invited audience of the first performance, the rich audience of the second (when orchestra seats cost $5.50), the left-wing-intellectual audience of the third, the drama critics—everybody felt in his own fashion that there was something wrong with it, some fault on which he could perhaps put his finger. And, having shared this feeling, I should like to give my own diagnosis, which perhaps differs more in words than in content from some of those already presented.

MacLeish has obviously come down from his ivory tower; this fact was mentioned several times in the symposium that followed the performance. He has decided to write about the life of his own time, about events in which all of us participated. Yet he still chooses the one theme that has been most popular among ivory-tower poets. Essentially he is writing about the Artist and the World, about the conflict between a sharply realized individual and a vaguely depicted and terrifying collectivity. There is only one real character in *Panic*, and the only conflict is within the mind of the hero-villain. Everything else is nebulous. The street crowd, representing "the external world against which the action of the play takes place," is composed of shapes in darkness, speaking as A Man, A Woman, An Old Woman, A Girl. The bankers who betray McGafferty are likewise wooden and symbolic figures, "rigid in the short black jackets and piped trousers (London model). They move and gesture together, but not with mechanical precision." The radicals who come to badger him are "all young, all bareheaded, all in leather jackets; one of them blind with a white ecstatic face. Like the bankers they move and gesture roughly together: speak one after the other in rotation." Even Ione, who appears in several scenes, is not really a person; she is simply the Woman, the Eternal Mistress, the depersonalized object of McGafferty's lust. *Panic* might be called a passion play of capitalism, but it is a passion play without Judas, without Pontius Pilate, without Mary Magdalene.

This failure to visualize or humanize the people who surround McGafferty is, I think, the real weakness of the drama. MacLeish is coming down from his tower; he is close enough to earth to perceive that men's fates are not independent of their times, that even the most powerful financial leaders cannot guard themselves against a general catastrophe. He sees that their destruction as a class would bring a vast sense of release to the people over whom they have ruled. But he still is not close enough to see that their struggles are human struggles, not against symbolic figures or forces looming invisibly "like the wind in curtains," but against living people. It is true, as MacLeish says, that in times of panic a formless apprehension goes creeping through the streets like fog or flood; yet this mysterious fluid finds living vessels for itself, and each of these vessels is different, and each is a man. The dramatist has the task of seeing and presenting them in their infinite variety.

All this may seem like a principle high in the air, vague and difficult, yet it has specific applications. If MacLeish had followed it, he would have written a longer and better play. His bankers would not have been identical figures in short black London jackets; they would have had personalities; perhaps one of them would have been a Falstaff (or a W. C. Fields) and one a Uriah Heep. His radicals, too, would have been a chorus speaking in harmony and counterpoint rather than dryly "in rotation." Ione would have been a woman, not a mere foil. And the voices in the street would have differed one from another; some would have lagged behind the emotions of the crowd as a whole, some would have leaped ahead, so that the transition from mood to mood would have been less abrupt and more intelligible. The whole play would have been richer in character and texture without losing its effect of inevitable disaster; it would have been based on human conflicts. Even a poetic drama has to be drama first of all.

Faulkner: Voodoo Dance

THE REAL plot of *Pylon*, if told straightforwardly, would run something like this:

Roger Shumann, the son of an Ohio country doctor, was supposed to study medicine, but his one lively interest was tinkering with engines, and his father bought him a second-hand airplane with the money saved to put him through medical school. He joined a flying circus. In Kansas, he met and carried off Laverne, a girl of fifteen who had been seduced by her brother-in-law. Laverne afterwards fell in love with a parachute jumper named Jack, but without separating from Roger. In California her baby was born, on a parachute unfolded in a hangar. She didn't know who the father was, but Roger and Jack rolled dice and Roger won, so Laverne became Mrs. Shumann. This family of air gypsies wandered over the country, risking their lives on aviation fields and starving in jerkwater hotels. After six years Laverne was expecting another child. She knew it was Jack's, this time, and Roger also knew, but he was determined to raise money for her confinement at the cost of any danger to himself. At an aviation meet in New Orleans, during Mardi Gras, he flew an old plane in the first day's race and took second prize by cutting closer to the pylons than the other flyers. His plane crashed on the second day. A drunken reporter, who had fallen in love with Laverne, helped him to get another plane, fast and notoriously unsafe. The aviation authorities knew that Roger was likely to be

Pylon, by William Faulkner. New York: Harrison Smith and Robert Haas. (*NR*, Apr. 10, 1935.)

killed, but they allowed him to enter the big race on the principle that the public was entitled to its thrills. When the plane went to pieces in the air, Roger managed to steer the wreckage away from the grandstand and into the lake before he fell. His body was never recovered. Laverne and Jack took the little boy to Shumann's father in Ohio and then continued their hopeless and hungry wanderings. . . .

This is a plot that fifty novelists might have chosen to treat in fifty different fashions—as a chronicle of the Shumann family, as an American panorama, as a gallery of strange types, as romance, as adventure. Faulkner has found a fashion of his own, but at the cost of forcing the real plot into the background and revealing it only in scattered dialogues. The direct action of his novel is confined to five days during the New Orleans carnival. The principal character, instead of being Roger or Jack or Laverne, is the drunken and sentimental reporter. Many of the episodes are seen through his half-glazed eyes, and are thereby refracted and distorted; the story proceeds in what military historians call "the fog of war." For the rest, the general construction is that of a play rather than of the usual novel. The story moves in two directions as in a tragedy by Racine—that is, toward a future catastrophe and also toward a fuller understanding of the past. The characters are easy to recognize: every time they walk on the stage, the author identifies them by phrases that have the same function as the catch lines or gestures of actors doing character bits. Thus, the reporter is known by his flapping coat, Jiggs the mechanic by his bouncing walk, and Laverne by her "savage mealcolored hair." The action is quick, sharp, condensed; the mood is unified and is sustained by noises offstage—by a loud-speaker reporting the results of the air races, by the shouts and horn-blowing of the Mardi Gras crowds. There is even a Greek chorus of newspaper men to comment on Shumann's death.

And not only is the novel dramatic in structure; it is also a poetic drama, in the sense that Faulkner's style is often closer to verse than it is to prose. This fact is not apparent on a first reading. One is likely to be confused by the way he runs words together—sometimes forming unnatural and illegible combinations like "robin'segg," "pavilionglitter," "electrodeitch"—and by his fashion of omitting commas even where they are needed. But one finds after reading a few paragraphs aloud that his style is extraordinarily resonant, that the accents fall naturally at the ends of phrases, and that the pauses for breath recur at regular intervals. Many of his descriptions, even the more prosaic ones, can be broken into verses and printed as songs:

> *Above the shuffle and murmur*
> *of feet in the lobby*
> *and above the clash and clatter*
> *of crockery in the restaurant*
> *the amplified voice still spoke,*
> *profound and effortless. . . .*

I have not changed a word or a punctuation mark, but have merely divided part of a sentence into separate lines at places where the voice instinctively breaks. I might have continued in the same fashion. There are poems like this all through the novel, and their steady pulse-beat ends by having the effect of the tom-tom booming offstage in *Emperor Jones;* it is the stylistic device that Faulkner uses to orchestrate his voodoo dance of human passions.

There is one question that remains to be answered. Why did Faulkner choose this particular plot to dramatize with obvious care and to clothe in lovely rhythms? No matter how much he is interested in barn-storming aviators, they are still not his own people, not the sort of characters he can write about from the inside. Of course one can say that they lead picturesque lives and meet violent deaths, but I suspect that there is some other reason for their hold on him. I suspect that either consciously or unconsciously he reads a symbolic meaning into the lives of people like Roger and Laverne and the parachute jumper.

Consider again the nature of their adventures. They live among machines, and these become a symbol of sex transmuted into speed, of sex interfused with danger. The most sensational passage of the novel is a description of two people making love in an airplane high above the ground. Laverne in her daily life is conscienceless; she shares herself between two men, but "it ain't adultery," the reporter says; "you can't anymore imagine the two of them making love than you can two of them airplanes back in the corner of the hangar, coupled." This, however, is exactly what the reporter does imagine; it is one reason for his hopeless and bloodless and impotent devotion to a woman from another world.

There is another symbol, this time hidden in the character of Roger Shumann. He comes nearer to being a hero than any other character in Faulkner's eight novels. He preserves his integrity in the midst of disorder; he is capable, strong, devoted, ready to sacrifice himself and to protect others even when his plane is crashing. He is also the technician, the type of modern demigod. And he is killed partly by the businessmen who control the Airport Commission and partly by the interference of a literary weakling. Thus, in two senses *Pylon* becomes a legend of contemporary life. The trouble is that the legend seems to have exerted more emotional power over the author than it exerts over his readers. Perhaps that explains the chief defect of what is otherwise an impressive novel—I mean the lack of proportion between stimulus and response, the air of gratuitous violence and horror.

The Mid-Victoria Cross

THERE ARE FIVE Pulitzer prizes in literature and the drama. Two of them went, this year, to writers who clearly deserved them. Of the other three awards, one was debatable, one was a cagey compromise and one was downright silly.

The two good choices were those of the biographer and the historian. Douglas Southall Freeman has collected all the existing material on Robert E. Lee, including much that was overlooked by other scholars, and has used it as the basis for a four-volume authoritative life. A $1,000 prize seems a pretty modest recompense for twenty years spent behind the bars and gratings of a library. Charles McLean Andrews, a former president of the American Historical Association, is writing what will be a still longer work on *The Colonial Period of American History*, a subject to which he has devoted almost his whole career. Louis Hacker tells me that nobody else except the late Frederick J. Turner has had a wider influence on recent American historians. I might add that the Pulitzer awards in history have been consistently better than the others, even though there have been occasional lapses like the choice of General Pershing in 1932 and of Herbert Agar in 1934. The biography awards have been fair to middling. Several times they have gone to stuffed shirts or to men in the business of stuffing them, but usually they have been offered as a reward for patient scholarship. The Pulitzer committees are more capable of judging scholarship, which is a measurable thing, than they are of recognizing taste or feeling or imagination.

The best of this year's awards in the field of imaginative literature is the one I called debatable. It was given to Josephine W. Johnson for *Now in November,* a novel that tells the story of a Missouri family, of its fight to pay off a mortgage, and of what happened one year when the crops were destroyed by drought and fire. The book is written with deep feeling, in an extraordinarily smooth and unified style. Indeed, the style is its chief defect, for it presents such a bright, impermeable surface that one loses the full force of the struggle underneath—it is as if a circus tent blew down, as if the animals clawed at each other while the audience tried wildly to escape, and as if we saw nothing of their struggles except great billows under the canvas. It seems to me that the Pulitzer Prize should have gone to a book conceived more as a novel, to a book in which the emphasis was on character and conflict, rather than on a beautifully subdued and all-subduing style that holds everything together by allowing nothing to stand out sharply. . . . Incidentally, the Pulitzer novel committee cannot be proud of its record since 1918. Among the writers who have contributed most to the development of American fiction—Dreiser, Anderson, Lewis, Dos Passos, Hemingway— it has chosen only Lewis, the most popular, and he refused to accept the prize.

There is no real debate, this year, about the award to Zoë Akins for her dramatization of Edith Wharton's *The Old Maid:* everyone except Clayton Hamilton seems to regard it as a neat compromise. Almost everyone agrees that the best plays of the season were either revolutionary (like *Awake and Sing, Stevedore* and *Waiting for Lefty*) or else were improper (like *The Children's Hour*). The play that won the prize was neither, and it had the additional merit of dealing with New York in the 1850's, so that it reflected not the faintest shadow of contemporary disputes. Sometimes in the past the Pulitzer drama committee has shown real courage in its choices and has had them overruled by the bigwig publishers and editors of the Advisory Board. This time it played safe.

But it is this year's poetry award that is indefensible, and for reasons that are older than our recent quarrels over sex and revolution. Back in 1916, when I was a member of the Harvard Poetry Society, there were two schools of thought among us—there were those who believed that we ought to write in our own language about things we had felt or seen, and those who believed that we ought to write about things we had read, in the language of Lord Alfred Keats-Rossetti. I thought that the victory of the first school had been acknowledged years ago, even by the Pulitzer poetry committee. But the award to Audrey Wurdemann's *Bright Ambush* makes me wonder whether we haven't gone back to the days of Bliss Carman and Richard Hovey—the old days when E. A. Robinson was a disreputable realist and Sandburg couldn't be mentioned in polite society.

Miss Wurdemann wasn't born till 1911. She comes from Seattle and has traveled extensively in the Orient, the Philippines, Hawaii and throughout the United States. But there is, in her poems, no sign of her birthplace or her travels. There are very few personal observations and not a single emotion that she makes indubitably her own. You would suspect from reading her that she was born somewhere in a provincial library, that she had moved no farther than from Elizabeth Barrett Browning to E. A. Housman, and that she sank every night into tender dreams after wrapping herself in the proof-sheets of Edna St. Vincent Millay.

All in all, this year's awards for imaginative literature are a discouraging spectacle, a drama that has turned into a comedy of intrigue and a kitchen farce without amusing its audience. The Pulitzer committees have proved after eighteen years that they are unable to produce good results under the system to which they are held: it is time for them to go out of business. Or, if the awards for poetry, drama and fiction are still to be made, I suggest that their terms be modified so that nobody

will be fooled by them. I suggest that Nicholas Murray Butler, when making his presentation address, should speak somewhat as follows:

"We members of the Advisory Board have great difficulty
in making our choices. Individually some of us are fairly
brave, but we begin to quiver and quake as soon as we come
together. We are afraid of sex, afraid of ideas, afraid of blood,
revolution and coarse language. We are even afraid of the
recommendations made by our own committees, which are
sometimes careless in tracking down heresies.

"Under these circumstances you will understand that it is
practically impossible for us to give prizes to the best novel or
drama or book of poems. The best in literature always has
about it something dangerous. Even the second best is likely to
be disturbing, and these prizes are being awarded on the basis
of our not having been disturbed. What they really imply is a
guarantee to the American public that the two chosen books
and the chosen play have nothing in them to shatter conventions or shake the state, nothing to drive the stock market
down or interrupt the sleep of virgins.

"Pulitzer prizemen, we had a hard time finding you this
year. Some of you we had to take very young, for fear that if
we waited too long you would become intellectually troubled
and emotionally troubling. We may have a harder time next
year, when the battle lines are more clearly drawn. Now, as a
token of our joy in discovery, let us present you with these
Mid-Victoria Crosses, worth each a thousand dollars. Take
them and bear them and let them always remind you that the
better part of valor is discretion."

Directions for Making a Genius

I PREDICT that within the next ten or fifteen years we
shall watch the development and slow recognition of an American literary genius. For nearly a century the critics have been

NR, July 24, 1935.

praying for a glimpse of him. Now our literature has reached a stage at which he can finally appear.

I don't know his name or where he was born or whether he writes poetry or prose, drama or fiction. I suspect that he is still under twenty-five, since almost all the older writers have disqualified themselves for the sort of life he will have to lead. I also feel strongly that he has working-class sympathies and, quite possibly, a working-class background. For the rest, I can sketch in the outlines of his probable career, on the assumption that it will resemble the careers of his predecessors in Europe. Great men like little ones run true to type.

He will have at least a moderate success quite early in life, so that he can devote the best of his time to his work, instead of hack-writing or selling Fuller brushes. On the other hand, he will arouse the fierce anger of most critics, who will be repelled by the freshness and violence of his writing: critics like a book to be not too different from others they have admired. He will be attacked for being revolutionary, illiterate, obscure or obscene, or perhaps for all these qualities simultaneously. The authorities may interfere with his books or suppress them altogether, but the public will somehow continue to read them. Eventually, as his reputation grows, the critics will fall in at the end of the parade, cheering and hoping that nobody noticed their absence. His literary rivals, forgetting their jealousy, will say, "I detest most writers of that school, but of course Everett Schmidt"—if that is his name—"stands out from the rest of them." Soon there will be Everett Schmidt reading clubs and college courses and Everett Schmidt boulevards, perhaps, in the new socialist cities, and young writers will be issuing manifestoes against the pernicious and stultifying influence of Everett Schmidt. At his death early in the twenty-first century—assuming that our civilization survives until then—he will be apotheosized in windy speeches as the American Goethe, the American Hugo, Dickens, Tolstoy and who knows what besides.

It is in this rich atmosphere of post-mortem reverence that great writers are usually approached and described. Their careers are presented as a mixture of hard work and the I Will spirit with three parts of ineffable mystery. I think we have a right to be more realistic about them. The literary great man, the recognized genius (as opposed to geniuses neglected during their lifetimes, like Blake, Melville and Baudelaire) is a writer who comes to express and embody the ideals of a nation or of a rising social class. He is a leader who never goes so fast that he leaves his followers behind. Indeed, he lives in a peculiarly close relationship with those who read his books—Victor Hugo once said that there is a sort of "fluid" between them, a living stream from which both of them draw strength. This relationship, rarely established, goes far toward explaining the apparent mystery of the great writer's career. His readers help to create his work; they read into it meanings that the author may or may not have intended to be there; eventually their pride of possession leads them to glorify the genius as a means of glorifying themselves. But they also expect him to give them something in return, to clarify their own ideas, give shape to their dreams and act as their literary conscience. Genius, in other words, is something more than a state of divine grace. The great man of letters has a function, a role in society —to put it baldly, a job.

That the job has never been filled in America is not, I think, the fault of our writers. It is the necessary audience that has been lacking in the past, rather than the speakers able to address it. The audience now seems ready. At the same time, literature is becoming more involved with public life, with reaction and revolution. Authors are being called on more and more to play the part of national and even international figures —inspirers, protesters, rebels or buffoons. Critics more and more anxiously are scanning the horizon. There are always bright-eyed watchers among them to tell us that the genius is here at last—he is Thornton Wilder, he is Louis Bromfield, he is Hervey Allen, this summer he is Thomas Wolfe, next fall he will be some new prodigy greater and even wordier than his predecessors, who will thereupon be classed with last year's bathing beauties. There is something more than fashionable snobbery in the present custom of high-hatting and old-hatting the writers to whom hats have been reverently raised. There is also resentment against them for failing to be the genuine long-hoped-for genius. Soon I think he will be created, if only by the manifest desire for him.

Meanwhile a position is waiting to be filled. What do you

think about it, young writers under twenty-five: is there one of you that would like to be a genius? The qualifications for the job are strict and difficult, but not impossible to meet. The writer preparing to be a genius must have imagination, sensitiveness, narrative power, all the qualities expected of other writers, but he also must have special gifts. For example, he must have a simple-mindedness that enables him to reduce problems and situations to their bare essences. He must be able to make himself heard by the masses. He must be curious about the lives of everyone he meets, and must give them the sort of sympathy that broadens and deepens his own emotions. He must serve some cause that is independent of his personal ambitions. More than this, he must have the instinctive shrewdness that keeps him from making a fool of himself, even though abundant opportunities are offered him. Chiefly he must avoid messianism—the belief, I mean, that his position of intellectual leadership has been attained solely through the mysterious powers residing within himself, and that he is therefore entitled to speak with the voice of a prophet. But he must also avoid the opposite vice of becoming an institution, a simple mouthpiece for proper sentiments.

In any case he must write a great deal; he must be nearly as prolific as the late Edgar Wallace, but without following an easy formula. He must work sixteen hours a day, like James Joyce when he was composing *Ulysses*, but without Joyce's contempt for his audience. There is no labor union of geniuses, no code authority to limit their working week. Even in their leisure time, if any remains, they are required to make speeches, correct the manuscripts of young writers, give advice to people who won't use it, make statements and, in general, play the part of public figures.

Such is the job, if anyone is able to take it and hold it. As for the pay, it will scarcely be that of a corporation lawyer. The American genius won't receive the Pulitzer Prize or the Nobel Prize, except by accident; he may not even be printed in magazines of the quality group. On account of his political opinions, he may be jailed or forced to live abroad, like Hugo and Gorky and Thomas Mann and others who have played the role. He won't starve to death—that is perhaps the only promise that can be made in regard to his economic position.

On the other hand, he will be certain of one privilege that very few American writers have enjoyed. He will have a sense of communion with his readers; he will know that his words are something more than echoes in the wasteland.

Poem for Amy Lowell

ONE DAY when Amy Lowell was sixteen, a Boston schoolgirl—"ugly, fat, conspicuous, and dull," she told her diary—

"Oh Lord please let it be all right, & let Paul love me, & don't let me be a fool"—

One day in her father's library she found *Imagination and Fancy*

(A book by Leigh Hunt, subtitled *Selections from the English Poets, illustrative of those first requisites of their art; with markings of the best passages, critical notices of the writers, and an essay in answer to the question "What Is Poetry?"*).

She read it, she devoured it, she seized upon the poets quoted: Shelley, Coleridge, Beaumont and Fletcher, Keats;

Keats most of all.

Then in her busy school days and again in her young womanhood, jilted, ill, despondent, she forgot herself in Keats.

All her life she was in love with John Keats, she was the sweetheart, the disciple, the wife, the adoring aunt, the invalid mother of John Keats,

Who was not an atheist like the man Shelley, author of books that were forbidden to enter her father's library,

Who was not a rebel or a rake,

But was instead a responsible young man, loyal to his family, capable in his two professions of surgery and rhyming.

He was someone you could ask for dinner and be sure that

Amy Lowell: A Chronicle, by S. Foster Damon. Boston: Houghton Mifflin Company. (*NR*, Jan. 8, 1936.)

your sheepdogs wouldn't attack him, as they did the hunch-back Randolph Bourne and the disreputably dressed Maxwell Bodenheim.

He was "the only English poet I can think of who was quite without moral preoccupation of any sort, and yet who never fell into licentiousness." Keats was the bridge between Brookline and Parnassus, between the Boston Athenaeum and eternal Pan.

For his dear sake she befriended and scolded dozens of young poets, most of them neither grateful nor talented;

For his dear sake she assembled manuscripts and letters, the world's largest collection of Keatsiana;

For his dear sake she wrote a memorial biography, work-ing night after night to decipher the almost illegible notes he left on the margins of his books, and rupturing the blood vessels in her eyes from too much study.

Three months after publishing her two-volume life of Keats she had a fatal stroke.

She died from overwork, she died for the love of John Keats.

Reading Foster Damon's record of her fifty-one years,

A book somewhat too reverent for my taste, but studious and fair and candid,

I remembered how we used to go to Sevenels for dinner, Foster and I and sometimes Roy Snow,

Taking the blue Chestnut Hill car, getting off at Heath Street, just past the old reservoir, and walking up a long snowy driveway to the house that for me was always shrouded in night.

I remembered the warmth inside, the reading of manu-scripts, the good laughter, the light-brown Manila cigars dressed in tight robes of tinfoil and petticoats of tissue paper.

I remembered Miss Lowell polishing her glasses, Miss Lowell demolishing her enemies.

I remembered the Poetry Renaissance and the great war between the new poets and the old, the passionate Vers Libristes and the pallid Sonneteers, the battle between the frogs and the mice.

It is all set down here, every move in the campaign.

Miss Lowell was the commanding general of the new poets.

It was a post that nobody asked her to take and nobody wanted to take away from her.

They said, All right, let Amy do it.

Amy could bring together an audience by her grotesque reputation and hold it by her good sense;

Amy could read pretty good poems as if they were masterworks;

Amy could expound, elucidate, make everything sound reasonable, make herself heard.

"She has everything but genius," one poet said of her.

She had genius too, but genius for organizing, genius for human relations, genius for command.

She wrote to Donald Evans, "Being a soldier, I should wish to be a general; being a cook, nothing but the chefdom would satisfy me."

She wrote to the editor of *The New York Tribune*, "I am as bad as Napoleon, I believe in my star."

Every new book of hers was a campaign planned with Napoleonic strategy, and every campaign was successful.

She was sure that she could conquer England, too, if only she could get there.

Never did poet more deliberately plan

To scale Parnassus, seize the Castalian fountain, blockade the Corcyrean nymphs in their cavern and snatch the laurel wreath from Apollo's hand.

Miss Lowell besieged the mountain of the Muses

With every available weapon: talent, wealth, family, shrewdness and charm, and flattery, and tears.

She buttered and bullied the editors, she had the reviewers round to dinner.

She told her publishers, "You advertise so much in *The Times* that you ought to force them into a somewhat less hostile attitude toward one of your authors."

She told her audience after reading a poem, "Well? —Clap or hiss, I don't care which; but do something!"

The audience laughed and applauded her, the editors printed her, the reviewers wrote very long reviews.

The new poetry was heard everywhere, and Miss Lowell's books of poems sold seven thousand copies each.

The encyclopedias tell us that Parnassus—*a mountain (8,070 ft. high) of Phocis, anct. Greece*—

Parnassus has two peaks,

Only one of which is haunted by Apollo and Dionysus and the Muses.

The other peak is sacred to the false gods of literature,

The puffers, the prize-winners, the professors, who gather there at banquets of artificial ambrosia and drink toasts in false nectar to the success of freshly fabricated classics.

They are bigger than the true gods, they are more imposing in their boiled shirts and academic robes, they have splendid funerals.

When they die, they die.

Miss Lowell was too warm and real, she did not belong with the false gods, but she was climbing in a great hurry.

It is so hard never to lose one's way.

It is hard to be a true poet when one is a Lowell of the eleventh generation, the daughter of a big cotton manufacturer, the sister of Percival the astronomer and Abbott Lawrence the president of Harvard.

Poets exult and lament, but the Lowells keep their troubles to themselves.

It is hard to write true poems when one is blanketed with four-percent debentures and rocked to sleep in a cradle of sound common stocks.

Not many sounds of human misery or passion can pierce the walls thickly insulated with tax-exempt government bonds.

One has to find other subjects . . . for example, Chinese legends in which "I cannot feel with you," Miss Lowell said, "that the action has human significance";

For example, Yankee monodramas rubbed and polished like old Yankee kitchen furniture in an antique shop on Beacon Hill;

For example, laments over the lost soul of Lady Emma Hamilton (1761–1815);

For example, Japanese lacquer prints, of which D. H. Lawrence wrote, "*Don't* do Japanese things, Amy, if you love us. . . . It isn't you at *all*, it has nothing to do with you, and it is not real."

And again he wrote: "If it doesn't come out of your own

heart, real Amy Lowell, it is no good, however many colors it may have. I wish one saw more of your genuine strong, sound self in this book, full of common sense & kindness and the restrained, almost bitter, Puritan passion. . . . How much nicer, finer, bigger you are, intrinsically, than your poetry is."

Of the real Amy Lowell there is not much left in her poems—

In "Lilacs," yes, and "Patterns," and "Rode the Six Hundred,"

But little of her in the others, no flesh or blood,

Not even the dried bones of her among the Chinese porcelain figures, the Mexican jade figures, the Italian eighteenth-century ivory figures pulled with string.

There is more of her in Foster Damon's book—

Of the stout little moon-enamored girl in love with Paul H—— and John Keats;

Of the debutante jilted, starving herself and breaking her health in the effort to be not-ugly;

Of the motherly woman who loved her nephew Jim Roosevelt, and her friend Ada Russell, and Mrs. Russell's grandchildren—

Keats, and her garden, and Winky her cat; who only mourned to Winky and her flowers as death, her own death, came with even stride—

Amy Lowell, the life-greedy, the laughter-greedy, terror of editors, imp of the drawing room,

"Full of common sense & kindness and the restrained, almost bitter, Puritan passion,"

Full of little-girl humbleness and Brahman pride.

In this book she scolds at us from the tomb,

"Well, clap or hiss!" she cries to us, having died.

Baudelaire as Revolutionist

TO SAY that George Dillon and Edna St. Vincent Millay have made the best available translation of *Les Fleurs du Mal* is mild and niggardly praise when you stop to consider the faults of their predecessors. Most of these have used the conventional language of late-Victorian poetry, the "whilom" and "eftsoons" dialect that transforms Baudelaire into a sort of Ernest Dowson with a lisp and a foreign leer. Moreover, they have exhibited a curious mixture of mealy-mouthedness and sensationalism—they have been evasive where Baudelaire was shockingly definite, yet at the same time they have tried to make his perfumes more sweetly cloying and his sins more scarlet. Arthur Symons in particular talks of "biting" at so many places where the word does not occur in the French text that he makes Baudelaire's women seem to suffer less from passion than from hydrophobia. Many other translators have been like him in emphasizing the "decadent" side of Baudelaire, the side that now seems mannered and out-moded. On the other hand, Miss Millay and Mr. Dillon try to write in the language of our own times, without ambiguity. They deserve more than perfunctory praise for revealing a side of Baudelaire that is above fashions.

Most of their versions, if one forgets the originals, are satisfying as English poems. My trouble on reading them for the first time was that I could not forget the originals, could not help glancing at the French text printed on the opposite page, could not keep myself from comparing words and measuring effects and being perhaps unduly irritated by English phrases that seemed unworthy of Baudelaire. I forgot the good lines in my anger at the bad ones; perhaps it will be several months before I can judge the translation fairly and as a whole. In the meantime, there are a few general observations to be made about it.

Miss Millay and Mr. Dillon have translated not quite half of the 158 poems that compose *Les Fleurs du Mal*. Consider-

Flowers of Evil, by Charles Baudelaire. Translated by George Dillon and Edna St. Vincent Millay. New York: Harper and Brothers. (*NR*, Apr. 15, 1936.)

ing the difficulties they had to overcome at every step, nobody could blame them for not completing the book. On the other hand, they are open to serious criticism for the order—or lack of it—in which they have printed their 72 selected poems. Baudelaire always thought of his book as forming something more than a random collection of lyrics; he said that it "must be judged as a whole, in which case there results from it a terrible morality." Speaking of the new poems inserted in the second edition, he told his mother, "It was easy for you to see that they were all composed for a plan." But both the morality of the whole and the plan that held it together are lost in the present arrangement, which places the first poem at the end of the book and lets the others come where they may.

Moreover, I find it hard to understand some of the omissions. There is, for example, "Femmes Damnées," the longer of the two poems bearing this title, the one that describes the unnatural love of Delphine and Hippolyte. The translators may have rejected it on the ground of its being too mannered and sententious, yet it is the most "Baudelairean" of all the poems, the one that best combines his moral intensity with the cold perfection of his verse; I think the last six stanzas are unexcelled in French literature. There is also "Une Charogne," which describes a putrefying corpse in terms that no other French poet since Villon had dared to use. There is the apostrophe to the little old women of Paris, "Les Petites Vieilles"; perhaps it is not among the best of Baudelaire's poems, but it is one of the tenderest, and without reading it one can hardly appreciate his realism. And there is "Abel et Caïn," the one poem in which Bauledaire was explicitly revolutionary —after describing the bourgeois sons of Abel and, over against them, the proletarian sons of Cain, he adjured the latter to climb into heaven and cast God to earth. In any collection from which these poems are omitted, Baudelaire loses a great deal of his richness; he becomes a simple sinner who repents in middle age, a poet like a thousand others.

There is a final criticism that deals with the verse itself rather than the selection. It seems to me that Miss Millay and Mr. Dillon are absolutely mistaken in their idea that English hexameter is the closest equivalent of the French alexandrine. Both lines are of twelve syllables, but that is their only real resemblance, and it is partly canceled by the fact that the French syllables are shorter on the average; many of them are silent in the spoken language and, even in verse, are barely pronounced. English hexameter contains more letters, more words and, if it is well written, more meaning. In order to render Baudelaire's alexandrines into hexameters, the present translators had to pad out their lines, sometimes with words that nobody could mistake for anything else than padding. Here are two random samples:

> *Old spavined horse, old nag not worthy of thy keep . . .*
> *Are but mirrors, mirrors cloudy and obscure . . .*

Both lines would be better if they were shortened, the first by omitting "old nag" and the second by omitting one of the "mirrors." In that case they would become pentameters, which means that they would be written in the measure usually employed for translating Baudelaire.

So much for the poems in their new English version. It is more interesting, I think, to discuss a neglected aspect of the man who wrote them. During the seventy-odd years since his death, Baudelaire has been praised as a romantic Satanist (especially when Satanism was in fashion), as a discoverer of new symbols (by the Symbolists), as a devoutly Christian character (by the neo-Catholics) and as a marvelous case history (by psychoanalysts specializing in the Oedipus complex). Almost nobody has talked about Baudelaire as a revolutionist, in spite of the fact that he risked his life three times on the barricades.

I can easily understand why the subject has been avoided. The poet himself changed his political opinions in later years and preferred not to talk about his earlier activities. The revolution in which he became involved was one that failed and therefore it has been played down by historians. Yet the French revolution of 1848 came as the result of a long intellectual and social ferment in many ways comparable with that which the world is passing through today. Its effect on French literature was perhaps more decisive than that of the World War. And Baudelaire took part both in the agitation that preceded it and in the political struggles that followed.

For six years he lived among revolutionaries. Beginning in 1845, when he lost control of his small fortune, he ceased to be a bohemian by choice and became a bohemian by necessity; he was a comrade of the struggling poets and painters and shared their hopes for overthrowing the bourgeois government. Courbet, the revolutionary painter, was one of his friends; another was Pierre Dupont, who wrote songs of revolt to be sung by the factory workers. In those days Baudelaire was influenced by their socialism, though it is hard to say how much of it he was willing to accept. He announced a volume of poems to be published in 1848 under the title of *Les Limbes* (Limbo). This title has mildly puzzled most of his biographers, but Enid Starkie explains that it probably referred to the "limbic" periods which, according to Fourier, marked the death of capitalism and the beginning of socialism. It would follow that the violence of Baudelaire's poems could be explained and excused to his contemporaries as the violent birthpangs of a new order. Critics seem to have expected that the book when it appeared would consist of socialistic poems.

Meanwhile the actual revolution had broken out. It included two periods of bloody streetfighting and Baudelaire took part in both of them. In February he helped to loot a gunsmith's, came running out with a new rifle and shouted, "Let's go shoot General Aupick"—his stepfather, whom he hated for many personal reasons. There was a great deal of malice and theatricality mixed with his revolutionary enthusiasm, though perhaps not so much as was implied by his conservative acquaintances who saw him during the fighting. In June, when the working-class quarters rebelled again, this time without the help of the petty bourgeoisie—in June Baudelaire was again fighting on the barricades, and now he was in deadly earnest. Indeed, he was saved from arrest and possible execution only by the appearance of a friend who managed to pass him through the lines.

His political activity did not end with the defeat of the proletariat. In February he had helped to edit a revolutionary newspaper, only two issues of which appeared. Later in the same year he tried political journalism in the provinces, writing for a conservative paper, but interlarding his editorials with praise for Robespierre and Marat. As late as 1851 he was listed as responsible editor of a paper called *The People's Republic*. But at the end of the same year came Louis Napoleon's coup d'état, with Baudelaire again under fire by government troops. That was his last revolt, for he was becoming thoroughly disillusioned. The proletariat had lost the fight, lost confidence in itself, lost the friends so easily gained among the intellectuals. From that time Baudelaire was interested only in his individual salvation.

Yet even though he became aloof and conservative—even though he wrote in his intimate journals that "Progress is a doctrine of idlers and Belgians," that "there is no form of rational and assured government save an aristocracy"—still the effects of his revolutionary years survived in his life and in his poems. For him to turn violently away from politics was already one effect that he shared with other poets—indeed, the whole Symbolist movement was partly an outgrowth of the defeated revolution. But beyond this a new quality appeared and persisted in his work, a tenderness toward the poor and a deep sympathy with people who suffer. It might even be said that the physical realism of his poems was connected with his revolutionary experiences; he sometimes writes with a direct earthiness very close to the spirit of the French working classes. And that realism helps to explain his literary excellence. Often I have wondered why people who try to imitate Baudelaire have always fallen so far short of him. Lack of talent? That cannot be urged against Swinburne or Symons or Dowson or any one of twenty poets who have adopted what they thought was the Baudelairean pose. No, I think that what they lacked was his human sympathy and his effort to depict heart and body just as he saw them, even if he had to use exact, sharp, humble words instead of the round words that people admired. The other poets tried to reproduce his loftiness without building the homely brick foundation above which it soared.

Afterthoughts on T. S. Eliot

T. S. ELIOT's early poems are beginning to seem less cosmically important than they did in 1925, when they first appeared in a collected volume. It is harder now to admire their deliberate obscurity, and this is particularly true in the case of *The Waste Land*, which has been discussed and eluci-dated at greater length than any other modern poem, without answering half the questions that it raises. Just what is the function in it of the drowned man, Phlebas the Phenician? Why are we told in a note that he suggests the Western asceticism of St. Augustine? Are we meant to identify Eliot himself with the Fisher King—that is, with the legendary monarch of a country that had been rendered waterless and desolate at the very moment when its king was struck with impotence for the sin of falling in love with a pagan maid? In that case, has the pagan any connection with the Russian noble-woman remembered longingly by Eliot in the first episode? The more I study the poem as a whole, the more it seems personal and arbitrary, not so much the embodiment of a great contemporary problem as a private diary written in rebuses.

On the other hand, it is quite possible that both *The Waste Land* and other poems of the same period have been partly spoiled for me by all the imitations they have called forth. Some of these are actually better written than Eliot's own work, in the sense of being more sustained in mood and richer in images: he is threatened with being lost among the crowd of his gifted followers. Moreover, I am beginning to doubt whether his enormous influence over his contemporaries is an accurate measure of his own poetical achievement. Some of the very greatest poets—Shakespeare, Milton, for example—have had a less tangible effect on other writers than anyone would judge from their personal eminence. A possible explanation is that they did their work too well: nobody else was impelled to do it again or felt sure of doing it better. Eliot, with his habit of making suggestions that he seldom develops and of changing every subject without exhausting it, has tempted others to

Collected Poems, 1909–35, by T. S. Eliot. New York: Harcourt, Brace and Company. (*NR*, May 20, 1936.)

continue his work. In the past, his very faults have attracted disciples.

The poems he has written since 1930, which occupy more than half of the new collected edition, have been less widely imitated. Most of them are devotional poems, a fact which many critics of our time might assume to be connected with their indifferent quality as verse. But the connection here, which really exists, is a result of Eliot's personal reaction to his new faith. He has developed into a peculiarly doleful type of Christian, given more to describing the sorrows of this world than to celebrating the joys of the next. Even when he writes a Christmas poem, "Journey of the Magi," he fills it with lamentations—it was the worst time of the year for such a long trip, the camel men were mutinous, the inns were dirty and expensive, and the very birth of the Christ Child was "hard and bitter agony for us, like Death, our death." Yet this is one of Eliot's happier and more factual pieces; elsewhere he loses himself in a mist of abstract sorrows. During the last half-century there have been several distinguished Catholic poets in France, but their best works have been poems of repentance, of pity, or of abuse directed against the infidels. Eliot has simply not sinned enough to make his repentance interesting as literature. He writes poems of pity for nobody but himself, and he is too frigidly polite to abuse his enemies. His Anglo-Catholicism has so far been intellectual rather than emotional or sensuous, with the result that his religious poems have hardly more color than a New England sermon. As compensation for this lack of appeal to eye and touch and taste, he has tried to give his verse a more complicated music, but in achieving this effect he depends too much on simple repetition:

> *Only through time time is conquered . . .*
> *Distracted from distraction by distraction . . .*
> *World not world but that which is not world . . .*

But *Murder in the Cathedral*—his latest work and the only one not included in this volume—seems to show that his talents are being revived. There are still too many repeated words, too many abstract words; there is an almost terrifying absence of sensuous impressions; but there is also more energy and more deftness in meter than he has shown since *The Waste Land*.

The murder of Thomas Becket, which is the central incident
of the play, is handled with a whole sequence of surprising
effects. First the chorus chants while the Archbishop is being
killed, then the four murderers come forward and excuse
themselves to the audience in the language of modern politicians (and the satire here is exceptionally keen), then the First
Priest asks who shall guide us now that the Church lies bereft,
then finally the Third Priest, after answering that the Church
is only fortified by persecution, thunders a malediction against
the assassins:

> *Go, weak sad men, lost erring souls, homeless in earth or heaven.*
> *Go where the sunset reddens the last gray rock*
> *Of Brittany, or the Gates of Hercules . . .*
> *Or sit and bite your nails in Aquitaine.*

It is a magnificent curse, yet it forces comparison with
another passage that I vastly prefer to it, the passage in
"Femmes Damnées" where Baudelaire, after reporting the
courtship of two Lesbians, suddenly rises in his own person and
thunders against them:

> *O lamentable victims, go ye down,*
> *Down, down the pathway to eternal hell—*

In Baudelaire's passage there is no mechanical listing of
countries to which the culprits might flee: Gibraltar, Morocco,
Norway, Aquitaine. Instead there is indignation bursting forth
in sometimes extravagant and sometimes homely metaphors;
there is a warmth of feeling that makes the climax of Eliot's
poetic drama seem chilly and academic. Yet *Murder in the
Cathedral* is the best verse that he has written since 1922. The
shorter pieces collected in this new volume make me feel for
the first time that Eliot is a minor poet; that his apparent
greatness was forced upon him by the weakness of his contemporaries and their yearning for a leader.

The Last Great European: Thomas Mann

THE LINE that divides Symbolist or "art" novels from social novels is probably not so straight or definite as people seemed to think a few years ago, when the subject was being vehemently argued. It is a border without guards or customs officials, and doubtful travelers are privileged to stand with one foot in either country. They can even become leading citizens of both, as witness the example of Thomas Mann, who is probably more respected than any other living writer. During the last twenty-five years, Mann has gradually become a social novelist, in an admirable sense of the word, yet he has not abandoned the technique or the emotional color of the Symbolists. He has never made the gesture of violently deserting an ivory tower.

His career can be traced in *Stories of Three Decades*, an omnibus volume containing everything he has written for publication except his essays and his four big novels. The book includes two long stories, "Death in Venice" and "Tonio Kröger," which Mann says in his introduction that he is inclined to reckon "not with my slighter but with my more important works." It includes two other long stories which, with much hesitation, I should be willing to place above Mann's favorites: these two are "Tristan" and "Mario and the Magician." "Blood of the Walsungs," describing a family of rich, hateful, pitiable Jews, is a shorter story almost as good; so too is "Disorder and Early Sorrow," in which all the hysteria of the German inflation is distilled into the tears of a six-year-old girl. There are stories still shorter than these last; there are episodes, sketches and a long, beautifully accurate biography of Mann's dog, recommended as corrective reading to people who believe that dog stories are childish. There is the first chapter of a novel, "Felix Krull," that Mann did not continue; and there is "Fiorenze," a historico-philosophical drama that had some success on the stage, but not enough to make its author a professional playwright. In all there are twenty-four pieces, written at every stage of his life—from the

Stories of Three Decades, by Thomas Mann. Translated by H. T. Lowe-Porter. New York: Alfred A. Knopf. (*NR*, June 24, 1936.)

year 1896, when he was twenty-one, to the year 1929, when he won the Nobel Prize. In their chronological order they give a fairly clear picture of his development.

His early work was centered round the familiar Symbolist theme of the artist's solitude. "There are two worlds," Mann always seemed to be saying. "There is the world of happy, normal people, to be envied even for their stupidity, and there is the lonely world in which the artist tries to bridle his nightmares, but often lets them run away with him." Almost all his stories dealt either with artists or else with moral or physical cripples (and he tended to place all these people in the same category, little Herr Friedemann the hunchback, Detlev Spinell the dilettante and Felix Krull the swindler).

His nearest approach to a hero is Tonio Kröger, the young, successful, hard-working novelist; yet this autobiographical character is the one who says most forcibly that art is a product of decay and that artists by their calling are barred out of ordinary society. "Literature is not a calling, it's a curse," Tonio tells his good friend Lisabeta Ivanovna. "It begins by your feeling yourself set apart, in a curious sort of opposition to the nice, regular people; there is a gulf of ironic sensibility, of knowledge, skepticism, disagreement, between you and the others; it grows deeper and deeper, you realize that you are alone." Both the artists and their audience are "always and only the poor and suffering, never any of the others, the blue-eyed ones. . . . The kingdom of art increases and that of health and innocence declines on this earth." It is curious to find that Tonio does not feel in the least angry or contemptuous toward the world that half rejects him; in this respect he is unlike Joyce's Stephen Dedalus and Huysmans' des Esseintes and almost all the other Symbolist heroes. He really loves and envies the ordinary people, "the blue-eyed ones" who have no need of art. His good friend tells him, "You are really a bourgeois on the wrong path, a bourgeois *manqué*."

"Tonio Kröger" is an unusual story, warm and open-hearted in mood, skillful in craftsmanship, the first work in which Mann learned to interweave his themes like a composer writing a symphony. Yet with the passage of years it is losing part of its effectiveness: the ideas behind it are beginning to seem localized in time and space. In writing it Mann did not foresee that the conflict between artist and bourgeois would not be an eternal subject, nor that it would soon become impossible to use the upper middle class as a symbol of health. He would soon be forced to go into his material more deeply.

That is exactly what he did in writing "Death in Venice," which was finished eight years later. Ostensibly it is another story of the relation between life and art, between art and self-discipline. Gustav von Aschenbach, the hero, is a distinguished novelist who has sustained himself through fifty years by obeying his Prussian sense of duty. Then, in the late afternoon of his life, he yields to the dissipation that is, for Mann, both a symbol of art and a symbol of death. He finds that Venice is a plague-stricken city, but he has fallen in love with a beautiful Polish boy and refuses to go northward until it is too late for him to escape. The story is extraordinary for its musical structure and for the complicated suggestions it evokes. But among these suggestions is one of a historical nature. "Death in Venice" was published two years before the War, and Mann is inclined to believe that its popularity was due to its "intense timeliness"—the delirium in which Aschenbach foundered belonged to the mood of the day and was a prophecy of the general delirium in which Europe would shortly founder. Aschenbach was not merely a picture of the artist yielding to his vices: he came to represent a moment of the European mind.

I am trying to describe the process by which a Symbolist novelist developed into a social novelist without greatly changing his aims or his methods, but chiefly by broadening his human sympathies. In another story—it is the last in the volume and appeared in 1929—the point becomes much clearer. "Mario and the Magician" relates the misadventures of a German family at a little Italian watering place. They do not like Torre di Venere; the chip-on-the-shoulder nationalism of the Italian tourists makes their lives mildly but persistently disagreeable. Nevertheless they remain, by inertia, and get themselves involved in the dangerous affair of the Cavaliere Cipolla. This magician, as he advertises himself—this hypnotist, as he is in reality—proves to be crippled and hateful and compelling. At his one performance he overawes and insults the audience, forcing one man after another to obey him, and the audience likes it; even the German children laugh and clap without quite knowing what is taking place. But Cipolla goes too far and one of his victims shoots him down, thus clearing the air of hysteria and constraint.

"Mario and the Magician" is not on the face of it a political story, in spite of occasional references to Mussolini and Italian pride. It deals with one episode witnessed by an ordinary German family. Yet it conveys, more strongly than anything else I have read, the atmosphere of Europe in these days of dictatorship and mass insanity: it suggests in miniature the great meetings at the Sport Palace in Berlin where Hitler sways the crowd like wind-bowed aspens; it gives us the essence of the Blood Purge, the Saar Plebiscite, the Ethopian war—everything is there, if only in the germ, and it was there six years before most of it was printed in the morning papers. We should not demand that poets be prophets; this is not part of their trade. But sometimes it happens that a writer, by going into his subject deeply, finds in it the spiritual tendencies that grew out of yesterday's events and will become the political tendencies of tomorrow. Thomas Mann, like Tolstoy, has done this more than once, and not for his country alone. In this age of crazy nationalisms, he is almost the last great European.

Van Wyck Brooks
and the New England Legacy

TOWARD THE END of the fine essay on Van Wyck Brooks printed in this issue of *The New Republic,* it seemed to me that Bernard Smith did less than justice to *The Flowering of New England.*

He might of course urge that he was discussing a literary career of almost thirty years, in which this new book was a single episode. He might urge that *The Flowering of New England* was deficient in the qualities he most admired in

"The Puritan Legacy." A review of *The Flowering of New England, 1818–1865,* by Van Wyck Brooks. New York: E. P. Dutton and Company. (*NR,* Aug. 26, 1936.)

Brooks' earlier work—conviction, indignation, moral force—
and that it seemed overtolerant, even fatalistic. Beyond this he
might urge that it presented the great New England era as a
dramatic pageant of growth and sudden decay, without sufficiently explaining the forces behind one or the other. But he
was wrong, I think, to characterize the book as "purely description and narration"; these words apply to its method, not its
purpose. And he was totally wrong to dismiss it as "scholarly
story telling"; for the story told by Brooks is capable of
changing our conception of American literature.

The book repairs a bridge into history that had seemed to
be broken; it recovers for us a "usable past." Lewis Mumford
had attempted something of the sort when he wrote *The
Golden Day*: he had assured us that our culture had its morning star in Emerson, its dawn in Thoreau, its high noon in
Whitman, its twilight in Hawthorne and Melville. But Mumford's book was purely an essay, a stimulating outline that
remained to be filled in. Brooks has taken a somewhat similar
though less symbolic group of ideas and has expressed
them so completely, documented them so carefully from the
books and letters and memoirs of the New England writers,
that they cease to impress us as ideas at all; we read them as a
narrative of people and events that places them in a new focus.
More than any other writer, Brooks makes us feel the strength
and richness—and the continuing effect—of American literature during its one great period.

He achieves that aim by painting a series of carefully vivid
pictures. First he gives us New England in 1815, serene in its
revolutionary heritage and its faith in the future. Then come
the Yankee scholars working twelve hours a day in the German universities, paying long visits to Goethe and Lafayette
and finally sailing back to Harvard with books and ideas and
foreign languages, the spoils of a continent to lavish on their
students. Then we learn of the desire for education and self-
improvement that infected all ranks of society, from John
Quincy Adams, who rose at four o'clock to read his Bible with
English, French and German commentaries, down to Elihu
Burritt, the learned blacksmith of Worcester. (Burritt wrote in
his diary for June, 1837: "*Monday*, headache; forty pages
Cuvier's 'Theory of the Earth,' sixty-four pages French,

eleven hours forging. *Tuesday,* sixty-five lines of Hebrew, thirty pages of French, ten pages Cuvier's 'Theory,' eight lines Syriac, ten ditto Danish, ten ditto Bohemian, nine ditto Polish, fifteen names of stars, ten hours forging.")

Out of all this self-confidence and labor and infiltration of new ideas, something had to be born; and thus the first half of the book creates in us a mood of expectancy. The second half creates a mood of exultation, with its picture of the years from 1840 to 1860 when the New England mind was blossoming like New England lilacs—first the Boston lilacs, then those in the Concord dooryards, then a blaze of purple and white and false-blue from the Housatonic Valley to Penobscot Bay. Those were the days when a dozen men of genius gathered in the Saturday Club and talent seemed to be everywhere; but Brooks makes us feel how much of this talent was going to be wasted. He foreshadows the end of blossom time, the beginning of the midsummer drought, in another fine series of pictures—and notably in a sketch of Hawthorne's last years, when the novelist was so obsessed with doubts and scruples that "life shook before his eyes, like the picture on the surface of a pond."

But although it is generally believed that the New England mind grew thinner and less fertile after the Civil War— that its best fields were abandoned like Green Mountain farms —still it seems to me after reading this book that more of its vitality has survived than is recognized by most critics, even by Brooks himself. The trouble is that we have been looking for the New England spirit in the wrong places. If we believe that it is fully embodied in poets like Robinson and Frost, or in the hooked-rug and lobster-pot novelists of the Maine coast, then we can be certain of its decline. Frost is a Whittier without the fiery earnestness (though with more subtlety); Robinson was a blank-verse Hawthorne still more fettered by still more shadowy scruples; as for the hooked-rug novelists, they would have to stand on tiptoe to touch the skirts of Sarah Orne Jewett. But the New England spirit has also appeared, without being recognized, in writers born thousands of miles from Beacon Hill. I should say that its purest representative today was T. S. Eliot, of St. Louis and London, whose Catholicism is partly Calvinist and partly Buddhist, strictly in the Concord tradition. I should say that Conrad Aiken (born in Savannah) and George Santayana (born in Spain) and even John Dos Passos (by descent half Portuguese and half Virginian) are all New Englanders by virtue of their scrupulousness and Harvard diffidence and half-concealed moral fervor, and still more by virtue of a thin, stubborn integrity that has carried them through the years when so many other writers were being flashily successful.

Van Wyck Brooks, born in New Jersey, is a Yankee at least by education. During his long career he has even been two kinds of Yankee. He belonged at first to the tradition of Channing and Emerson and Wendell Phillips, the men of social purpose, the exhorters and prophets; during this period he wrote the books that Bernard Smith most admires. But *The Flowering of New England*, which will be the first volume in a general history of American literature, suggests another type of Yankee tradition, that of Bancroft and Prescott and Motley, the patient yet worldly scholars and historians. Prescott's father said, "If you wish to be happy, always have ten years' work laid out before you"; that is the Yankee way of planning one's future. At fifty, Brooks seems to have laid out before himself a labor that will occupy more than ten years. One can prophesy already that when the series is even half complete it will be compared with Prescott's narratives of the Spanish conquest and with Motley's book on *The Rise of the Dutch Republic*.

But these great scholarly works almost always have a meaning not directly expressed by the author, a meaning that inheres in the subject itself. Writing of Bancroft, for example, Brooks makes it clear that his *History of the United States* was inspired by the confident nationalism of the young republic. Writing of Motley, he explains that the Dutch republic was Motley's subject because the modern business man, the archetypical Yankee, had first appeared in Holland. If he had written of the purpose behind his own work, Brooks might have told another story. Today when the American republic is no longer lusty and crowing; when it feels that its fate is involved with that of Western civilization as a whole, which in turn is threatened by world upheavals that threaten to destroy all inherited culture—when the guns are booming one day in

Addis Ababa, the next on the outskirts of Madrid, the next, perhaps, along the Rhine—today many sensitive men like Brooks are turning back to the great past in order to see the real nature of the traditions that we are trying to save and to gain new strength for the struggles ahead.

Afterthoughts on Dos Passos

FOUR YEARS AGO in reviewing *1919*, the second volume of John Dos Passos' trilogy, I tried to define two types of fiction that have been especially prominent since the War. An *art novel*, I said, was one that dealt with the opposition between a creatively gifted individual and the community surrounding him—in brief, between the Poet and the World. Usually in books of this type the Poet gets all the attention; he is described admiringly, tenderly, and yet we learn that he is nagged and broken and often, in the end, driven to suicide by an implacably stupid World. Dos Passos' earlier novels had applied this formula, but *The 42nd Parallel* and *1919* belong to a second category: they were *collective novels*, whose real hero was American society at large, and this fact helped to explain their greater breadth and vigor. I added, however, that certain elements in these later books—and notably the autobiographical passages called the "Camera Eye"—suggested the art novel and therefore seemed out of place.

But after reviewing *The Big Money* and rereading the trilogy as a whole, it seems to me that this judgment has to be partly revised. I no longer believe that the art novel is a "bad" type of fiction (though the philosophy behind it is a bad philosophy for our time), nor do I believe that the collective novel is necessarily a "good" type (though it has advantages for writers trying to present our period of crisis). With more and more collective novels published every year, it is beginning to be obvious that the form in itself does not solve the writer's problems. Indeed, it raises new problems and creates

new disadvantages. The collective novelist is tempted to over-
emphasize the blindness and impotence of individuals caught
in the riptides of history. He is obliged to devote less space to
each of his characters, to relate their adventures more hastily,
with the result that he always seems to be approaching them
from the outside. I can see now that the Camera Eye is a
device adopted by Dos Passos in order to supply the "inwardness" that is lacking in his general narrative.

I can see too that although the device is borrowed from the
art novel—and indeed is a series of interior monologues resem-
bling parts of Joyce's *Ulysses*—it is not in the least alien to the
general plan of the trilogy. For the truth is that the art novel
and the collective novel as conceived by Dos Passos are not in
fundamental opposition: they are like the two sides of a coin.
In his art novels the emphasis is on the individual; in his
collective novels it is on society as a whole; but in both we get
the impression that society is stupid and all-powerful and fundamentally evil. Individuals ought to oppose it, but if they do
so they are doomed. If, on the other hand, they reconcile
themselves with society and try to get ahead in it, then they
are damned forever, damned to be empty, shrill, destructive
insects like Dick Savage and Eleanor Stoddard and J. Ward
Moorehouse.

In an earlier novel, *Manhattan Transfer*, there is a paragraph that states one of Dos Passos' basic perceptions. Ellen
Herf, having divorced the hero, decides to marry a rich politician whom she does not love:

> Through dinner she felt a gradual icy coldness stealing
> through her like novocaine. She had made up her mind. It
> seemed as if she had set the photograph of herself in her own
> place, forever frozen into a single gesture. . . . Everything
> about her seemed to be growing hard and enameled, the air
> bluestreaked with cigarette smoke was turning to glass.

She had made up her mind. . . . Sometimes in reading
Dos Passos it seems that not the nature of the decision but the
mere fact of having reached it is the unforgivable offense. Dick
Savage the ambulance driver decides not to be a pacifist, not to
escape into neutral Spain, and from that moment he is forever
frozen into a single gesture of selfishness and dissipation. Don
Stevens the radical newspaper correspondent decides to be a

good Communist, to obey party orders, and immediately he is stricken with the same paralysis of the heart. We have come a long way from the strong-willed heroes of the early nineteenth century—the English heroes, sons of Dick Whittington, who admired the world of their day and climbed to the top of it implacably; the French heroes like Julien Sorel and Rastignac and Monte Cristo who despised their world and yet learned how to press its buttons and pull its levers. To Dos Passos the world seems so vicious that any compromise with its standards turns a hero into a villain. The only characters he seems to like instinctively are those who know they are beaten, but still grit their teeth and try to hold on. That is the story of Jimmy Herf in *Manhattan Transfer;* to some extent it is also the story of Mary French and her father and Joe Askew, almost the only admirable characters in *The Big Money*. And the same lesson of dogged, courageous impotence is pointed by the Camera Eye, especially in the admirable passage where the author remembers the execution of Sacco and Vanzetti:

> America our nation has been beaten by strangers who have turned our language inside out who have taken the clean words our fathers spoke and made them slimy and foul
>
> their hired men sit on the judge's bench they sit back with their feet on the tables under the dome of the State House they are ignorant of our beliefs they have the dollars the guns the armed forces the powerplants . . .
>
> all right we are two nations

"The hired men with guns stand ready to shoot," he says in another passage, this one dealing with his visit to the striking miners in Kentucky. "We have only words against POWER SUPERPOWER." And these words that serve as our only weapons against the machine guns and tear gas of the invaders, these words of the vanquished nation are only that America in developing from pioneer democracy into monopoly capitalism has followed a road that leads toward sterility and slavery. Our world is evil, and yet we are powerless to change or direct it. The sensitive individual should cling to his own standards, and yet he is certain to go under. Thus, the final message of Dos Passos' three collective novels is similar to that of his earlier novels dealing with maladjusted artists. Thus, for all the vigor of *1919* and *The Big Money,* they leave us wondering whether the author hasn't overstated his case. For all their scope and richness, they fail to express one side of contemporary life—the will to struggle ahead, the comradeship in struggle, the consciousness of new men and new forces continually rising. Although we may seem at the moment a beaten nation, the fight is not over.

Louis Aragon

A FEW MOMENTS after Louis Aragon came striding into a restaurant on the Kurfürstendamm, I was ready to admit that he was more brilliant than anyone else I had known. It is possible that the scene of our first meeting contributed not a little to my enthusiasm. Berlin West in the autumn of 1922 was peopled with cripples and fairies, with bacon-fatty Polish profiteers, with hungry street girls (half of them Lesbians), with demobilized and demoralized German officers who looked as if they belonged in a hospital rather than a night club. The general atmosphere was that of a frenzied carnival in an asylum for incurables. When Aragon came striding in, with his proud head and his ingratiating white-toothed smile, he looked like a first intruder from the world of living men, like Orpheus in hell.

Yet my first impression of him, though changed in detail, was not at all weakened during the year that followed, when I saw him almost daily. He had an astonishing combination of fancy, of quick, cruel wit and literary erudition. I never heard him enter a conversation without transforming it. But what impressed me most was the consistent point of view revealed even in his jokes. He belonged to that lucky group of Frenchmen who were young enough to have served only during the last year of the War, and thus to have been disillusioned without being physically and morally broken. Some of them had

The Bells of Basel, by Louis Aragon. Translated by Haakon M. Chevalier. New York: Harcourt, Brace and Company. (*NR*, Oct. 7, 1936.)

learned to enjoy postwar Europe, even including Berlin West, as a spectacle of "the most admired disorder." It was also a field in which to test their own coolness and strength of will— for each of them had his rigid personal standards, as if to compensate for the anarchy of the world outside. Aragon, for example, was as abstemious in his habits as a Boston divinity student. He would not or could not surrender himself completely to any passion—not even to his love for literature, which was his nearest approach to a religion. Everyone admired his style, even then, but he was a writer of brilliant fragments that seemed to be chipped off from his personality. They were not the sort of works, complete in themselves, that make one forget the author.

I haven't seen him since leaving France in the summer of 1923, but often I have heard about him from the friends we had in common. He was helping his classmate André Breton to set forth the doctrines of Surrealism. He was in Kharkov, at the Soviet writers' congress; he had married a beautiful Russian. Back in France he was being tried and given a suspended sentence of five years for writing a poem that insulted the French flag. He had quarreled with Breton over politics. He was an editor of *Humanité*, the French Communist daily. He was helping to organize the intellectual allies of the People's Front and was proving to be as skillful in healing quarrels as he had once been in fighting them to the end. . . . It was a little surprising to think that Aragon, the literary anarchist, had become a disciplined party functionary. It was more surprising, however, to learn that he had written a social and collective novel, *The Bells of Basel*. For the social novelist has to be not only the master of his characters but also their humble servant. He has to do what Aragon always refused to do: he has to surrender himself in order to create a work that will have an independent life.

The Bells of Basel, which Haakon Chevalier has translated into easy-running English, is a novel of the class struggles in France that preceded the Great War. The subject is similar to that which Romains is treating in *Men of Good Will*; there are even characters that seem to be copied from the same living originals. But Aragon is approaching his subject from a different angle, with more emphasis on labor unions and financial intrigues and the social position of women. His story centers on four major characters. There is first of all Diane de Nettencourt, a society whore whose lover belongs to a group of French capitalists plotting to get control of Morocco, even at the cost of another Franco-German war. There is Catherine Simonidze, a lovely Georgian girl whose uncertain working-class sympathies get her involved with the Bonnot gang of anarchists and bank robbers. There is Victor, a leader in the taxi strike that the police are trying to break by allowing Bonnot's gang to commit new crimes and then getting anarchists and strikers confused in the public mind. Finally there is Clara Zetkin, who attends the great Socialist peace congress in Basel and speaks for the mothers of Europe. Just as Diane had represented the rich women of the old order, and Catherine the half-emancipated women who hesitated between the old and the new, so Clara Zetkin represents, to Aragon, "the woman of tomorrow. . . . The equal. The one to whom this whole book points, in whom the social problem of women is solved and left behind. . . . The woman of modern times is born and it is of her that I sing."

Reading the novel I could not help thinking that Aragon as a socialist realist was acting an alien part; yet he has too much talent not to play any part with high distinction. His story of Diane de Nettencourt is a beautifully cruel picture of the financial world. Catherine Simonidze is convincing both as a symbol and in her own person. The police intrigues around the Bonnot affair are described with a political acumen that no other novelist has surpassed. But gradually we begin to feel that the author is distracting our attention from his own characters. He seems to be angry at their meanness and vacillation. The baldness of his style makes us guess that he is tiring of the taxi strike. Suddenly he breaks off the story and bursts into a splendid apostrophe to Clara Zetkin's sea-blue eyes—"those measureless, magnificent eyes, the eyes of the whole working population of Germany, blue and mobile like deep waters crossed by currents."

In those earlier romantic stories of his, Aragon had often done something like this: he had swept his puppets into the wings and appeared on the stage in his own person, speaking with that disdainful eloquence for which he is famous. This time he surpasses himself, but uselessly; for his characters are more than puppets and we do not like to see them swept aside. We are a little disappointed to find that Aragon in spite of his new life has remained what he was in the beginning: a sharp, engaging writer who has never produced anything cheap or dull, but also a writer whose personality as revealed in his books is more brilliant and coherent than the books themselves.

A Portrait of James T. Farrell as a Young Man

HAVING READ James T. Farrell's new novel, I turned back to the *Studs Lonigan* trilogy and for the first time recognized its really unusual virtues. The author deserves my apologies for this belated praise, but he will probably understand that Studs is not my type of hero: I do not naturally enjoy the lives of tough and hairy and pitiable gangsters, especially when they are magnified beyond life size and presented with a sort of revulsion that is hard to distinguish from pure zest. But Studs finally justifies himself to the reader by that same quality of zest in the author.

As I explain the matter in my own mind, Farrell was probably an obedient and studious boy, not like Studs Lonigan at all, but rather like the hero of his new novel. In school he learned to rebel against his dingy surroundings and against the terrible lack of human dignity in the domestic quarrels of his neighbors. But he also rebelled against his schooling, with its perpetual lessons of godliness and politeness. He admired the older boys like Studs Lonigan who thieved and fornicated and generally defied the whole system of rules observed by himself, but he also feared and hated these baby hoodlums. Thus, a whole tangle of emotions went into his first long novel. Part of them were as simple as the behavior of the good boy in

A World I Never Made, by James T. Farrell. New York: The Vanguard Press. (*NR*, Nov. 18, 1936.)

Sunday School who writes dirty words in the toilet, and part of them were psychologically complicated—the death of Studs, for example, seems to be a symbolic murder in which one of Farrell's selves is the victim. But the point is that all the emotions worked in the same direction, that Farrell in this book was revenging himself not only on the sordidness of South Chicago but also on its pious hopes, and not only on the bullies from whom he had suffered but also on the heroes whom he had outgrown. It is this complete emotional integration that explains the power of the book. The author had such a good time writing it that he conveys this feeling to the reader, even in scenes that appear to be mean and revolting. The hero is presented with such gusto that he becomes a legendary as well as a real figure. Even though he is not of the same stature as Crusoe and Huckleberry Finn, he shares their quality of being truer than life.

But in his new novel—the beginning of a series that will probably continue through four or five fat volumes—Farrell is presenting a different type of hero altogether. Danny O'Neill is his name, and he had appeared several times in the background of the *Studs Lonigan* trilogy. We heard of him as a baseball player marvelously skilled at catching fouls, as a kid boxer who could outpoint Studs's heavy-footed friends, as a student at the big Protestant university, finally as a radical, with a younger brother and a sister marching among the Communists—but always as the bright boy who pointed Stud's follies by contrast, like the industrious apprentice in Hogarth's fable. Studs is now forgotten for the moment. In *A World I Never Made* we are carried back to Danny's boyhood, to the year when he left his own home crowded with rats and younger children and was taken to live with his mother's somewhat more prosperous family. He goes to a baseball game, he spends his first unhappy days in parochial school, he learns the facts of life at too great length, he gets sick from eating Christmas candy. Usually he stays in the background and watches the intrigues of his relatives—his two uncles rising as shoe salesmen, his pretty Aunt Peg sinking as the mistress of a broken financier, his grandmother puffing her clay pipe and the whole family quarreling like fishwives and lobstermen. Among these characters, Danny himself is the least vivid, and for a reason that is not hard to find. Danny is supposed to arouse our sympathy and admiration, whereas his author has always been most successful in arousing terror and revulsion. Danny is a "plus" character, and Farrell is presenting his life with a "minus" equipment.

And this lack of integration explains many of the weaknesses in the novel. Thus, it explains why Danny is usually kept in the background and why the passages that deal with him directly are written without much fire. It explains why the author shows such evident relish when he describes the degrading quarrels of the O'Flahertys and the O'Neills, writing in a language that sometimes makes *Studs Lonigan* seem as innocent as a Sunday School tract. The dirty words used by Studs were an integral part of the story. But when pretty Aunt Peg O'Flaherty says to herself, "Well, if he wants to look at my ass moving when I walk, let him, the poor goddamn fish," one feels that she is being forced to speak out of character. A fairly high-class prostitute like Aunt Peg would never think of her own body in these terms—other people would have "asses," but she would have "shapely hips" or at the very worst a "backside."

In any case, the fury of the language cannot hide the fact that Farrell, this time, is writing an essentially tender and wholesome story. He is writing about an Irish family that is mean and quarrelsome but still united by deep loyalty, so that every member of it is willing to sacrifice his own comfort in order to push ahead a talented nephew. And he is writing about this boy of talent—how he suffers in poverty and has his mind stuffed with hatreds and superstitions, yet how he struggles upwards not toward wealth, as his family desires, but toward always wider horizons. In other words, he is writing again the story of David Copperfield and Stephen Dedalus and all the impoverished but highly gifted heroes whose sorrows have been described in a thousand great, nearly great or unspeakably bad novels. Here again Farrell is faced with a problem that had scarcely existed in *Studs Lonigan*. He had been dealing there with an almost completely new background: the material itself seemed more important than the author's way of handling it. But in *A World I Never Made* he is challenging his readers to compare him technically with

Dickens and Joyce, and of course his faults are emphasized by such a comparison. His style is hackneyed and threadbare, with too many "he said pointedly's" and "Lizz rejoindered's" and only an occasional phrase that has music or color. It gives us the impression that the author is not trying to reveal life in quick flashes, but is simply slogging ahead through low-pressure areas of prose, trying to carry out his great design and write three thousand words per day.

It would be rash to predict the future of this long novel from the first volume. In *Studs Lonigan* Farrell showed a considerable inventiveness, an ability to present fantastic scenes and make them real. There is something here of the same nature, in the quarrels between Aunt Peg and her mother, and there may be more of it in the books that follow. The hero should become more interesting as he grows toward manhood. Still, I should guess that in treating the life of Danny O'Neill, Farrell has tackled the wrong sort of problem.

Yeats as Anthologist

AS A MIRROR of our age, as a compendium of the best English and Irish poems written since 1892, *The Oxford Book of Modern Verse* suffers a little from the virtues of its editor. William Butler Yeats is too great a poet to be the perfect anthologist. He is too sure of his opinions, formed and fixed by half a century of reflection, to be very tolerant of opinions with which they conflict. His taste has been refined by twenty thousand hours of writing and revision and self-criticism. In general it is superb, but he follows it too far and struggles a little too weakly against its occasional lapses.

There are, at any rate, a dozen or more contemporary poets whom he has never learned to appreciate at their full value. I am not thinking of the Americans omitted here (with the exception of Eliot and Pound, two poets "who by subject, or by

The Oxford Book of Modern Verse, chosen by W. B. Yeats. New York: Oxford University Press. (*NR,* Dec. 16, 1936.)

long residence in Europe, seem to English readers a part of their own literature"). Yeats explains, quite reasonably, that he could not hope to acquire sufficient knowledge of American poetry to make a representative selection. But he is less convincing when he explains his treatment of certain English poets—Wilfred Owen, for example, of whom he gives us not a line. "I have rejected these poems," he says in his introduction, "for the same reason that made Arnold withdraw his 'Empedocles on Etna' from circulation; passive suffering is not a theme for poetry." But passive suffering is not the beginning or end of Owen's poetry, which can better be defined as an active and even violent attempt to make people see and hear and feel the wartime suffering of others. T. S. Eliot gets much better treatment, with seven poems printed in full. But there is nothing from *The Waste Land*—nothing except four lines quoted by Yeats in the introduction, with an unfavorable comment. "I was affected, as I am by these lines, when I saw for the first time a painting by Manet. I longed for the vivid color and light of Rousseau and Courbet. I could not endure the gray middle-tint." So instead of "A Game of Chess" and "The Fire Sermon"—the gray middle-tint of Eliot at his best—we are given the early "Preludes" and the later religious poems. D. H. Lawrence is not mentioned in the introduction, but I doubt that Yeats feels any deep sympathy for his work; the six poems quoted here are lacking in his peculiar intensity. These three men, with Yeats himself, are probably the most important figures in recent English poetry, and Yeats is unjust to all of them—even to himself, for he completely omits his early work in favor of poems written since the Irish revolution.

On the other hand, he proclaims a vast enthusiasm for several minor poets whom I find it hard to admire even mildly. W. J. Turner is one of these. There are twelve of his poems quoted, and they fail to justify Yeats's comment that they exhibit "a control of plastic material, a power of emotional construction, Pound has always lacked." Except in his earlier lyrics, Turner seems prosy and philosophically muddled. Edith Sitwell gets even more space, and is even worse. Indeed, the anthology contains entirely too much and too many of the Sitwell tribe, as if Yeats had been overawed by their high opinion of themselves. Oliver St. John Gogarty (Joyce's Buck Mulligan) is another elegant poet rated at more than his true value. He makes me think of words like *sang-froid* and *chic* and *savoir-faire*—in a word, he makes me think of Mr. Lucius Beebe, the night-club editor of *The New York Herald Tribune.* Yeats's appreciation of all these minor figures seems less critical than creative. He reads his own qualities of ripeness and melody and precision into poems that possess them not at all.

Quite possibly an editor who was a third-rate instead of a first-rate poet might have compiled a better anthology—better, that is, in the sense of being more representative and more useful to students of contemporary literature. Still, I doubt that such a book would be as good for the general reader. It would not delight or infuriate him, as Yeats does on every page of the long introduction; and neither would it surprise him by presenting the work of poets who are sneered at or unknown. No matter how many faults one may find in *The Oxford Book of Modern Verse*, it has the quality of being continually alive; and it makes the English poetry of the last forty years seem more exciting than the picture of it that had slowly been forming in our minds.

But was it so exciting in reality? Yeats believes that "England has had more good poets from 1900 to the present day than during any period of the same length since the early seventeenth century. There are no predominant figures, no Browning, no Tennyson, no Swinburne, but more than I have found room for have written two, three or half a dozen lyrics that may be permanent." I wonder whether a critic of the distant future would agree with him. Let us imagine that a thousand years have passed and that Yeats's anthology has luckily been saved from the last burning of the books. Let us imagine that inscriptions in stone or bronze have also survived (along with our primitive machine guns) and that the critic of the future can decipher the general outlines of our era. What would he say about the English poets of the early nineteen-hundreds?

Wouldn't he say first of all that they lacked conviction? That they were skilled in manipulating a language they had learned from books, but that they seldom appeared to be deeply interested in the subjects with which they were ostensibly dealing? The subjects were chiefly nature, history and religion. But the poets did not praise nature for its own sake, as it had been praised by the Elizabethans. Always understood in their descriptions of country lanes bright with hawthorn buds and sweet with songbirds was the fact that the lanes were being invaded, the buds and birds destroyed, by a factory civilization that the poets were trying to escape. It was the same with their treatment of history. When they wrote about Samarcand or Alexander or the Spanish Main, they were not trying to present the real past. Instead they were fleeing into a realm of myth, hoping to find there a sense of dignity or a reason for living that was absent from their daily environment. Even their religious poems were not written out of belief, but rather out of the feeling that disbelief was uncomfortable. They seemed to be saying, "Yes, I do really believe, in spite of what you say."

And so—the future critic would continue—those early twentieth-century poets had the vice of divided attention. They talked about one thing while brooding over another. The real subject was their personal lives—their lives that were lacking in beauty (thus driving them to nature), lacking in dignity (thus driving them into the past) and lacking in value (thus driving them into the church). Their real subject was the predicament of the individual in a society that affronts his pride, that keeps him walled within himself, but they rarely had courage to face that subject. That is why the poets of this age (with the exception of a few honest ones like Yeats and Lawrence and Eliot) were forgotten even before the collapse in war of the civilization that had nourished them.

Hemingway: Work in Progress

CHIEF AMONG Hemingway's virtues as a writer is his scrupulous regard for fact, for reality, for "what happened." It is a rare virtue in the world of letters. Most writers want to please or shock, to be "accomplished craftsmen" or to be "ori-

To Have and Have Not, by Ernest Hemingway. New York: Charles Scribner's Sons. (*NR*, Oct. 20, 1937.)

ginal"; in both cases their work is determined by literary fashions, which they either follow or defy. From the very first, Hemingway did neither, since his aim was simply to reproduce the things he had seen and felt—"simply," I say, but anyone who has tried to set down his own impressions accurately must realize that the task is enormously difficult; there is always the temptation to change and falsify the story because it doesn't fit into a conventional pattern or because the right words are lacking. Hemingway himself had to find a whole new vocabulary, one in which old or popular words like "good," "nice" and "rotten" are given fresh values. But it always makes me angry to hear people speaking of his "lean, hard, athletic prose." Sometimes his prose is beautiful, poetic in the best sense, in its exact evocations of landscapes and emotions. Sometimes it is terse and efficient. Sometimes, with its piling up of very short words, it gives the effect of a man stammering, getting his tongue twisted, talking too much but eventually making us understand just what he wants to say.

During the last ten years Hemingway has been imitated more widely than any other American or British writer, even T. S. Eliot. You find his influence everywhere from the pulp-paper true-detective-story weeklies to the very little magazines making no compromise with the public taste. You find it in newspapers and the movies, in English highbrow novels and even in this weekly journal of opinion. Partly it has been a bad influence. It has made people copy the hard-boiled manner of "The Killers" and "Fifty Grand"—this latter being the cheapest story that Hemingway ever signed. It has encouraged them to boast in print of their love affairs and drinking bouts—though God knows they needed little encouragement. Worst of all, it has caused many young writers to take over Hemingway's vocabulary and his manner of seeing the world, thereby making it impossible for them to be as honest as Hemingway. But in general I think that his influence has been excellent. It has freed many writers—not only novelists but poets and essayists and simple reporters—from a burden of erudition and affectation that they thought was part of the writer's equipment. It has encouraged them to write as simply as possible about the things they really feel, instead of the things they think that other people think they ought to feel. Critics in particular owe a debt to Hemingway; and many of them, including myself, have been slow to acknowledge it. So let me put the record straight. I don't think that he is as great as Tolstoy or Thomas Mann, but I do think that he is perhaps as good as Mark Twain, and that is saying a great deal. In our own generation he is the best we have.

His new novel I found easy to read, impossible to lay down before it was finished, and very hard to review. It contains some of the best writing he has ever done. There are scenes that are superb technical achievements and other scenes that carry him into new registers of emotion. As a whole it lacks unity and sureness of effect.

Part of its weakness is a simple matter of plot structure, a department in which Hemingway was never strong. The book falls apart at the beginning and the end. It begins with two long stories about Harry Morgan—both of them, I think, were first published in *The Cosmopolitan*—and it ends with a fine soliloquy by Harry Morgan's widow. In the intervening pages, Hemingway deals with his principal theme, which is really two themes in counterpoint—on the one side, the life of the Have-Nots, that is, the Key West fishermen and relief workers who surround Harry Morgan; on the other side, the life of the Haves, that is, the wealthy yachtsmen and the drunken writers who winter in the Key West bars. These two themes never quite come together.

But a more serious weakness lies in the characters themselves, or rather in the author's attitude toward his characters. Some of them—the writers for example—are the same sort of people, leading the same sort of lives, that he described in *The Sun Also Rises*. In those days Hemingway was unhappy about the lives they were leading, yet he approached the people with sympathy, going to great pains, for example, to explain to himself why Robert Cohn was really a villain in spite of all his admirable qualities. But this time Hemingway really hates the people; he pictures them not as human beings but as the mere embodiments of lust or folly, as wolves or goats or monkeys disguised with little mustaches and portable typewriters. "All right," Helen Gordon says to her husband. "I'm through with you and I'm through with love. Your kind of picknose love. You writer." It is the final insult. But since Hemingway is a

writer himself, this aversion is also a self-aversion and prophe-
sies a change in his own career—not from literature to fishing,
for example, but rather from one kind of writing to another
kind. And that change, that transition, is already foreshadowed
in his characters. Among the very few that he portrays sympathetically are two Catholics and a communist war veteran.
Harry Morgan himself begins as a tough guy capable of killing people in cold blood, either to get money or to save his
hide, but he dies as a sort of proletarian hero.

There is a story behind this novel perhaps more interesting
than the story that Hemingway has told. Someday we may
know the whole of it; at present I have to reconstruct it from
word-of-mouth information and from internal evidence. Hemingway has been working on the book for several years—at the
very least, since 1933. It was practically finished a year ago,
before he left for Spain. At that time it was a longer novel
than in its present version, and it ended in a mood of utter
discouragement. When Hemingway returned, full of enthusiasm for the Spanish Loyalists, he must have felt dissatisfied
with what he had written; at any rate he destroyed large parts
of it. It may have been then that he wrote a death scene for
Harry Morgan—the scene in which he stammers out with his
last few breaths: "One man alone ain't got. No man alone
now. . . . No matter how, a man alone ain't got no bloody
f——g chance." This might be the message that Hemingway
carried back from Spain, his own free translation of Marx and
Engels: "Workers of the world unite, you have nothing to
lose. . . ." The whole scene is beautifully done, but it doesn't
grow out of what has gone before.

There are other scenes that are even stronger, and better
integrated with the story—for example, the phantasmagorical
drinking and slugging bout of the veterans on relief, and the
quarrel between Helen Gordon and her husband, and Mrs.
Morgan's last soliloquy. Almost all the women in the novel
are portrayed with subtlety and sureness. As a whole, *To Have
and Have Not* is the weakest of Hemingway's books—except
perhaps *Green Hills of Africa*—but it is by no means the least
promising. For some years now the literary hyenas have been

saying that Hemingway was done for, but their noses have betrayed them into finding the scent of decay where none existed. From the evidence of this book, I should say that he was beginning a new career.

Thomas Mann's Joseph Legend

1. And Joseph was brought down to Egypt; and Potiphar, an officer of Pharaoh, captain of the guard, bought him off the hands of the Ishmaelites, which had brought him down thither.

2. And the Lord was with Joseph, and he was a prosperous man; and he was in the house of his master the Egyptian.

Almost the whole plot of *Joseph in Egypt* is contained in the first twenty verses of Genesis 39. It is true that Mann has borrowed several details from other versions of the Joseph legend—from that in the Koran, for example. But for the most part he confines himself to the familiar story of how Joseph was sold into Potiphar's household, how he became the chief steward there, how he was tempted by Potiphar's wife, how he was falsely accused and how, in the end, "Joseph's master took him, and put him into the prison, a place where the king's prisoners were bound." I have emphasized the word "how," remembering Mann's apology for telling the story at such great length. "Let no one think I am deaf to the reproach," he says, ". . . that the laconic terseness of the original text cannot be surpassed, and that my whole enterprise, which is already of such long continuance, is so much labor lost. But . . . is there not as much dignity and importance attached to the discussion of the 'how' as to the transmission of the 'what'? Yes, does not life first fulfill itself in the 'how'?" Here lies the key to Mann's purpose. In expanding twenty verses of Genesis into a novel of 664 pages, bound in two

"The Golden Legend" (*NR*, Mar. 16, 1938) and "Second Thoughts on 'Joseph' " (*NR*, Mar. 23, 1938). A two-part review of *Joseph in Egypt*, by Thomas Mann. Translated by H. T. Lowe-Porter. New York: Alfred A. Knopf. 2 vols.

volumes, he is trying to find the "how" that restores life to the Joseph legend and reveals it as part of our own experience.

This novel—or let us say the whole unfinished series of which it forms a part—is among the few masterpieces of our time. The word "great" that is so often misapplied can be used this time without embarrassment. But its greatness is not veiled in Orphic mystery. Mann makes no attempt to hide his theories of writing or his standards of workmanship; he is almost too willing to discuss them with his readers. In trying to revivify the story of Joseph, he has followed four methods which other writers can follow too—if they have the same breadth of understanding and the same capacity for taking pains.

His first method is one that biblical scholars have been using for at least a thousand years. He analyzes the text; he seizes upon its implications and tries to make them clear. Thus, the Bible says of Joseph, "he was in the house of his master the Egyptian." Why hadn't he been sent into his master's fields, to work and die under the lash with most of the other slaves? Mann finds the answer both in Joseph's character and in that of Potiphar's overseer, a new figure introduced into the story without disturbing its outlines. The Bible says of Potiphar's wife, "she spake to Joseph day by day." Mann develops this hint of continued action into a picture of slow moral disintegration. There are parts of the novel that apparently refer to modern Europe, but usually they are based on suggestions in the original narrative. Thus, Potiphar's wife makes a Jew-baiting speech to the men of her household. But she had made that speech in the Bible too. "See," she said, holding up Joseph's torn garment, "he hath brought in an Hebrew unto us to mock us." It was not Thomas Mann who imagined her talking like Goering at the Reichstag fire trial; it was the author of the Pentateuch.

But analysis of the text will carry him only so far; and where it stops Mann has to depend on a second familiar method—that is, on the novelist's talent for creating characters. Here he is on dangerous ground; he is approaching the sort of "fictionized biography" that might be defined as biography simplified and conventionalized by fiction. We have a lord to depict: let us make him lordly. Our hero is tempted: let us make the woman a temptress like Cleopatra. But Mann is a novelist much too subtle to fall into such a trap. Besides playing their proper roles in the story—and playing them superbly—his characters are in themselves complex, human and convincing. Potiphar, the great lord, is captain of the king's guard, but his office is a sinecure. Essentially he is powerless; his splendid career is built wholly on appearances. In the midst of them is a lonely, uneasy man trying to hide the secret that he has been emasculated by his parents, who offered his manhood as a sacrifice to the gods. His wife, Mut-em-enet, known to her friends as Eni, is cool, beautiful, indifferent, a virgin dedicated to the service of the temple. But when she falls in love with Joseph, her pride is broken and her character begins to degenerate, month by month. Even her body changes, till at the end—but only at the end—she becomes a furious hag.

These characters, modern in conception, are set against a definite historical background which also suggests the modern world. Mann imagines that Joseph was sold into Egypt during the reign of Amenhotep III, at the end of the eighteenth dynasty. It was a time when the Egyptian empire, which had reached its height a century before, was rapidly declining: the Hittites were attacking from the northeast; the desert tribes were drifting into Palestine. At home there was a bitter conflict between the priests' party—the bitter nationalists, the reactionaries, the worshipers of Amon—and the king's party of internationalists who worshiped Aton the Sun as the only true god. This conflict burst forth into civil war during the reign of Ikhnaton (Profitable-to-Aton), the next Pharaoh and the one who would release Joseph from prison. As a foreigner and a leader in the king's party, Joseph would be deeply involved in Egyptian politics—which in sober truth were not unlike the German politics of our own century.

But Mann has a fourth method of adding richness and weight to his story. Continually he draws on a field of modern thought that lies on the borderland between science and speculation. Freud and the Gestalt school, in their different branches of psychology; Frazer and Durkheim, in their outlines of primitive religion; Spengler, in his "morphology of history"—all these men had something in common, no matter how deep their conflicts. All of them were seeking for patterns or configurations or forms of experience, rather than for causes in the strict logical sense of the word. Mann borrows some of their theories, psychological or anthropological, but chiefly he uses their general attitude. To him the story of Joseph is a master pattern of human experience. It includes the episodes that recur in other legends—the miraculous birth, the strife among brothers, the descent into the pit (a symbolic death), the wandering in exile, the tempting, the labors, the triumph. In a sense it repeats the stories of Abraham, Isaac and Jacob (not to mention Osiris, Tammuz, Adonis). In another sense it foreshadows the adventures of heroes in our modern world.

By all four methods—analytical, fictional, historical and morphological—the author enriches his story without necessarily bringing it any nearer to the Joseph-who-lived. But did he ever live? On that point, tradition is eloquent while history holds its tongue. Joseph may have been a slave in Egypt under the Hyksos, the Shepherd Kings, three hundred years before the date that Mann has chosen. He may have been several figures, vaguely remembered and merged into one by the Hebrew story-tellers; or he may have been a culture hero who never existed on earth. For Mann's purpose, it doesn't really matter. What he is seeking is not the Joseph-who-lived but rather the legend that has never died—the legend repeated through the centuries and shaped by popular wisdom, so that even in its errors it reflects the living nature of man.

ii

I found the first hundred pages of *Joseph in Egypt* rather hard going. In the little caravan of Ishmaelites that bought him from his brothers, Joseph is being taken across the Sinai peninsula into the delta of the Nile. He passes through Per-Sopdu, the city of clove-pinks, and Per-Bastet, the city of cats, and On, the golden city of the sun; he camps for a night beside the Sphinx; and slowly, day by day, he learns about the complexities of Egyptian religion. Says Dr. Harry Slochower in his book called *Thomas Mann's Joseph Story*, "The first chapters of *Joseph in Egypt* are thoroughly epic in their slow rhythm. So 'Egyptian' is the mood created that in parts the story does not seem to move at all and time appears to stand still, as in sleep." Dr. Slochower's essay is helpful and discerning and I recommend it to anyone who wants to study the novel. But at this point I suspect him of turning a fault into a virtue on the ground that Mann is above criticism. One might also say that time stands still in these first two chapters because the story is overburdened with atmosphere and exposition.

In the third chapter Joseph reaches the gate of Potiphar's mansion, and the story comes to life as a tired horse does when his head is turned toward home. From this moment—from the middle of page 132—it trots ahead almost without pausing, at first by formal narrative and then by a really magnificent series of confrontations that resemble the scenes of a Racinian tragedy—Joseph and Potiphar in the garden; Joseph and Montkaw at the old steward's deathbed; Potiphar and his wife Mutem-enet, also called Eni; and midway in the second volume Eni and Joseph in the scene of the tempting, perhaps the richest and subtlest that Mann has written. Here the tempo changes again. The mood, the characters having been established, there is no further need for exposition. The story no longer trots, it gallops with a loose rein through a whole series of comic or terrifying situations to that final scene, told at a calmer pace, where Potiphar pronounces judgment. Joseph will be sent to the island prison of Zawi-Re, the place where the king's prisoners are bound; he will be one of Pharaoh's slaves.—"So then Joseph went down a second time to the prison and the pit. The story of his rising again out of this hold to a still higher life may be the subject of future lays."

Through all these scenes, the story moves forward on different levels, psychological, social, symbolic, legendary. On the topmost level, Joseph's adventure is a psychological drama of a type that might recur in any age, including our own. There have always been great ladies, married to weaklings, who fell in love with their husband's steward or his gamekeeper (Lady Chatterley) or his handsome uniformed chauffeur. But Joseph and Mut-em-enet were also, in a sense, the first to find themselves in that situation. They would be the figures of a legend, and Joseph was conscious of his role—"It may easily be that we are the stuff of history," he says to Eni. "Therefore have a care for yourself and take pity upon your story, that you do not become a warning in it and the mother of sin." Eni belonged to an old and tired civilization, incapable of creating new forms; to Joseph she represented a sort of death. And there was a whole series of conflicts implicit in their meeting—matter against spirit, the old against the new, paganism against puritanism, the many gods against the one true God. Eni and Joseph are symbols, but they are not abstract figures of vice and virtue; first of all they are living people. That explains why the symbolism is complicated and extraordinarily rich in meanings.

It may be that there is an allegory of the author's life to be read in the story. Thomas Mann is an exile like Joseph. Not so long ago he was tempted with the promise of high official honors if only he would praise that new German government which, in its spirit of hierarchy and its complete subservience of the people to the state, is not essentially different from the old Egyptian government. Like Joseph he thought that if he consented he would be surrendering spirit to matter and life to death. Late in his career Mann has developed a keen sense of social responsibility, to supplement his earlier sense of artistic responsibility; Joseph is an archetype of the social man. These are of course vague and questionable comparisons, but of one thing there can be no doubt: the Joseph cycle is written more lyrically than Mann's earlier novels and with a deeper feeling of personal urgency. "Why do I turn pale," he asks in the Prelude, "why does my heart beat high—not only since I set out but ever since the first command to do so—and not only with eagerness but still more with physical fear? . . . The past into which I now shudderingly descend [is] the past of life, the dead and gone world, to which my own life shall more and more profoundly belong." In telling the legend of Joseph he is telling his own legend too, and writing his testament.

But the chief virtue I find in the novel is one that has always distinguished his work, though never more than in the present series—that is, its complete and amazing coherence. From the first page of *Joseph and His Brothers* (1934) through the whole of *Young Joseph* (1935) to the last page of these two new volumes—and of the "future lays" that will doubtless follow—in the whole project everything fits together like the parts of an enormously intricate puzzle. Philosophy, action, character, style, symbolism, dream, history, legend, everything contributes to the same effect. This does not mean that the books were written mechanically to plans and specifications drawn up in advance. They grew in the writing: the figure of Jacob came forward, the ten older brothers retreated into the background (Mann simply can't get interested in them), and the drama with Potiphar's wife assumed more importance, so that this book once meant to end the series is now only a resting place along the way. But no matter how much the story grows, it remains true to its own nature. One might say that the whole of it is present by implication in every part.

One might say more than that. The system of relationships created by Thomas Mann is so complete and persuasive that one is tempted to accept it as a whole, the faults along with the virtues, the dreams and miracles along with the drama. In this lies a danger that I don't want to exaggerate. If I venture to give a warning, it is not addressed to Thomas Mann, who does not need our advice or even our admiration, but to those who accept his work with a complete surrender of their critical faculties. On such readers, the effect of his recent books is sometimes to induce a fog of exalted sentiments. Anything can happen in a fog: for example soldiers might wander into the ranks of the enemy.

The philosophy that Mann develops in the Joseph story is a noble structure, full of wisdom, but it is also full of dark rooms and calculated mysteries. This is an age in which mysteries are to be distrusted. When reasonableness and good sense are being threatened on all sides by all sorts of myths—as they are today—and by glorifications of force, instinct, blood, race, the soil, it is dangerous to praise legends at the expense of history. It is dangerous to confuse truth with error on the ground that both reveal the essential nature of man. The next step might be to praise tradition in general and to justify despotic governments on the ground that they are rooted in tradition. Mann would never take this step, but others inspired by him might do so; and they would find some arguments to support them in the Joseph cycle. It is a great work, and one that expresses the sickness of the modern mind as well as its persistent strength.

The Maugham Enigma

THERE IS a Somerset Maugham enigma, one that has always puzzled me. Why has he never written another book that was half so good as *Of Human Bondage?* Since 1897 he has been a professional writer, since 1907 a successful playwright, since 1916 a famous novelist. On the flyleaf of his latest book is a list of thirty-eight that preceded it—best-selling novels, short stories, travels, plays that were smash hits in London, New York, Berlin—and these are only the books he wants to remember; there are half a dozen others he is willing to forget. More than a collection of separate works, he has produced a unified body of work, an *œuvre*, something that very few living writers have achieved in our language. Yet there has been a suspicion among critics that the *œuvre* was artificial and the production of a second- or a third-rate artist. The critics have usually been unjust to Maugham; they have neglected his great achievements as a craftsman. He has never fallen so low as Arnold Bennett at his worst or Sinclair Lewis at his third-best. Even when writing for the sort of public he despised, he was upheld by the strict morality of the prostitute who told him years ago that she was proud of always giving honest value. Still, there were times when his heart wasn't in the work. Why did he write one book that was full of candor and human warmth? Why did he never climb back to the same level?

In *The Summing Up* he gives a partial and indirect but still a convincing answer to these questions. Of course that wasn't his aim in writing the book. Having reached the age of sixty-three, he wanted to take an inventory—"to sort out my thoughts on the subjects that have chiefly interested me during the course of my life." He didn't propose to write an autobiography or a book of confessions—"I have no desire to lay bare my heart, and I put limits to the intimacy that I wish the reader to enter upon with me." But without being frank, in the cant use of the word, he intended to be personal and completely truthful; and the result is the most interesting book he

The Summing Up, by W. Somerset Maugham. New York: Doubleday, Doran and Company. (*NR*, Mar. 30, 1938.)

has published for twenty years. Incidentally it tells us a great deal about the sources and the psychological effects of his one great novel.

Of Human Bondage was written when Maugham was forty years old; his literary apprenticeship was over. He had learned four languages and studied masterpieces in all of them; he had worked to develop a prose style; he had written several novels, most of which were pure technical exercises; he had enjoyed the rare experience of having four plays running during a single London season. But in the midst of his success as a popular playwright, he began to be obsessed—the word is his own—by the teeming memories of his past life. "It all came back to me so pressingly, in my sleep, on my walks, when I was rehearsing plays, when I was at a party, it became such a burden to me that I made up my mind that I could only regain my peace by writing it all down in the form of a novel. I knew it would be a long one and I wanted to be undisturbed, so I refused the contracts managers were anxious to give me and temporarily retired from the stage."

Novels written after such an apprenticeship and out of such a necessity are almost certain to be good novels. But why didn't Maugham produce others of the same rank?

There are at least two answers and one of them is purely psychological. The clue to it lies in his use of the word "obsessed." Maugham was obsessed, haunted by the past—by his mother, kind and beautiful, who died when he was eight; by his lonely boyhood in the vicarage at Blackstable; by his schoolmates jeering at his stammer (which was the psychological equivalent of Philip Carey's clubfoot); by the suffering humanity he saw at St. Thomas's Hospital; and finally, I should guess, by a love affair as prolonged and unhappy as Philip Carey's love for Mildred. He was under a compulsion to tell the whole story, to perform the rite of public confession and so receive absolution. "The book," he says, "did for me what I wanted, and when it was issued to the world . . . I found myself free forever from those pains and unhappy recollections. I put into it everything I then knew and having at last finished it prepared to make a fresh start." He would never again return to the material that was closest to his heart.

But there is a second answer that lies in a field between the psychological and the social. The coldness and externality of Maugham's later novels was partly a result of his success—"the greatest danger that besets the professional author":

> Success . . . often bears within itself the seed of destruction, for it may very well cut the author off from the material that was its occasion. He enters a new world. He is made much of. He must be also superhuman if he is not captivated by the notice taken of him by the great and remains insensible to the attractions of beautiful women. He grows accustomed to another way of life. . . . How difficult it is for him then to move freely still in the circles to which he has been accustomed and which have given him his subjects! His success has changed him in the eyes of his old associates and they are no longer at home with him. They may look upon him with envy or admiration, but no longer as one of themselves. The new world into which his success has brought him excites his admiration and he writes about it, but he sees it from the outside and can never so penetrate it as to become a part of it. No better example of this can be given than Arnold Bennett. . . .

But Maugham himself is another example of the author separated by success from the circles that gave him his best subjects. They were not the upper-middle-class circles with which his later books have dealt. He was born into the upper middle class—his father was solicitor for the British Embassy in Paris—and he will die in it too, but he has never felt at home with its members. Except in a few early plays like *Jack Straw*, he has always observed them as a faintly hostile stranger. His best subjects were the poor people he met when he was a down-at-the-heels medical student and a starving writer.

There is a story here with which his future biographer will have to struggle. My own idea is that when Maugham left Paris at the age of ten, an orphan speaking broken English—when he was neglected by his uncle the vicar and tormented by his schoolmates because of his timidity and his stammer—he became psychologically alienated not only from church and school but from his own class in English society. A few years later, at St. Thomas's Hospital, he met the people who lived in the Lambeth slums and all hostility vanished. Philip Carey had the same experience in *Of Human Bondage;* he found that "he was less shy with these people than he had ever been with others; he felt not exactly sympathy, for sympathy suggests condescension; but he felt at home with them."

At this point the path of the hero diverged from that of the novelist. Philip Carey fell violently in love with a waitress, lost her and married a seamstress instead. After becoming a doctor he chose to practice in a poor fishing village, partly because it was his first opening but also because he liked the people and they liked him in return. Somerset Maugham, as soon as his plays made money, bought a house in Mayfair, but only because he liked the neighborhood as a symbol of success; he was irritated by the people. And that, I should guess, is the trouble with his work during the last twenty years. He has been writing stories—accurate and workmanlike and dramatic stories—about a class from which he had been spiritually alienated, and about people with whom he doesn't care to live. One reads in his character an impulse toward generosity and fellow-feeling that he hasn't given himself much chance to display. The faintly disagreeable aftertaste in his books is the milk of human kindness, half-soured.

Yeats and the "Baptism of the Gutter"

ONE OF THE PROBLEMS that set Yeats to writing about his own relatively happy life was the broken and tragic lives of his early friends. Lionel Johnson, Ernest Dowson, Arthur Symons, Oscar Wilde, Aubrey Beardsley, John Davidson, Francis Thompson, almost all his associates of the Rhymers' Club and The Savoy, were artists of unusual talent and personal modesty. "Why," he asks, "should men who spoke their opinions in low voices, as though they feared to disturb the

"Poet in Politics." A review of *The Autobiography of William Butler Yeats*, consisting of *Reveries over Childhood and Youth* (1914), *The Trembling of the Veil* (1922), and *Dramatis Personae* (1936). New York: The Macmillan Company. (*NR*, Sept. 21, 1938.)

readers in some ancient library, and timidly as though they knew that all subjects had long since been explored, all questions long since decided in books whereon the dust settled— live lives of such disorder?" And why should they all seek early deaths, one or two by drink, one by drink and whoring, one by scandal, one by drugs, one at least by suicide, more than one by insanity, or by bodily diseases that they did not struggle against, and all, so it seemed, by some disease of the will?

Yeats in his autobiography suggests not one but several reasons for the end of what he calls the Tragic Generation. Most of them, he says, were poor men, strained and broken by their poverty (though he tells us that Lionel Johnson and one or two others had private means). Their effort toward intense and lyrical emotion may have made them emotionally unstable (though he tells us that the first of them to go insane was a man without any lyrical gift). Again, they may have been weakened by their philosophy of life for art's sake and art for its own pure self. They made "what Arnold has called that 'morbid effort,' that search for 'perfection of thought and feeling, and to unite this to perfection of form,' sought this new, pure beauty, and suffered in their lives because of it."

This last would apply to other tragic poets as well—Poe, Baudelaire, Rossetti—and therefore is the most convincing of the reasons that Yeats offers for their decline. A still more convincing reason is one that he often suggests but never mentions explicitly: their self-imposed and utter isolation. When Lionel Johnson was asked whether his irregular hours "did not separate him from men and women, he replied, 'In my library I have all the knowledge of the world that I need.' "—"That room was always a pleasure to me," Yeats himself continued, "with its curtains of gray corduroy over door and window and bookcase . . . and a general air of neatness and severity; and talking there by candle light it never seemed very difficult to murmur Villiers de l'Isle Adam's proud words, 'As for living, our servants will do that for us.' " The truth is that these poets were completely cut off from living, screened from the world by their curtains of neat gray corduroy. They had very few human sympathies and no instinctive attachment to birthplace or class or nation. They had to draw song from their inner resources, like water from a cistern that was never renewed from the outside, till at last, as it dwindled, it became stagnant and poisonous.

Back in the first days of the Rhymers' Club, Yeats had told his friends, "None of us can say who will succeed, or even who has or has not talent. The only thing certain about us is that we are too many." There was no doubt even then that some of them would fail disastrously; but nobody could have guessed that within a comparatively short time the Rhymers would be swept off the scene as if by a virulent plague. And nobody could have guessed that the young Irishman who addressed them—awkward, embarrassed, lost in his private world, given to experiments in spiritualism and black magic—would be the only one of them to show practical wisdom and, after twenty years, almost the sole survivor.

During those years, Yeats had followed a different path from his friends. It was chiefly his interest in Irish literature that led him to found the Irish Literary Society (London, 1891) and the National Literary Society (Dublin, 1893). But the question of reviving poetry in Ireland was intimately connected with the question of restoring the Irish nation, which in turn was connected with the colonial question and the land question—and the result was that Yeats for a few years became an effective political agitator. He went on lecture tours through England and Scotland, he spoke at tumultuous Dublin conventions, he presided over committee meetings in the back rooms of Irish pubs, and he was rumored—though falsely —to have instigated the riots against Queen Victoria at the time of her Jubilee visit. His own story is that he was merely lost in the window-breaking Dublin mob. "In a battle like Ireland's," he wrote to Lady Gregory, "which is one of poverty against wealth, we must prove our sincerity by making ourselves unpopular to wealth. We must accept the baptism of the gutter."

That was a romantic way of conceiving the part he played; and it was inevitable that Yeats would be unhappy when he found that "the gutter" too was divided into factions, most of them hostile to visitors from the upper world. The Irish national movement in the 1890's was almost like the American radical movement in the 1930's, with Parnellites hating Anti-Parnellites and both sides hating the Irish Unionists almost more than the British. "Most of us were prosecuting heretics," Yeats says, "and our conventions . . . were dominated by little groups, the Gaelic propagandists being the most impassioned, which had the intensity and narrowness of theological sects."—"A movement first of poetry, then of sentimentality, and land hunger, had struggled with, and as the nation passed into the second period of all revolutions, given way before a movement of abstraction and hatred." Slowly the poet became disillusioned; and after his allies the Nationalists had rioted against *The Playboy of the Western World*, which was written by his best friend and produced in a theatre that Yeats himself had founded, he withdrew almost completely from political life.

The truth is that Yeats had always been of a divided mind about his participation in politics. His eagerness to change people's minds and his pride in success were mingled with his shame at having surrendered himself "to the chief temptation of the artist, creation without toil."—"Politics, for a vision-seeking man, can be but half achievement, a choice of an almost easy kind of skill instead of that kind which is, of all those not impossible, the most difficult." He came to speak with revulsion "of the dirty piece of orange peel in the corner of the stairs as one climbs up to some newspaper office; of public meetings where it would be treacherous amid so much geniality to speak or even to think of anything that might cause a moment's misunderstanding in one's own party."

He believed that poetry and politics, abstraction and image, public life and private vision, were fixed in eternal opposition. Yet one can scarcely doubt that his own political life helped to save him from a broken career and an early death like those of his friends. . . . No, I am not trying to say what I was once mistakenly accused of saying, that a poet can be saved by adopting the right opinions. No poet can be saved by any opinions whatsoever. Those adopted by Yeats were in many cases the wrong opinions, even in his youth when he fancied himself a socialist and even in his young manhood when he was actively working for the Irish revolution. His mystical nationalism, with its talk of the Irish racial spirit and the Irish oversoul, could be used by some of Hitler's court and barrack-room philosophers. His fear of abstractions kept him ignorant of modern thought, except for Mallarmé and Madam Blavatsky. Later, after he had washed his hands of politics, he became almost as monarchistic and right-thinking as old William Wordsworth. No matter: there had been a time when he worked and fought among the Irish masses, shared their hopes and hatreds, learned to speak their language and transformed it into a medium for great poetry. He had broken his isolation, stepped out of his private world; he had found a subject and an audience. And the effect of that "baptism of the gutter" persisted in his later work, just as it persisted for a while with Wordsworth and longer with Baudelaire. Today when he peers from his lonely tower into the Irish mist, the visions he sees there are not disembodied, like Francis Thompson's or Lionel Johnson's visions; they are given shape and endowed with life by the passions of his active years.

Socialists and Symbolists

IN READING Yeats's autobiography, I was struck once more by the close connection between the technique of the Symbolist poets and their attitude toward life and art. They not only hated science and despised public affairs; they even went to crazy lengths in the effort to avoid any sort of generalized or abstract thinking. "I refused," Yeats says, "to read books and even to meet people who excited me to generalization. . . . I said my prayers much as in childhood, though without the old regularity of hour and place, and I began to pray that my imagination might somehow be rescued from abstraction. . . . For ten or twelve years more I suffered continual remorse, and only became content when my abstractions had composed themselves into picture and dramatization." Thus, the style that Yeats adopted, with its wealth of concrete images and its search for "precision of word and sound," was based on his dislike for scientific or political thinking. Even the

NR, Sept. 28, 1938. Yeats's autobiography is reviewed in the preceding essay.

rhythms of his poems can be traced to the same source, as he explains in a fine passage that has been quoted more than once:

> We make out of the quarrel with others rhetoric, but of the quarrel with ourselves, poetry. Unlike the rhetoricians, who get a confident voice from remembering the crowd they have won or may win, we sing amid our uncertainty; and, smitten even in the presence of the most high beauty by the knowledge of our solitude, our rhythm shudders.

There cannot be any doubt that this technique based on hesitating rhythms and on images that are precise yet infinitely suggestive has been successful in Yeats's own work and in that of other great Symbolists—Mallarmé, Eliot, Rainer Maria Rilke. The question is whether the same technique can be used convincingly by poets who, unlike the Symbolists, are interested in general ideas and in the social life of our times. Selden Rodman says that the younger poets are using it already. He believes that the most important, the dominating movement in contemporary verse, is the one he calls Social Symbolism. In a letter printed in this issue of *The New Republic*, he gives me a friendly scolding for doubting its success.

Though he brings forward some good arguments and an impressive list of names, he hasn't changed my mind. For I have lately been reading the poets he mentions, with many others like them, and though I am glad to recognize their talent, I am becoming more and more dubious about the value of the movement in which they are engaged. Most of their verse is spoiled for me by a fatal lack of agreement between manner and matter, between their shuddering rhythms copied from Yeats (or Eliot or Hopkins) and their subjects borrowed from the world today. Let me illustrate by quoting a few lines from Muriel Rukeyser, who is certainly among the best of the new writers (though I am using one of her weaker poems to prove my point):

> *John Brown, Nat Turner, Toussaint stand in this courtroom,*
> *Dred Scott wrestles for freedom there in the dark corner,*
> *all our celebrated shambles are repeated here: now again*
> *Sacco and Vanzetti walk to a chair, to the straps and rivets*
> *and the switch spitting death and Massachusetts' will.*

Here is a stanza made completely out of books and newspapers, which we are expected to have read, so that each of the names mentioned will press a button and light an incandescent hundred-watt emotion. The poet herself gives almost nothing but this catalogue of names, these faceless apparitions. It is true that even a catalogue can be effective, if presented skillfully. But Miss Rukeyser uses the worst possible meter for her purpose, writing in a long, loose, shambling blank verse better suited to lonely meditations than to the scene in the courthouse at the Scottsboro trial. (And why give us a phrase like "Toussaint stand," with its s's and t's piling up in a traffic jam?)

Or again, let me quote from Stephen Spender, whose early poems I still prefer to anything else written by the younger Englishmen. Last spring he completed a five-act tragedy in verse, *Trial of a Judge,* which was produced by the London Group Theatre and has now been published in this country. It is a dream play at many points suggesting Franz Kafka's dream novel, *The Trial.* It is also a political play about Nazis and Communists, which ends with the judge himself executed for trying to sentence the guilty and reprieve the innocent. There could scarcely be a clearer example of the Symbolist method applied to a political subject. The fourth act is a fine dramatic conception, and I have heard from friends in London that the whole play was effective on the stage. But the verse seems almost as weak to me as the stanza from Muriel Rukeyser's Scottsboro poem. Let me quote two passages:

> *We are driven to violence by violence*
> *Of groups hidden in crowds, like a ripe core*
> *Packed with black seeds driving outwards.*

Here the first line is excellent, but half the force of it is lost because the sense carries over into the second line, which is so weak that it falls apart in the middle. "Like a ripe core packed with black seeds" is a good figure of speech, but why should any seeds be "driving outwards"? At this point, the image grows faint and faltering; the poet has lost interest in it. Or take another passage, a Communist prisoner speaking in the fifth act:

> *Winning is our reality; that once gained*
> *Their freedom will push leaves from victory*

> *And in the borderless world of the many*
> *States and separate power melt away.*

Here is a four-line passage full of abstractions—eight of them, to be exact—and ambiguous phrases that should have been clarified. I had to read it twice before I realized that "many" didn't refer to "states"; "the borderless world of the many" is simply the workers' world. I still don't understand what Spender means by "separate power" in the last line, or how he pictures freedom pushing leaves from victory: is freedom the sap and victory the stem? Obviously he is rewriting Lenin's *The State and Revolution* in irregular iambic pentameters, but his language is less precise than Lenin's, and less poetic. There is a division or disharmony in the play that Lenin never had to face and Spender has failed to overcome. His theme is the conflict between two mass political movements, but the style in which he wrote the play is that of a lonely intellectual, tortured with doubt and unable to form a clear picture of the visions that throng his mind.

What I have just said about Spender and Muriel Rukeyser applies more forcibly to other poets who, with less talent, are working in the same field. Most of their verse is terribly bad verse, spoiled as a social weapon by its halting rhythms, its mannerisms and its desperate need to be individual; spoiled as poetry by its abstract sentiments and its incurable vagueness.

But what are poets to do if they want to write about the world in which they live? It seems to me that they have a choice between two general courses of action.

The poets who choose the first course will retain much of the Symbolist technique, but will develop it further by applying it to their whole field of interest instead of confining it to a few subjects, like disappointed love or regret for the past, that are carefully chosen for their esthetic "purity." Their poems will most certainly reveal an interest in social questions, but only at the points where those questions touch their own lives and work deeply on their own emotions. They will avoid the worst vice of their contemporaries, that of writing verses based on what they read in the daily papers. And they will not be social poets in the sense of expressing immediate social aims, in a language directed toward the broad public. Like the earlier Symbolists they will be working for a small audience, which they think of as existing in the past or the future. . . . Muriel Rukeyser and Stephen Spender at their best are poets to whom this description applies. It applies even better to Yeats himself —who, in his later years, has written many poems dealing with political and military struggles ("Sixteen Men," "Nineteen Hundred and Nineteen," "Meditations in Time of Civil War"), but has written them without exhortation or argument, in a style that resolves abstract issues "into pictures and dramatization."

There is, however, a second and bolder course for modern poets. Those who follow it will abandon Symbolism altogether, the technical method along with the philosophy, and will become social poets pure and simple. They will write the sort of verse that Yeats dismisses, quite unjustly, as rhetoric— battle songs, laments for the fallen, heroic ballads, satires against their enemies and perhaps ritual verses for a new society. Their rhythms will no longer "shudder" from the knowledge of their personal solitude, but instead will be confident, solemn or exultant, with the strength of a shared emotion. I should guess, for example, that they will largely abandon blank verse, which has become a meditative measure with the variations more important than the pattern; in place of it they will cultivate some of the trochaic and anapestic measures that have been neglected since the early nineteenth century. They will require a great fund of technical skill in order to raise their work above the level of the political jingle-makers. In spite of their skill, they are certain to lose much of the precision and suggestiveness that were achieved by the older poets; yet they might gain immeasurably from their closeness to a vast new audience whose language they speak and whose desires they express.

Tribute to Ben Franklin

AMONG HIS OTHER ACCOMPLISHMENTS, almost as varied
as Leonardo's, Benjamin Franklin was a great dramatist in
terms of his own life and a great tragic and comic player. He
applied the theory of the Mask, as it would later be expressed
by William Butler Yeats. That is, a great man may overcome
his weaknesses and redouble his influence by creating a false
character for himself, based on exactly those qualities in which
he is lacking. Franklin did more than that. He imagined and
wrote and acted not merely one character but a whole series, so
that it is hard to say which of them was the "real" Franklin.

He must have come nearest to revealing himself during his
youth in Boston, when he was a printer's devil apprenticed to
his brother James. At that time he was known to be proud,
disputatious, even quarrelsome, and eager to excel. In his
earliest writings he expressed two convictions that would later
be softened or concealed without ever disappearing: his profound disbelief in revealed religion and his profound hatred
for lords and royal officials. He regarded himself then and
afterwards as a "leather-apron man," a mechanic bent on rising
in the world without betraying his own class. Yet even in those
Boston days he wrote for *The Courant* under an assumed name
and character—as Prudence Dogood, the widow of a country
clergyman.

By the time Franklin opened his own printing shop in
Philadelphia, at the age of twenty-two, he had already created
a new mask, one that he used not only in his writing but also in
his daily life. He was now the honest tradesman, deferent to
those in authority, including royal governors, and respectful to
the churches whose power he still hoped to undermine. His
pride was transformed into apparent humility, his contentious-
ness into silence; and his real industry became a part to be
acted with gestures in the theatre of the streets. "I took care,"
he says, "not only to be in reality industrious and frugal but to
avoid all appearances to the contrary. I was seen at no places of
idle diversion. . . . To show that I was not above my busi-

Benjamin Franklin, by Carl Van Doren. New York: The Viking
Press. (*NR*, Oct. 26, 1938.)

ness, I sometimes brought home the paper I purchased . . . in a wheelbarrow."

I am not suggesting that Franklin was a hypocrite, or even that he was insincere. He had the gift of judging himself clearsightedly, and with no more indulgence than he showed to others. But he had learned that seeming goes farther in the world than being and that public men are judged like actors, by the parts they play. Franklin played different parts in different countries. Two of those he assumed in later life—one in England, the other in France—were so effective that they helped to build a nation and change the course of European history.

He was in England from 1757 to 1762 and from 1764 to 1774, as an agent for Pennsylvania and three of the other colonies, including rebellious Massachusetts. But the chief public part he played was that of a natural philosopher, the successor to Sir Isaac Newton. He was encouraged in this role by the British ruling class, which wanted to flatter the colonies and persuade them to accept new taxes; the cheapest method of conciliation was to honor their most prominent representative. Franklin was elected to all the learned societies and given degrees by Edinburgh and Oxford; there was even talk of a baronetcy and a pension. But the ruling class also wanted the British public to believe that Americans were ignorant half-savages, incapable of ruling themselves. That was an easy doctrine to preach; but how could it be reconciled with the fact that these Mohawks had produced the world's greatest scientist? Simply by playing the role that was thrust upon him, Franklin became a living plea for his countrymen. The British ministry decided that he was entirely too clever; they changed their tactics and tried to destroy him. By this time, however, Franklin's reputation was so well established that their great attack against him, delivered by the solicitor general in person, had the air of being a deliberate persecution; it won him more friends than it lost. Those friends were not without power in British politics. Their influence helps to explain the half-hearted tactics of the British armies during the Revolution.

In France, where he represented his country from 1776 to 1785, Franklin was also the great man of science, but he played a second role that was even more important. He was the perfect type of middle-class virtue, the archbourgeois. Voltaire and Rousseau had also attempted that role; but Voltaire had aimed too high, making himself the Count of Ferney; and Rousseau, insisting that he was a simple watchmaker, had aimed too low. At this point I am copying Bernard Faÿ, who explained that Franklin had found the happy medium. He was a bourgeois and quite deliberately he dressed the part, going to court "without wig or sword, in brown velvet, white hose, his hair hanging loose, his spectacles on his nose and a white hat under his arm." The bourgeoisie was highly favored in those days before the bourgeois revolution; and Franklin's face appeared in thousands upon thousands of reproductions. The king got so tired of hearing him praised by Diane de Polignac that he gave her a chamber pot of Sèvres china with Franklin's face in the bottom of it. But the king too was deeply impressed. Indeed, when you read this latest biography of Franklin, you wonder whether any other American could have negotiated the treaty of alliance with France.

We owe a considerable debt to Carl Van Doren for writing a full-length, scholarly life that incorporates the latest researches into Franklin's long career. There is no doubt that he has been neglected of recent years, not by historical students, who have continued to unearth new facts about him, but rather by literary fashion and by the public at large. There are signs that Franklin is ceasing to be a hero of the nation that he did more, perhaps, than any other single man to conceive and unite and launch on its career. The trouble is of course another mask, Poor Richard of *The Way to Wealth*, the role in which he is best remembered by his own countrymen. Poor Richard has made him the patron saint of thrift societies, building-and-loan associations and moss-backed Republican bankers who would be outraged to hear that they were quoting the maxims of a freethinker, an easygoing libertine and a revolutionary democrat. Says Mr. Van Doren at the end of his preface, "The dry, prim people seem to regard him as a treasure shut up in a savings bank to which they have the lawful key. I herewith give him back, in his grand dimensions, to his nation and the world."

His book has already been nominated by several critics for the Pulitzer Prize, and I should like to add my vote to theirs. Among all the lives of Franklin, it is the longest and best informed, and I doubt that any other biography of the year will be as useful. But there is a fault or limitation in the plan of the book that keeps it from telling a complete story. Mr. Van Doren explains in his preface that Franklin is known chiefly from his *Autobiography*, and is therefore insufficiently known, since that work stops short with his middle years. Franklin had always intended to write about his later life. The materials he would have used are still available, in his journals, letters and miscellaneous writings. "Here at last they have been drawn together and arranged in something like the order he might have given them. . . . In effect, Franklin's autobiography is here completed."

But is a new autobiography of Franklin what we really want or need in the twentieth century? It seems to me that in order to know the man "in his grand dimensions," we have to see him in perspective, against the background of his times, and this is a view that Mr. Van Doren fails to give. As compared with Bernard Faÿ's *Franklin*, published in 1929, his book is sounder at many points but conspicuously lacking in general ideas. He has written a behavioristic biography, one that tells us "what Franklin did, said, thought and felt," one that describes the successive roles he assumed. But how can we understand those roles, or their effect, without knowing the theatres where they were played and the audiences that hissed or applauded them?

Yeats and O'Faolain

A FEW WEEKS before the death of William Butler Yeats, I woke out of a restless sleep and found myself fuming at an essay that dealt with his work. The essay, printed in the winter number of *The Virginia Quarterly Review*, was well informed and sharply phrased; otherwise it wouldn't have stuck in my head. But I felt that it typified a weakness of much contemporary criticism, especially the sort that is written by polished and professional men of letters.

The title of the essay was "Æ and W. B." and its author was Sean O'Faolain. The sentence in it that first roused my sleepy resentment was, "The Marxist critic will never be able to do anything with Yeats." Although I had written two or three essays about him, there was no reason for my taking the statement personally. I am not and never was a Marxist critic, in the sense of wanting to judge all literature by its direct bearing on the class war and the proletarian revolution. Marx himself was not a Marxist in that sense, for he was careful not to confuse his literary with his political enthusiasms; the living writer whom he most admired was Balzac, a Royalist. It was Plekhanov, at the end of the nineteenth century, who began to consider novels and plays and poems as a department of revolutionary party politics, the department of agitation and propaganda—Agitprop. Most of the Marxist critics writing today have unfortunately followed Plekhanov and his Russian disciples rather than Marx himself. Yet for all their narrowness and, on occasion, their insensitiveness to literary values, they have contributed something to the discussion—new answers to old questions, new questions that remain to be answered and, most of all, a consistent method of interpretation and evaluation. Anyone who completely rejects their method should at least propose another to take its place. And so, when I remembered O'Faolain's flat statement that "The Marxist critic will never be able to do anything with Yeats," I wanted to ask him what the non-Marxist critic could do.

Lighting the bed-lamp, I read the essay again. My strongest impression was that it was beautifully written, in a slow and rhythmical early eighteenth-century style that survives only in Dublin, just as the early nineteenth-century style survives in our Southern universities. It showed what to me was an enviable knowledge of Yeats's work and personality and literary interests. It made several illuminating suggestions, and at times it seemed to be on the point of pronouncing some ineffable truth about Yeats. But the truth never got itself uttered, at least not in language that could be understood by the common reader, and I finished the essay a second time with a feeling of having somehow been cheated.

It seemed to me that O'Faolain, like other critics of his type, would flinch at the critical moments when one expected a clear statement of what he had been hinting at or preparing to say. Instead of a definition, he would write a beautiful phrase. For example, the essay begins with a fine impressionistic picture of spiritualism and theosophy—"spookism," in short—as practiced by literary men in the 1890's. This leads to a historical survey of the spiritualist movement, and this in turn to a paragraph dealing with the considerable part that was played in it by Yeats and Æ. But just what did it mean in terms of Yeats's poems? The road has been paved and the reader guided along it to a summit from which he is expecting a clear view of the countryside; but this is precisely the moment when O'Faolain chooses to hide in a literary mist:

> All that kind of thing one knows about; and, in so far as one bothers with it at all, one dismisses it as the natural caparison of young and febrile genius. What really is important is the subjection of mind to what these things symbolized. . . . This mental subjection is something more easily felt than defined. What synthesis Yeats managed to evolve out of his multifarious interests emerges, in so far as it ever emerges, in fits and starts, and was always subject to a kind of catalepsy.

Now the truth is that Yeats's interest in spooks and spectres led him to certain ideas which he later developed, with other ideas, into a fairly systematic philosophy; one can find it expressed in his essays and in *A Vision*. That philosophy—that mythology, if you prefer—is essential to anyone who wants to understand his later poems. In the summer number of *The Southern Review*, Cleanth Brooks Jr. discussed it a little pedantically but clearly and at great length, with the result that his essay tells you more about Yeats than a hundred "impressions" or "appreciations." O'Faolain dismisses the subject with a phrase. "A kind of catalepsy" is a good phrase, but it is neither accurate nor helpful to the reader. To the critic, I thought, it is positively harmful, since it tempts him away from the tedious but fruitful work of finding a definition.

Perhaps I was being unjust to O'Faolain. But I was trying to get at a quality of his essay, one that it shares with a great mass of critical writing—the quality of mistaking impressions for ideas and effective phrases for explanations, in a word, of making literature about literature. The critic insists on being a creator, a poet in his own right. He pretends to be looking at another author, but his stare is misty and abstracted; he is really thinking about the color and rhythm of his own style. That is the weakness, I thought, of a passage like the one in which O'Faolain tries to follow Yeats in his divagations between the real Ireland and the world of spooks:

> It was an extraordinary voyage and it had an unexpected conclusion; and naturally we can more easily observe the end than record the fluxive currents that had, before he alighted, blown him this way and that. We know, however, that having thus published three or four books with an Irish flavor, he floated off again into the symbolism of the Rose poems. . . . For the formative period of his life he was simply groping about here and there, happy with any kind of imagery or crude expression of his innate feeling that the duality of a man's nature is the germinating element in him.

This is an effective passage, better in the original than in the abbreviated version I have given, which omits all the skillfully chosen quotations. I suppose that I shouldn't complain if it tells us very little about Yeats's actual career as a poet and how it happened that one set of ideals succeeded another. My real grievance is that it obscures his story, dresses it up, whisks over it a veil of Keltic twilight—and see! there was no logic in it, none whatsoever; Yeats was "blown this way and that," he "floated off again," he was "simply groping about here and there." A Marxist critic could find reason and direction in these gropings of a poet who was the greatest of our time. But Yeats himself was something of a Marxist critic in his *Autobiography*, where he judged himself objectively against his background. His style—which has plainly influenced O'Faolain's—is a little difficult to follow in its ramifications, but if we read him carefully he makes us understand that each new stage in his thinking was a logical and almost necessary development out of his past. That understanding is precisely what his critic fails to give.

Or take another passage, one where the weakness of O'Faolain's approach is exposed more clearly. He has been making a distinction—rather hard to grasp, since I doubt that it is clear in his own mind—between character and personality. He has

also been saying that Yeats attempted to resolve a conflict
between two sides of his own nature, the solitary and the social.
Not being what O'Faolain would call a man of character, he
invented a personality for himself, in order "to unite his human gregariousness and his artistic loneliness." But this personality, this role that Yeats assumed, has been overdramatized:

> Yeats is not, by nature, either so romantic or so lonely as his
> role might suggest. He is a public figure, if a rather vague one.
> And when I think of the modern men who seem not to have
> lived by static character but by personality, the names that come
> to me are the names of other gregarious men—Johnson, Landor,
> Donne, Dick Steele, Sterne, Horace Walpole, Goldsmith; and to
> these, none romantics, the one romantic, Shelley. I think of men
> whose character was static, and I think of lonely Arnold,
> Wordsworth, Gray, Tennyson, Rousseau and possibly Browning
> —all romantics except Gray. And surely it is to the former
> company rather than the latter that Yeats belongs.

All that is nicely stated and very learned, and perhaps to
the specialist in literary biography it conveys an idea—but just
what idea, I wonder? What was the quality that Johnson,
Donne, Sterne and Shelley had in common? —that Gray, Rousseau and possibly Browning had in common? —except the quality of having "names that come to me" at the same moment.
Perhaps there are real links binding the writers in each group,
but I should like to see the links described in non-subjective
terms. Were they physiological, glandular? In that case, how
would O'Faolain define them in terms of medical science?
Were they psychological? In that case, how would he define
them in terms of psychoanalysis, behaviorism, Gestalt or any
other psychology with scientific pretensions? Or perhaps the
links were social and political? In that case, are they capable of
definition in terms of Marx, Weber, Mannheim, Pareto or any
other non-literary political scientist?

But those are only a few of the questions suggested by one
passage. How can one say that Wordsworth, for example, had
a static character and Goldsmith hadn't, considering that Goldsmith remained the same lovable child until his death, whereas
Wordsworth changed so completely that if, in his old age, he
had met the younger Wordsworth he would have thrown him
into jail for his radical opinions? And what does O'Faolain

mean by a romantic—that is, would he explain the word historically, psychologically, sociologically or in terms of pure literature? If it is being used in a literary sense, why weren't
Walpole and Gray romantics, considering that much of their
work belongs to the romantic movement? If it is being used
historically, how explain the mixture of centuries in both lists
of names? What light do these examples from the English
past throw on the work of a modern Irish poet? He was an
eighteenth-century figure, O'Faolain tells us, but was born out
of his time. That is the sort of remark often made by literary
critics when they can't think of anything better. If it really
applies to Yeats, how can we also believe, as O'Faolain seems to
do, that his character or nature or personality was molded by
the spiritualist movement of the 1890's, by the Irish literary
renaissance of the 1900's and by the Irish revolution?

There are other questions I might have asked. But at this
point in my long soliloquy, I began writing a letter to O'Faolain. I told him much of what has been said here about his
essay. I told him—and without being merely polite—that I
greatly admired his stories and novels; what I liked in them
especially was their power of suggestion and vague evocation.
"But why do you aim toward the same qualities in your critical
writing? That isn't," I said, "a question addressed to you alone.
Critics for at least a century have been trying to judge literature purely in terms of literature. When that line of thinking
gets them into trouble, as it is bound to do, they merely stop
thinking and write a finely evocative phrase. Or else they make
use of some abstraction—Beauty or Ecstasy, or Personality and
Character—to gloss over conflicts that couldn't be resolved
without hard thinking and tedious research.

"Rather than being scholarly or scientific or merely informative," I said, "many distinguished critics want to be the
high priests of a literary tradition. They go on repeating their
own errors and those of their predecessors, which custom has
rendered almost sacred. The result is that criticism in our times
has advanced scarcely farther than in those of Aristotle; much
of it is really pre-Aristotelian. And most of it won't amount to
more than a learned game until it consents to let its results be
tested by outside disciplines—by philosophy, psychology, sociology, medicine, and by history most of all.

"That explains the service rendered by the Marxist critics. They introduce non-literary standards that change the rules of the game, that make it more of a discipline, that bring it closer to the rest of life. The standards are often crude and impolite, especially in the beginning, but at least they can be tested and verified and altered at the points where they disagree with information from other sources; in other words, they are capable of further development. The trouble with abstractions is that they are capable of producing nothing but more abstractions. The trouble with beautiful writing, for a critic like yourself, is that it simply piles literature on literature, prayer on prayer, subjective mood on subjective mood, world without end."

Thomas Wolfe's Legacy

WHEN Thomas Wolfe died last year at the age of thirty-eight, he left no completed but still unpublished novel behind him. What he did leave was an enormous puzzle in the shape of a manuscript containing more than a million words, the length of a dozen ordinary novels.

Embedded in the manuscript were chapters or incidents from at least five of the novels that Wolfe had planned to write, and probably from several others as well. One of these books, dealing with his great unhappy love affair, was present in an almost complete draft, with many revisions. A second book concerned his relations with a publisher and a third described his trip across the country; these also were nearly finished. The remaining books were more fragmentary, though together they told a fairly connected story—Wolfe's own story, the subject of almost everything he had ever written. He sometimes thought of throwing all the books together into a single novel that would have been longer when completed than *Remembrance of Things Past;* he had made some

The Web and the Rock, by Thomas Wolfe. New York: Harper and Brothers. (*NR*, July 19, 1939.)

of the revisions that would have been necessary. Still, as a result of his changing plans—or rather of his inability to follow a consistent plan—the manuscript was as wildly confused as his life had been.

This was the problem he bequeathed to his publishers and his literary executor. After much hesitation they solved it in a fashion that I think was mistaken. They decided to publish almost the whole manuscript, divided into two very long novels. It is the first of these, *The Web and the Rock,* that has just appeared.

Judged as a piece of editing, it is able and conscientious. Judged as a new book by Thomas Wolfe, it is decidedly less successful. That is a fact one would hardly suspect from reading most of the reviews it has so far received. The critics have apparently been swayed by their warm personal regard for the author, which everybody shared, and by their hope that his astounding promise would somehow be fulfilled in spite of death. But the truth ought to be told, even in a review that reads like a letter of condolence; and the truth is that *The Web and the Rock* is by far the weakest of Wolfe's novels—is indeed so weak that there is a justified question whether most of it should have been published at all.

One of its obvious faults is that it breaks apart into two uneven sections. The first of these tells how Monk Webber grew up in the little city of Libya Hill in the state of Old Catawba—that is, in Buncombe County, North Carolina, where Wolfe himself was born and reared. He spends four years at Pine Rock College—that is, Wolfe's own University of North Carolina—then comes to New York in search of fame and a mistress. I understand that part of this section was written shortly before Wolfe died. Other parts of it are what he was able to salvage from the unpublished first draft of *Look Homeward, Angel* and from an abandoned novel about his mother's kinsfolk that he intended to call *The Hills Beyond Pentland.* The episodes from these various sources are loosely tied together. Some of them have a powerful organic life that is lacking in the section as a whole.

The second section, beginning on page 295, is much more unified. It tells how the hero, coming home from Europe—but how did he get there?—falls in love with a Jewish theatrical

designer named Esther Jack, a candid and charming woman
much older than himself. He is mothered by her for three
years, grows plump on her delectable cooking, meets and dislikes her literary friends, finishes a book that she inspired him
to write, fails to get it published, then quarrels with her
unjustly and—the word is not too strong—insanely for page
after page and chapter after chapter. Most of this section
seems to consist of a novel that Wolfe had written in 1936,
though at least one of the original episodes has disappeared,
leaving a gap in the story, and new material must have been
added in 1938. It is connected with the first section only by the
name of the hero. One could hardly say that it is connected by
his personality, since Monk Webber has changed almost beyond recognition.

In the title of the book as published, the Rock is Manhattan Island. The Web is the subtle and unnatural world of the
Jewish intelligentsia, in which the hero threatens to get involved through his love for Esther. Finally he escapes to
Munich, where he starts a drunken brawl, gets a broken head
that he fully earned, and finds spiritual rebirth in a hospital.

The novel as a whole contains many fine passages—for
example, the stories of Baxter Lampley, the butcher's son; of
Jim Randolph, the football hero who never got over it; of
Dick Prosser, the pious Negro who ran amok. The chapter on
Seumas Malone, the Irish critic, is a fairly effective piece of
satire, especially to those who recognize Seumas Malone. The
character of Esther Jack is one of the most careful and sympathetic full-length portraits that Wolfe has drawn; it is a
tribute to his honesty as a novelist that he makes one sympa-
thize with Esther instead of the hero in all their quarrels. But
the book is everywhere marred by bathos, bombast, painful
repetitions, middle-class prejudice and naïve but offensive anti-
Semitism. Whole chapters, like those on the hero's daydreams
("Alone") and on Horace Liveright's publishing house ("The
Philanthropists") are so gawkily written that it is a physical
discomfort to read them. Wolfe's novels have always presented this mixture of the nearly sublime and the silly. In this
new book, however, the best passages are less nearly sublime
than the best in *Look Homeward, Angel* and *Of Time and the
River*. The worst are sillier than anything he published dur-

ing his lifetime; indeed, they are almost without a parallel in
serious literature.

Here are a few examples of bad writing, chosen not at all
as the most flagrant but merely as the shortest:

> Some fifteen or more years ago (as men measure, by those
> diurnal instruments which their ingenuity has created, the im-
> measurable universe of time), at the end of a fine, warm, hot,
> fair, fresh, fragrant, lazy, furnacelike day of sweltering heat
> across the body, bones, sinews, tissues, juices, rivers, mountains,
> plains, streams, lakes, coastal regions and compacted corporosity
> of the American continent, a train might have been observed by
> one of the lone watchers of the Jersey Flats approaching that
> enfabled rock, that ship of life, that swarming, million-footed,
> tower-masted and sky-soaring citadel that bears the magic name
> of the Island of Manhattan, at terrific speed.

> . . . the heights of Jersey City, raised proudly against the
> desolation of these lonely marshes as a token of man's fortitude,
> a symbol of his power, a sign of his indomitable spirit that flames
> forever like a great torch in the wilderness, that lifts against the
> darkness and the desolation of blind nature the story of its
> progress—the heights of Jersey, lighted for an eternal feast.

> So all were gone at last, one by one, each swept out into the
> mighty flood tide of the city's life, there to prove, to test, to find,
> to lose himself, as each man must—alone.

> But, of such was youth. And he was young.

> The sight of her face, earnestly bent and focused in its work
> of love, her sure and subtle movements and her full, lovely figure
> —all that was at once both delicate and abundant in her, to-
> gether with the maddening fragrance of glorious food, evoked an
> emotion of wild tenderness and hunger in him which was unut-
> terable.

In most of these passages the fault is an undisciplined and
undirected energy that leads him to write about a train ride
across the Jersey marshes as if it were the charge of the Lost
Brigade and about Jersey City as if it were Periclean Athens.
The last passage presents a different and more illuminating
problem. It would be easy to defend if Wolfe really meant it
to be funny, for in that case the worst charge against it would
be that he used exactly the same language for burlesque humor
that he used for his serious writing and therefore left the

reader uncertain of the effect he was trying to achieve. But the context seems to show that Wolfe was as serious here as elsewhere; that in fact he regarded his wild tenderness and his hunger for glorious food as being of equal value; both were "unutterable" and therefore holy. In certain African tribes, even the fingernail parings of the king-god are sacred; and Wolfe had almost the same attitude toward his own least and tritest emotions. A train ride across the Jersey marshes really was the charge of the Lost Brigade, because Wolfe was taking it.

By now it ought to be obvious that the source of his weakness, and of his abounding energy as well, was his inordinate preoccupation with himself. He was not conceited in any familiar sense of the word; indeed he was realistic and humble about his own failings. On the other hand, he regarded his life as something more than that of an ordinary mortal; it was a sacrament, a miracle, a legend of man's eternal aspirations. All his thoughts and deeds were bathed in a supernatural light that was also reflected on the people around him. When he wrote about those people, he usually wrote well—unless he hated them—and sometimes he wrote superbly. He had a thirst for knowledge about their lives, a warm sympathy, a gift for seeing, "beneath their bright, unnatural masks, something that was naked and lonely." But when he wrote about himself, as he usually did, he lost all sense of proportion.

This was a fact he realized in his later years, and he intended his new book to be "a genuine spiritual and artistic change . . . the most objective novel I have written." But the attempt was doomed to failure by his whole personality. He liked to keep people at a distance and wrote about them most confidently when he was looking at them from a train window. When a character became too interesting and threatened to distract attention from the autobiographical hero, Wolfe dropped him instantly. It was the same impulse, I think, that made him quarrel with some of his oldest friends when they threatened to become an essential part of his life. Instinctively he was driven back on himself, driven back to writing books about himself, until his apparently endless resources were in fact nearly exhausted.

Though his editors have worked with care and even piety, I am not sure that in publishing the present version of *The Web and the Rock* they have done their best for his posthumous career. They have accepted the author's valuation of himself and his mania for bigness, whereas he was actually at his best in episodes and novellas. They have been tolerant of his faults, remembering how he used to howl with pain and exasperation when one of his weaker passages was omitted. This time they have included whole chapters that should have been decently forgotten. Had they been more ruthless toward the manuscript, they would have been a great deal kinder toward its author and its readers.

A Farewell to the 1930's

JUST AS THE 1920's were the postwar decade, so the 1930's were post-boom and post-crash. Just as the 1920's were ended by the depression, so the 1930's were ended by the new war in Europe. It is a neat pattern that we have to consider: a decade that actually lasted for nine years and ten months, that began on October 24, 1929—Black Thursday —and ended on the early morning of September 1, 1939, when the German armies marched into Poland; or perhaps had already ended on August 23, with the news of the Russo-German pact. The decade began for many writers with a sense of relief; they had been unhappy in the boom days, which were dominated by their enemies, the businessmen. It ended with a sense of defeat and disillusionment, when they saw the world falling into the hands of their other enemies, the generals and the power politicians. As one writer said, laying down his copy of *The New York Times*, "You can't expect good news in an earthquake."

There has never been a period when literary events followed so closely on the flying coattails of social events. In ordinary times, it takes a man of long memory to recognize that such and such a book may have been inspired by such and such a political struggle, now generally forgotten. The novels that we connect with the Populist movement were published in the early 1900's; the movement itself had been shattered in 1896, at the end of Bryan's first campaign. But during the

1930's, the time between event and expression was so short that no one could miss their connection—and least of all the author himself. The Gastonia strike was fought and broken in 1929; during the first three years of the crisis there were at least four novels and two plays with Gastonia as their background. As for the crisis itself, there was no end to its literary echoes. Almost all the books published after 1932 belonged to the literature of the depression, in the sense that they either revealed its effect on their authors, or studied its causes, or tried to evade it by fleeing to the ends of the earth and the depths of time—only to return with a lesson for tomorrow.

Yet the crisis in general is not much help to us in describing and separating the literary currents of the 1930's; it explains entirely too much. Before using it as a basis for interpretation, we have to divide it into three different clusters or series of events. There are first the political and social struggles rising out of the crisis—the strikes and demonstrations, the growth of radical and fascist groups, the fight over the New Deal. There are second the events resulting from the new position of the United States in world affairs, which in turn resulted from the crisis in Europe and left this country as the greatest and perhaps the final stronghold of bourgeois democracy. Third and last are the events connected with the closing of the frontier in American business—that is, the growth of larger corporations at the expense of smaller ones, the narrowing opportunities for pecuniary success and the changes that followed in middle-class ideals. Each cluster of events has been the background for hundreds of novels, essays, poems, plays; and each of them might be discussed in turn.

The political and social struggles that I mentioned were mirrored in proletarian writing—or, to use a milder academic term, in the literature of social protest. Strikes born of hunger and desperation were among the features of the new decade; and strikes were the usual subject of the earlier proletarian novels. The cotton mills, the coal mines, the garment industry, the California orchards, the West Coast lumber mills and logging camps, were assaulted each in its turn; in those days literature was a weapon of attack. Weapons grow to resemble one another; and very soon these strike novels began to follow a pattern almost as rigid and conventional as that of a Petrarchan sonnet. The hero was usually a young worker, honest, naïve and politically undeveloped. Through intolerable mistreatment, he was driven to take part in a strike. Always the strike was ruthlessly suppressed, and usually its leader was killed. But the young worker, conscious now of the mission that united him to the whole working class, marched on toward new battles.

In part this story reflected the pattern of actual strikes, like that in Gastonia. In part it echoed the slogans of the Communists in days when their chief contact with industrial workers was through the small revolutionary unions they had organized in fields where the struggle was so bitter and hopeless that ordinary trade unions were frightened off. In those days the Communists never won a big strike; and except in the fur trade they rarely or never succeeded in holding the gains sometimes made in smaller strikes. Their plan must have been to march on from defeat to defeat, always training more recruits—like the young worker of the strike novel—till they were strong enough to face the final conflict.

Midway in the 1930's, the Communist Party changed its policy, dissolved its revolutionary unions, softened its attacks on middle-class liberals and tried to win over all men of good will. It made converts of some writers and influenced many others, directly or indirectly. That helps to explain a literary development for which there were other causes as well. Briefly, the proletarian novelists began writing with greater freedom, finding different subjects and experimenting in new forms. There were sharecropper novels—of which *Tobacco Road* was the first and best—and shanty-Irish novels like *Studs Lonigan*. There were industrial novels in which the subject, instead of being a strike, was the daily monotony and seasonal insecurity of the men on the assembly line. There were intimate novels of working-class life, with the class struggle present only as a dim but pervasive background. There were collective novels in which the hero was not an individual but a group, usually the workers of a single factory or town. The most ambitious book of the decade—*U. S. A.*, by John Dos Passos—was a collective novel in which the hero was the country as a whole.

From the very beginning, the novels of social protest received a critical attention that was out of all proportion to their popularity, considering that very few had a sale of more than 2,500 copies. Even the worst of them were extravagantly praised in the left-wing press; even the best were bitterly attacked not only by conservatives but also by dissident radicals and former radicals. By 1936 a whole chorus was chanting that proletarian literature was dead and buried. Yet it was not until 1939 that a proletarian novel, *Christ in Concrete,* received an almost official recognition by being chosen as a Book of the Month. Another proletarian novel, *The Grapes of Wrath,* was not only a best seller but the most widely read book of the year.

I do not think it is the absolutely superb novel that some critics have called it. The plot is too weak for that—at least in the last two hundred pages—and the ending is theatrical and inconclusive. Yet it shows how proletarian literature had refined itself in the ten preceding years; had built itself a method, a tradition and finally a public. Although *The Grapes of Wrath* is not an imitative book, it could not have been written without a whole series of experiments to guide its author—for example those of Dos Passos, which must have suggested the interludes used to broaden the story of the Joads into that of a whole people; and those of William Faulkner in *As I Lay Dying,* where a sharecropping family travels obstinately with a corpse; and the drawling conversation of *Tobacco Road;* and the violence of Steinbeck's earlier novel, *In Dubious Battle,* where he first wrote about a strike among the fruit pickers—not to speak of what he learned from documentary films like *The Plow That Broke the Plains* and *The River.* A whole literature is summarized in this book, and much of it is carried to a new level of excellence.

A second cluster of events that affected literature during the 1930's grew out of our relations with the rest of the world. First it was the Russian Five Year Plan that impressed us, then the rise of Hitler that frightened us, then the war in Spain that engaged our sympathies. As crisis followed crisis in Europe; as parliaments were silenced and labor unions suppressed, people began to feel that this was one of the few countries able to solve its problems by democratic methods. But they also felt that our security was threatened—vaguely at first by fascism, them more definitely by war—and many decided that our fate was bound up with that of Europe and the world. Others preached our duty to stand apart, but that in itself was proof of our involvement. In the days when isolation was a fact and not a doctrine, nobody bothered to talk about it.

That is the general background, but the international situation also affected writers in their own persons. The depression brought hundreds of them home from Europe. Though their reason for returning was in many cases merely that their money had run out, they showed the usual tendency of writers to find historical motives and make a necessary action appear as a free and long premeditated choice. They rediscovered America, in one book after another, and it was a different America from the country they had deserted early in the 1920's. To carry the process one step further, European writers began to follow them westward, as political refugees or tourists, so that New York became a capital of world literature. Its importance began to be recognized abroad.

The effect of these events can be traced in hundreds of books. For example, it is evident in the long series of goodbyes —to Paris, to the south of France, to Majorca, to Moscow, to China—that were published after 1934. Most of them were written in an elegiac tone, but still with the feeling that America was somehow better and was at any rate our country. Again it is evident in the books dealing with the wars in Spain and China, by American observers or participants. It is evident in the anti-fascist novels, not all of which are melodramas. It is evident in the memoirs of foreign correspondents, among which Vincent Sheean's *Personal History* is still by far the best. But it is also hidden in books where world affairs are not directly treated, but where they deeply affect the intellectual and emotional background. Americans have begun to write with their eyes on the world overseas.

The third cluster of events was connected with the closing of the business frontier. Competition among small corporations was giving way to price-fixing and the division of territory among big corporations; in a word, risk and change were giving way to a small-visioned stability. What this means in terms of corporate structures, dividends, prices and wages has been studied in a whole series of economic monographs. What it means in terms of daily life has still to be explored. The truth seems to be that during the last ten years, the American middle class has slowly built up a different set of ideals. Once the whole aim was getting ahead, with hard work and privation willingly endured as the price of ultimate success. Now, as opportunities in business become fewer and less dramatic, the aim is security at a somewhat lower level—that and making the best of what one has. America is beginning to resemble Europe before the First World War. There is a growing interest in the amenities of life—in cooking and gardening and decoration, in bridge and croquet, in neighborhood gossip and community affairs. There is a growing determination to hold on to one's position in society; and there is a corresponding fear of change, of the private or public misfortunes that might lead to losing one's job.

The effects on literature of this process are a little harder to trace than those of the social struggles that began with the depression. Obviously we are dealing here with the middle class rather than the proletariat, and with a state of mind rather than the events that produced it. But the state of mind is revealed in a whole group of books—like *Rich Land, Poor Land* and *Deserts on the March*—that call for the preservation of our natural resources. It is revealed even more strikingly, I think, in the popularity of historical novels and dramas. *Abe Lincoln in Illinois* was the most successful play of 1939; *Anthony Adverse* and *Gone with the Wind* were the two most successful novels of the decade—and of the century as well, in dollar volume of sales. A man rising in the world is not concerned with history; he is too busy making it. But a citizen with a fixed place in the community wants to acquire a glorious past just as he acquires antique furniture. By that past he is reassured of his present importance; in it he finds strength to face the dangers that lie in front of him.

It is still too early to judge the literature of the 1930's, qualitatively and comparatively. The lasting works, those built, so to say, in stone, have not yet been disengaged from the plywood and tarpaper shacks that surround them. In 1905, hardly anyone could have guessed that the most important novel of that decade was a half-forgotten book called *Sister Carrie*, printed in a first edition of a thousand copies, most of which were then gathering dust in a publisher's warehouse. In 1939 we may be equally blind or ill informed as to the important books of the decade that has just ended. Yet certain features of those years can already be recorded. They will be known, I think, as lean years for poetry, with no major figures appearing. They will be known as middling rich years for the novel. They will be known as decidedly rich years for autobiography, and as lively years for criticism. They will be known as the years when Crane and Wolfe, those two heraldic beasts, projected their vast legends of America, without supplying the knowledge or sympathy that might have filled in the bold outlines created by an act of will. They will be known as the years of the hard-boiled novel. They will be known as the years when general magazines declined—and the profession of literary free-lance along with them—and when most of the comfortable incomes earned by writers were earned in Hollywood. They will be known as years when the public standing of literature improved, as a result of the greater leisure for reading. Beyond that, it is hard to fix their value. To me they seem more interesting than the 1920's and comparable in many respects with the period that preceded the First World War, though probably less fruitful.

And now they have ended, by an act of statesmanship, an act of violence and an act of the calendar.

As for the literature of the next ten years, I should prefer to write about it in 1949. It will continue to mirror what is happening in the world at large—that much is safe to say. Yet even if we had before us a complete chart of historical events during the 1940's, we still could not predict the nature of the poems and novels that such events would inspire; too much of literature depends on individual talent and simple human perversity. There will always be writers who

> *So much despise the crowd, that if the throng*
> *By chance goes right, they purposely go wrong.*

Normally we may expect that the principal tendencies of the 1930's will continue during the following decades, until they have exhausted their possibilities or, more likely, their public appeal, or else are halted by some such catastrophe as our entrance into the war, in 1917, which ended the promising first stage of what used to be called the American renaissance. The new war in Europe may be the occasion for another such disaster. But whatever happens, we may expect that newer tendencies will also be followed. For example, one can foresee a literature of disillusionment that was announced by Dos Passos' *Adventures of a Young Man* and that will certainly be encouraged by the mood growing out of the Russo-German pact. And one can foresee a new mysticism, already indicated by the growing interest in novelists like Kafka.

Whether great books will be written, no one can say. The only statement to be ventured is that we now have certain conditions for great books that were formerly lacking. As late as 1920 this country continued to labor under the domination of English standards and under a sense of inferiority that sometimes took the form of aggressive nationalism. The intelligent reading public was comparatively small; the amateur censors were active. There were many writers of talent, but few of professional seriousness and trained competence. All that has been changed in the last twenty years. Perhaps the greatest difference is in the number of writers who, by permanent standards, are second-rate and yet are intelligent and determined to do their best work. Although they will never produce great books, they help to produce them, by creating the necessary background and the tradition that may nourish greater writers in the future.

Richard Wright:
The Case of Bigger Thomas

Native Son is the most impressive American novel I have read since *The Grapes of Wrath*. In some ways the two books resemble each other: both deal with the dispossessed and both grew out of the radical movement of the 1930's. There is, however, a distinction to be drawn between the motives of the two authors. Steinbeck, more privileged than the characters in his novel, wrote out of deep pity for them, and the fault he had to avoid was sentimentality. Richard Wright, a Negro, was moved by wrongs he had suffered in his own person, and what he had to fear was a blind anger that might destroy the pity in him, making him hate any character whose skin was whiter than his own. His first book, *Uncle Tom's Children*, had not completely avoided that fault. It was a collection of stories all but one of which had the same pattern: a Negro was goaded into killing one or more white men and was killed in turn, without feeling regret for himself or his victims. Some of the stories I found physically painful to read, even though I admired them. So deep was the author's sense of the indignities heaped on his race that one felt he was revenging himself by a whole series of symbolic murders. In *Native Son* the pattern is the same, but the author's sympathies have broadened and his resentment, though quite as deep, is less painful and personal.

The hero, Bigger Thomas, is a Negro boy of twenty, a poolroom loafer, a bully, a liar and a petty thief. "Bigger, sometimes I wonder why I birthed you," his pious mother tells him. "Honest, you the most no-countest man I ever seen in all my life." A Chicago philanthropist tries to help the family by hiring him as chauffeur. That same night Bigger kills the philanthropist's daughter—out of fear of being discovered in her room—and stuffs her body into the furnace. This half-accidental crime leads to others. Bigger tries to cast the blame for the girl's disappearance on her lover, a Communist; he

Native Son, by Richard Wright. New York: Harper and Brothers. (*NR*, Mar. 18, 1940.) Reprinted by permission of *The New Republic*, © 1940, Harrison-Blaine of New Jersey, Inc.

tries to collect a ransom from her parents; after the body is found he murders his Negro mistress to keep her from betraying him to the police. The next day he is captured on the snow-covered roof of a South Side tenement, while a mob howls in the street below.

In the last part of the book, which is also the best, we learn that the case of Bigger Thomas is not the author's deepest concern. Behind it is another, more complicated story he is trying hard to explain, though the words come painfully at first, and later come in a flood that almost sweeps him away. "Listen, you white folks," he seems to be saying over and over. "I want to tell you about all the Negroes in America. I want to tell you how they live and how they feel. I want you to change your minds about them before it is too late to prevent a worse disaster than any we have known. I speak for my own people, but I speak for America too." And because he does speak for and to the nation, without ceasing to be a Negro, his book has more force than any other American novel by a member of his race.

Bigger, he explains, had been trained from the beginning to be a bad citizen. He had been taught American ideals of life, in the schools, in the magazines, in the cheap movie houses, but had been denied any means of achieving them. Everything he wanted to have or do was reserved for the whites. "I just can't get used to it," he tells one of his poolroom buddies. "I swear to God I can't. . . . Every time I think about it I feel like somebody's poking a red-hot iron down my throat."

At the trial, his white-haired Jewish lawyer makes a final plea to the judge for mercy. "What Bigger Thomas did early that Sunday morning in the Dalton home and what he did that Sunday night in the empty building was but a tiny aspect of what he had been doing all his life long. He was *living*, only as he knew how, and as we have forced him to live. . . . The hate and fear which we have inspired in him, woven by our civilization into the very structure of his consciousness, into his blood and bones, into the hourly functioning of his personality, have become the justification of his existence. . . . Every thought he thinks is potential murder."

This long courtroom speech, which sums up the argument of the novel, is at once its strongest and its weakest point. It is strongest when Mr. Max is making a plea for the American Negroes in general. "They are not simply twelve million people; in reality they constitute a separate nation, stunted, stripped and held captive *within* this nation." Many of them— and many white people too—are full of "balked longing for some kind of fulfilment and exultation"; and their existence is "what makes our future seem a looming image of violence." In this context, Mr. Max's talk of another civil war seems not so much a threat as an agonized warning. But his speech is weakest as a plea for the individual life of Bigger Thomas. It did not convince the judge, and I doubt that it will convince many readers.

It is not that I think Bigger "deserved" the death sentence for his two murders. Most certainly his guilt was shared by the society that condemned him. But when he killed Mary Dalton he was performing the first free action in his whole fear-tortured life; he was accepting his first moral responsibility. That is what he tried so hard to explain to his lawyer. "I ain't worried none about them women I killed. . . . I killed 'em 'cause I was scared and mad. But I been scared and mad all my life and after I killed that first woman, I wasn't scared no more for a little while." And when his lawyer asks him if he ever thought he would face the electric chair, "Now I come to think of it," he answers, "it seems like something like this just had to be." If Mr. Max had managed to win a life sentence for Bigger Thomas, he would have robbed him of his only claim to human courage and dignity. But that Richard Wright makes us feel this, while setting out to prove something else— that he makes Bigger Thomas a human rather than a racial symbol—shows that he wrote an even better novel than he had planned.

Faulkner by Daylight

The Hamlet is a new sort of novel for William Faulkner, less somber, more easygoing and discursive. Except for a few short stories, it makes better reading than anything else he has written since *Sanctuary*.

Until now, almost all his books have been war novels—Civil War novels, in a sense, although most of them have been laid in the twentieth century. They have been based on aspects of the same plantation legend that appears in *So Red the Rose* and *Gone with the Wind*. This seems a curious statement, considering that Faulkner is usually described as a realist and a rebel against the Southern tradition. In reality he accepts the tradition, but in an altered form, making it less material than moral. He does not insist in his books that ante-bellum life was glamorous, and he is not interested in white-pillared plantation houses except as symbols of decay. What he does tell us is that there used to be men in the South who were capable of good and evil, who observed or failed to observe a traditional code of ethics. These men, he says, were defeated in the Civil War, but not by the Northern armies. Surviving into a new era, they were weakened by a sense of guilt resulting from their relations with the Negroes; and they were finally destroyed by new men rising from among the Poor Whites. The point is made symbolically in *Absalom, Absalom!* where the plantation owner is killed after the war by a white squatter. His only surviving descendant is a half-witted mulatto.

But in Faulkner's novels the war has never ended. It has merely been transformed into another struggle, between the heirs of the slaveholders, who try rather feebly to live by the old code, and the new bankers and demagogues, who have absolutely no standards but pecuniary success. Instead of the South fighting the North, it is Southerners fighting each other, the caste of Sartoris against the new and miserable clan of Snopes. Faulkner thinks of himself as a Sartoris, but always in his novels it is the old order that goes down to defeat.

The Hamlet, by William Faulkner. New York: Random House. (*NR*, Apr. 15, 1940.) Reprinted by permission of *The New Republic*, © 1940, Harrison-Blaine of New Jersey, Inc.

This in itself is an important theme, and Faulkner is one of our few important writers. I have always felt, however, that theme and treatment were somehow disharmonious; that instead of writing the tragedy of a ruling caste he was writing allegorical melodramas dressed up with stormy but second-rate romantic poetry. His books about the Sartoris family are fascinating to analyze, if one tries to separate the conscious symbolism from the obsessive dream beneath it, or tries to explain Faulkner's need for writing violent prose and creating violent situations—rape, murder, incest, miscegenation—that seem disproportionate to the characters involved. But one's interest is psychological rather than literary; one admires the author while feeling that most of his books are Gothic ruins, impressive only by moonlight. Until now *Sanctuary* has been the one novel where, in spite of hasty writing, he has suggested the full range of his effects—including not only terror and pity but also homely realism, Freudian illogic and wild humor.

The Hamlet is different from any of the novels in the Sartoris cycle. Reading it one feels that Faulkner has suddenly emerged from his Gothic midnight into the light of day.

The scene is a community so humble and remote that it is outside the plantation system; it might exist almost anywhere in the American backwoods, from Florida to Oregon. There are no surviving heirs of the slaveholding caste in Frenchman's Bend, and there are comparatively few Negroes. Most of the natives are white and poor, but they are too self-respecting to be called Poor Whites. Only the Snopes family, which has come from richer land to the westward, has been corrupted by living among people with higher economic—and moral—standards.

The principal theme of the novel is the rise of Flem Snopes, by consistent meanness, from clerking in the village store to lording over the whole community. Very soon he has peopled Frenchman's Bend with a whole swarm of his relatives, little men gnawing at money like rats at cheese. One of them, Mink Snopes, commits a murder for pure spite. Another, Ike Snopes, is an idiot boy who falls in love with a cow (and this passage is the least effective in the novel because it seems deliberately intended to be shocking). Flem Snopes himself cheats the shrewdest man in the county by making him dig for

an imaginary treasure. The book is composed of separate episodes like these, tragic, sensational or hilarious. Some of them
have little to do with the Snopes family; and they are bound
together chiefly by dealing with a community where Faulkner
seems to have known every single inhabitant from birth to
deathbed.

The new quality I find in this book—new to Faulkner at
least—is friendliness. Pity he has often shown in the past, but
never before the amused liking that he extends to almost all
the people of Frenchman's Bend. He likes their back-country
humor, he likes the clean look of their patched and faded
shirts, he likes the lies they tell when swapping horses. In a
curious way, he even likes the invading tribe of Snopeses; at
least he likes to write about them. And Flem Snopes himself—
with his little bow tie, his mud-colored eyes, his jaws rolling a
cud of tobacco till the suption is out of it—is made so unfail-
ingly mean, so single-hearted, that he arouses a sort of admiration. When he exhausts the resources of Frenchman's Bend
and moves on to the county seat, one feels sorry to see him go
and relieved at the promise of meeting him again.

The Hamlet was written as the first volume of a Snopes
trilogy. In the novels to follow, Flem will certainly become a
leading banker—that much has been promised—and possibly a
Senator as well. Anything, one believes, is possible to a man so
tight-fisted and empty-minded. Twelve years ago we had a
President Snopes, from Vermont.

Hemingway's "Nevertheless"

IN ADDITION to being a fine novel, *For Whom the Bell Tolls* is also an interesting and very complicated political and moral document. More attention should be paid to this side of it, for all the able reviews that the book has already received. The truth is that Hemingway has always been concerned with ideas, even when his critics took it for granted that he was dealing with purely visceral processes; and for many years his work had more effect on the thinking of young Americans than that of any professional philosopher. In his latest book, the ideas are handled more directly. He is trying here not only to write his best novel, but also to state and justify an attitude toward the Spanish revolution, and toward the whole set of beliefs that dominated the 1930's, besides implying an attitude toward what has happened since his story ended. It is an ambitious undertaking, but then Hemingway has written a very long book, and everything is there if you look for it.

The hero, Robert Jordan, is an American college instructor who had always spent his vacations in Spain and could speak the language without an accent. He joined the Loyalists when the war broke out, "because it had started in a country that he loved, and he believed in the Republic and that if it were destroyed life would be unbearable for all those people who believed in it." He had no politics, as he often told himself; his only creed was liberty, equality and fraternity. And yet, "He was under Communist discipline for the duration of the war . . . because, in the conduct of the war, they were the only party whose program and whose discipline he could respect."

That explains the nature of the People's Front in Spain, but it is not by any means the whole story. For Jordan was also united to the Communists by a deeply religious emotion, "something like the feeling you expected to have and did not have when you made your first communion. It was a feeling of

"Death of a Hero." A review of *For Whom the Bell Tolls*, by Ernest Hemingway. New York: Charles Scribner's Sons. (*NR*, Jan. 20, 1941.) Reprinted by permission of *The New Republic*, © 1941, Harrison-Blaine of New Jersey, Inc.

consecration to a duty toward all the oppressed of the world," and it gave you "a part in something that you could believe in wholly and completely and in which you felt an absolute brotherhood with the others who were engaged in it. . . . Your own death seemed of complete unimportance; only a thing to be avoided because it would interfere with the performance of your duty. But the best thing was that there was something you could do about this feeling and this necessity too. You could fight."

That explains the spirit of the International Brigades, but again it is not the whole story. For Jordan also discovered that "in the fighting soon there was no purity of feeling for those who survived the fighting and were good at it. Not after the first six months." The gradual corruption of the survivors, including himself, is a point he makes often and with great subtlety. He has noted that the Republican leaders are mostly vain and incompetent and capable of betraying the people they are supposed to be saving; he has noted that the people themselves, whom he loves, are cruel and irresponsible; and especially he has noted that the Russians coming to help them are living in well-guarded luxury at Gaylord's Hotel while joking about the hardships suffered by the Spanish soldiers. "He liked to know how it really was; not how it was supposed to be"; and meanwhile he was trying to fit all these elements together into a private philosophy of action.

It might be called the philosophy of Nevertheless, and I suppose it is the only possible philosophy for a fighting man who also wants to remain intelligent and clear-sighted. Jordan tells himself that there are good and evil on his side; *nevertheless* he has balanced them together and has found that the good predominates. He will not reveal the evil he has seen, because by doing so he would injure his cause; *nevertheless* he will not close his eyes to it. And although his whole course of action may eventually prove useless, *nevertheless* he will continue fighting till the end of the war. Then, at some later date, he will satisfy his political and literary conscience by writing a book—"only about the things he knew, truly, and about what he knew. But I will have to be a much better writer than I am now to handle them, he thought. The things he had come to know in this war were not so simple."

We can take for granted that *For Whom the Bell Tolls* is the sort of "true book" that Robert Jordan would have written if he had survived. And because he belongs to the long line of Hemingway's semi-autobiographical heroes, we can take for granted that he is speaking for the author, who also played his part in the Spanish war. But this, once again, is not the whole story. Jordan cannot speak for him completely, since the author himself has changed since the defeat of the cause for which his hero died. Something of his later philosophy or his changed feeling toward life has also gone into the book, and that is what makes it such a complicated document.

The new attitude is never directly expressed, but it is implicit in the choice of characters and events and in the whole mood of the story. From the first chapter to the last, one feels a continual sense of doom, so that reading the book is almost like watching an express train pounding at full speed toward an open drawbridge. The hero has to die by emotional necessity, because he has become the symbol of a dying cause. But most clearly of all, Hemingway's new feeling about the war is revealed by the double irony of this death. Robert Jordan pays with his life for dynamiting a bridge, in order to assure the success of a Loyalist offensive, although he already knows that the offensive will be a failure. That is the first irony. But even at the moment of his death, he wants to carry on the fight, telling himself that if he holds the enemy back a little while or merely shoots the officer, "that may make all the difference." Painfully wounded, fighting back the desire to kill himself and thus avoid being taken and tortured, he lies there with his submachine gun pointed at the road. Now it happens that among the Rebels mentioned in the book, one officer has been singled out as a modest, brave and religious man, exactly the sort that Jordan admires. By the second irony, this is the officer killed with Jordan's last clip of bullets.

Years ago, in an often quoted passage of *A Farewell to Arms*, Hemingway had said that he "was always embarrassed by the words sacred, glorious and sacrifice, and the expression in vain." Now apparently he has written a whole book to explain the meaning of the word "sacrifice" and the phrase "in vain." Yet even that is not the whole story. For Hemingway also seems to be saying that human beings are not in vain;

that they are worth more than any cause for which they die. He seems to be saying, less persuasively, that love is not in vain, especially when enjoyed in the face of danger. And finally, by the immense care with which he has written this book, the best and richest of his novels, he seems to be saying that honesty and craftsmanship are not in vain. These apparently are the principles to which he clings in the ruin of our times.

Roger Martin du Gard: The Next-to-Longest Novelist

WITH GLAZED EYES and swollen lids, I have just finished *The World of the Thibaults* in the complete English translation—both volumes and all the 1,900 pages. It isn't fair to blame Roger Martin du Gard, a kindly man and a conscientious writer, for the dull headache that comes from reading too much. Yet I wonder whether this business of writing oversize novels hasn't been carried much too far since Marcel Proust first set the fashion. Is there any human subject that can't be treated in a hundred or at most two hundred thousand words, instead of spinning the story out to nearly a million? Is there any reason for believing that a novel published in eleven books —as this one was in France—is eleven times or even twice as good as a novel in one reasonably large volume with a beginning, a middle and an end, and not too many extraneous incidents? Isn't it possible that giantism in fiction is quite as unhealthy a symptom as giantism in business or architecture or armies?

The least one can say is that the author who writes an inordinately long novel is like the orator who delivers an

"The Next-to-Longest Novel." A review of *The World of the Thibaults*, by Roger Martin du Gard. Translated by Stuart Gilbert. New York: The Viking Press. (*NR*, Mar. 10, 1941.) Reprinted by permission of *The New Republic*, © 1941, Harrison-Blaine of New Jersey, Inc.

inordinately long speech: he is disregarding the capacity for attention of his audience. Either the book must be leisurely sampled over a period of weeks, in which case the reader is likely to have forgotten the beginning before reaching the end; or else it must be read as a reviewer's chore, hour after hour and day after day, in which case it leaves one with aching eyes and perhaps a blurred picture of the author's intentions. And the author, too, is running a risk. Any man who sets out to write a 2,000-page novel is betting against fate and human experience that he can remain unchanged until the book is finished. He is also betting that the world he describes will remain unchanged, instead of being shattered to pieces. After starting a novel of contemporary life, he may end by writing ancient history.

Something like that has happened with Jules Romains, whose *Men of Good Will* is far from being completed, although it is already the longest serious novel of all time. Martin du Gard is more fortunate, since he had finished *The World of the Thibaults* before Paris fell. Yet the book was twenty years in the writing, with the first of its eleven volumes started not long after the Armistice and the last published in the midst of another war. We should not be surprised that the theme of it changed in the middle, or that it can best be approached as two separate novels.

The book started out as what the French call a "river novel," flowing on from volume to volume. Apparently the author intended to make an extended study of family life in the *haute bourgeoisie*, choosing as his examples the Thibaults and their neighbors the Fontanins. He would show how Oscar Thibault, a rich and pious Catholic, tyrannized over his two sons without ceasing to love them. He would show how the sons hated their father and rebelled against him—Antoine, the elder, becoming a rather commonplace atheist, while Jacques, the younger, transformed his private emotions toward the family into a revolt against bourgeois society as a whole. At the same time he would make it clear that both Antoine and Jacques were molded in their father's image. He would portray the Fontanins as a Protestant family ruled by the mother, who was a kindlier soul than Oscar Thibault, yet in her own way just as domineering. The novel would be written—quite consciously, it seems—under the influence of André Gide. It would embody a good deal of his philosophy, would present several characters modeled after those in *The Counterfeiters,* and would even repeat some of his characteristic phrases.

Seven books of the novel had been finished by 1929; all of them are included in the first of the two big American volumes. In writing them, Martin du Gard had remained moderately faithful to his plan—but, like a moderately faithful husband, he had found other interests outside the family. Some of the independent episodes—like the love affair between Antoine and the equestrienne—had become almost as important as the main theme. Already one could say that the novel as a whole was not so much a river as a chain of lakes—some deep and clear, others shallow, and with only a rivulet connecting them.

In 1930, the author had finished an eighth book, dealing with the adventures of Jacques Thibault among the international revolutionists. The manuscript was never delivered to his publishers. For Martin du Gard had a moral crisis, during which he decided that his novel was moving in the wrong direction, was failing to treat the real issue of his time. He tore up the book he had called "Under Sail" and started to work on the three volumes of *"Summer 1914."* Here, family matters have retreated into the background, even though the author finds room for a desperate love affair between Jacques Thibault and Jenny de Fontanin. Jacques instead of Antoine is now the principal character, and the principal subject is the coming of the war.

Through his Socialist group, which has members in every European capital and a private intelligence service, Jacques is kept almost as well informed of international maneuvers as the diplomats themselves. From Geneva he has an eagle's-eye view of the events that follow the murder at Serajevo. Moreover, he is sent on missions to Berlin, to Brussels, and twice to Paris, where he haunts the meeting places of Socialist politicians and hears the shot that killed Jaurès. His information is almost too complete to be completely credible, as fiction. In one sense, *Summer 1914* might be read as a fair-minded and impressively documented treatise on war guilt. But it is also, in the end, a surprisingly effective novel.

The influence of Gide has practically disappeared from its

philosophy and its method. In this section of his work, Martin du Gard's fictional technique is at least as old as Zola's: it consists in the simple and realistic treatment of events, with nothing left to chance, with no experimental or poetic writing, and with the author's personality kept strictly out of the picture. Scrupulously fair, he presents all points of view—those of Cabinet Ministers, of the conservative middle classes, of the fire-eating Royalists, of the international Socialists and Anarchists, of the workingmen in the streets. Sometimes one gets pretty impatient with him for trying to say everything; part of his exposition might have been left to the historians. Yet slowly he rises to the emotional level of his subject, writing with more and more intensity as the story continues. Day by day he notes the changes in the collective mood of Paris—from indifference to alarm, from alarm to gestures of rebellion, from rebellion to surrender in the face of what seems inevitable, from surrender to a mad patriotic fervor. And the tempo of his story grows more clearly marked from page to page, until everything is timed to the tramp of hobnailed boots and the clank of guns through the Paris streets, all moving toward the front.

Then comes an episode that is pure nightmare. Jacques, who has remained faithful to his international ideals when almost everyone else has abandoned them, plans a last suicidal attempt to stop the war. He will fly over the lines in an airplane, scattering leaflets that call upon the soldiers of both sides to lay down their arms. But the plane has hardly left the Swiss border when it crashes in Alsace. Horribly mutilated, unable to speak but still breathing—an object wrapped in bandages and splints from a packing case, so that the soldiers refer to him as "Chinaware"—Jacques is carried along in the vast disorder of the French retreat, until finally a gendarme puts a bullet through his head. That is the real end of the novel. The epilogue, designed to round off the story and unite the two themes of war and family, impressed me as being a somber and rather tedious anticlimax—though by the time I reached it, my eyes were too tired to make me a fair judge.

Summer 1914 is the work for which Martin du Gard will be remembered and for which he deserved to receive the Nobel Prize. In the easy-running translation by Stuart Gilbert, it can be enjoyed almost as much as in the author's sometimes pedestrian French. Yet it would have been better, I think, if it had been written quite independently, without regard to the family affairs of the Thibaults and the Fontanins. Standing alone, without seven other books as an introduction and without an epilogue, it would be even more impressive. It could be read for itself, and with clearer eyes.

Mr. Churchill Speaks

BEFORE THIS WAR, Winston Churchill was often called Cassandra, but the comparison was hardly exact. Cassandra had been endowed with the gift of true prophecy by Apollo, in return for a promise that handsome young women are often asked to make. When she refused to carry out her part of the bargain, the god revenged himself by decreeing that not one of her prophecies should be heeded. She foretold the Trojan War and the fall of the city, and nobody bothered to listen. Churchill also foretold dire misfortunes for his people, and the present volume of his speeches, including those he made from May, 1938, to February, 1941, shows that he had Cassandra's gift for true prophecy. But unlike her, he used all the wiles of Apollo in order to make himself heard. He argued, he cajoled, he asked searching questions, he revealed facts that everybody else was hoping to disregard, yet at the same time he tried not to wound the vanity of his opponents; he wanted to make it easy for them to change their policies. Eventually they did change them; they followed Churchill's advice item by item. The tragedy was that they followed it half-heartedly and almost always too late.

After the invasion of Poland, Churchill became a responsible member of the War Cabinet, a position that Cassandra never held in Troy. We can assume that he did not lose his gift

Blood, Sweat and Tears, by Winston S. Churchill. New York: G. P. Putnam's Sons. (*NR*, Apr. 21, 1941.) Reprinted by permission of *The New Republic*, © 1941, Harrison-Blaine of New Jersey, Inc.

of foresight, but for the moment he had to keep it hidden and loyally execute the policies of Neville Chamberlain. The result was that his public remarks for the next eight months had an air of complacency that was totally unjustified by the extent of the British war effort. It was not until he became Prime Minister, on May 10, 1940, that his speeches revealed the seriousness of the situation. Since then, they have been a surprisingly complete and candid history of the war from the British point of view, besides being a means of uniting the nation for always greater efforts. I don't like to use superlatives, but Churchill has earned the right to be called the best public speaker in the world today.

Others better qualified will use the present volume as an opportunity to analyze his policies of war and peace; in essence they are simple enough, being aimed at the one goal of preserving Britain and her empire. My own impulse is to make a few comments on his manner of writing. Churchill is one of the few professional authors who have ever been chosen to rule a great nation. He not only makes laws for his people but writes their songs as well, in the sense that his speeches are battle cries, dirges for the fallen and hymns of victory. Since his style reflects and helps to shape the mind of the Englishman at war, it is a subject of more than literary interest.

One notes first of all that the language he uses is spoken English, as opposed to the literary jargon of the universities and the technical jargon of statesmen. Almost all the memorable phrases that he has put into circulation are expressed in the simplest possible words: "Never in the field of human conflict was so much owed by so many to so few."—". . . if necessary for years, and if necessary alone."—"We shall go on to the end . . . we shall fight on the beaches, we shall fight on the landing grounds, we shall fight in the fields and in the streets, we shall fight in the hills; we shall never surrender." Phrases like this show by their choice of words a hatred of pedantry and a willingness to call disagreeable things by their common names. Sometimes Churchill blunders into the false simplicity of Hemingway's early style at its worst: "We tried again and again to prevent this war, and for the sake of peace we put up with a lot of things happening that ought not to have happened." More often the simplicity is true and unaffected, as in the famous statement to Parliament from which the title of this book is taken: "I have nothing to offer but blood, toil, tears and sweat."

A second characteristic of his writing is the continual use of irony, often in the form of understatement. This rhetorical device is safe to use only in a society so unified that its members understand one another even when they are saying less than half of what they mean. Churchill, for example, introduced what was in 1939 probably the largest naval budget in history by saying, "I come before the House on behalf of the navy to ask for a few men, some ships and a little money." The Reichstag might have taken him at his word. Sometimes the effect of his understatement depends on an elaborate build-up: "If after all his boasting and blood-curdling threats and lurid accounts trumpeted round the world of the damage he has inflicted"—and so on for several lines—"if after all this his whole air onslaught were forced after a while tamely to peter out, the Führer's reputation for veracity might be seriously impugned." More often the point is simply made: "There is a general curiosity in the British fleet to find out whether the Italians are up to the level they were at in the last war or whether they have fallen off at all." This was said on June 18, 1940, eight days after Italy had declared war and one day after Pétain had sued for peace. Even when everything seems hopeless, Churchill has a vitality that bursts forth in sanguinary humor. "In the brown hours, when baffling news comes, and disappointing news, I always turn for refreshment to the reports of the German wireless."

A third characteristic is his sense of English history as a continuing process, a book that the living nation is helping to write. The heroes of the English past are always standing at his elbow. "We must regard the next week or so," he says, "as a very important period in our history. It ranks with the days when the Spanish Armada was approaching the Channel, and Drake was finishing his game of bowls." And British history extends for him into the distant future. "Let us therefore brace ourselves to our duties," he said on that same June 18, "and so bear ourselves that, if the British Empire and its Commonwealth last for a thousand years, men will still say, 'This was their finest hour.'"

Lacking almost entirely from these speeches is a picture of the world that Churchill would like to see after the war. One can take for granted that England, old England, would play a great part in it. He is, after all, an English Tory, head of the party, and distinguished from Tory colleagues like the late Mr. Chamberlain chiefly by the fact that he has always and instinctively put national interests above class interests. This, however, is more than a minor difference. If it seems to Churchill that national interests require a drastic remodeling of society to the profit of the broad masses, he will end by supporting the necessary measures. Meanwhile his war aims, as opposed to his peace aims, are more directly stated in this volume of speeches than I had expected before reading them. The first aim is victory—"victory at all costs, victory in spite of all terror, victory however long and hard the road may be." The second and more questionable aim is the carrying out of all British pledges to the conquered nations of Europe. "We abate nothing of our just demands; not one jot or tittle do we recede. Czechs, Poles, Norwegians, Dutch, Belgians have joined their cause to our own. All these shall be restored." He neglects to say whether all shall be restored to full economic anarchy.

His third and last point—mentioned as frequently since the war began as was the German danger in his earlier speeches—is the need for the closest coöperation with the United States. In connection with other statements, one passage that was widely quoted in this country acquires a more definite meaning. He has been saying that the British Empire and the United States "will have to be somewhat mixed up together in some of their affairs. . . . For my part," he continues, "looking out upon the future, I do not view the process with any misgivings. . . . Like the Mississippi, it just keeps rolling along. Let it roll. Let it roll on in full flood, inexorable, irresistible, benignant, to broader lands and better days." Is it too much to say that these words are a direct invitation to join with Britain in winning the war and writing the peace and later enforcing it by something like a Federal Union?

What the Poets Are Saying: 1941

PERHAPS the chief reason for predicting a revival of poetry is the critical state of this country and the world. During a crisis, there is more community life in workshops and armies, but the briefer moments of solitude are prized more highly. Individuals are stirred by the public danger, but at the same time they find themselves driven back on their inner resources: on the emotions and memories and aspirations that are naturally expressed in verse. The situation that encourages the writing of poetry is favorable to its reading as well. There is less opportunity to enjoy novels of a thousand pages or more; these became popular during a period of enforced idleness. In times of crisis, the demand is rather for something short and memorable: a first-hand narrative, an appeal for action, a lyric poem in three or four stanzas. One discovers that the admirable workmanship of a poem, even if its mood is sombre, somehow restores one's faith in the value of human effort.

In comparison with the present, the 1930's in America already seem to have been a rather drab period for the art of verse. It is true that a number of interesting poets appeared in this country—Horace Gregory, Kenneth Fearing, Josephine Miles, Winfield Townley Scott, Muriel Rukeyser, Maria Zaturenska, Delmore Schwartz, Elizabeth Bishop, Ben Belitt, and Edwin Rolfe, to mention only a few. These and others have done sound work in the past and can be depended upon to do more of it in the future. Yet since Hart Crane's *The Bridge*, in the spring of 1930, there has not been published a single volume of poems that greatly altered or expanded our picture of American literature. During the same time there has been somewhat more, I think, than the usual proportion of dull or pretentious or totally misdirected poetical writing.

It is a question why American poets accomplished so little during the 1930's, as compared with American novelists or autobiographers. Perhaps their chief difficulty was the conflict between the subjects they wanted to write about and the literary tradition in which they insisted on writing. The subjects were drawn largely from the world of political struggles and social movements. The tradition was that of the hermetic poets —Eliot most of all, but after him Pound, Hopkins, Cummings and Crane—all of them Symbolists, all bent on crowding an infinity of allusions into every phrase. Crane once sent a letter of five closely typewritten pages to the editor of *Poetry* explaining what he had intended to say in a poem of four short stanzas called "Melville's Tomb"; Miss Monroe had accused him of writing nonsense. The letter was a lucid and eloquent statement of his intentions; it proved that each of the poem's sixteen lines was an extraordinary collection of telescoped images. But it also proved that "Melville's Tomb" could appeal only to an audience patient enough to search for his meanings; or at most and worst to an audience of snobs who thought they could understand it intuitively, or liked to be mystified. Yet similar methods were being employed all during the 1930's by poets who were hoping to express the aspirations of struggling humanity and who dreamed of being read by the masses.

From their experience, some critics have drawn the lesson that it is impossible to write good verse about political subjects. That view is at least short-sighted, considering that such verse has been written almost since the beginning of literature. Most of the great Latin poets were politicians of a sort. Blake and Shelley, Heine, Baudelaire, Swinburne and Rimbaud, all are represented in anthologies of revolutionary poetry. But the amount of good political verse produced in the 1930's was surprisingly small, at least in this country, considering the widespread hopes of a proletarian revolution. Looking back on the decade, one feels that the "social" poets would have been more effective if they had used suitable techniques—for example, those of ballad or folksong or Skeltonian doggerel or neat Swiftian satire. Interesting poems of all these types were actually written by W. H. Auden, with his talent for adapting old methods to contemporary themes. Too many poets, however, wanted to be not only social but symbolist as well—which is like saying that they wanted to make public proclamations in a private language or whisper confidentially to a crowd.

And there were other reasons, as the decade went on, for the general absence of good verse. A set of beliefs that began by opening new horizons had ended by becoming as rigid and confining as the dogmas of older faiths. Certain inconsistencies in those beliefs were not to be noticed, or if noticed were not to be put into words. Certain ideas were not to be questioned. Certain feelings were almost compulsory, even if they could be felt only with the tips of the nerves and expressed only in terms of political rhetoric. It is no wonder that some poets became unconscious hypocrites—which is to say that they wrote bad verse—and that others ceased writing entirely.

But the situation has changed during the last two or three years. The Marxian dogmas have ceased to exert much influence on poetry, notwithstanding the place they still hold in political thinking. As yet no other dogmas have taken their places, even though one can see the shadow of new orthodoxies just over the horizon. Poets feel more at liberty to follow their instincts and, in particular, to deal with the inner world that many of them had been neglecting. For ten years, a great deal of American poetry had consisted of private speech about public matters. More of it deals with private matters today, but in a somewhat more public fashion.

Meanwhile the literary traditions of the new era are more in harmony with the subjects that poets are treating. The writers most generally praised are Yeats, Auden, Kafka; and the influence exerted by all of them seems for the moment healthy. Yeats's later verse, with its short, clean, deceptively simple lines and its use of concrete images, is an admirable model to follow. Auden, with his ability to write in different styles, is a literature in himself; behind him one glimpses a whole line of dead English poets and a group of poets now writing, not to mention a body of philosophical ideas still unfamiliar in this country. As for the novelist Franz Kafka, his influence on poets has been to free their imaginations. I cannot remember a time at which American verse was so full of impossible but compelling dreams and visions.

But if it be admitted that conditions are favorable for a poetry revival, and even that such a revival is now beginning, what is its nature likely to be? In particular, what are the new poets saying? Are they as difficult and as far from ordinary life as many poets of the 1920's? Does their work offer any reward to the average intelligent reader?

As the best way of answering those questions, I had once thought of drawing up a simple outline explaining to the best of my ability what each of several poets was trying to tell us. It would not have been an impossible plan to carry out, considering that most of the new poets have pretty definite ideas about themselves and the world, but it might have proved monotonous. I soon found that the messages of different poets, if printed side by side, would prove in many cases to be the same message. That isn't because the poets are lacking in personality or write in the same style—they aren't and don't—but rather because many of them have had the same reactions to the same sort of world. Such being the case, I decided to follow another method. Instead of treating the poets one by one—first Auden, then George Barker, then Frederic Prokosch, then Richard Eberhart, then Randall Jarrell, Weldon Kees, Harry Brown, and so down the list—I would mention a few of the motives or themes or basic ideas that appear in the work of several writers. An outline of this second type would read somewhat as follows:

THE SENSE OF DOOM. — Most of the writers mentioned seem to feel that a revolution is in progress which will violently put an end to everything good and bad in their familiar world. A few years ago the word "revolution" suggested hope; but what it now suggests to them is apathy or despair. The fate that rules the immediate future is pictured as a huge automaton striding through heaps of the slain, or perhaps— and both these images are from the same poet, Randall Jarrell —it is a gas-masked machine gunner:

> *Our times lie in the welded hands,*
> *Our fortune in the rubber face—*
> *On the gunner's tripod, black with oil,*
> *Spits and gapes the pythoness.*

THE SENSE OF THE INCONGRUOUS. — But the doom that they foresee is to most of them unreasoning and, against the background of our present society, incongruous. From this basic idea springs a whole collection of poems about death intruding suddenly into the midst of petty affairs, about murder in the schoolroom or bombs dropping on a college football field where a team of criminals is playing against a team of maniacs. Or again, a poet like Weldon Kees, who ought to be published more widely, will write a sort of fugue in which visions of destruction, expressed in dignified blank verse, are interrupted by the deliberately trivial remarks of Bones and Sambo. A great deal of the perplexing and nightmarish poetry of these times becomes simple enough if we approach it as an effort to depict a world that is itself a nightmare.

PSYCHO-SOCIAL PARALLELISM. — The conflict between violence and reason does not exist merely in the world outside. The same conflict is repeated in each man's heart; and the inner and outer struggles mirror each other by a sort of psycho-social parallelism. Thus, Frederic Prokosch says in one of his recent poems, "The Reapers":

> *The evil implicit in our age like dust falls everywhere.*
> *Even in these flowing, flickering sheaves of wheat I see it.*
> *I see it in the singing faces, I feel it in the August air.*
>
> *For that is all our fever. It is a fever of the spirit,*
> *And it lies deep. It will heal again, but certainly not soon.*
> *We cannot localize it, we cannot even see or hear it.*
>
> *The smart, efficient, petrifying flavors of our age*
> *Lie scattered all around us, not only in the lies and bullets,*
> *But here, in the hot touch of a hand, or the turning of a page.*

THE SENSE OF PERSONAL GUILT. — If that is true—if the fever of the world is also a fever of the individual spirit—then it follows that each of us in his own heart is partly responsible for the world catastrophe. Here again is an idea now being expressed by many poets. "Whenever we kissed we cocked the future's rifles," says George Barker in a sonnet addressed "To any member of my generation." But it is W. H. Auden who has treated the theme of personal guilt most often and most effectively. When he came to write about the new war, he did not burst forth against Hitler for having invaded Poland, or against Chamberlain for having tried to make peace with Hitler; instead he emphasized the general blame that rests on all of us. His poem "September 1, 1939" contains a good deal of his recent philosophy. It is too long to summarize in full, but I might try to give the gist of it in prose:

Accurate scholarship can reconstruct the whole offense, from Luther to the present day, that has driven our civilization mad. But that is unnecessary, since even schoolchildren know that those to whom evil is done do evil in return. In one sense, all of us are children, lost in a haunted wood and afraid of the night; children who have never been happy or good. Our error has been to crave what we cannot have: not universal love, but to be loved each for himself alone; from this guilty pride come our present misfortunes. Meanwhile the Just exchange their messages like points of fire in a night of terror; and like them I wish to show an affirming flame.

COMRADESHIP. — And what is the affirmation that Auden and poets like him wish to make? Auden himself has called it Love, but the word has so many meanings, sexual, sentimental and religious, that I should prefer to use a less multicolored expression like comradeship or communion. He has kept insisting that no one can exist alone, that all of us must learn to break through the walls of our separate egoisms, that "we must love one another or die." It is this need for comradeship that led several of the younger English poets toward communism—as note Stephen Spender's address to the "young men, oh young comrades"—and it is now leading some of them by devious paths toward Christianity. This at least would seem to be the lesson of Auden's latest and longest poem, "The Double Man."

To this list of basic ideas that I have given, a few others might be added. There is, for example, the wish to honor greatness that was first expressed by Spender ("I think continually of those who were truly great") and later carried out by Auden in his poems to Yeats and Melville and Freud. There is the idea that the first need of this world is a restoration to psychological health. There is the interest in ritual and ceremonial that is best exemplified in the work of Paul Goodman. Taken together, these ideas serve as a logical framework for the new poetry. They can be criticized for intellectual vagueness, for sentimentality and even defeatism, but not at all for being beyond the comprehension of the average intelligent reader.

Sholokhov's Black Earth

OF THE RUSSIAN AUTHORS I have read, Sholokhov is almost the only one with a highly developed sense of locality. The others—and of course I speak with an American reader's limited knowledge of Russian literature—are either concerned with universal human nature, like Dostoevsky, so that their novels are situated in "the provincial town of N——," or in "our district," which we can take for granted is any provincial town or any district; or else they present some abstract theme like the Five Year Plan; or finally these authors may give the impression of being city intellectuals going out into the country for the first time and being overwhelmed by the undifferentiated vastness of the Russian land—as if they were New Yorkers rhapsodizing over "the mountains" or "the prairies," whereas a native would speak of one particular mountain or one prairie township, in his eyes essentially different from any other. That is how Sholokhov regards the village of Tatarsk, which does not exactly resemble any other Cossack *stanitsa*, let alone any Russian *yar* or any community of Ukrainian peasants. And the country he loves is not the "wide Russian land," but rather a certain district on the banks of the Don, with its wooded ravines, its black-earth steppe, its wheatfields and its melon patches. The story he tells could have happened nowhere else.

Besides his sense of locality, he also has a sense of people that is somewhat commoner in Russian fiction, though rare enough in the literature of any country. He writes about them as if he had always known and loved them and wanted the outside world to understand just why they acted as they did. They are of course his own people, the community or nation of the Don Cossacks, and another writer might have a hard time making them seem plausible. They are peasants tied to the soil, and yet until the end of the civil wars they were soldiers wandering over the face of the earth. They are miserly with

The Silent Don, by Mikhail Sholokhov. Translated by Stephen Garry. New York: Alfred A. Knopf. 2 vols. (*NR*, Aug. 18, 1941.) Reprinted by permission of *The New Republic*, © 1941, Harrison-Blaine of New Jersey, Inc.

their wheat, yet prodigal with their money and their lives; they are heavy drinkers, brawlers, wife beaters and, on occasion, looters and killers, yet they are full of simple kindliness; they are honest citizens descended from outlaws and ready in any period of disorder to resume the life of their ancestors. Another writer might have insisted on combing the lice from their hair and wiping the blood from their hands before admitting them to his hygienic fiction. Sholokhov pictures them just as they are, without even washing their faces, but without making us feel that he is collecting specimens for an ethnological museum. They are simply people to him; he lives in a Cossack village and these are his neighbors.

He has been working on his Cossack novel since 1925, when he was twenty years old and had just finished his first collection of stories. It grew longer as he went along; there were always more incidents to crowd into it. The first volume to appear in English was *And Quiet Flows the Don*, published in 1934. The second volume, called *The Don Flows Home to the Sea*, is advertised as being complete in itself—can you remember any second volume that wasn't?—but it is part of the same work, the continuation and tragic end of the hero's story.

After his unhappy marriage and his unhappier love affair with Aksinia; after serving three years at the front and becoming an officer; after fighting for the Reds and then deserting them—all this was told in the first volume—Gregor Melekhov comes home. He distrusts both sides in the struggle; his only loyalty is to the Cossack nation and his only desire is to live in peace on his own farm; but that is what neither Reds nor Whites will permit him to do. First the Cossacks rise and drive out the Reds, but the Reds come back again. Then the Cossacks rise a second time and Gregor, called once more into service, becomes the commander of a whole division. The Whites march into the Donside, where the Cossacks are forced to join them by the logic of the struggle. But the White army disintegrates, after marching nearly to Moscow, and Gregor joins the Reds again, fighting under Budienny in the Polish war. His services are not enough to protect him when he comes back to the village, and after learning that he is to be arrested by the Cheka, he escapes into the steppes to join a rebel band.

But the story is not primarily one of military campaigns, even though these are described with painstaking accuracy. Sholokhov's underlying theme is how a Cossack soldier was deprived step by step of everything and everybody he loved—first his brother, taken prisoner and killed by the Reds; then his wife, then his parents, then his always loving but unfaithful Aksinia, then his farm and even the right to live in his own village. Along with this went a moral denudation: he lost his scruples one by one and his belief in the rightness of what he was doing; he drank to forget, he robbed and stole and murdered his prisoners like other rebel Cossacks; finally he lost even his animal courage, so that after the massacre of the Fomin band he was only an outlaw hiding in the forest, afraid of every cracking twig. And Gregor in his utter destitution seems to represent the whole Cossack people, who during the civil war lost not only their goods and most of their land—other Russians did that—but also their profession as soldiers, half or more of their numerical strength, and for a long time their national existence. It was not until twenty years had passed—and then partly through the influence of Sholokhov's novels—that they were once again recognized as a separate community.

But there is a great deal more than Gregor in the story. There are of course his mistress and his wife, both memorable figures; and not far in the background are all the other robust and sharp-tongued Cossack women, about whom Sholokhov writes as if he did nothing but listen to their gossip. There are the old men, sly, boastful, drunken and faithful to the Tsar; Sholokhov seems to deplore them as a Communist, while honoring them as a Cossack is taught to honor his elders. There is more wild humor than one would expect to find in such a tragic story. There are a hundred scenes and incidents that stick in one's mind—the trenches along the Don where the Cossack wives came to wash their men's clothing, the flight of the peasants, the embarkation of the defeated White army, the typhus epidemic (during which Gregor uncovers his dead father's face to find it crawling with lice), the drinking bout with the English officer (although this episode is missing from Mr. Garry's translation) and scene after scene of death in battle, death in the village, death behind the lines by firing squad or

Cossack saber; death always at one's elbow until it no longer arouses a twinge of horror. After the executioner chosen by Fomin's band comes back from shooting a young Red soldier, somebody asks him, stifling a yawn, "What's the weather like, Chumakov? Is it clearing up?" Today the weather is stormy again over the steppes, and the new war gives this book a contemporary quality; it is news from the Eastern Front; it shows how bitterly and resourcefully the Russians will fight in defense of their land. Meanwhile the land itself is the real protagonist of the novel. "Beloved steppe!" the author exclaims, for the first time interrupting his story. "Winding ravines, dry valleys, ruddy cliffs, expanse of feather-grass worked with darker traces of horse-hoofs, mounds rising in a wise silence, preserving your former Cossack glory. Low I bow and filially kiss your fresh earth; I kiss the Don Cossack, unresting, blood-soaked steppes."

Apparently *The Silent Don* is the greatest of all the novels that have been written about the Russian revolution; and I say "apparently" for the one reason that it is hard to tell just how good the book may be in the original. Stephen Garry's translation is by no means the worst that I have read during the past few years; at least he has a feeling for English prose. But to judge from sections of the novel that appeared in *International Literature*, it is far from being complete; and it is full of meaningless expressions and apparent misunderstandings of the Russian text. Not for a single page does it let you forget that it is being translated from a very foreign language.

Virginia Woolf: England Under Glass

AMERICAN TRAVELERS in England before this war often felt that they were strolling—no, were being wheeled in comfortable chairs—past neat showcases of a museum. These trains that always ran on time were obviously toy trains, built and kept in order by some retired millionaire. These fields were covered with excelsior dyed green; no grass was ever so free from weeds. These earthen dykes that surrounded the fields—and kept them from being worked by machinery—were preserved as a relic of Saxon times; and the wild flowers that grew on the dykes were planted there by the same pious hands that had thatched the cottages and painted a soft mist over the horizon. Even the people sometimes looked like wax figures dressed in authentic costumes and labeled Mine Host or Farmer Hobbs or The Costermonger. The general supervision of this country was by a political subcommittee of the Society for the Preservation of British Antiquities; one pictured them as kindly men who met on the steps of the British Museum with their umbrellas raised to protect them from the gentle rain. The oldest of them would say, "We must break no glass," and the next-to-oldest, "We must shatter no illusions," while even the pigeons would be cooing, "Peace in our time."

This England under glass, this England where people of breeding were sometimes not quite sure whether they were themselves or their family portraits, is the subject of Virginia Woolf's last novel. The local scene is Pointz Hall, outside an English village; the time is a summer's day in 1939. The plot —well, *Between the Acts* has no plot, strictly speaking, but the action is concerned with a pageant, given for the benefit of the local church, which deals with the history of England from the earliest times. The pageant is brilliantly written, and while it lasts it holds the audience together, after a fashion. When it ends, the spectators and the actors disperse to their homes, their daily papers and their daily quarrels; for each of them,

Between the Acts, by Virginia Woolf. New York: Harcourt, Brace and Company. (*NR*, Oct. 6, 1941.) Reprinted by permission of *The New Republic*, © 1941, Harrison-Blaine of New Jersey, Inc.

"the curtain rises." A summer day has passed and much has been revealed, but nothing has been changed.

It has often been pointed out that Mrs. Woolf's method has little to do with that of the ordinary novel. There is no conflict in her books, no sense of drama or dialectic; there is no progress through difficulties toward marriage or a deathbed. There is not even a story, in the usual sense of the word. Mrs. Woolf in her heart did not believe in stories; she thought of herself as living in a world where nothing ever happened; or at least nothing that mattered, nothing that was real. The reality was outside the world, in the human heart. Her literary method, based on this philosophy, was not to deal explicitly with a situation, but rather to present the shadows it cast in the individual consciousness. When the last shadows had moved across the screen and when the attentive reader had caught a glimpse of something motionless behind them—"this peace, this rest, this eternity"—Mrs. Woolf had nothing more to say. Her story had ended without having begun.

This method—as I think William Troy was the first to observe—is that of lyric poetry rather than fiction, and *Between the Acts* is the most lyrical of all her books, not only in feeling but also in style. The historical pageant is written chiefly in verse; the characters in their private meditations are always breaking into verse; and even the narrative passages have an emotional intensity and a disciplined freedom in the use of words that one does not associate with prose. Moreover, Mrs. Woolf uses almost as many symbols as Yeats does in his later work. The first scene in the book is a meeting to discuss a new cesspool for the village—nobody could overlook her meaning here—and the pageant is being held to buy a new lighting system for the church. It is enacted by the villagers themselves, as if to indicate the continuity of English life; Queen Elizabeth after all must have looked like Mrs. Clark the tobacconist. The village idiot wanders across the scene, playing no one but himself. In the last tableau, entitled "The Present Time—Ourselves," the characters bring mirrors on the stage and hold them up to the audience, while a voice howls from a megaphone that they are nothing but "scraps, orts and fragments."

The coming war is scarcely mentioned. Once a dozen airplanes fly overhead in military formation; twice the heroine finds herself thinking—she doesn't know why—about a newspaper story she had just read of a girl raped by soldiers. Yet the spirit of war broods over the novel, and one feels at every moment that bombs will soon be crashing through the museum cases. Factories will rise on the site of the wrecked cottages; the green lawns will be an airfield; the "scraps, orts and fragments" will be swept away.

Virginia Woolf herself would soon become a war casualty, though not in the simple manner that was suggested by the first accounts of her suicide. A phrase in the coroner's report led to an exchange of letters in *The Sunday Times;* a bishop's wife was superior, and Leonard Woolf wrote a frank and dignified answer. It seems that Mrs. Woolf had suffered a mental breakdown during the First World War and, after her recovery, had been haunted by the fear of relapsing into madness. This fear was especially vivid during the period of tension that always followed the completion of a novel. In other words, it was the mental strain of writing *Between the Acts* and not the physical strain of living under bombardment that caused her death. But the book itself is her comment on the war, or rather her elegy for the society the war was destroying, and so we are back at our starting point. When the bombs crashed through the glass that covered England, she was one of the people—and they were not the weaklings or the cowards —who were too finely organized for life in the wind and the rain.

Her books, too, are not written for this new age. If one rereads several of them in succession, as I did recently, one is as likely to be impressed by their narrow range of characters and emotions as by their cool wit and their warm imagination. The outside world has made itself real to us as it never was to the people in her novels. It would be wrong, however, to treat the judgment of our moment in time as if it were that of history. The days will come again when people have leisure to appreciate her picture of the inner world and her sense of the living past. The essential spirit if not the body of Georgian England endures for future readers in her novels.

Epilogue: Adventures of a Book Reviewer

THIS BOOK was Dan Piper's idea and undertaking. Of course I had suggestions about what should go into it, but it was Piper who assembled the book. When reading the manuscript, I remembered how I had written these pieces and a hundred others like them. "Pieces" will do for want of a better word: some of them are essays, some are reports, some are editorial pontifications, but more are unabashed book reviews—and why not? The relatively short book review was my art form for many years; it became my blank-verse meditation, my sonnet sequence, my letter to distant friends, my private journal. I did not fall into the illusion that it was a major form; no, it was dependent for its subject matter on the existence of novels or plays or poems worth writing about. Nevertheless it was *my* form: and for years I neglected my obligations to family and friends in order to get the review written. As writers tend to do with any form imposed on them by accident, I poured into it as much as possible of my adventures among events and opinions.

The accident that imposed the form was a change in my status on *The New Republic*. I had been doing a good deal of editorial work, besides running the book department since 1930, the year when Edmund Wilson decided to become a roving reporter. I had also been writing articles and reviews for the paper when there was time, but that wasn't every week; I never learned how to dash them off. Then in the autumn of 1934 Bruce Bliven and George Soule, my senior colleagues, decided that I should do less editing and more writing. They proposed that I should contribute a weekly book review and that, to have more time for it, I should spend only Tuesdays, Wednesdays and Thursdays in the office.

From that autumn the review gave a definite rhythm to my week. It started—not the week but the review—on Thursday afternoon as a vacancy at the beginning of the book section, all the rest of which was in galley proof. I knew what book I was going to discuss, but often I hadn't read beyond the first chapter.

"How much space will you need for your piece?" Betty Huling would ask me as she pasted up the galleys. Betty was in charge of make-up and copy editing.

"Oh—one page and five lines," I would answer with a false air of decision. (Or again, if I hoped there might be more to say, the answer would be, "One page and exactly a column on the next.") Then I would go back to dictating letters, another chore that was left to the last moment. In my three days at the office I never had time for everything.

FRIDAY. It was my day for reading the book, that is, for being confronted in solitude with a new personality and a subject matter that might be totally unfamiliar. What should I, what could I say about them? A general reviewer is supposed to have been endowed at birth with challenging opinions on every topic, but the good fairies had neglected me. Instead of starting with opinions, I had nothing but a pretty wide range of interests and a few presuppositions: as notably that literature is a part of life, not subordinate to other parts, such as politics and economics, but intimately affected by them and sometimes affecting them in turn. All the parts were interwoven, I believed, in the web of history. That was a serviceable belief, but only as a background for opinions about the book at hand. Those I must find by going deeper into the book and into myself. What was the author really saying, as opposed to what he intended and appeared to say? What light did he cast on the drama of our times? What did I truly think about him? It seems to me now that I was writing not so much to express my opinions as to discover what they were.

Parenthetically. That search for opinions, consistent ones if possible, goes a long way toward explaining the popularity of Marxism in the 1930's, particularly among reviewers, commentators and foreign correspondents. The secure world of their childhood had fallen apart. They were looking for a scheme of values, a direction, a skeleton key that would unlock almost any sort of political or literary situation (and help them to write a cogent page). Marxism, in a more or less rudimentary form, was the key that many of them found. Uncompromisingly materialistic as it purported to be, it served the same unifying purpose for writers of the depression years that Emerson's uncompromising idealism had served for New England rebels of an earlier time. Emerson wrote in 1837, ". . . let me see every trifle bristling with the polarity that ranges it instantly on an eternal law . . . and the world lies no longer a dull miscellany and lumber-room, but has form and order; there is no trifle, there is no puzzle, but one design unites and animates the farthest pinnacle and the lowest trench." Writers of the depression years also believed in an all-pervasive design and in a law of universal polarity which they called the class struggle. Adopting that "long view," as it was called, I wrote in 1934 an essay called "Art Tomorrow," reprinted in this volume.

> Two housewives [I said] gossiping on the back porch about their husbands' jobs and the price of groceries, a small merchant bankrupt in the next block, a love affair broken off, a mortgage foreclosed, a manufacturer's rise to power—all these incidents take their place in a historical pattern that is also illuminated by revolts in Spain, a new factory in the Urals, an obscure battle in the interior of China. Values exist again, after an age in which they seemed to be lost; good and evil are embodied in men who struggle.

I did not realize that I was being less Marxian than Emersonian—though without Emerson's poetic force; or again that my companions of the 1930's would be more bitterly disillusioned than the rashest of his disciples at Brook Farm. Close parenthesis.

SATURDAY. In the rhythm of the week, that was the day when I confidently expected that the review would write itself. I set to work in the morning, then found again that nothing wrote itself, not even the first sentence. After staring at the typewriter, which had assumed a hostile face, I would go back to the book, reading parts of it more attentively and taking pages of notes that there would never be space to use. In the afternoon I would go for a long walk. After the first mile I found my opinions taking shape in words, as if tramped out of clay, and on happier Saturdays I might come back with a first sentence and even an outline of what I hoped to write.

SUNDAY. In the end that became my day for writing, simply because the review had to reach the Steinberg Press in Brooklyn by ten o'clock on Monday morning; otherwise I might have spent another week on it. I started early, in the deluded hope that I might be finished by late afternoon; then for once we could go out for dinner and the movies. But there was always something to add or delete, something to rephrase, and the result was that I worked late into the night. Why did I make everything hard for myself? One reason, I suspect, was that I had been trained as a poet, not a journalist, and that I instinctively tried to combine the qualities of sound journalistic prose with those of a poem or a short story. That is, I tried to make an accurate report that would place the book in our momently changing world, but at the same time I hoped that the report would have strength in itself to outlast the moment. I wanted it to stand as a balanced structure, fashioned with an economy of materials, a richness of internal relations, a beginning that set the tone, and a cadenced march to an inevitable conclusion. The problem, I found, was largely one of sequence. Each statement had to follow another logically—for I was presenting an argument—but there also had to be an associative or temporal connection between them, as in a poem. Somehow I had to unite "then" and "therefore," the *post hoc* of narration and the *propter hoc* of exposition, if I wanted to produce a reasoned criticism that could be read like a story.

Of course I did not often succeed in reconciling those contradictory purposes, but I would keep trying through the night, while facing the additional demands of space and time. Space was the easier to meet of those two inexorable conditions. When I said off-handedly on Thursday afternoon, "One page and five lines," or, "One page and a column on the next," I had issued a challenge to myself and, in effect, had given a form to the review, as if I had undertaken to write the fourteen lines of a sonnet or the twenty-eight of a ballade. On Friday and Saturday I was haunted by that vacancy of precise dimensions: how could it ever be filled? By Sunday, however, I had always assembled too many notes, and the problem became one of selection. It seems to me now, in memory, that I solved the problem by omitting my best paragraphs; usually these are the easiest to omit because they are more personal or general and less essential to the immediate argument. As for revising to an exact number of lines, that became a simple matter as soon as I learned to set the margins of my typewriter to the average character count of a *New Republic* column. Betty Huling told me that I never went wrong by more than a line.

Time was a more difficult requirement. My stubborn habit of revision, combined with what seems to me an invincible sluggishness of spirit, kept me working into the early morning hours. I would glance at my watch to make sure there was still time to catch the last mail train for New York, then write another version of the final paragraph. Always it threatened to become either briefly dogmatic or wordily sententious; one or the other of those faults was hard to avoid when I was filling exactly ten lines at three in the morning. Sometimes I saw the full moon setting from my study window, and in summer I might still be at my desk when the room was brightened with dawn.

That was after we moved to the country in 1936. Earlier reviews had been written in a variety of places: our Greenwich Village apartment (till we found that my typing disturbed the baby and vice versa); a room in the Hotel Chelsea, where the walls are thick; at Yaddo, the artists' colony in Saratoga Springs; or in the very old Riverton Inn, thirty miles from Hartford. I became a virtuoso in mail trains and post-office schedules. There was a train from Saratoga at two in the morning; from Hartford at three (I nearly missed that one after a dash over icy roads); from South Norwalk at four (but that was a forty-five mile drive); then at last I discovered that I could give my special-delivery envelope to the mail clerk on the six-o'clock train from Pawling, New York, only ten miles from our house. Once I missed the train at Pawling and raced it twenty miles down the line, till I caught up with it at Croton Falls. Once I nearly didn't get home. It was a lovely June morning alive with birds, and the train was half an hour late. On the drive back I began to fall asleep. That had happened before, and I had parked by the roadside and taken a brief nap. This time I was so close to home that I thought I could hold out. "It's only a mile," I said to myself, biting my lip hard. "I can keep awake . . . awake." Suddenly I woke and found the car on a bank twenty feet above the highway with its left front wheel in the air. I wrenched at the steering wheel, saved the car from falling, and bumped my way along the bank till it sloped over rock ledges to the level of the road.

Thanks to the postal service, which must have been more reliable in the depression years, the review always reached the Steinberg Press before the Monday-morning deadline. Betty

Huling was there to read it, and she turned it over to the linotyper without changing a word (though sometimes she ventured a comma). Nobody else saw the review until copies of *The New Republic* were delivered to the office on Wednesday morning. Often Bruce Bliven and George Soule must have been dismayed by what they read, but as gentlemanly colleagues they never complained and never suggested that I might show them the manuscript before sending it to the printer. In effect I was speaking for myself, on my own responsibility, to what had become my own circle of readers. It was an extraordinary privilege for which, if I could have afforded the gesture, I would gladly have paid *The New Republic* instead of accepting a salary.

I like to think that the personal tone of these reviews and reports—with the extra hours that went into each of them and the accumulation of notes that could not be used, but that still became implicit in what I said—has given them a certain durability. Perhaps, by making things harder for myself, I also made them harder for other reviewers and thereby contributed a little toward raising the standards of the profession. As for the subject matter of the pieces, they deal with past events and with an assortment of authors among whom some are lastingly famous, but others are out of fashion; they express judgments that in some cases are embarrassingly simple and far from those I would express today; but I think they have their value as part of the historical record. To keep the record straight, I made no changes in the text beyond striking out some adjectives, adverbs and conjunctions, of which there were too many, and omitting two or three of those questionable last paragraphs. The opinions stand as dredged from my mind on Fridays and Saturdays; the judgments stand as revised on those long-ago Sunday midnights. I think Dan Piper was right to arrange the pieces in chronological order. As a result they tell the story of how a rather unsophisticated young man, endowed by accident with a degree of independence, confronted the social and literary issues of the depression years, and how he gradually learned that they were a great deal more complicated than they had seemed in the beginning. Perhaps the young man's story might stand for that of many others.

Malcolm Cowley